D1406982

INTERNATIONAL COMMODITY DEVELOPMENT STRATEGIES

# International Commodity Development Strategies

Edited by Budi Hartantyo
Hidde P. Smit

VU University Press
Amsterdam 1993

VU University Press is an imprint of:
VU Boekhandel/Uitgeverij bv
De Boelelaan 1105
1081 HV Amsterdam
The Netherlands

tel. (020) - 644 43 55
fax (020) - 646 27 19

layout by Jacques de Swart
        and Hanneke van Wouwe
cover by D PS, Amsterdam
printed by Wilco, Amersfoort

isbn 90-5383-268-8
nugi 835

# FOREWORD

The Common Fund for Commodities conducted in Brussels, from 22 to 25 June 1993, the second of its seminars, this one devoted to the subject of Commodity Development Measures in the Context of International Commodity Strategies. The Proceedings of this Seminar are made available in this publication. Documents by International Commodity Bodies (ICBs) on the specific issues of their commodity, and by international organizations, are published as their own, with the Fund claiming neither right nor taking responsibility, and are presented in the form submitted to the Seminar. They constitute the first part of this publication. Presentations by guest speakers, which focus on specific areas relevant to various commodities, form the second part of the publication. Some of these presentations have been adapted since their presentation at the Seminar.

The Fund expresses its gratitude to the Belgian Government, and especially to Mr. Erik Derycke, Secretary of State for Development Co-operation, for the hosting of this Seminar. A word of thanks should also go to the Moderator of the Seminar, Sir Alister McIntyre, Vice Chancellor of the University of the West Indies, and to Mr. Carlos Fortin, Deputy to the Secretary-General of the United Nations Conference on Trade and Development, to the guest speakers and participants, and to all those that worked hard to make this Seminar a success.

# ABBREVIATIONS

| | | |
|---|---|---|
| ACP | - | Africa, Caribbean and Pacific |
| CFC | - | Common Fund for Commodities |
| CGIAR | - | Consultative Group on International Agricultural Research |
| CIS | - | Commonwealth of Independent States |
| EC | - | European Communities |
| FAO | - | Food and Agriculture Organization of the United Nations |
| GATT | - | General Agreement on Tariffs and Trade |
| ICA | - | International Commodity Agreement |
| ICAC | - | International Cotton Advisory Committee |
| ICB | - | International Commodity Body |
| ICCO | - | International Cocoa Organization |
| ICO | - | International Coffee Organization |
| IGET | - | Intergovernmental Group of Experts on Tungsten |
| IJO | - | International Jute Organisation |
| ILZSG | - | International Lead and Zinc Study Group |
| INRO | - | International Natural Rubber Organization |
| IOOC | - | International Olive Oil Council |
| ITC | - | International Trade Centre (UNCTAD/GATT) |
| IRSG | - | International Rubber Study Group |
| ISO | - | International Sugar Organization |
| ITTO | - | International Tropical Timber Organization |
| IWC | - | International Wheat Council |
| LDC | - | Least Developed Countries |
| NIC | - | Newly Industrialized Country |
| OECD | - | Organisation for Economic Co-operation and Development |
| OPEC | - | Organization of the Petroleum Exporting Countries |
| SDR | - | Special Drawing Right |
| STABEX | - | Stabilization of Export Earnings |
| UNCTAD | - | United Nations Conference on Trade and Development |
| UNIDO | - | United Nations Industrial Development Organization |

vi

# CONTENTS

# PART I

---

# EXECUTIVE SUMMARY

# EXECUTIVE SUMMARY
## OF THE PROCEEDINGS OF THE COMMON FUND SEMINAR ON COMMODITY DEVELOPMENT MEASURES IN THE CONTEXT OF INTERNATIONAL COMMODITY STRATEGIES

From 22 to 25 June 1993, the Common Fund for Commodities conducted a Seminar on Commodity Development Measures in the Context of International Commodity Strategies.

The Seminar, held in Brussels, was hosted by the Belgian Government with Mr. Erik Derycke, Secretary of State for Development Co-operation, as its Honorary Chairman. The Managing Director of the Common Fund addressed the Seminar. The Seminar was moderated by Sir Alister McIntyre, Vice Chancellor of the University of the West Indies and a former Deputy Secretary-General of UNCTAD with wide experience on commodity matters. Mr. Carlos Fortin, Deputy to the Secretary-General and Director for Commodities of UNCTAD, was the keynote speaker of the first session. Around 75 participants and observers attended the Seminar.

The objective of the Seminar was to maximize the benefits of International Commodity Bodies (ICBs) from the Fund's Second Account operations by providing guidance for preparing appropriate project proposals in the context of commodity strategies. The Seminar had special significance in view of the increasingly important role that development projects are assuming in ICB activities. For this purpose, the Fund issued a Project Preparation and Management Manual which served as the basis for discussion. It is hoped that the use of this Manual will facilitate the selection, preparation and implementation of appropriate projects and save scarce resources of the ICBs.

Emphasis has been placed on the importance of adopting commodity strategies for each commodity. Such strategies identify the perennial problems of the commodities and direct persistent and long-term efforts through projects and programmes to address these problems.

The Fund also stresses the priority that it attaches to specific commodity development measures such as local processing of commodities and diversification of exports of developing countries, natural resource management, research and development for new end-uses, improvement of quality and productivity as well as assisting the Least Developed and small producer/exporter countries. Most LDCs depend on only one or two commodities for the bulk of their export earnings. While these countries comprise 8.2% of the world's population, they account for only 1.4% of the total export earnings (goods and services) of all developing countries, and under 0.3% of world exports of goods and services. Consequently, they are the most vulnerable and the most seriously affected by the present depressed commodity markets. It is the Fund's priority to assist the Least Developed Countries in their efforts to diversify their exports. Diversification measures will, undoubtedly, boost the earnings of the LDCs and reduce dependence on a very limited number of commodities that are subject to major price and volume fluctuations or declining price trends. It was the Seminar's objective to sensitize the ICBs of the plight of this category of countries and small producer/exporters and the Fund's policy concerning them.

The Seminar further provided an occasion for ICBs, international organizations and other participants to meet and, through interaction, exchange ideas on world commodity problems faced by the developing countries, in particular, the least developed among them, and ways and means of overcoming these problems.

A summary of the proceedings and discussions is given below.

## 1 COMMODITY DEVELOPMENT MEASURES IN THE CONTEXT OF INTERNATIONAL COMMODITY STRATEGIES

Mr. Carlos Fortin described developments in the 1980s, as documented in the Report of the Secretary-General of UNCTAD to the UNCTAD VIII Conference. There had been a clear weakening of efforts to agree upon and implement policy actions for a number of reasons. The Report concluded that the formulation of a strengthened international commodity policy must take account of the changed circumstances and identify strategic areas where action can remove the main obstacles to international co-operation. The revitalization of producer cooperation was deemed crucial given the over-supply situation for many commodities. The Cartagena Commitment of UNCTAD VIII and its follow-up provided both a reaffirmation of the will of the international community to persevere in the attainment of enhanced co-operation in the area of commodities, and a number of concrete orientations and guidelines to implement that will.

According to the speaker, the more concrete operational areas identified for producer-consumer and producer-co-operation include:

- supply management and rationalization;
- improvement in market transparency;
- research and development;
- promotion of local processing;
- market promotion;
- improvement in, and rational use of, marketing systems and practices; and
- ensuring the sustainability of commodity-based development.

Producer co-operation should aim at objectives catering for immediate improvement (such as the elimination of stocks overhanging the market) and/or for long-term improvement (such as investment and production policies, marketing strategies and research and development). The most striking positive development in the 1980s was the growing awareness of the need to co-operate internationally to improve transparency in commodity markets and industries, and the growing number of concrete efforts in this direction that are taking place, e.g. in various metals and minerals and in a number of agricultural commodities. Also striking is the movement that has taken place in the field of international co-operation for supply management and rationalization. As both consumers and producers have come to conclude that depressed prices in the long term are in nobody's interest, production policies and supply rationalization measures deserve strong support from the international community. Especially promising is the upsurge of interest in co-operation for improvement in, and rational use of, marketing systems and practices. This should include training activities in the marketing areas.

Mr. Fortin concluded by stressing that in all of the preceding, support by international organizations is essential. Both the Common Fund for Commodities and UNCTAD have a special role to play in this connection. The Fund should play an important role in the mobilization of financial support for co-operative development activities in the field of commodities, while UNCTAD should continue to concentrate on the areas of market transparency, financial instruments for commodity risk management and participation in international commodity exchanges and domestic processing.

The Chief Operations Officer of the Fund, Mr. H. Skouenborg, explained the operation of the Second Account. His presentation focused on a number of issues, among which, specifically, the need for ICBs to articulate international commodity strategies in which projects submitted by the designated ICBs would fit. The Project Manual indicates some elements relevant for formulation of such strategies. The speaker suggested that one or more scenarios should be identified which would apply to a commodity and would go some way towards selecting, as a first step, the wider objectives to be included in a strategy. These could include, among others, the demand-supply-price scenario, the trade policy scenario, the value-added scenario and the sustainability scenario. In concluding, the speaker stressed that the formulation of a strategy should not be seen as an additional burden or a straight-jacket as it would help in better formulating activities to be pursued by the ICB.

In the ensuing discussion, it was remarked that the Fund should make itself more known in Africa by giving seminars or workshops in Africa. Some questions were raised as to the criteria applied by the Fund for rejecting project proposals, as formulating project proposals is costly. It was questioned on how to reconcile different strategies as formulated by different organizations as, in line with the Integrated Programme for Commodities, consistent and coherent strategies between ICBs are essential. It was remarked that it is important to take note of the changes brought about by globalization, and by the fact that some governments are not as attached to commodity production and consumption as in the past.

The afternoon session was devoted to brief presentations by ICBs on the core problems affecting their individual commodities. Presentations were made by the International Olive Oil Council, the International Jute Organisation, the International Natural Rubber Organization, the International Tropical Timber Organization, the International Lead and Zinc Study Group, the Intergovernmental Group of Experts on Tungsten, the Intergovernmental Group on Bananas, the Intergovernmental Group on Citrus Fruit, the Intergovernmental Group on Hard Fibres, the Intergovernmental Group on Hides and Skins, the Intergovernmental Group on Tea, the Intergovernmental Sub-Committee on Fish Trade, the Intergovernmental Group on Rice, the Intergovernmental Group on Meat and the Intergovernmental Group on Oil, Oilseeds and Fats. Written statements were received from the International Wheat Council and the International Rubber Study Group.

The ICBs gave a review of the problems their commodities faced. Without dealing with each ICB separately, a few themes emerged which appeared common to many commodities. Almost all commodities suffer from the recession in the industrialized world, enhanced by the strong reduction in the market in Eastern Europe. This leads to situations of sometimes severe over-supply. Efforts are being made or designed to increase demand through market promotion and the elimination of trade barriers, and to manage supply. Enhancing the current over-supply are the improvements in productivity which many producers have pursued in the last decade. Special problems occur in the areas of investment in research and development, pest control, diseases, low productivity, processing, marketing, packaging and waste disposal. The elimination of commodity boards as part of structural adjustment programmes creates transition problems in areas such as quality control and marketing. The policy emphasis continues to shift towards production policy and promotional strategies.

From the discussion, it emerged that the current seminar was greatly appreciated by ICBs and that such an exchange of information should be organized regularly. This would allow ICBs to be well-informed of policies applied by the Fund regarding preferred subjects for projects, desired themes, co-financing etc. The Fund does not, it was confirmed, finance general training or institution building programmes, though it was remarked that the policy not to finance training should perhaps be refined. Representatives from the Fund should participate in meetings of the ICBs, so as to remain at all times aware of developments in policies and strategies of the ICBs. More use could be made of co-operation between ICBs, the Fund and the regional Economic Commissions of the United Nations.

## 2 CHALLENGES, OPPORTUNITIES AND STRATEGIES FOR COMMODITIES

Various elements included as *'components in a commodity strategy'* were introduced by guest speakers, and subject of discussions. Dr. Fernando A. Bernardo, Deputy Director-General of the International Rice Research Institute (IRRI), Philippines, introduced the topic of *'productivity improvements in agriculture'*. He put this in the perspective of the stages between producer and final consumer, converting inputs into primary products, primary into processed products, and processed products into consumer goods through marketing efforts. He saw five challenges for research: increasing productivity; enhancing profitability; achieving sustainability; protection of the environment and, finally, addressing social equity issues. Drawing on the experiences of the IRRI, he dwelt upon each of these five challenges.

Because of population increases and decreases both in the land that is available for production and in the rural-urban population ratio, increasing productivity is mandatory to meeting future increasing demand. With hybrid varieties and new varieties of rice, the irrigated rice yield plateau can be lifted by 25 to 30 per cent. Improved farming systems would also make a considerable contribution. To enhance profitability, less labour, water and fuel should be used. There is scope for decreased use of fertilizer, even up to 50 per cent, while biological control of weeds and nitrogen fixation in cereal crops hold promises for the future profitability of cereal cultivation. Achieving sustainability would require ecosystem-oriented research and development. Each ecosystem would require development of its own production system. For the existing ecosystems, finding solutions for the decline in yield when inputs are held constant is a major challenge. Reduction of environmental damage can be achieved by integrated pest management, the development of durable pest resistant varieties, and the elaboration of production systems that prevent water and land degradation. Finally, the well-being of producers and consumers, in particular those with low income, calls for low-input varieties that have some tolerance for drought and floods and are early maturing. The problem with hybrid varieties is the necessity to purchase the seed, making the seeds an external input to the farm. An improvement would be the introduction of a-sexual seed production that can internalize the seed production.

Implementation of research projects requires partnership and sharing of responsibilities between international institutes, national agricultural research networks and universities and like institutions. IRRI distinguishes between research consortia, research networks and technology evaluation networks. Consortia, involving a few top institutes, develop the new technology that can be evaluated in the research network, and adapted through contacts with national research organisations and the private sector. Embedded within a long-term strategy in which participation of key players and target beneficiaries is assured, this approach provides the conditions for both high-quality research and large-scale applicability of the results.

A central question in the discussion that followed was whether productivity improvements would lead to more revenues: the immediate response to higher production might be a decrease in price which could offset the gain in productivity. Some participants emphasised that without production improvements, other producers would come in, as illustrated by the inroads that Malaysian cocoa producers made when African producers reduced their investments, or as otherwise market share would be lost to competitive products. In the case of mineral products, hardly any scope appears to exist for gainful productivity improvements at the primary level, but productivity improvements in processing with concomitant reduction of prices should enable development of new end-uses.

Mr. Jose A. Cerro, Executive Secretary of the Group of Latin-American and Caribbean Sugar Exporting Countries (GEPLACEA), Mexico, introduced the topic of *commercial utilization of waste products and by-products'*. The speaker pointed at the fluctuating world market prices of sugar due to the extremely high share of fixed costs in sugar production, and to economic policies reducing the world market to a residual market and causing a chronic surplus of sugar. In these circumstances, the strategy followed by GEPLACEA was: (i) to defend prices and markets; (ii) aim at diversifying the end-uses of sugar cane; and (iii) productivity improvements, while improving the environment. The first part of the strategy involves marketing efforts, including research, information collection, and training of marketing officers in co-operation with major market players. It also involves political work, including co-ordinated action concerning GATT negotiations. Diversification is envisaged at growers' levels by enabling more intercropping, and at industry level by developing new products, such as alcohol, bagasse, and molasses as animal feed, plastics and paper. Such diversification would not be possible if productivity were not increased.

The search for reducing environmental damage, combined with the integral approach to sugar cane processing, has led to the formulation of a project now submitted to the Common Fund for Commodities: the project for treatment of residues at alcohol distilleries using sugar cane molasses to recover Saccharomyces yeast and produce biogas.

Dr. Gabriel Kouthon, Senior Officer, Food and Agriculture Industries Service, FAO, whose presentation was on the topic of *'ways of proceeding towards increased local processing in developing producing countries'*, provided evidence of the beneficial impact that the establishment of processing industries can have for regions and countries. Through the application of appropriate technologies for the processing of crop, livestock, fisheries and forest products, local processing industries can improve food supplies and reduce imports; add value to raw material and increase export earnings; provide employment and reduce income gaps;

assure better market opportunities and provide a stimulus to increase production; reduce population migration; improve standards of nutrition; and increase opportunities for investment in rural areas.

Dr. Kouthon identified the following as major impediments to agro-industry development in developing countries: limited financial ability to purchase inputs; land tenure problems; lack of credit for seeds, fertilizers, implements and other inputs; inefficient links between industry, government and research institutions; limited technical knowledge; erratic labour availability and managerial skills; lack of road infrastructure and transport; inappropriate handling of containers, and a neglect of food handling and packing in technical training and assistance programmes; poor facilities; lack of utilities; irregular supply of raw materials and inefficient quality control; insufficient product publicity; lack of market information, retail opportunities and outlets; lack of attractive packaging materials used in most developing countries, and unsuitability to good preservation of the products; irregular supply of products; short shelf-life; price fluctuations and a lack of product quality assurance; lack of trained personnel and of training facilities for middle-level manpower required for technological activities; lack of industrial extension services and maintenance and operation of machinery and training for graduates in food and agricultural processing technology; lack of extension facilities to convey research results to the users of technologies; absence of national institutions involved in research and development and training in the field of food and agro-industries in some countries, and lack of adequate facilities for these activities in other countries; absence of national institutions involved in product quality control to promote a safe and honestly presented supply to protect consumers from products which are injurious to health, unfit for human consumption, adulterated or presented in a deceptive manner, and to encourage the orderly development of food and agro-industries which can stimulate increased foreign earnings through the export of commodities which comply with acceptable standards.

In the discussion, major issues highlighted were the financing of processing capacity and the guiding policies of governments. Indonesia was mentioned as an example of a successful policy-induced creation of a plywood industry, and Taiwan was mentioned as an example of how domestically raised finance helped setting up the agro-based industry there. In addition to the list of constraints given by Dr. Kouthon, the high effective rates of protection in many developed countries were specifically mentioned.

Tan Sri Dr. B.C. Sekhar, Secretary-General of the International Rubber Study Group (IRSG), spoke on *'the global era - quality concepts'*. The speaker stressed that quality is an essential and critical element in the market stability of industrial commodities. There are basically two distinctive parts in the total quality concept. The first relates to the intrinsic quality as defined by acceptable specification and the second arises from consistent quality through standardised application of quality management checks and balances as in the ISO 9000 series of quality management principles. There is universal acceptance for the need to implement fully the elements of ISO 9000. The speaker illustrated the above using the example of natural rubber (NR). The advent of the synthetic rubber (SR) sector as a consequence of the Second World War brought about motivation on the part of the producers as, like in most industries, it is the 'consumer pull' that brings about quality changes. The tyre sector, consuming about 70% of NR, was traditionally prepared to accept the traditional form of NR, sheets packed in bales, as the all-important competitive feature was price. Because of the competition from SR and vertical integration between SR production and tyre production, the NR sector had to change. The first step was the introduction of a number of grades of Technically Specified Rubber which, however, differs among countries depending on the way the rubber is produced. The net effect was, unfortunately, that manufacturers wanted the better grades for the lower price. It is, therefore, the marketing approach that needs to be improved. The basic approach for NR producers should be to reduce the number of grades, to offer quality as 'free' and let the market follow the fundamentals of supply and demand. 'Producer push' in the case of NR should receive an enthusiastic welcome; NR producers can ill-afford to wait for further 'consumer pull'.

In the discussion, it was remarked that in the case of metals, higher quality leads to higher prices, which is not necessarily the case for soft commodities. The story of quality also applies to different commodities with different modalities; e.g. coffee has to consider hygiene, while natural rubber has to worry about substitution. It was stressed that quality improvement is an area in which the Fund should specifically help.

In the session on *'marketing'*, two papers were presented. The first paper, *'Promoting and limiting factors to expand demand for commodities toward the 21st century'* was presented by Dr. T. Haseyama, Chuo University, Tokyo. The speaker reviewed some limiting factors to expand demand for primary and related commodities, mentioning, among others, the economic stagnation, structural changes in industrialized countries, increased recycling and new materials. The speaker then discussed the correlation between energy-resource consumption and industrial activity as well as the trade-off between energy-resource consumption and economic growth. There is a shift towards an energy-saving industrial structure. The speaker then addressed the main theme of promoting and limiting factors to expand demand for commodities. Case studies were presented on the huge potential demand for cereals for feed-use, and Japanese efforts to exploit the overseas demand market for primary commodities. The conclusion based on the latter case study was that the success is due to some intensive efforts by producers, exporters and such institutional bodies as co-operatives, implying a concerted effort of all actors. Such 'self-help' efforts, or similar strategies on the part of countries exporting primary commodities, would make for more favourable breakthrough in the demand market for their products.

The second paper in the session on marketing, *'Promotion of demand for commodities through multinational action'*, was presented by Mr. B. Olsen, Chief Market Development Section, International Trade Centre. After discussing the need for demand stimulation and the possibilities for doing so through intergovernmental co-operation using generic promotion, the speaker briefly described case studies on generic promotion for commodities regarding: (i) promotion of jute geotextiles; (ii) promotion of sisal harvest twine; (iii) promotion of the health aspects of tea; and (iv) promotion of spices in the United States. The speaker concluded that the planning and implementation of generic promotion must be done in close collaboration with the trade and industry in the target markets. The promotion programme has to be designed specifically for the commodity and, in most cases, for the specific target market, although many elements of a generic promotion campaign can be common in different target markets. ICBs can play an important role in drawing the attention of their members to the options existing for generic promotion of their particular commodity and in the preparation of project proposals. The ICBs also have an important role to play in identifying potential financing sources and in negotiating agreements on generic promotion actions with the trade and industry in exporting and consuming countries.

Participants raised the problem of how to evaluate market promotion projects, how to measure the effect, and how to mobilize the private industry. In the case of industrial commodities such as natural rubber and jute, the question was raised of whom to approach when using the environmental friendliness argument: the manufacturer, or the final consumer?

Ms. Janet Farooq, Chief, Diversification, Processing, Marketing and Distribution Section, UNCTAD, presented the paper *'The challenge of marketing commodities from developing countries'* written by herself and Mr. Lamon Rutten. The paper focused on the problems arising in the marketing of commodities related to marketing structures, the mechanisms used and the associated government policies. It was written with the intention of identifying activities that need to be reinforced or initiated in order to assist commodity traders in developing countries who are in a weak bargaining position. In this regard, three basic models of commodity production can be identified: large-scale production; small-scale, but organized production (such as through co-operatives); and small-scale, fragmented production. Large-scale production units are in a position to have their own sophisticated marketing department. The second way in which production can be organized is through co-operatives or producer associations which group together several small or medium-sized producers for the purpose of providing some common services. One of these services is usually in the marketing area and can range from informal arrangements to co-ordinate shipments, to obtaining more favourable transport rates, or improving export logistics to have a common marketing service which acts as agent for the group. The third scenario involves a multitude of small-scale producers who usually sell their output to middlemen. These are the groups who often do not have access to market information on an ongoing and up-to-date basis to credit lines for sales, or to other marketing services.

These production scenarios lead to at least four marketing scenarios which have different implications for producer price formation: direct sales by producers to buyers abroad, purchases from producers by agents of local and foreign firms, centralized market places such as auctions, electronic tender systems or forward markets, and government purchases, through a marketing board. Marketing boards recently have often fallen victim to IMF/World Bank-assisted structural adjustment programmes. Depending on the functions of the former board this may lead to increasing price instability, reduced or lacking quality control and inexperience in trading by the emerging private traders. At the same time, the role of futures and options has increased in the international markets. With more complicated markets, there is a growing importance of knowing how to obtain and use information, especially as practically all commodity markets are segmented in various ways. Concomitant with the above developments, there have been some important changes in the world trading structures. The concentration among trade houses of many commodities has significantly increased. This has given the remaining houses considerable market power and increased knowledge about market plans of major suppliers.

Approaches by developing country governments in handling the policy aspects of this new marketing situation have taken three forms. Firstly, the liberalized internal market in a country can be left to sort itself out with only the more viable and experienced traders surviving. This is a high-cost solution with export earnings for the country taking a beating for some years. A second approach is to encourage domestic traders to work together through an association of exporters. The third approach, which is complementary to the other two, is to develop an internal market place such as an auction, electronic tender system or a forward market. Under any of these approaches, producers and exporters are more visibly exposed to price risks. Many have expressed interest in learning to cope with these risks by becoming actively involved in using commodity price risk instruments. The last issue is, then, to assess what assistance is available to developing countries. The first need for assistance is in the area of improving market transparency. This has been supported through market reviews and statistical work of study groups and international commodity organizations. A second area of assistance which has expanded tremendously over the last few years is training for traders, covering a variety of important topics. UNCTAD has taken a slightly different, though complementary, approach in developing its commodity trading packages. The focus has been on computer-based training for using risk management instruments (futures and options) by traders in relation to their specific commodity in order for them to be able to execute trade deals efficiently, and to provide advice to their companies on marketing opportunities. Work has also included courses for executives of companies and policy-makers in governments, and advice on the organization and operation of internal and regional market places.

The discussion stressed the possible adverse effects of the abolition of marketing boards, the possibly ineffective or adverse government policies regarding the operation of co-operatives, the need to set up appropriate marketing systems with adequate staff to be trained, the need for assistance in training and the question of whether such training should be self-financed or require assistance from outside, e.g. from the Fund; and finally, what the policy of the Fund is, or should be, regarding projects including training. In particular, the development of course material requires funding. The futures market should play a more important role and actors in the market should be better acquainted with the alternatives, physicals, futures, options. More liquidity was deemed needed in this respect which may sometimes create some instability, but will not affect the long-term tendencies or use.

Dr. Uma Lele of the University of Florida presented a paper which she prepared together with James Gockowski and Kofi Adu-Nyako entitled *'Economics, Politics and Ethics of Primary Commodity Development: How Can Poor Countries and Peoples most in Need Benefit?'*. In her introduction she stated that the poorest countries depend preponderantly on a limited number of agricultural commodities. It means that commodities must receive high priority in improving production or exports if overall economic transformation is to be achieved. The speaker discussed the inhospitable international market environment, with inelastic world demand for specific products of LDCs, rapid technological change in production in competing countries, growth of substitute products in importing countries, growing environmental concerns associated with their production, health concerns associated with their consumption, and not the least important, the protectionist policies of OECD countries. A combination of these conditions is generating surplus production, increased price and supply volatility, artificially low international prices, displacement of export markets of developing countries, the dumping of food aid, and a spoiling of production incentives for rural households in poor countries.

The speaker further discussed supply response, and the roles of price and non-price factors as well as the record of macro-economic and sectoral adjustment during structured adjustment. Particular attention was paid to the record of price adjustments, the movement of input prices, the availability of credit the performance of countries with regard to public expenditures. As regards economic diversification (within and outside agriculture) and the fallacy of composition, the speaker drew lessons from recent history, e.g. the importance of emphasizing the development of the food and export crops in which a country already has a strong demonstrated comparative advantage, but doing so by understanding the location-specific costs and benefits of alternative strategies as the most effective means of diversifying out into new crops, and/or undeveloped regions. Lessons of successful agricultural development at the micro level were, according to the speaker, in the area of food insecurity and labour constraints, the role of infrastructure in market integration, the need for stable prices at the national level in selected cases only, the need for research and extension, and for input intensification and environmental concerns.

The speaker concluded that agricultural development requires a deep understanding of the highly diverse location-specific technological, institutional, management, pricing and marketing needs of individual commodities, households and natural resources associated with them. Even though a commodity-based approach to development is currently out of fashion, past successes with smallholder commodity development throughout Africa all offer numerous important lessons. They stress the importance of high-quality, location-specific research and extension, an excellent rural feeder roads network, producers' and processors' access to finance, high-quality planting material, processing and marketing arrangements that take into account economies of scale in processing, and a price incentive system which rewards quality. Most importantly, production of commodities in developing countries requires a competitive global market environment. Similarly, broad-based access of households, handlers, processors, packagers and exporters to information is critical to developing a thriving export sector.

This implies firstly the need for a pragmatic partnership of the public, private and the community level institutions rather than ideologically-based preferences for the role of the private or the public sector. Secondly, it calls for predictable and pluralistic institutions and sophistication on the part of governments to allow the development of the necessary institutions that can bring to bear the most modern, but cost-effective, technologies. It also requires a commitment to the collection and dissemination of relevant information to all concerned actors. International personnel with the necessary know-how must often be important partners in the development and implementation of that strategy because of the access to technology and new forms of management, training, information systems and export strategies that they can bring to bear. Governments need to be skilled to employ the right international personnel, and such partnership must often be distinguished from the ill-equipped, inexperienced technical assistance provided with little institutional memory that has often accompanied foreign aid programs. Industrial country governments who both influence agricultural policies of their own countries and the aid policies towards Africa need to undertake a fundamental assessment of the implications of the current global and African circumstances for both trade and aid policies which would place the low income countries of Africa on a sustained growth path. Most importantly, the governments of African countries need to review the experience of others in the developed and developing world to change the fundamental way in which African agriculture now operates.

The discussion on the paper stressed the need to be careful regarding devaluing exchange rates, as over-valued exchange rates favour the urban sector. It is essential to aim for quality, to maintain and improve the infrastructure and to take into account the complementarity between production of food and cash crops for a better income. In the long-run, countries are moving from some commodities to others, diversifying horizontally and vertically; more vertical diversification appears to be the best solution for the long-term. Governments often do not understand smallholder policy and do not put emphasis on the agricultural sector; this, however, is the lifeline for most poor people in most LDCs. Co-operatives have to be grassroot co-operatives to survive and be effective. Projects in the above areas should be financed by the Fund and, to this effect, the Fund should gather and organize a network around the world of excellent commodity experts because it was felt that such network does not exist in other international organizations. There is a strong need to translate research into practice.

## 3 HOW TO PREPARE GOOD PROJECTS

Members of the Consultative Committee introduced the Manual for the Preparation and Management of Projects to be Financed through the Second Account. Generally, the issuance of the Manual was much welcomed by the ICBs as a substantive strengthening of information on how to prepare projects that would qualify for financing under the Fund's Second Account. In the discussion, five areas were touched upon by ICBs commenting. Firstly, on *'financing policies'*; several ICBs reiterated their preference for grant financing for the following reasons: (i) by their nature, many project types such as research and development, human development, dissemination, or environment-oriented projects, have no direct commercial return; (ii) many ICBs are still not allowed, by their statutes, to sign loan agreements. In addition, a number of ICBs' members have expressed strong reservations about guaranteeing loans; and (iii) the economic and financial situation of many countries, especially the LDCs, does not allow for an increase in their debt burden; bringing in the required counterpart contributions is, for many of these countries, already a severe burden.

Some ICBs, e.g. the International Tropical Timber Organization (ITTO), stated that they had already developed their own procedures for project formulation, supervision and accounting, of which some elements were based on the Fund's Project Manual.

With regard to *'selection of projects'*, it was remarked that the formulation of a comprehensive statement on commodity strategy is both time- and resource-consuming. However, the formulation of an overall strategy, it was stressed, was not a quantitative issue but a qualitative one. Further, it was stated that in some cases technical assistance is required to assist in the formulation of a strategy paper.

Referring to the *'preparation and submission of project proposals'*, it was underscored that the present Standard Format is of great value. A few modifications were requested to be considered:

- adjustment of Parts I and II to avoid duplications;
- an indication of requirements for the completion of project profiles; and
- more elaboration on the management structure in case the ICB is not the Supervisory Body. In such case, a definition of the obligations of the four parties involved, with special emphasis on the responsibility of the ICB, was requested.

Early dialogue between the ICBs and the Fund was considered to be of prime importance. The majority of ICBs expressed an interest in submitting project ideas and profiles for first comments by the Secretariat and the Consultative Committee before an official submission. In principle, Part I of the Standard Format could serve as a Project Profile.

Serious concerns were expressed by the FAO about the high cost of project preparation, supervision and monitoring and these concerns were supported by all the ICBs present. A request was formulated stressing the need for assistance in this regard, and the proposal made for the establishment of a Technical Assistance Facility within the Fund was much welcomed and supported.

Regional institutions such as ECA and ESCAP offered assistance in the preparation of profiles or proposals and this offer was appreciated very much, in addition to the proposal to possibly act as Project Executing Agency or Supervisory Body and to otherwise assist ICBs at all stages of the project cycle.

As regards *'appraisal and approval of project proposals'*, a request was made for a clear timeframe for the appraisal and approval process.

Finally, on the subject of *'management of projects'*, including monitoring and evaluation, it was remarked that, for a few cases, an alternative project management structure should be considered by the Fund. If, for very specific reasons, the ICB itself is the Project Executing Agency, the Supervisory Body could, so it was remarked, be an international institution or even a consulting firm. For project evaluation, advice from the Secretariat was requested on the participation of the Project Executing Agency, the ICB concerned and the Fund, in order to calculate the financial implications into the project budget. It was also remarked that an impact assessment in the framework of the project evaluation should be carried out by an independent consultant.

## 4 SUMMARY AND CONCLUSIONS BY THE MANAGING DIRECTOR OF THE COMMON FUND FOR COMMODITIES

The Conclusions of the Moderator of the Seminar[1] are eloquent and need not be repeated here. They offer thoughts and recommendations that are critical and worthy of consideration. Without paraphrasing any of them, let me add some of my own conclusions as observations.

The Seminar may be deemed an unqualified success in that it accomplished its stated objectives. It brought together most ICBs and organizations active, or interested, in commodity development measures. The exchanges of information and views were useful and effective in clarifying points of view, and focusing on action. The *'role of the Fund as a forum for co-ordination and consultation in commodity measures'* was highlighted as deserving more attention, and in need of proposals and action to concretely fill in this function.

The *'changing role of ICBs'* with an increasing emphasis on their function as originators of commodity development measures and projects, beyond their current administrative and data-gathering roles, was stressed. To fulfil their new function, ICBs will need to formulate effective and sustainable *'commodity strategies'*, which fit in the Integrated Programme for Commodities in a coherent way. Here again, the role of the Fund as a forum for co-ordination comes to the fore. As originators of commodity development projects within the framework of commodity strategies, ICBs will need *technical assistance*. The issuance of the Manual was a small step, but more is to be done to ensure that scarce resources of ICBs are

---

[1] The Conclusions of the Moderator of the Seminar are included at the end of these Proceedings.

not spent on project proposals that come to nought. A network of commodity expertise and financial assistance to develop good projects effectively are key to building a viable pipeline of project proposals to the benefit of the ICBs' members, especially the Least Developed ones. In this regard, the proposals for the creation of a *Technical Assistance Facility* deserve urgent consideration. The history of other International Financial Institutions (IFIs) points to the need, especially at the start, of being able to offer technical assistance facilities to beneficiaries. The Fund cannot fail to draw lessons from this experience. In this regard also, the Fund cannot fail to ignore that other IFIs offer to this day project preparation facilities.

Finally, the need for *training* of *'Least Developed Countries' participants in using market instruments'* is a subject that requires action, in concert with other organizations and ICBs. At a time when the number of trading houses diminishes, creating in some commodities effective oligopolies; at a time when commodity agreements no longer effect price stability in the face of continuously declining commodity prices and exports, and with high effective rates of protection in developed countries; at a time when bankers estimate that more than USD 25 billion is invested in Managed Futures Funds, access to market information and instruments is critical to all developing countries but especially in the poorest ones.

We are rejoicing in that the new Presidency of the European Community Council desires to promote the strengthening of the dialogue on commodity measures which, we wholeheartedly agree, was too long neglected. This is because commodity matters do not belong to the *arcana* of trade negotiations, they are increasingly vital to most of the population of this earth. To ignore their demand is to ignore one's own future well-being.

# PART II

---

# OPENING STATEMENTS

# OFFICIAL OPENING STATEMENT BY
## MR. ERIK DERYCKE,
## SECRETARY OF STATE FOR DEVELOPMENT CO-OPERATION

**Mr. Chairman, Dear Sir, Ladies and Gentlemen:**

It's a great honour for me to welcome all of you today to this seminar of the Common Fund for Commodities here at the Egmont Palace in Brussels. The importance that Belgium attaches to this seminar in particular, and to the development of the commodity sector in general, is underlined by this impressive location. We are all aware of the profound crisis which the commodity sector experiences today and the severe consequences for the commodity dependent developing countries with their millions of inhabitants. I hope this seminar will, ultimately, make a worthwhile contribution to the strengthening and revitalization of the international commodity co-operation.

Allow me to reiterate some of the more striking premises. Most commodity prices have fallen to almost unprecedented levels. The prospects for recovery remain vague. The traditional strategies of price stabilization agreements and arrangements have failed. On the other hand, the commodity dependent position of many developing countries, particularly the least developed ones, is even more pronounced over time. For these countries, commodities will have to continue to form the engine of economic growth, because the same constraints that generally keep these countries in this position - lack of human resource development, of good infrastructure, and of access to investment flows - also limit the overall economic development and growth.

Against this background, the necessary development efforts for the commodity sector should be characterized by the following principal objectives:

- the establishment of an equilibrium between supply and demand
- the improvement of the competitiveness through an increased productivity and cost-effectiveness.
- the reduction of excessive dependence on primary commodities through

vertical and horizontal diversification
- an improved access to and transparency of the international markets
- a better management of the natural resources to ensure a surtainable development.

Improved international commodity agreements, at the same time viable and more efficient, are of primary importance for a continued international co-operation in the sector. Therefore, the current negotiations should receive all necessary attention and support. All international agencies involved in the commodity sector and present here should remain strong advocates of sustainable international agreements and should make their voices heard.

At the same time, all other instruments and facilities for commodities development should be constantly monitored, improved and fine-tuned to ensure optimal results. Research institutions, produces associations, compensatory financing facilities, commodity information systems ... among others would be valorized up to their maximum.

Therefore, the Common Fund for Commodities in particular, given its unique focus and objectives, has to produce all necessary efforts that can lead to the full realization of its potential capacities. It should play an important central and catalytic role in world commodity issues.

The need for a coherent international commodity policy tackling the issues for each specific commodity is clearly felt at all levels. This seminar, aiming to prepare the groundwork for the development of global strategies for individual commodities, can be considered as the first step in this direction. Consequently, I do urge all participants to enter in a positive interactive exchange of views and discussion in order to meet the goals set for this seminar.

The elaboration of a coherent long-term strategy for each commodity will enable both the International Commodity Bodies and the Common Fund to screen and identify in a more effective way projects and development actions to be financed through the Second Account. The presentation of, and the subsequent discussion on, the 'Project Manual' should facilitate an efficient communication between the ICBs and the Common Fund.

All this should lead to a well-functioning Second Account facility for the financing of development efforts in the commodity sector.

This unique gathering of organizations, active in the field of commodities should, in my opinion, be able to offer additional results to what is stated in the objectives of this seminar. There is the issue of the Common Fund First Account facility. The absence of buffer-stocking arrangements has left the resources of this account unused. This seminar will offer an informal opportunity for a reflection on alternative uses for this facility. I, therefore, invite all participants in this seminar to share any new ideas they may have acquired in their specific involvement with the commodity sector.

**Mr. Chairman, Dear Sir, Ladies and Gentlemen, Distinguished Participants:**

Devising a global strategy for specific commodities is only a first step in a whole process. To valorize this effort to its full extent, these strategies should be reflected in the international and national commodity development policies of organizations, producer and consumer countries.

Therefore, I do hope that this seminar and the quality of its results will enable the Common Fund for Commodities to come forward and play its role as a key instrument in this sector. It's only by making a worthwhile contribution to the amelioration of the current dismal situation that the Common Fund will assume its full place on the international commodity development scene.

What's left for me to do now, is to declare this seminar officially open. I wish you fruitful discussions and I shall be interested to hear your conclusions at the end of this week. Till then.

# STATEMENT BY
## MR. BUDI HARTANTYO,
## MANAGING DIRECTOR OF THE COMMON FUND
## FOR COMMODITIES

**Mr. Derycke, Sir Alister, Distinguished Representatives of International Commodity Bodies and other international organizations, Ladies and Gentlemen:**

First of all I should like to express, on behalf of all the participants and on my own behalf, our deep appreciation to the Government of Belgium for hosting this Seminar and for providing this magnificent Egmont Palace as its venue.

I also should like to thank the Secretary of State for Development Cooperation, Mr. Erik Derycke, for taking a personal interest in the Seminar and for having so graciously accepted to be its Honorary Chairman. His inspiring address and his thoughts on world commodity issues will undoubtedly serve as a valuable element on which to base our discussions in the Seminar. I further should like to thank the guest speakers for the time they took off from their busy schedules to join us, and I am sure that their valuable contributions will be very worthwhile.

We are fortunate today to have also with us Mr. Carlos Fortin, Deputy to the Secretary-General and Director of the Commodities Division of UNCTAD, who will be addressing us later this morning. As you may be well aware, the Common Fund for Commodities was born out of the Negotiating Conference on a Common Fund held under the auspices of UNCTAD, and our two organizations have kept a very close and special relationship with each other since.

Last but not least, I am grateful to Sir Alister McIntyre for agreeing to be the moderator of the Seminar. Sir Alister is currently the Vice-Chancellor of the University of the West Indies in Jamaica. He has served as Deputy Secretary-General and Officer-in-charge of UNCTAD, and is quite familiar with the objectives and functions of the Fund. Although Sir Alister has been away from UNCTAD for some time now, I believe that his heart is still with the Common Fund and that he retains a keen interest in its work and developments.

**Distinguished Participants:**

Since the Common Fund held its first seminar for ICBs in 1991, the situation in the world commodity market has not improved. In fact, the plight of the commodity exporting developing countries has even worsened. Prices of commodities in the world market keep falling and supply overhang remains as serious as ever. At the same time, there has been little relief from heavy external debt burden.

The 1980s were referred to as the 'lost decade for development' for the developing countries. This apt characterization of the situation derives its origin from UNCTAD under the then Officer-in-charge, our moderator of the Seminar, Sir Alister McIntyre. That situation has spilled over into the 1990s until to date.

Among the main causes for the depressed state of the economies of the majority of developing countries is the prevalence of very low and declining real prices for most commodities on international markets and a resulting contraction of commodity export earnings. Virtually all developing countries experienced shortfalls in export earnings. Highly commodity dependent countries suffered the most. Africa's commodity export earnings, for instance, contracted by about 40% between 1979 and 1989.

Although some developing countries, notably those in Southeast Asia, have been successful in reducing their dependence on commodities, the importance of commodity exports to Africa, other Asian countries, Latin America and the Caribbean continues to be vital.

Forty out of 47 countries in Africa depend for more than 70% of their export earnings on commodities, while in Latin America and the Caribbean 17 out of 31 countries also depend heavily on commodity exports. In the 1988-1990 period, out of 113 developing countries, 42 depended for over 70% of their export earnings on only one or two commodities. Almost two-thirds of them were African countries. This heavy dependence on commodities renders them highly vulnerable to the vagaries of the market. Unfortunately, at least for the foreseeable future, most of these countries will have to continue to depend on commodities for their revenues and as engine for growth, as there are no short-cuts. Nevertheless, in my view, all is not lost. The experience of East and Southeast Asian countries shows that diversification in the traditional commodity sector and improvements in productivity and quality and, consequently, competitiveness vis-à-vis substitutes is the way to reducing dependence and maximizing earnings.

It is here that the Common Fund can play a significant role in assisting the commodity producing developing countries in developing and diversifying their respective commodity sectors.

As the only multilateral institution of global dimension that has emerged from the North-South dialogue of the Seventies, the Common Fund for Commodities is unique in the sense that it is alone among international development institutions in that it deals solely with commodity issues and that its operational activities emphasize commodity focus as opposed to country focus.

As you are well aware, the Fund was established to support, through its First Account, the financing of buffer stocks held by international commodity organizations for stabilizing prices of their respective commodities at remunerative and equitable levels. Its other function is to finance, through the Second Account, commodity development measures aimed at improving the structural conditions in markets and at enhancing the long-term competitiveness and prospects of particular commodities.

However, the collapse of many price stabilization agreements during the past decade has left few customers to take advantage of the facility offered through the First Account. The absence of buffer-stocking agreements necessitated focal attention to be devoted to Second Account Operations. Nevertheless, various options are being considered on how the resources of the First Account can be best used to cushion the volatile commodity sector. One of these is providing assistance to developing countries, particularly to the least developed among them, in training manpower in the use of market instruments. Training of manpower from developing countries in the use of market instruments constitutes a primary step for a possible future involvement in market-related activities. It will introduce developing countries to the use of appropriate hedging mechanisms that guarantee them predictable price levels and that enable them to reasonably plan their activities. In this regard, I would like to invite participants from the International Commodity Bodies as well as the other participants to take the opportunity provided by this Seminar to advance any ideas they may have for the use of the resources of the First Account.

Efforts are now being intensified towards the other goals of the Integrated Programme for Commodities of UNCTAD. These include in particular the optimization of the contribution of the commodity sector to the national economies through, inter alia, activities aimed at improving productivity and cost-effectiveness, long-term competitiveness, the gradual reduction of excessive dependence on primary commodities as a source of export revenues through vertical diversification efforts, improving market access, and ensuring proper and sustained management of natural resources.

The shift in emphasis from price stabilization efforts to development measures has boosted the importance of Second Account activities and the potential role it can play in alleviating the problems faced by developing countries.

Second Account operations, after a somewhat slow start, are now taking off vigorously. This is not unusual in the operational development of international institutions. It is particularly true with regard to Second Account operations of the Common Fund with its unique commodity focus. Neither the Fund nor most of the ICBs had previous experience in this regard and there was no earlier model to follow. Many things had to be done on a trial and error basis. Those of you who have attended the first seminar that the Common Fund had organized with the ICBs in September 1991, may recall the discussions that took place in that seminar. Although the seminar could be considered successful and had achieved the objectives for which it was organized, it had left many questions unanswered. That year, in 1991, only one project ('Design and Prototype Fabrication of Shipping Containers for Rubber Bales') was approved for financing through the Second Account.

It might be interesting for you to note that even a large and prestigious international financial institution as the World Bank went through similar childhood illnesses as the Common Fund.

In this respect I would like to quote an extract from Mason and Asher's book 'The World Bank since Bretton Woods' on the history of the Bank three years after its establishment:

*"The hope that well-conceived, well-prepared project applications would come cascading into headquarters was dashed almost as soon as the Bank opened for business. It quickly became clear that applicants needed technical assistance in preparing project proposals."*

Those words may sound very familiar both to the ICBs and the Fund with regard to project proposals from ICBs to the Fund.

Nevertheless, I think that, since we had that first seminar, a lot of water has gone under the bridge and that both the ICBs and the Fund have gained considerable experience in project preparation and project appraisal respectively. Last year five projects have been approved for financing by the Fund and it is my hope that this year we will be able to approve at least ten projects. Around forty project proposals are currently in the pipeline for consideration by the Consultative Committee at its next two or three meetings.

There is better understanding now on the side of the ICBs with regard to the policies and requirements of the Fund, while on the side of the Fund there is also better appreciation of the constraints and capabilities of ICBs. The Fund has also strengthened its relationship and cooperation with other, well-established development institutions such as the World Bank and the Consultative Group on International Agricultural Research (CGIAR), among other things with respect to the co-financing of projects.

However, further efforts are required to reach on optimum level of interaction and mutual understanding, not only between the ICBs and the organs of the Fund (in particular the Consultative Committee and the Secretariat), but also with the various relevant international organizations involved in commodity development issues.

The present Seminar is intended to advance that goal.

The immediate objective of the Seminar is to maximize the benefits that ICBs can derive from the facilities of the Second Account by providing them guidance in preparing appropriate project proposals in the context of commodity strategies and which will meet with the policies and criteria set by the Fund. For this purpose, the last day and a half of the Seminar will be devoted to discussing the 'Manual for the Preparation and Management of Projects' which was recently issued by the Fund.

However, the Seminar has a special significance in view of the increasingly important role that commodity development measures are assuming in ICB activities. It would be a milestone, if I may use this much abused word, if this Seminar could provide a further impetus to the ICBs to assume, in addition to their traditional roles, a new role in developing international strategies for their particular commodities. Such a role would include becoming promoters and designers of projects related to commodities with the objectives of generating added-value and enhancing the market structures for the benefit of the developing countries, in particular the least developed among them.

The above-mentioned goal of the Seminar is reflected in the choice of topics to be discussed in the Seminar:

- productivity improvement
- quality improvement
- commercial utilization of waste- and by-products
- diversification/local processing
- competitiveness

- new applications/end uses
- new consumers
- the domestic and international marketplace
- how to reach the countries and peoples most in need of help

For that purpose, the Fund has invited prominent experts to speak on the commodity development measures referred to above which, I hope, will generate a stimulating and fruitful discussion among the participants.

I am fully convinced that, with the uniqueness of the Fund, in strong partnership with the ICBs, the cooperation of other development institutions, and the full support of its Members, together we will make our mark in international development efforts.

For many developed countries, commodity issues may not appear of importance today, but for a large number of developing countries improvements in the commodity sector are vital. To neglect the needs of a majority of mankind may prove to be shortsighted and one day we might be haunted by our failure to give them the importance they deserve.

Around this table today are gathered representatives of almost all the international commodity bodies and other international organizations involved in commodity issues. It is my sincere hope that this Seminar may somehow, even if in a modest way, help turn around the situation for the better.

I wish you fruitful deliberations and a successful Seminar.

## ADDRESS BY
## MR. CARLOS FORTIN
## DEPUTY TO THE SECRETARY-GENERAL AND
## DIRECTOR FOR COMMODITIES OF UNCTAD

The promotion of international cooperation has always been one of the cornerstones of UNCTAD's approach in the commodities field. The integrated Programme for Commodities was essentially an effort at mobilizing the cooperative will of producers and consumers to address the problems of the international commodity economy. This is indeed one element of the IPC that remains unquestionably valid, irrespective of the vicissitudes of some of its other, more specific components.

It is therefore little wonder that the issue of international commodity co-operation was very much present in the thinking of UNCTAD's secretariat in the preparations for the eighth Conference in February 1992. In particular, the Report of the Secretary-General of UNCTAD to the Conference devoted a good deal of attention to the issue and offered an assessment of producer-consumer and producer co-operation in the 1980s and an analysis of the factors explaining the level of co-operation achieved.

The assessment of developments in the 1980s pointed to some serious problems. The report stated that, despite broad agreement in the international community as to the central objectives of international commodity policy, the translation of those objectives into implementable measures and actions had been sporadic and no coherent international commodity policy had been evolved. It then went on to state that the most significant factor accounting for that situation was the weakening of the content of producer-consumer and producer cooperation in the 1980s. While the 1980s had witnessed the emergence of a number of new producer-consumer and producer arrangements, including ICAs without economic provisions and study groups, there had been a clear weakening of interest in systematic efforts to agree upon and implement policy actions. Disillusionment with the operations of price stabilization arrangements had set in, notably following the collapse of the International Tin Agreement and weak producer responses to mounting surpluses. The membership of certain commodity arrangements had declined entailing the absence of important actors on both the producer and consumer sides. Budgetary and other financial difficulties had tampered the operations of commodity organizations and the establishment of new study groups. As a result of these problems, no marked improvement had taken place in the transparency of commodity markets.

The Secretary-General's report suggested that the weakening of producer-consumer and producer co-operation in the 1980s was due to a number of factors. Perhaps the main one was that, contrary to the situation which prevailed in the 1960s and 1970s, international commodity markets were characterized by depressed real prices rather than price instability around an upward trend. The main determinant of depressed prices was over-supply rather than insufficient demand. The problem of over-supply did not lend itself easily to approaches through producer-consumer and producer co-operation. This situation favoured consumers who were no longer concerned with the issue of security of supplies, and it also led to divergencies amongst producers on the types of co-operative action that might be taken. A further significant factor influencing the policies of countries in this regard was the growing emphasis on reliance on market forces as opposed to government intervention.

Structural changes in developed and developing countries also affected producer-consumer co-operation. A huge expansion of production in both groups of countries, resulting from substantially increased productivity and the successful diversification efforts of new entrants, led to important changes on the importer and exporter sides alike and made the dynamics of co-operation more difficult. Moreover, some major actors in international commodity markets became less dependent on specific commodities and consequently less dependent on co-operative action for these commodities.

For developing countries, a variety of factors introduced additional complexities. As a result of debt service obligations and the adoption of structural adjustment programmes which called for the expansion of the export sector, developing producer countries came under pressure to expand commodity production and exports. This aggravated the problems of over-supply. For many developing countries the economic crisis that they underwent in the 1980s weakened considerably the chances of meaningful producer co-peration. In addition, certain developing countries became important consumers and importers of a number of commodities.

In developed countries, domestic policies and protectionism stimulated production as well as the export of commodities, reduced their imports and led to conflicts both among them and with developing country producers. In addition, some countries in Central and Eastern Europe became major consumers and importers of commodities, mainly under special bilateral arrangements.

The Secretary-General's report concluded this discussion stating that the formulation of a strengthened international commodity policy must take account of the changed circumstances and identify strategic areas where action can remove the main obstacles to international co-operation. The revitalization of producer co-operation is crucial given the over-supply situation. For this to happen, it is essential that an overall approach be adopted whereby cross-commodity trade-offs can occur in order to take account of the growing diversity of interests among and within producer countries. In this context, efforts would have to be made at introducing forms of supply management. The purpose here should not be to perpetuate inefficient production but rather to facilitate the transition to a new division of labour among producer countries based on comparative advantage and on diversification. Strengthened producer co-operaton is also a precondition for the revival of a producer-consumer dialogue. The inclusion in such a dialogue of particular issues of concern to consumers, including, for example, the influence of environmental considerations on the consumption and use of particular commodities, should provide a new impetus to strengthened international co-operation on commodities.

At UNCTAD VIII the issue of producer and consumer co-operation was amply discussed on the basis of the Secretary-General's report, and the conclusions of the discussion, embodied in the relevant paragraphs of the Cartagena Commitment, reflected the fundamental orientations of the report. The Conference urged producers and consumers of individual commodities to make an examination of ways and means for reinforcing and improving their co-operation in order to contribute to the solution of problems in the commodity area. Significantly, the Conference recognized that such co-operation could take various forms, and it consequently stressed that producers and consumers should take into account the particular characteristics and situation of each individual commodity.

The Conference recommended that an optimal functioning of commodity markets should be sought, *inter alia*, through improved market transparency involving exchanges of views and information on investment plans, prospects and markets for individual commodities. Substantive negotiations between producers and consumers should be pursued with a view to achieving viable and more efficient international agreements, that take into account market trends, or arrangements, as well as study groups. In this regard, particular attention should be paid to the agreements on cocoa, coffee, sugar and tropical timber. The Conference underlined the importance of full and active participation by consumers and producers in international commodity agreements and arrangements. Occupational health and safety matters, technology transfer and services associated with the production, marketing and promotion of commodities, as well as environmental considerations, should be taken into account.

Co-operation among producers and consumers should be strengthened, especially in situations of large stock overhangs.

The Conference welcomed the coming into force of the Common Fund for Commodities and its potential contribution to support international commodity co-operation. It urged exploitation of its resources. It also urged an increase of efforts for the elaboration and consideration of appropriate project proposals, including those on diversification, to be financed through the Second Account, particularly to benefit the least developed countries and the commodities of interest to developing countries, particularly those of small producers-exporters.

The broad orientations agreed by the Conference were reflected later on by the Trade and Development Board of UNCTAD when it adopted the Terms of Reference of the Standing Committee on Commodities, the intergovernmental organ of UNCTAD charged with the promotion of sound, compatible and consistent policies at national and international levels in the commodities field. The Standing Committee was specifically mandated to follow and facilitate, as appropriate, intergovernmental consultations and action among interested countries on the problems of particular commodities or groups of commodities; to analyse the need for, and encourage when considered necessary, the achievement of viable and efficient international agreements or arrangements that take into account market trends, as well as study groups, both autonomous and within UNCTAD.

UNCTAD VII and its follow-up, therefore, provided both a reaffirmation of the will of the international community to persevere in the attainment of enhanced co-operation in the area of commodities and a number of concrete orientations and guidelines to implement that will. What has, in fact, happened in international commodity co-operation since?

In front of this audience I do not need to engage in a detailed account of developments in commodity negotiations in the last 18 months. Many of you have in fact been directly involved in such negotiations. Let me simply state that the process has been complex and that the results are, so far, mixed. Unresolved problems remain in some such major negotiations as those in cocoa, coffee, timber and natural rubber; by contrast, negotiations were successfully concluded in the cases of sugar, olive oil and table olives, and copper, and co-operation continued and was in some cases strengthened in a number of other commodities. One way to attempt an overall balance may be to assess developments against some of the more specific orientations for international policy action in the field of commodity co-operation that were considered in UNCTAD VIII. This way of proceeding would have the additional advantage of allowing focussing of the directions for the future that international policy on commodity co-operation should take.

Precisely this more concrete identification of operational areas for producer-consumer and producer co-operation was proposed in another document submitted to UNCTAD VIII, namely the analytical report of the UNCTAD secretariat to the Conference. There it is stated that efforts to achieve and maintain a better balance between supply and demand must continue to be the major component of producer-consumer co-operation. The actions to be taken will need to include research and development to reduce costs of production and to identify new end-uses, market promotion to increase demand and improvements in the processing, storage, transportation and handling, quality control, grading, packaging and marketing of the commodities. The report recognizes that a listing of the areas for producer-consumer co-operation varies from commodity to commodity. It does, however, identify the following as deserving particular attention:

- Supply management and rationalization
- Improvement in market transparency
- Research and development
- Promotion of local processing
- Market promotion
- Improvement in, and rational use of, marketing systems and practices.
- Ensuring the sustainability of commodity-based development.

In connection with producer co-operation, it is suggested that it has a fundamental role to play, whether as a catalyst for launching co-operation with consumers, or as complementary to, and an effective tool for strengthening producer-consumer co-operation when the latter exists, or finally as a substitute to the latter when it does not exist.

The more specific objectives of producer co-operation overlap substantially with those of producer-consumer co-operation. They include, on the supply side, such action aimed at immediate improvement as management

and rationalization measures, through such schemes as indicative voluntary production and export quotas. These measures are particularly called
for in situations where there are excessive stocks overhanging the market
which depress prices to unremunerative levels. On the demand side,
intensified co-operation among producers is called for in order to undertake generic advertising and market promotion campaigns aimed at
providing immediate relief by expanding the markets for their export
commodities.

For the long term, producers should co-operate in order to improve the
structural characteristics and promote the development of their commodity
markets. Such co-operation would need to cover:

- Research and development activities aimed at lowering the costs of
  production and improving the quality of their commodity in order to
  enhance its competitiveness.
- Enhanced market transparency through the building of efficient systems
  of gathering and transmission of comprehensive, reliable and up-to-date
  information that would allow producers to evaluate market opportunities
  objectively and efficiently.
- Improvement of marketing techniques including greater use of commodity exchanges and futures trading.
- Joint procurement of imported inputs used for the production, local
  processing or marketing of commodities (fertilizers, pesticides, equipment, packing and packaging and complementary materials, etc.)
- Harmonization of production policies and marketing strategies. In order
  to avoid large market imbalances and a waste of scarce financial
  resources, regular and systematic exchange of information and consultations among all producers are required with a view to harmonizing their
  investment, production and marketing plans.

When viewed against this broader panoply of policy objectives and
modalities, the assessment of developments in international commodity co-
operation since UNCTAD VIII appears considerably less bleak than it was
at the end of the 1980s. The most striking positive development is the
growing awareness of the need to co-operate internationally to improve
transparency in commodity markets and industries, and the growing
number of concrete efforts in this direction that are taking place. Improvements in the availability of market and industry data and in the
mechanisms for exchange of information are a feature of all the agreements already renegotiated or currently being negotiated. In addition,
particularly in the field of minerals and metals, there has been an upsurge

of interest in study groups, whose main purpose is to improve transparency. Concentrating for a moment only on those cases in which UNCTAD has been directly involved, as already indicated, an International Copper Study Group was formally established in January 1992 and started effective operations in the course of 1993. A dialogue between bauxite producing and consuming countries, including also alumina and aluminium, was initiated in UNCTAD in 1991 when an Ad hoc Review Meeting on Bauxite was held. A second meeting took place in April 1993, which discussed the need for a continuing effort to increase transparency of the market. The Intergovernmental Group of Experts on Iron Ore, operating under the auspices of UNCTAD, has continued to serve the goal of improving market transparency and providing a forum for regular dialogue between iron ore producers and consumers. A similar role is played by the Intergovernmental Expert Group on Tungsten, also operating under UNCTAD. Exchanges of information and of experiences have also become intensified among commodity producers, notably in sugar, bananas, cocoa, tin and natural rubber.

Also striking is the movement that has taken place in the field of international co-operation for supply management and rationalization. This is a sensitive area, which evokes fears of attempts at manipulating markets. Also, as indicated, the short-term advantages of oversupply for consumers and of expansion of export volumes for some producers conspired until recently against international co-operation in this field. This is now changing. Consumers have now come to perceive the medium and long-term dangers of persistently depressed markets, which lead to under-investment and future scarcity. Producers have also realized that, given the price elasticities of different commodities, they are often better off by selling less at a better price than more at a much lower price. As a result, the notion of supply rationalization is gaining acceptance. The most visible example is, of course, the introduction of production policy as the central economic clause of the proposed cocoa agreement, but similar ideas have been floated in the negotiations on coffee and, among producers on natural rubber. It is sadly ironic that a pioneer effort in this front, the supply policies introduced by the Association of Tin Producing Countries, are at the moment under pressure in the market. Production policies and supply rationalization have emerged as a highly promising avenues for international co-operation in commodities, and deserve strong support from the international community.

Equally promising is the upsurge of interest in co-peration for improvement in, and rational use of, marketing systems and practices. It is now widely recognized that an improved producer-consumer dialogue aimed at reviewing marketing systems being used for a commodity, including risk management instruments, would assist in the better functioning of commodity markets. Such a review should also cover problems in regulatory systems affecting physical and futures trading and changes in marketing structures in terms of major actors involved. Co-operation should encompass training activities in the marketing areas, especially for developing country exporters and importers, and exchanges of experience on the use of various practices, such as options, swaps and countertrade.

Again, this is an area that offers interesting possibilities and challenges for international co-operation.

The balance in connection with the other objectives of international co-operation enunciated above is mixed. In research and development there has been positive movement both at the level of producer-consumer co-operation and of co-operation among producers. Most ICAs include this co-operation among their objectives, and producer organizations such as UPEB and GEPLACEA have also been active in this area. By contrast, insufficient progress has been made in the use of international co-operation for purposes of diversification. This is regrettable in that such co-operation is doubly necessary: to help producer countries to identify and take advantage of opportunities for diversification, and to improve exchanges of information in order to allow more informed investment decision, and avoid future over-supply problems.

An area in which some progress has been made but much more is possible is that of co-operation to improve marketing. This involves on the one hand actions designed to open up new markets and expand consumption of commodities, including in semi-processed and processed forms, whether for traditional or new uses. Strengthened co-operation between consuming countries, where most of the promotion outlays are incurred, can facilitate the design of joint projects in this area that could attract financing from bilateral and multilateral sources.

In all of the preceding, support by international organizations to producer-consumer and producer co-operation in commodities is essential. Both the Common Fund for Commodities and UNCTAD have special roles to play in this connection.

The Second Account of the CFC should play an important role in the mobilization of financial support for co-operative development activities in the commodities' field. This calls for an intensification of joint efforts among producers for the elaboration of a collective long-term strategy for the commodity and for the identification, within a framework of this strategy, of programmes and projects on developmental measures which could be sponsored by the competent international commodity bodies.

UNCTAD, on the other hand, has been particularly active in supporting efforts at improving market transparency. This activity has been based on an assumption that full advantage should be taken of new technologies in data processing and communications. UNCTAD's micro-computer based commodity analysis and information system (MICAS) is an effort at providing both producers and consumers with a powerful and flexible tool to store and manipulate commodity information for policy making. The system is currently being installed in some countries in South East Asia. UNCTAD is also very active in production and dissemination of statistical information in the minerals and metals field.

Another area of major involvement of UNCTAD in promoting and supporting international co-operation concerns the use of financial instruments for commodity risk management and participation by producers and consumers in international commodity exchanges. The first of a two-part expert group meeting on commodity exchanges took place in May 1993, attended by experts representing the various participants in the market (producers, consumers, traders, dealers, brokers, the exchanges themselves, international organizations and governments and independent experts.) Possibilities for strengthened co-operation both in policy research and in training and dissemination of information on the use of commodity exchanges were identified and will be the subject of proposals to be considered at the 2nd part of the meeting in September 1993.

UNCTAD is also active in efforts at promoting domestic processing of commodities, and is in the process of identifying ways and means in which international co-operation in this field could help the goal of commodity diversification.

One area in which international co-operation is only beginning to develop is that of ensuring the sustainability of commodity-based development. Here, a major issue on which international co-operation is called for is the internalization of environmental costs and resource values in the prices of commodities. UNCTAD is currently undertaking an examination of this issue, from which proposals for co-operative action might stem.

In sum, international co-operation in the commodities field has experienced something of a revival in the 1990s. This is due to a number of factors, some of which have been discussed above: one, non-negligible one, is the clear commitment of the interntional community at UNCTAD VIII to make co-operation a central component of international commodity policy.

Still, there is a long road ahead, and efforts should be intensified both on the part of producers and consumers and of international organizations that can provide support. Producer-consumer and producer co-operation remains a major instrument for the achievement of the overriding goal agreed by the international community at UNCTAD VIII, namely, to put in place sound, compatible and consistent commodity policies at national and international levels.

PART III

---

**PRESENTATIONS BY**

**INTERNATIONAL COMMODITY BODIES**

# COCOA:
# THE CURRENT WORLD SITUATION AND OUTLOOK[1]

## 1 INTRODUCTION

Cocoa is a commodity produced in the developing countries of the tropics but consumed mostly in the middle and high income countries of the world's temperate zones. A number of cocoa-producing countries rely on cocoa exports for a significant proportion of the foreign exchange earnings they need to finance economic development projects and to service external debt obligations. In Ghana, for example, export earnings from cocoa, until recently, accounted on average for nearly two-thirds of its total foreign exchange earnings. In Côte d'Ivoire, it accounted for around 35% of foreign exchange earnings. Therefore, cocoa appears not only as a natural candidate for international co-operation, but also as a perfect vehicle of aid transfer from rich countries to developing countries, and one that qualifies entirely for the support of the Common Fund.

## 2 WORLD COCOA SUPPLY/DEMAND SITUATION

### Overview

During most of the past decade or so, world cocoa production has persistently outstripped consumption, often by large tonnages, resulting in a relentless build-up of stocks, a collapse of cocoa prices and a serious setback to export earnings. The market impact of seven years of successive production surpluses (1984/85 to 1990/91) has been such that, despite an appreciable production shortfall in 1991/92 and expectations of an even larger deficit in 1992/93 cocoa year, world cocoa prices have remained trapped at historically low levels. Currently, world cocoa prices are, in real terms, the lowest since 1960/61 and for some cocoa-producing countries, prices received at the farm level are, in real terms, the lowest

---

[1] A general background information paper presented by the International Cocoa Organization (ICCO).

ever on record. In recent years annual drops in these prices of up to 59 percentage points have been experienced.

Various aspects of the world cocoa economy have continued to be characterized by a high degree of concentration. Thus, for the five-year period ended 1990/91, top ten countries accounted for 92% of world cocoa production, 95% of exports, 78% of imports and 70% of grindings.

## Production

From a level of 1.5 million tonnes in 1983/84 cocoa year (the last year with a production deficit before 1991/92), world *production* of cocoa beans had increased to 2.46 million tonnes in 1988/89. After a fall to 2.4 million tonnes in 1989/90, production recovered to reach an all-time record of some 2.5 million tonnes before falling back to 2.3 million tonnes in 1991/92. Production is forecast to stay at around 2.3 million tonnes in 1992/93.

The remarkable increase in production has been assisted by a number of factors including: (i) the officially-sponsored cocoa development and rehabilitation programmes undertaken in many countries in the late 1970's and early 1980's; (ii) the rapid growth of cocoa as a plantation crop in South East Asia; and (iii) the programmes of economic restructuring and revitalization undertaken in a number of major producing countries.

The geographical distribution of world cocoa production has undergone notable changes in recent years. The average share of the African region dropped from some 60% in 1988/89 to 54% in 1991/92. In contrast, the share of the Americas increased from 24% to 26% while that of Asia and Oceania rose from 16% to 20% over the same period. Thus Asia and Oceania have become the fastest growing source of supplies although the bulk of the total world supplies still originates from Africa.

## Consumption

World cocoa *consumption* (as measured in grindings of cocoa beans) over the same period had also increased steadily, but at a slower rate than production, rising from 1.70 million tonnes in 1983/84 to 2.3 million tonnes in 1991/92. Consumption is forecast to reach a new all-time record of 2.4 million tonnes in 1992/93. The regional distribution of grindings witnessed significant changes in recent years. Western Europe increased its share of world grindings from 39% in 1988/89 to 44% in 1991/92. The share for Asia and Oceania rose from 9% to 13%, but Eastern Europe saw a dramatic drop in its share from 14% to 4%. The shares of the Americas (31% in 1991/92) and Africa (8% in 1991/92) were little changed as was the share of cocoa producing countries as a group (32%).

The political and economic developments in the former Soviet Union and Eastern Europe have reduced cocoa consumption in that region and the prospects of a continued substantial growth in world consumption will, in the absence of suitable countervailing measures, probably remain uncertain for the foreseeable future. At the global level, the contraction in the number of key market players, partly as a result of the world recession but also attributable to a number of company mergers, may be introducing new uncertainties in market behaviour which are yet to be fully evaluated.

### Stocks

The balance between world production and world grindings show, from the 1984/85 cocoa year, a seven-year run of production surpluses ranging from 67,000 tonnes in 1986/87 to 299,000 tonnes in 1988/89. These were followed by two successive years of production deficits of 64,000 tonnes in 1991/92 and a projected 102,000 tonnes in 1992/93. The persistence of production surpluses between 1984/85 and 1990/91 resulted in large accumulation of *world stocks*, both in absolute terms and as a proportion of world consumption. From 532,000 tonnes or 28.6% of world consumption in 1984/85, global stocks of cocoa beans had grown to 1.56 million tonnes or 66.9% of world consumption in 1990/91. The production deficit in 1991/92 was estimated at 64,000 tonnes reducing world stocks to 1.50 million tonnes or 64.8% of world consumption. A deficit of 102,000 tonnes forecast for 1992/93 implies a further decline in world stocks to 1.39 million tonnes or 57.8% of projected consumption (See Tables 1 and 2.).

Despite this fall in world stocks, the general view must still be that the present level of global stocks is excessive. Compared with the 1970's and early 1980's, there appears in recent years to have been a decline in essential stock requirements as a proportion of total world consumption of cocoa. This decline is believed to reflect a change in the stock-holding behaviour of the major market players. The change has been attributed partly to more efficient stock management and has been associated with the effect of high levels of interest rates, the contraction in the number of trade houses and the predominance of multi-national companies in the chocolate manufacturing industry. There was also the factor of generally improved availability of supplies. In economic terms, this process is equivalent to a downward shift in the cocoa market's stock-demand curve and implies that the market would be prepared to hold any given levels of cocoa stocks only at cocoa prices which are below what they would have been if there had been no change in the market's behaviour.

*Table 1:* Global supply/demand balance in the world cocoa market

| Period/ year | Production (gross crop) | | Grindings | | Surplus/ Deficit | Total Stocks[1] | Ratio St/Gr | ICCO daily price SDR/tonne | |
|---|---|---|---|---|---|---|---|---|---|
| | 1000 tonnes | % | 1000 tonnes | % | 1000 tonnes | 1000 tonnes | % | In current terms | In constant 1991/92 terms |
| 1980/85 | 1 681 | (+11.8) | 1 669 | (+15.0) | | 625 | 37.9 | 1 953 | 2 639 |
| 1985/90 | 2 208 | (+31.4) | 2 013 | (+20.6) | | 917 | 47.6 | 1 340 | 1 576 |
| 1985/86 | 1 971 | (+0.8) | 1 847 | (-0.6) | 104 | 636 | 34.4 | 1 886 | 2 315 |
| 1986/87 | 2 008 | (+1.9) | 1 910 | (+3.4) | 78 | 714 | 37.4 | 1 607 | 1 936 |
| 1987/88 | 2 194 | (+9.3) | 1 984 | (+3.9) | 188 | 902 | 45.5 | 1 269 | 1 487 |
| 1988/89 | 2 462 | (+12.2) | 2 130 | (+7.4) | 307 | 1 209 | 56.8 | 1 035 | 1 167 |
| 1989/90 | 2 406 | (-2.3) | 2 192 | (+2.9) | 190 | 1 399 | 63.8 | 902 | 973 |
| 1990/91 | 2 514 | (+4.5) | 2 329 | (+6.3) | 160 | 1 559 | 66.9 | 863 | 891 |
| 1991/92 | 2 266 | (-9.9) | 2 307 | (-0.9) | -64 | 1 495 | 64.8 | 831 | 831 |
| 1992/93 | 2 332 | (+2.9) | 2 411 | (+4.5) | -102 | 1 393 | 57.8 | 742[2] | 728[2] |

*Notes:* Figures in parentheses represent the percentage change from the previous period.
[1] Total stocks include ICCO-held buffer stock.
[2] Average October 1992-March 1993.

*Source:* ICCO Secretariat.

*Table 2:* Evolution of world cocoa stocks in relation to world grindings, 1981/82 - 1991/92

| Year | Grin-dings | Closing stocks | | Ratio St/Gr | |
|------|------------|----------------|---|-------------|---|
| | | Incl. Buffer Stock | Excl. Buffer Stock | Incl. Buffer Stock | Excl. Buffer Stock |
| | | (thousand tonnes) | | (percentage) | |
| 1981/82 | 1 598 | 787 | 687 | 49.2 | 43.0 |
| 1982/83 | 1 629 | 670 | 570 | 41.1 | 35.0 |
| 1983/84 | 1 703 | 461 | 361 | 27.1 | 21.2 |
| 1984/85 | 1 859 | 532 | 432 | 28.6 | 23.2 |
| 1985/86 | 1 847 | 636 | 536 | 34.4 | 29.0 |
| 1986/87 | 1 910 | 714 | 539 | 37.4 | 28.2 |
| 1987/88 | 1 984 | 902 | 652 | 45.5 | 32.9 |
| 1988/89 | 2 130 | 1 209 | 961 | 56.8 | 45.1 |
| 1989/90 | 2 192 | 1 399 | 1 154 | 63.8 | 52.6 |
| 1990/91 | 2 329 | 1 559 | 1 317 | 66.9 | 56.5 |
| 1991/92 | 2 307 | 1 495 | 1 262 | 64.8 | 54.7 |

*Source:* ICCO Secretariat.

*Table 3:* Degree of concentration in the production, grindings and trade in cocoa (based on five-year average 1987/88 - 1991/92)

| | Production | | Grindings | | Imports[1] | | Exports[2] | |
|---|---|---|---|---|---|---|---|---|
| | 1000 tonnes | % | 1000 tonnes | % | 1000 tonnes | % | 1000 tonnes | % |
| Top 3 countries | 1 352.1 | 57.1 | 784.7 | 35.9 | 987.5 | 50.1 | 1 248.7 | 59.5 |
| Top 4 countries | 1 579.3 | 66.7 | 1 020.1 | 46.6 | 1 122.4 | 56.9 | 1 465.1 | 69.8 |
| Top 5 countries | 1 728.3 | 73.0 | 1 145.7 | 52.4 | 1 255.6 | 63.7 | 1 606.1 | 76.6 |
| Top 10 countries | 2 158.2 | 91.1 | 1 540.3 | 70.4 | 1 577.1 | 80.0 | 2 003.9 | 95.5 |
| Top 15 countries | 2 274.6 | 96.0 | 1 760.9 | 80.5 | 1 729.3 | 87.7 | 2 049.1 | 97.7 |
| Top 20 countries | 2 305.2 | 97.3 | 1 912.8 | 87.4 | 1 812.4 | 92.0 | 2 073.1 | 98.8 |
| World | 2 368.4 | 100.0 | 2 188.3 | 100.0 | 1 971.1 | 100.0 | 2 097.6 | 100.0 |

*Notes:* [1] Net imports of cocoa beans plus net imports of cocoa products converted to beans equivalent using the following conversion factors: cocoa butter 1.33; cocoa powder and cake 1.18; cocoa paste/liquor 1.25.
[2] Net exports of cocoa beans plus net exports of cocoa products converted to beans equivalent using the following conversion factors: cocoa butter 1.33; cocoa powder and cake 1.18; cocoa paste/liquor 1.25.

## 3 COCOA PRICES AND INCOMES

As would be expected, the persistence of production surpluses for most of the past decade has ensured that world cocoa-bean prices have followed a downward trend, reaching an all-time low in 1991/92 in real terms, and likely to be even lower in 1992/93 (see Tables 5 and 6). The nominal ICCO daily price, which averaged SDR 2320 per tonne in 1983/84 has declined each year to reach SDR 831 in 1991/92 and is expected to be lower still in 1992/93.

The impact of the relentless weakening of international cocoa prices on farm-level prices has been predictable. In constant domestic-currency terms, producer prices have shown consistent annual declines in Brazil and Malaysia since 1985, in Cameroon and Côte d'Ivoire since 1986, in Nigeria since 1988 and in Ghana since 1989 (see Table 4).

The value, in US dollar terms, of exports of cocoa beans and cocoa products has been on a downward trend for almost all the major cocoa producing countries since 1986 (see Table 7). Although this tendency is traceable also to fluctuations in the volume of exports, the sustained fall in international prices has been a significant contributory factor. The situation has proved particularly painful in a number of producing countries where the dependence on cocoa exports for foreign exchange earnings is specially high.

*Table 4a:* Producer prices in selected cocoa-exporting countries in local currency, 1965 - 1992, in current terms.

| Year | Brazil[1] | Cameroon[2] | Côte d'Ivoire[2] | Ghana[3] | Malaysia[4] | Nigeria |
|------|-----------|-------------|------------------|----------|-------------|---------|
| 1965 | .. | 85.0 | 70.0 | .. | .. | 249.10 |
| 1970 | .. | 85.0 | 82.0 | 8.8 | .. | 310.00 |
| 1971 | .. | 87.0 | 85.0 | 8.8 | .. | 310.00 |
| 1972 | .. | 90.0 | 85.0 | 10.1 | .. | 310.00 |
| 1973 | .. | 93.0 | 93.0 | 11.6 | .. | 340.00 |
| 1974 | .. | 107.0 | 126.0 | 14.6 | .. | 470.83 |
| 1975 | .. | 123.0 | 175.0 | 17.2 | .. | 632.50 |
| 1976 | .. | 137.0 | 177.0 | 20.2 | .. | 660.00 |
| 1977 | .. | 173.0 | 198.0 | 31.2 | .. | 752.50 |
| 1978 | .. | 233.0 | 250.0 | 53.3 | .. | 1030.00 |
| 1979 | .. | 268.0 | 263.0 | 100.0 | .. | 1100.83 |
| 1980 | 0.001 | 293.0 | 300.0 | 120.0 | 4374 | 1216.67 |
| 1981 | 0.002 | 303.0 | 300.0 | 160.0 | 3436 | 1300.00 |
| 1982 | 0.003 | 315.0 | 300.0 | 360.0 | 2954 | 1300.00 |
| 1983 | 0.012 | 360.0 | 338.0 | 540.0 | 4176 | 1375.00 |
| 1984 | 0.047 | 380.0 | 356.3 | 750.0 | 4853 | 1425.00 |
| 1985 | 0.138 | 412.5 | 381.3 | 1299.0 | 4774 | 1525.00 |
| 1986 | 0.271 | 420.0 | 400.0 | 2550.0 | 4294 | 1600.00 |
| 1987 | 0.835 | 420.0 | 400.0 | 3450.0 | 3850 | 6500.00 |
| 1988 | 4.123 | 420.0 | 400.0 | 4612.5 | 3176 | 7500.00 |
| 1989 | 33.908 | 377.5 | 312.5 | 5091.0 | 2582 | 10750.00 |
| 1990 | 902.265 | 242.5 | 200.0 | 6348.0 | 2590 | 8500.00 |
| 1991 | 4961.668 | 220.0 | 200.0 | 7128.0 | 2443 | .. |
| 1992 | .. | 220.0 | 200.0 | 7128.0 | 2443 | .. |

*Notes:* [1] cruzeiros per arroba (one arroba is equivalent to 15kg).
[2] CFA francs per kg.
[3] cedi per headload (a headload is equivalent to 30kg (66 lb)).
[4] Malaysian ringgit per tonne.

*Table 4b:* Producer prices in selected cocoa-exporting countries in local
currency, 1965 - 1992, in constant 1990 terms.

| Year | Brazil | Cameroon | Côte d'Ivoire | Ghana | Malaysia | Nigeria |
|------|--------|----------|---------------|-------|----------|---------|
| 1965 | .. | 509 | 429 | .. | .. | 8085 |
| 1970 | 1394 | 472 | 386 | 9252 | .. | 7666 |
| 1971 | 996 | 467 | 407 | 8502 | .. | 6598 |
| 1972 | 1278 | 446 | 405 | 8797 | .. | 6388 |
| 1973 | 2512 | 417 | 399 | 8602 | .. | 6638 |
| 1974 | 3044 | 410 | 461 | 9144 | .. | 8150 |
| 1975 | 2424 | 415 | 574 | 8328 | .. | 8211 |
| 1976 | 3321 | 420 | 519 | 6267 | .. | 6882 |
| 1977 | 6410 | 462 | 455 | 4538 | .. | 6904 |
| 1978 | 4740 | 554 | 509 | 4462 | .. | 7752 |
| 1979 | 4073 | 598 | 459 | 5387 | .. | 7424 |
| 1980 | 3263 | 597 | 457 | 4290 | 6026 | 7468 |
| 1981 | 2423 | 557 | 420 | 2644 | 4317 | 6593 |
| 1982 | 1789 | 511 | 391 | 4865 | 3506 | 6126 |
| 1983 | 3142 | 501 | 416 | 3272 | 4781 | 5258 |
| 1984 | 4121 | 475 | 420 | 3252 | 5345 | 3903 |
| 1985 | 3677 | 509 | 442 | 5108 | 5242 | 3960 |
| 1986 | 2952 | 481 | 432 | 8048 | 4682 | 3942 |
| 1987 | 2755 | 454 | 430 | 7788 | 4161 | 14537 |
| 1988 | 1737 | 418 | 402 | 7927 | 3366 | 12133 |
| 1989 | 1030 | 385 | 311 | 6988 | 2661 | 11514 |
| 1990 | 902 | 243 | 200 | 6348 | 2590 | 8500 |
| 1991 | 917 | 225 | 197 | 5996 | 2341 | .. |
| 1992 | .. | 220 | 175 | 5117 | 2242 | .. |

*Table 4c:* Producer prices in selected cocoa-exporting countries in local currency, 1965 - 1992, in constant 1990 terms (index).

| Year | Brazil | Cameroon | Côte d'Ivoire | Ghana | Malaysia | Nigeria |
|------|--------|----------|---------------|-------|----------|---------|
| 1965 | .. | 210 | 215 | .. | .. | 95 |
| 1970 | 155 | 195 | 193 | 146 | .. | 90 |
| 1971 | 110 | 192 | 203 | 134 | .. | 78 |
| 1972 | 142 | 184 | 203 | 139 | .. | 75 |
| 1973 | 278 | 172 | 200 | 136 | .. | 78 |
| 1974 | 337 | 169 | 230 | 144 | .. | 96 |
| 1975 | 269 | 171 | 287 | 131 | .. | 97 |
| 1976 | 368 | 173 | 260 | 99 | .. | 81 |
| 1977 | 710 | 191 | 228 | 71 | .. | 81 |
| 1978 | 525 | 228 | 255 | 70 | .. | 91 |
| 1979 | 451 | 247 | 229 | 85 | .. | 87 |
| 1980 | 362 | 246 | 228 | 68 | 233 | 88 |
| 1981 | 269 | 230 | 210 | 42 | 167 | 78 |
| 1982 | 198 | 211 | 196 | 77 | 135 | 72 |
| 1983 | 348 | 206 | 208 | 52 | 185 | 62 |
| 1984 | 457 | 196 | 210 | 51 | 206 | 46 |
| 1985 | 407 | 210 | 221 | 80 | 202 | 47 |
| 1986 | 327 | 198 | 216 | 127 | 181 | 46 |
| 1987 | 305 | 187 | 215 | 123 | 161 | 171 |
| 1988 | 193 | 172 | 201 | 125 | 130 | 143 |
| 1989 | 114 | 159 | 156 | 110 | 103 | 135 |
| 1990 | 100 | 100 | 100 | 100 | 100 | 100 |
| 1991 | 102 | 93 | 99 | 94 | 90 | .. |
| 1992 | .. | 91 | 88 | 81 | 87 | .. |

*Tabel 5a:* Evolution of ICCO daily prices in SDRs, in US dollars and in the currencies of selected cocoa-exporting countries in constant 1990/91 terms, 1970/71 - 1979/80[1], (Index 1990/91 = 100)

| Crop year | SDRs | US dollars | Cameroon '000 CFA francs | Côte de'Ivoire '000 CFA francs | Ecuador '000 sucres | Ghana cedis | Malaysia ringgit | Nigeria naira |
|-----------|------|------------|--------------------------|--------------------------------|---------------------|-------------|------------------|---------------|
| 1970/71 | 217 | 166 | 268 | 238 | 118 | 159 | 136 | 102 |
| 1971/72 | 193 | 159 | 232 | 221 | 108 | 175 | 122 | 90 |
| 1972/73 | 289 | 262 | 330 | 318 | 169 | 251 | 176 | 146 |
| 1973/74 | 359 | 343 | 422 | 406 | 200 | 306 | 205 | 185 |
| 1974/75 | 292 | 286 | 329 | 321 | 157 | 219 | 183 | 128 |
| 1975/76 | 354 | 334 | 368 | 358 | 181 | 187 | 225 | 125 |
| 1976/77 | 725 | 690 | 761 | 673 | 349 | 229 | 463 | 238 |
| 1977/78 | 587 | 582 | 567 | 496 | 282 | 110 | 377 | 164 |
| 1978/79 | 554 | 563 | 522 | 417 | 272 | 145 | 357 | 163 |
| 1979/80 | 399 | 400 | 374 | 288 | 197 | 88 | 272 | 106 |

*Notes:*[1] Based on average exchange rates and relevant index of consumer price inflation quoted in IMF, *International Financial Statistics*.

*Sources:* IMF, *International Financial Statistics*; ICCO Secretariat.

*Tabel 5b:*  Evolution of ICCO daily prices in SDRs, in US dollars and in the currencies of selected cocoa-exporting countries in constant 1990/91 terms, 1980/81 - 1991/92[1] , (Index 1990/91 = 100)

| Crop year | SDRs | US dollars | Cameroon '000 CFA francs | Côte de'Ivoire '000 CFA francs | Ecuador '000 sucres | Ghana cedis | Malaysia ringgit | Nigeria naira |
|---|---|---|---|---|---|---|---|---|
| 1980/81 | 293 | 268 | 312 | 236 | 126 | 31 | 194 | 70 |
| 1981/82 | 262 | 222 | 312 | 249 | 117 | 19 | 164 | 65 |
| 1982/83 | 275 | 223 | 330 | 287 | 129 | 11 | 165 | 63 |
| 1983/84 | 338 | 266 | 410 | 387 | 157 | 73 | 197 | 58 |
| 1984/85 | 314 | 236 | 389 | 375 | 122 | 121 | 191 | 53 |
| 1985/86 | 260 | 223 | 290 | 265 | 150 | 159 | 188 | 64 |
| 1986/87 | 217 | 204 | 214 | 202 | 163 | 176 | 175 | 193 |
| 1987/88 | 167 | 165 | 153 | 155 | 150 | 157 | 148 | 126 |
| 1988/89 | 131 | 124 | 131 | 131 | 125 | 134 | 119 | 101 |
| 1989/90 | 109 | 105 | 105 | 104 | 111 | 109 | 103 | 90 |
| 1990/91 | 100 | 100 | 100 | 100 | 100 | 100 | 100 | 100 |
| 1991/92 | 93 | 95 | 95 | 95 | 86 | 98 | 89 | 93 |

*Notes:*[1] Based on average exchange rates and relevant index of consumer price inflation quoted in IMF, *Int. Fin. Stat.*.

*Sources:* IMF, *International Financial Statistics*; ICCO Secretariat.

*Tabel 6a:* Evolution of ICCO daily prices in SDRs, in US dollars and in the currencies of selected cocoa-importing countries in constant 1990/91 terms, 1970/71 - 1979/80[1]

| Crop year | US dollars | French francs | Deutsche mark | Japan yen | Netherlands guilders | Pounds sterling | USSR roubles |
|---|---|---|---|---|---|---|---|
| 1970/71 | 166 | 225 | 226 | 368 | 241 | 246 | 78 |
| 1971/72 | 159 | 197 | 192 | 303 | 202 | 216 | 73 |
| 1972/73 | 262 | 286 | 277 | 432 | 296 | 358 | 115 |
| 1973/74 | 343 | 377 | 373 | 524 | 358 | 469 | 163 |
| 1974/75 | 286 | 281 | 276 | 434 | 276 | 359 | 145 |
| 1975/76 | 334 | 340 | 344 | 496 | 334 | 455 | 184 |
| 1976/77 | 690 | 725 | 670 | 938 | 634 | 957 | 400 |
| 1977/78 | 582 | 563 | 513 | 650 | 559 | 718 | 327 |
| 1978/79 | 563 | 504 | 543 | 620 | 460 | 623 | 345 |
| 1979/80 | 400 | 349 | 350 | 526 | 338 | 388 | 271 |

*Notes:* [1] Based on average exchange rates and relevant index of consumer price inflation quoted in IMF, *International Financial Statistics.*

*Sources:* IMF, *International Financial Statistics*; ICCO Secretariat.

*Tabel 6b:* Evolution of ICCO daily prices in SDRs, in US dollars and in the currencies of selected cocoa-importing countries in constant 1990/91 terms, 1980/81 - 1991/92[1]

| Crop year | US dollars | French francs | Deutsche mark | Japan yen | Netherlands guilders | Pounds sterling | USSR roubles |
|---|---|---|---|---|---|---|---|
| 1980/81 | 268 | 283 | 300 | 343 | 288 | 269 | 221 |
| 1981/82 | 222 | 269 | 274 | 327 | 261 | 259 | 200 |
| 1982/83 | 223 | 304 | 292 | 340 | 283 | 299 | 213 |
| 1983/84 | 266 | 398 | 387 | 397 | 376 | 393 | 284 |
| 1984/85 | 236 | 383 | 388 | 377 | 377 | 385 | 283 |
| 1985/86 | 223 | 279 | 284 | 264 | 275 | 303 | 233 |
| 1986/87 | 204 | 218 | 215 | 207 | 210 | 259 | 195 |
| 1987/88 | 165 | 168 | 166 | 151 | 163 | 184 | 154 |
| 1988/89 | 124 | 139 | 138 | 118 | 137 | 141 | 125 |
| 1989/90 | 105 | 107 | 107 | 114 | 108 | 114 | 106 |
| 1990/91 | 100 | 100 | 100 | 100 | 100 | 100 | 100 |
| 1991/92 | 95 | 93 | 92 | 92 | 92 | 94 | 95 |

*Notes:*[1] Based on average exchange rates and relevant index of consumer price inflation quoted in IMF, *International Financial Statistics.*

*Sources:* IMF, *International Financial Statistics*; ICCO Secretariat.

Tabel 7: Value of exports of cocoa beans and cocoa products by major producing countries

| Year | Brazil | Cameroon | Côte d'Ivoire | Dom.Rep. | Ecuador | Ghana | Malaysia | Mexico | Nigeria | Papua New Guinea |
|------|--------|----------|---------------|----------|---------|-------|----------|--------|---------|------------------|
| | | | | (thousand dollars) | | | | | | |
| 1971 | 91757 | 60163 | 117384 | 12584 | 28724 | 209943 | 1930 | 3861 | 216428 | 15580 |
| 1972 | 99293 | 59605 | 110624 | 18016 | 29906 | 249645 | 3139 | 11305 | 172280 | 12950 |
| 1973 | 143507 | 98856 | 153997 | 23951 | 34549 | 339706 | 7458 | 10392 | 201999 | 14528 |
| 1974 | 322849 | 160149 | 315029 | 26928 | 125465 | 489557 | 14736 | 11928 | 295056 | 34424 |
| 1975 | 293510 | 151000 | 293334 | 27841 | 68168 | 553950 | 15424 | 11221 | 334507 | 54852 |
| 1976 | 312166 | 128619 | 390008 | 48741 | 94356 | 516027 | 26493 | 31771 | 380159 | 36467 |
| 1977 | 604601 | 221347 | 551981 | 94940 | 228857 | 797000 | 53578 | 25852 | 577311 | 70097 |
| 1978 | 632840 | 286269 | 924400 | 87578 | 265675 | 947000 | 69000 | 29563 | 756800 | 107175 |
| 1979 | 945024 | 265870 | 706394 | 75412 | 269907 | 739050 | 85796 | 33701 | 763029 | 85403 |
| 1980 | 696586 | 272471 | 925312 | 53827 | 210130 | 791102 | 91911 | 91914 | 309390 | 69368 |
| 1981 | 596758 | 185598 | 857415 | 48321 | 138796 | 430985 | 93174 | 8622 | 196869 | 50759 |
| 1982 | 428992 | 145620 | 609992 | 57657 | 113636 | 410318 | 104205 | 15472 | 256944 | 43151 |
| 1983 | 554588 | 151070 | 525656 | 58988 | 33546 | 268600 | 122019 | 33814 | 361112 | 49610 |
| 1984 | 661734 | 184326 | 1073854 | 73875 | 145191 | 383356 | 195577 | 27158 | 294719 | 75437 |
| 1985 | 778856 | 160951 | 1093390 | 64175 | 188122 | 399264 | 218564 | 28090 | 268046 | 60687 |
| 1986 | 630612 | 213360 | 1211877 | 65397 | 153962 | 497884 | 248710 | 25176 | 320914 | 58346 |
| 1987 | 584297 | 237310 | 1222400 | 72213 | 127712 | 530189 | 340750 | 32874 | 195900 | 61995 |
| 1988 | 518729 | 219601 | 840861 | 67906 | 103616 | 470035 | 340109 | 29544 | 346679 | 53613 |
| 1989 | 335591 | 181348 | 817000 | 45810 | 99273 | 414901 | 260045 | 14004 | 144873 | 53744 |
| 1990 | 335808 | 168977 | 909000 | 43717 | 124247 | 369700 | 256635 | 17178 | 149570 | 33662 |

Notes: All export value data are on f.o.b. basis.

Sources: FAO, Trade Yearbook; IMF, International Financial Statistics.

*Tabel 8:*   Share of cocoa-derived earnings to total value of exports by major producing countries

| Year | Brazil | Cameroon | Côte d'Ivoire | Dominican Republic | Ecuador | Ghana | Malaysia | Mexico | Nigeria | Papua New Guinea |
|------|--------|----------|---------------|--------------------|---------|-------|----------|--------|---------|------------------|
| | | | | (per cent) | | | | | | |
| 1971 | 3.16 | 29.06 | 25.74 | 5.18 | 14.43 | 58.97 | 0.12 | 0.26 | 11.93 | 12.88 |
| 1972 | 2.49 | 26.97 | 20.00 | 5.18 | 9.17 | 59.58 | 0.18 | 0.67 | 7.90 | 5.83 |
| 1973 | 2.32 | 28.00 | 17.97 | 5.42 | 6.49 | 54.09 | 0.24 | 0.46 | 5.83 | 2.82 |
| 1974 | 4.06 | 33.50 | 25.97 | 4.23 | 11.16 | 66.88 | 0.35 | 0.40 | 3.21 | 5.26 |
| 1975 | 3.39 | 33.78 | 24.84 | 3.11 | 7.00 | 68.47 | 0.40 | 0.39 | 4.18 | 12.44 |
| 1976 | 3.08 | 25.17 | 23.90 | 6.81 | 7.50 | 62.02 | 0.50 | 0.93 | 3.53 | 6.62 |
| 1977 | 4.99 | 31.44 | 25.59 | 12.17 | 15.94 | 78.60 | 0.88 | 0.62 | 4.88 | 10.26 |
| 1978 | 5.00 | 35.69 | 39.81 | 12.96 | 17.05 | 86.64 | 0.93 | 0.49 | 7.60 | 15.01 |
| 1979 | 6.20 | 23.49 | 28.09 | 8.68 | 12.83 | 74.28 | 0.77 | 0.38 | 4.43 | 9.67 |
| 1980 | 3.46 | 19.69 | 29.52 | 5.60 | 8.47 | 62.94 | 0.71 | 0.59 | 1.19 | 6.73 |
| 1981 | 2.56 | 16.80 | 33.85 | 4.07 | 5.66 | 40.47 | 0.79 | 0.04 | 1.10 | 6.06 |
| 1982 | 2.13 | 13.69 | 25.96 | 7.51 | 4.88 | 47.00 | 0.87 | 0.07 | 1.99 | 5.60 |
| 1983 | 2.53 | 15.48 | 25.14 | 7.51 | 1.43 | 39.97 | 0.86 | 0.15 | 3.49 | 6.10 |
| 1984 | 2.45 | 20.80 | 39.67 | 8.51 | 5.54 | 72.61 | 1.18 | 0.11 | 2.49 | 8.46 |
| 1985 | 3.04 | 22.29 | 34.19 | 8.73 | 6.48 | 64.71 | 1.42 | 0.13 | 2.14 | 6.65 |
| 1986 | 2.82 | 27.28 | 36.13 | 9.11 | 7.09 | 57.69 | 1.81 | 0.15 | 5.63 | 5.65 |
| 1987 | 2.23 | 29.44 | 39.54 | 10.16 | 6.62 | 54.27 | 1.90 | 0.16 | 2.66 | 5.34 |
| 1988 | 1.54 | 23.77 | 30.30 | 7.63 | 4.73 | 46.24 | 1.61 | 0.14 | 5.04 | 3.70 |
| 1989 | 0.97 | 18.79 | 29.10 | 4.94 | 4.22 | 40.77 | 1.04 | 0.06 | 1.84 | 4.14 |
| 1990 | 1.07 | 13.52 | 34.30 | 5.96 | 4.58 | 39.33 | 0.87 | 0.06 | 1.09 | 2.92 |

*Notes:* All export value data are on f.o.b. basis.

*Sources:* FAO, Trade Yearbook; IMF, *International Financial Statistics.*

## 4 OUTLOOK

In a recent study published by the ICCO Secretariat entitled 'The World Cocoa Market: An Analysis of Recent Trends and of Prospects to the Year 2000', an attempt was made to project the likely developments in the world cocoa market up to the end of the decade. The projected developments are summarised in Tables 9 and 10 which present a low cocoa-consumption growth scenario and a high cocoa-consumption growth scenario, respectively. It is felt that the two sets of results define the limits of a range within which the actual market trends could lie.

The general conclusion from the study is that the period of structural production surpluses which lasted until and including the 1990/91 cocoa year, is now at an end. The period from 1991/92 to the end of the decade is seen as likely to produce more of production deficits than surpluses. Both production and consumption should, however, continue to trend upwards, but the rates of growth will be much slower than those achieved during the 1980's. The associated draw-down in stocks is not expected to be large enough to liquidate quickly and completely the excess stock currently over-hanging the market. Consequently, although significant recovery in prices is expected, it will be slow and prices by the year 2000 are likely to be less, in real terms, than the corresponding levels in 1987.

There would appear, therefore, to be a need for an effective world production management scheme, supported by appropriate and realistic consumption promotion measures in order to further improve the fortunes of the world cocoa economy.

These features of the world cocoa economy, especially in the cocoa producing countries, have helped to focus attention on the root causes of the problem. At the on-going negotiations for a fifth International Cocoa Agreement under the auspices of the United Nations Conference on Trade and Development (UNCTAD) a consensus appears to be emerging that appropriate mechanisms should be devised to deal with the underlying structural imbalance without ignoring the problems posed by short-term or temporary market imbalances. Thus an internationally co-ordinated production policy is under serious consideration and there are indications that consumption promotion may be given an enhanced status in a possible fifth international cocoa agreement.

The adjustments to production and consumption which are being contemplated for the world cocoa economy will not be easy or painless. Cocoa, as a commodity, can do with all the assistance it can get in this regard. Already, the Common Fund has given an earnest of its goodwill, having recently approved two projects on cocoa. One is encouraged, therefore, to look to continued co-operation with the Fund and to a better future for cocoa.

*Tabel 9:* World cocoa market development through to 2000/01; scenario based upon the localized consumption models (low consumption-growth scenario)

| Crop year | World production | | World seasonal grindings | Total world stocks | | | | Prices in 1991 terms | | Average consumer income growth |
| | Gross | Net | | Annual change | End-of-season | Ratio St/Gr | | Average | in June | |
| | | | (thousand tonnes) | | | (%) | | (SDRs/tonne) | | (%) |
| 1991/92 | 2 266 | 2 243 | 2 307 | -64 | 1 495 | 64.8 | | 818 | 699 | 0.9 |
| 1992/93[1] | 2 401 | 2 377 | 2 463 | -86 | 1 325 | 53.8 | | 786 | 806 | 2.6 |
| 1993/94 | 2 412 | 2 388 | 2 521 | -134 | 1 192 | 47.3 | | 925 | 959 | 2.9 |
| 1994/95 | 2 442 | 2 418 | 2 514 | -97 | 1 095 | 43.6 | | 1 043 | 1 070 | 2.9 |
| 1995/96 | 2 499 | 2 474 | 2 500 | -26 | 1 069 | 42.8 | | 1 088 | 1 096 | 3.0 |
| 1996/97 | 2 558 | 2 532 | 2 508 | 25 | 1 094 | 43.6 | | 1 074 | 1 067 | 3.1 |
| 1997/98 | 2 587 | 2 561 | 2 538 | 23 | 1 117 | 44.0 | | 1 059 | 1 055 | 3.1 |
| 1998/99 | 2 594 | 2 568 | 2 574 | -6 | 1 111 | 43.2 | | 1 078 | 1 082 | 3.1 |
| 1999/00 | 2 594 | 2 568 | 2 601 | -33 | 1 078 | 41.4 | | 1 131 | 1 143 | 3.1 |
| 2000/01 | 2 594 | 2 569 | 2 616 | -47 | 1 031 | 39.4 | | 1 202 | 1 222 | 3.1 |

*Notes:* [1] forecasts

*Tabel 10:* World cocoa market development through to 2000/01; scenario based upon the global consumption model with price-level effects (high-consumption-growth-scenario)

| Crop year | World production | | World seasonal grindings | Total world stocks | | | Prices in 1991 terms | | Average consumer income growth |
|---|---|---|---|---|---|---|---|---|---|
| | Gross | Net | | Annual change | End-of-season | Ratio St/Gr | Average | in June | |
| | | | (thousand tonnes) | | | (%) | (SDRs/tonne) | | (%) |
| 1991/92 | 2 266 | 2 243 | 2 307 | -64 | 1 495 | 64.8 | 818 | 699 | 0.9 |
| 1992/93[1] | 2 401 | 2 377 | 2 469 | -91 | 1 320 | 53.5 | 792 | 813 | 2.6 |
| 1993/94 | 2 413 | 2 389 | 2 541 | -151 | 1 168 | 46.0 | 959 | 995 | 2.9 |
| 1994/95 | 2 451 | 2 426 | 2 578 | -152 | 1 016 | 39.4 | 1 174 | 1 222 | 2.9 |
| 1995/96 | 2 536 | 2 511 | 2 611 | -101 | 916 | 35.1 | 1 381 | 1 428 | 3.0 |
| 1996/97 | 2 648 | 2 621 | 2 653 | -32 | 884 | 33.3 | 1 507 | 1 531 | 3.1 |
| 1997/98 | 2 739 | 2 711 | 2 712 | -1 | 883 | 32.6 | 1 569 | 1 578 | 3.1 |
| 1998/99 | 2 800 | 2 772 | 2 779 | -7 | 876 | 31.5 | 1 636 | 1 648 | 3.1 |
| 1999/00 | 2 839 | 2 811 | 2 843 | -33 | 843 | 29.7 | 1 762 | 1 788 | 3.1 |
| 2000/01 | 2 871 | 2 843 | 2 897 | -54 | 789 | 27.2 | 1 949 | 2 002 | 3.1 |

*Notes:* [1] forecasts

# THE WORLD COTTON ECONOMY IN 1993
# AND LIKELY DEVELOPMENTS TO 2000[1]

## 1 INTRODUCTION

At the Common Fund seminar in September 1991, in a background paper it was pointed out that the world cotton market is a mixed market, which is hard to characterize in a dogmatic way. Raw cotton is produced and traded by both the wealthiest and poorest countries in the world. Technologies vary from extreme capital-intensity, employing computer technology to deliver water and plant nutrients to the roots of the plant and to monitor and determine pest and weed control requirements, to extreme labour-intensity, employing seed saved from a previous crop, no machines and no fertilizers or chemicals. Similarly, cotton is processed in textile industries in countries which produce cotton and in countries which import cotton from halfway around the world. The processor countries may also be among the world's wealthiest, where textile companies compete with high-tech industries for their resources. Or they may be poor countries using textiles as an engine for economic growth and development. As opposed to the usual assumption that developing countries produce raw materials used in developed countries, in cotton many developed countries produce the raw material which is then processed in developing countries. Other non-producing developed countries may purchase raw materials from developing countries and produce textile products, utilizing their specialized resources, which are then sold in developing countries.

It was also noted that there are many government interventions in the marketing of a product like cotton, with market arrangements varying from state monopoly trading to totally free enterprise, from trade unfettered by barriers to country-delineated quotas for both raw cotton and textile products. Given the vast array of different technologies and different institutional arrangements, the eventual development of the

---

[1] Background information from the International Cotton Advisory Committee (ICAC).

market in a post-Uruguay Round world of greatly diminished agricultural subsidies and textile trade barriers is not completely clear but seems likely to include the same mix of rich and poor countries, importing and exporting both raw materials and processed products.

## 2  THE CURRENT SITUATION

In 1993, the cotton world is being buttressed by most of the economic and political changes shaping our world. World per capita consumption of textile fibres is estimated at 7.3 kg, out of which 3.6 kg are cotton. Total world cotton consumption is forecast at 19.2 million tonnes. World production is forecast at 19 million tonnes, based on normal weather conditions through the season which will continue until May 1994 in the Southern Hemisphere. Production has varied from 15 to 21 million tonnes in the last seven years. Consumption on the other hand has been relatively unchanging, varying only from 18.1 million tonnes to 18.8 million tonnes.

With varying levels of world production and static demand, cotton prices (which are traditionally measured in US cents per pound) have fluctuated from 52 cents to 87 cents. Despite the expectation that world consumption and production are expected to be balanced in 1993 and that world stocks in most countries are not excessive, prices have been in the low part of this range at around 60 cents for the first half of 1993. Statistical models suggest that prices would normally be expected to be in the upper part of this range, if supply and demand were behaving in a fashion similar to that of the last 20 years. However, the cotton market, like many commodity markets, is adjusting to the changing conditions which have accompanied the dissolution of the former Soviet Union, changes which are likely being exaggerated by the policies of various countries important in world cotton supply and demand.

The cotton producing Republics of Central Asia, which formerly supplied the raw fibre for the textile industries of Russia, Ukraine, the Baltics and other eastern European countries, have found their markets greatly diminished by the low level of buying power in the new and restructured countries in this part of the world. The trading arrangements of the past, internal transfers and Comecon barter, have not yet been replaced by money transactions, and inefficient and uncertain trading arrangements involving many entities with little knowledge of the value of cotton currently prevail. Large supplies of cotton from these Republics have been placed on the international market in competition with the usual suppliers.

Some of the largest usual suppliers have not retreated from the competition, instead utilizing the means available to them to compete. Some low cost suppliers, who have traditionally not passed the full value of international prices to producers, have been able to continue to offer cotton at below average prices by foregoing the surplus which they have enjoyed in past years. Other wealthier suppliers have been able to use their domestic policies to provide support payments to cotton farmers to allow them to achieve nearly full returns despite low international prices. In some cases, these domestic policies have even offered support to traders and domestic textile mills to prevent the distortions caused by agricultural subsidies from destroying the market prospects of other sectors of the textile pipeline.

Nearly two-thirds of the international trade in raw cotton is today accounted for by either the new competitors in the Central Asian Republics or countries where domestic prices are insulated from the international market by domestic interventions. The resulting situation for the countries supplying the remaining one-third of the market has been one of desperation. In some countries, governments preferring to follow free trade policies have been forced to implement support programs of their own in order to prevent widespread damage to the economy and the social fabric of regional areas where cotton is the only alternative cultivation. Other countries have at least initially let their cotton sectors decline.

## 3 THE SITUATION IN 2000

In time, one can expect the international cotton market to adjust to the new supplies from Central Asia and that the economies of Eastern Europe and Russia will grow rather than decline. At the moment, however, developing cotton producing countries and developing cotton processing countries are suffering from reduced world markets and low prices for their products.

By the year 2000, we should see expanded markets for cotton and increased cotton production, assuming average rates of world economic expansion. Production and consumption of cotton are expected to rise to 23 million tonnes, growing at an annual average rate of 2%. Developing countries are expected to represent 66% of the production of cotton in 2000. Very little change is anticipated in the structure of production in the next seven years. Developing countries represented 64% of world cotton production in the late 1980s.

Developing countries are anticipated to be a larger force in the use of cotton. 70% of world textile mill consumption of cotton is likely to be in the developing countries in 2000, up from 64% in the late 1980s. Developing countries will also represent 54% of the end-use consumption of cotton in 2000, up from 49% in the late 1980s. As a larger share to total fibre use will take place in developing countries in the future, there will likely be incentives to locate processing activities in closer proximity to growing final product markets in developing countries, although actual market arrangements are still likely to be complex. In sum, the outlook for cotton markets in the remaining part of this decade will be quite bright. A graphical presentation is shown in the Figures below.

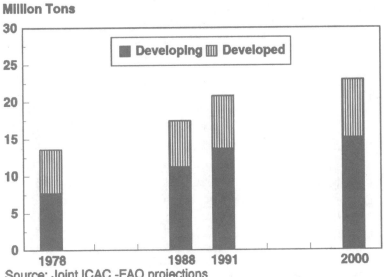

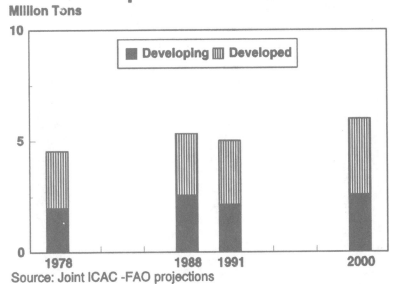

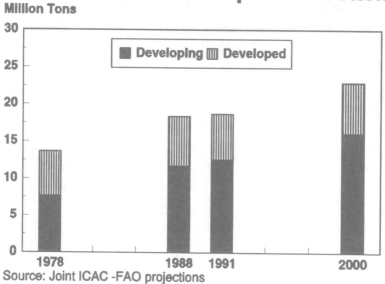

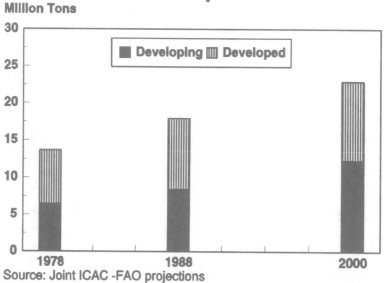

## 4 THE CHALLENGE FOR DEVELOPING COUNTRIES

In order to survive current market conditions to be able to get to the year 2000, developing countries will have to lower their costs. In today's market of low prices, reducing costs is a necessity for the producing country without resources to subsidize producers.

### Reduced costs

Cotton producers have indicated that costs associated with the use of chemicals to control insect pests are the major cause of high production costs and low producer returns. Reducing these costs through biological means (by instituting biological controls, use of beneficial predators, genetic engineering of insect-resistant varieties) or by changes in crop management practices are given the highest priority by producing countries. Insect control costs represent from 1 to 30% of total costs according to surveys of the cost of production conducted by ICAC. It should be noted that even the country with the lowest insect control costs is threatened by the spread of a major insect pest and places highest priority on insect control management. Countries using irrigation to produce cotton are also greatly concerned about the increasing cost of using water and its diminishing supply. Any cost-effective improvement to yields (physical output per unit of land) will increase producer returns per unit of land and reduce costs of producing a kilogram of cotton lint, thus assisting higher-cost developing countries compete in the world market for fibres.

### Increased processing?

As indicated above, the arrangements which have evolved over time between developing country and developed country suppliers of raw material, processors of textile products and end-consumers are not simple. While the ICAC looks forward to a world in which barriers to trade and trade-distorting practices are eliminated, it is not clear that increased processing of raw cotton fibre into yarn in developing producing countries would be the result in a world without government interventions. It may be observed that developing cotton producing countries processing a significant portion of their production have had strong governmental incentives for domestic consumption. It may also be observed that some developing cotton-producing countries do little processing in the absence of government incentives.

**Utilizing by-products**

The production of cotton involves production of a variety of by-products, the value of which can contribute to producer returns. Historically, however, producers have concentrated on the production and marketing of cotton fibre. For each kilogram of lint produced, there are approximately two kilograms of cottonseed, which can be used for edible oil and feed for ruminant animals. It also can be shown that non-cotton waste can be used for power generation at cotton ginneries, that short fibres removed in ginning and spinning can be further processed and that cotton plant stalks can be used for household fuel. In general, the value of these by-products is low. Given market structure (a large number of suppliers of the by-products and a small number of processors of by-products) and the availability of many substitutes for oil and animal feed, exploiting cottonseed and other by-products may produce returns for small producer-exporters but they are likely to be marginal.

**Remaining competitive with chemical fibres**

Of paramount importance in cotton is the need to remain competitive with chemical fibres produced either by utilizing cellulose in wood products to produced acetate or rayon (viscose) fibres or by extruding a number of plastics in fibre form (polyester, nylon, polypropylene). Cotton is currently estimated to account for 49% of the total market for textile fibres. This share is down from 50% in the 1986-1987 period. Projections made jointly by the ICAC and FAO assume that cotton will be able to hold onto this share in the period to 2000.

Cotton's share of market is rising in the USA, where farmers conduct a major research and development effort to promote cotton use, but it has declined significantly in Japan and Italy, major fibre markets. There is now no effective international attention given to the promotion of cotton as a fibre, outside of efforts of the US industry and government to promote US produced cotton in export markets. Developing countries probably benefit indirectly from US promotion of cotton but have, in the past, been unwilling in sufficient numbers to commit resources to an effective international cotton promotion program.

In these circumstances, the major step which developing country producers of cotton can take to protect their markets is to assure buyers (the textile industry processors of cotton) of a regular supply of cotton of a good quality for spinning. Synthetic fibres can be produced on demand in a factory and are uniform and predictable in quality. Cotton is a natural product which is produced once a year and which varies in supply due to lack of control of producers over all the inputs used in production (namely the weather).

While consumers at present are interested in natural products, textile processors are not interested in a raw material which is not uniform and which presents problems in the spinning mill. Cotton when it is planted theoretically possesses properties to produce a fibre of a certain length with certain fineness and strength. The process of growing, ginning and transporting the fibre destroys a part of this potential. Fibre may be contaminated by various non-cotton materials. The process of ginning may break fibres and reduce their hypothetical length and strength. Furthermore, insect deposits of sugar on open cotton can make the fibre sticky and essentially unusable at the spinning mill. Efforts to minimize these reductions in quality are important if cotton is to remain the major textile fibre.

Producers and consumers in the forum of ICAC have indicated the high priority which they give to the maintenance and improvement of cotton quality, from ways to deal with the stickiness problem in the field, at the gin and in the textile mill to providing cotton breeders with information regarding the spinning properties of the varieties they are developing so that highly-spinnable and not just high-yielding varieties will be grown.

## A continued need for market information

Improved transparency in the market place and increased flow of information to both producers and consumers of cotton will be needed for developing countries to assess their opportunities. Better information regarding supply and demand conditions of both the quantity and qualities of cotton will help the participants in the market make the decisions which will lead to a sufficient and regular supply of raw material of the quality required by the world textile industry.

# THE WORLD JUTE ECONOMY, TRENDS AND PROJECTS[1]

## 1 INTRODUCTION

Jute and kenaf, comprising Corchorus and Hibiscus species are soft bast fibres whose production is concentrated is South and South-East Asia. The four largest producers - Bangladesh, China, India and Thailand - accounted for 94% of the world average output of 3.4 million tonnes during the past three crop years. Due to the high variability in the acreage and yields, the change in world jute production from one season to the next has ranged from +85% to -42% over the 1973-90 period.

The main traditional use of jute and kenaf has been for the packaging market. Cloth, sacks and bags made of these fibres are widely used for the transport and storage of agricultural products, fertilisers, cement and some chemical products. With the advent of bulk handling and synthetic packaging materials, the markets for these traditional jute and kenaf materials have been seriously affected, particularly in the developed world.

However, growing concern over the impact on the environment of the use and disposal of synthetic material has recently led to renewed interest in the possible advantages of natural fibres. Along with traditional uses, a number of new uses of jute and kenaf have been developed in recent years which, although accounting for relatively small quantities of fibre at present, seem to offer potential for future development. Such items include geotextiles for erosion control, various types of jute composites, jute laminates, paper pulp and paper, car panels made of non-woven fabrics, as well as many types of decorative fabrics, furnishings, carpets and handicrafts.

---

[1] Statement of the International Jute Organisation (IJO)

## 2  TRENDS OF PRODUCTION, IMPORT AND PRICES

### Production prospects: production to fall in major producing countries

World jute production increased reasonably fast during the 1973-80 period (1.7% per year) but declined slowly during 1980-90 period (0.2%) although substantial year-to-year crop fluctuations occurred during these periods. Jute production expanded at more than 1% annually until the late seventies, in the eighties the growth rate fell to 0.4%. World total production during 1992/93 has been estimated at 3 million tonnes, 11.8% lower than the last year and 32.2% lower than the average of the years 1985/86 - 1987/88.

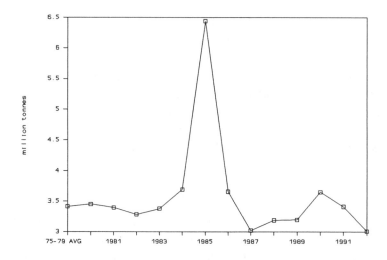

*Figure 1:* World production of jute, kenaf and allied fibres

Jute production prospects in the medium and longer term, based on the demand for traditional jute products, indicate a declining trend. However positive results from marketing non-traditional jute products suggest that this trend could be moderated.

### Consumption to grow in producing countries only

From 1973 to 1990, traditional jute products lost market share to bulk handling in the transport and to synthetics materials substituting for jute sacks and fabrics. Over the 1973-90 period, the slight upward trend in world apparent consumption of jute reflected mainly the growth of markets in the jute producing countries themselves. Thus, while global consumption rose at an average annual rate of 0.5%, the rate of growth in Bangladesh, China and India taken together was in excess of 3.5% per year; their share of world apparent consumption increased from 38% during the early seventies to more than 55% in recent years.

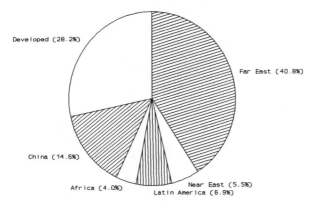

*Figure 2:* Consumption of jute, kenaf and allied fibres, 1980

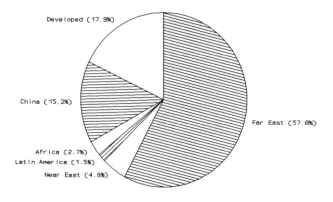

*Figure 3:* Consumption of jute, kenaf and allied fibres, 1990

World consumption of jute during 1991 has been estimated at 3.2 million tonnes, 9.2% lower than previous year and about 21% lower than the average level of the period 1985-87. Apparent consumption of jute in developed countries as a group declined by more than 3.5% per year. Future prospects for jute demand growth are most promising in the producing countries themselves.

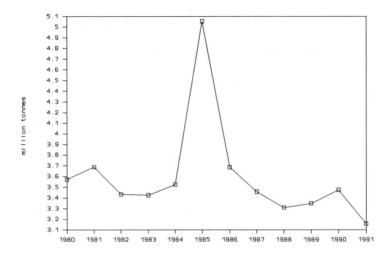

*Figure 4:* World consumption of jute, kenaf and allied fibres

### Import Demand for Jute and Jute Goods will Decline

According to a study by FAO on the trend of import of jute goods, the percentage of jute products traded internationally compared to apparent consumption accounted for only 27% in 1990 against 42 percent in the mid-sixties. The study suggests that imports of jute products into developed regions fell by 23 percent during the period 1980-90. Some rise in imports of yarns was offset by declines in those of hessian, sacking and other products. The decline in imports of jute products of the developing regions by 20 percent during the above period was mainly accounted for by the sharp decrease in imports to Latin America and near East regions which offset some recovery in Africa in some recent years. World Bank and FAO in their study forecast that the volume of jute traded internationally could amount to less than 30% of global production by the year 2000, compared to about 40% in 1987-90, reflecting the increasing concentration of consumption in the producing countries themselves.

World trade in jute fibre and products could amount to about 1.0 million tonnes compared to 1.4 million tonnes in 1985-90, reflecting smaller exports from all major supplying countries. Demand for raw jute is expected to continue declining as importing countries opt for imported jute products or install capacities for domestic production of substitute synthetic products. During 1991/92, world total export of raw jute fell for the second consecutive year to about 360 thousand tonnes, far below the 1989/90 peak of 501 thousand tonnes and were the lowest volume since 1984/85.

Although jute consumption outside the jute producing countries is increasingly dependent on imports of manufactures, the trade volume of jute goods is still expected to decline due to the overall retrenchment in jute use in the importing countries. Apparent consumption prospects imply only a small increase in jute goods imports in the low-middle income countries of Asia, modest declines in Europe, and more substantial declines in other regions. The four largest jute producing countries will continue to be the primary providers of jute products to the world market.

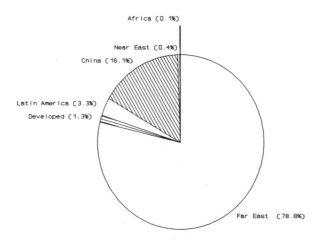

*Figure 5:* Production of jute, kenaf and allied fibres, 1980

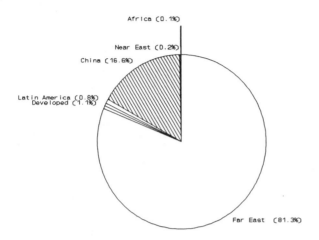

*Figure 6:* Production of jute, kenaf and allied fibres, 1990

### Price prospects - real jute prices continue to decline

The world jute market is subject to severe supply/price cycles. During the current cycles the indicator price (Bangladesh white, D Grade, f.o.b. Bangladesh) increased from its low average of $270 per tonne in 1986/87 - due to sharp increase of stocks from the extremely large 1985/86 crop - to 475 per tonne in 1990/91 as excess stocks were gradually liquidated. The price started to fall rapidly in 1991/92 and the declining trend continued in 1992/93. In September 1992 it was recorded at US$290 per tonne and it fell further to US$260 in December 1992 and continued to prevail at this lowest ever level until April 1993. During the 1991/92 season, this price which was recorded at US$392 was below the lower band of the indicative price range forecasted by the FAO Inter-governmental Group on Jute, Kenaf and Allied Fibres in November 1991 and still below the lower band of the indicative price set by the Group in October 1992.

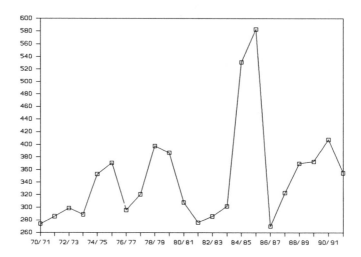

*Figure 7:* Prices of raw jute; export price BWD Grade US$/tonne

Real jute prices have declined over the past two decades. These reductions
have not been offset by improved productivity as in the case of some of
the crops competing for land and production inputs with jute. During the
coming decade, jute prices will continue to be strongly influenced on a
year to year basis by annual crop fluctuations and, over the longer run,
by structural changes in the market as described in the sections above
dealing with consumption. The price implications of this analysis suggest
that real prices will continue to decline in the period to 2000. Reductions
are expected to be particularly severe in the period to 1995, with some
recovery occurring in the latter part of the decade.

## 3  STRATEGIES FOR INTERNATIONAL DEVELOPMENT

### IJO's intervention

Over the decades jute has become an integral part of the cropping system
in the jute growing belt of the south and the south east Asian countries.
Presently around 2.5 million hectares of land are under jute cultivation.
More than 12 million farmers, mostly small and marginal, earn their

livelihood from jute cultivation, jute being the major cash crop in the belt. The jute industry in the producing countries employ a few hundred thousand workers. Exports of jute and jute products are also quite important for the producing countries. As a result jute has assumed a high socio-economic importance in the producing countries which are in the categories of developing and least developed countries. Keeping in view the interests of the millions of small and marginal jute farmers, who have to grow jute either as rotation crop or due to lack of alternatives, IJO's intervention in the form of regional and international co-operative and collaborative efforts to develop the jute sector has assumed importance. This intervention is in addition to the national level interventions that are present in most jute producing countries. In this connection it may be mentioned that although jute and allied fibres are field crops they have not so far received any significant development and funding attention as compared to, for example, field crops being dealt with by the International Agriculture Research Centre under Consultative Group of International Agricultural Research (CGIAR).

**Improvement in Productivity and Quality**

On account of the slow development of appropriate production technology jute farmers continue to use traditional practices as a result of which jute yields have remained low, a little over a tonne per hectare. In terms of technical focus high yielding varieties of jute seed, appropriate low cost production practices, improved retting and fibre extraction techniques are the needs of the day. IJO has developed a number of projects covering these aspects. The following project of IJO has already been successfully completed:

- Jute Seeder Development

The following projects are under implementation:

- Collection, Conservation, Characterisation and Exchange of Germplasm for the Development of Improved Varieties of Jute, Kenaf and Other Allied Fibres - Germplasm Project Phase II.
- Strengthening Jute and Kenaf Seed Programmes
- Improved Retting and Extraction of Jute

The following projects have been approved by the Council, but have so far remained unfunded:

- Support for Varietal Improvement of Jute and Kenaf for Increased Productivity
- High Yield Cultivation Technology Development for Jute and Kenaf
- Collaborative Research for the Exploration and Exploitation of Genetic Variation for the Improvement of Jute and Kenaf Production and Fibre Quality
- Application of Biotechnology in the Improvement of Jute, Kenaf and Allied Fibres

**Search for new applications, commercial utilisation of waste and by-products, and increased processing**

In the Industrial sector the main thrust of IJO activity has been on development of new products from jute. The following two projects are now under implementation:

- Development of Non-woven Products from Jute and Jute Blends and Test Marketing (Phase II).
- Improvement of Physico-chemical Properties of Jute/Kenaf Fibre, Yarn and Fabrics for the Production of Value Added Diversified Products.

Another project - 'Pilot Scale Demonstration of Enzymes Use for the Improvement of Low Grade Jute Cuttings for their Large Scale Utilisation' has become fully funded recently and will commence soon.

The following projects have been approved by the Council but have so far remained unfunded:

- Technical Survey and Market Study of the Potential of Jute Geotextiles.
- Improvement of Existing Spinning Processes including Fine Yarn Manufacturing.
- Development of Jute-based Packaging and Jute Intermediates as Substitutes for Wooden/Plywood and other Packaging.
- Blending of Jute with other fibres for Diversified Uses.
- Conversion Kit for the Introduction of Flexible Rapier Weaving on Ordinary Flat Jute Looms.

**Defence against competing products, improvements in domestic and international markets**

In view of the stiff competition from synthetic substitutes, markets for jute packaging materials have been under tremendous pressure. Promotional activities based on market research need to be taken up by IJO. Moreover, for new products, market promotion activities are essential as soon as commercial production is established. These activities should cover consumer survey, design support, publicity and advertisement. The following two projects are currently under implementation:

- Jute Market Promotion in Japan 1992/93-1994/95.
- Jute Market Development in Selected European Countries (1992/93 - Interim Programme).

The following three projects have been approved by the Council but have so far remained unfunded:

- Market Promotion for Jute Carpet Backing in the United States of America.
- Market Promotion of Jute Products in Australia and New Zealand.
- Jute Market Promotion in Japan 1992/93 - 1994/95 (funds for 2 years available).
- Market Promotion in Western Europe - Interim Programme.

## Environmental Implications of Jute

In its 1989 session the Intergovernmental Group of FAO on Jute, Kenaf and Allied Fibres noted that natural fibres like jute and kenaf might enjoy more favourable market conditions in the future on account of increasing concern with environmental issues all over the world. It was felt that there was need to analyze the environmental implications of using jute as compared to synthetics, to focus attention on the advantages of natural fibres. In its 1990 session the Group commissioned a study to be undertaken by an independent research body which it considered would be helpful. The study suggests that a natural fibre like jute is more environmentally sound and thus, less costly to society than its competing synthetic material. It also suggests in the life-cycle the disposal stage of synthetic material is most harmful to the environment causing highest direct economic and social costs. It further suggests that the environmental advantage of natural products would grow when input factors now available freely are duly costed. Eco-tax based legislation on the principle 'Who pollutes, pays' could modify the present cost and price relations in favour of natural fibres. In this context, the market promotion of jute has assumed greater significance.

IJO will present a paper based on the independent study and observations obtained from the member countries to the Consultation on Jute and Environment to be held in The Hague on October 26-28 1993 under the auspices of FAO.

**Status of Funding of Approved Projects - CFC's role**

In short, IJO has now 13 approved projects whose implementation cannot start due to lack of funds. The total requirement of funds for these projects is US$7.04 million out of which US$460,590 has been committed. The Special Account of IJO which is meant to support projects has been low and as a result IJO has to solicit funds from donors for any new project which is approved by the International Jute Council. So far IJO has presented 7 projects to CFC for approval out of which 2 projects have been approved, 3 projects have not been favoured by CFC and 2 projects are under their consideration.

Now, a few suggestions for extending CFC's role in funding IJO projects are made. It appears from the reports of the Consultative Committee that the Common Fund prefers projects where substantial co-financing is available. For IJO projects co-financing has largely come from member countries. Since most of them are also members of the Common Fund, questions are now being raised as to why they should contribute funds to CFC and at the same time commit funds to Commodity Bodies. It is suggested that the Consultative Committee should examine project proposals on the basis of its technical merits, co-financing being a plus point only. On the basis of technical merits the Consultative Committee may recommend a certain level of financing rather than rejecting the proposal in the absence of co-financing.

It appears that the Common Fund favour project proposals showing quick results. As an International Commodity Body, IJO also wants quick results but there may be good projects, especially in the agriculture and market promotion sectors, which do not necessarily show short term results.

It has been noted that the decisions of the Consultative Committee are largely influenced on occasions by the views of its consultants engaged to examine the project proposals submitted by the ICBs. Consultants engaged by the ICBs or by UN agencies like FAO, ITC, UNDP to prepare their projects are persons or firms of international standing and their views should be given due weight. In the case of IJO the project proposals are examined by the Council after detailed scrutiny by the Committee on Projects. The task of the Consultative Committee may be easier if the Common Fund is equipped with qualified professionals in its staff, but in any event it would be appreciated if the reports of the Consultants engaged by the Fund are sent to the ICBs for comments before the proposals are submitted to the Consultative Committee. Such prior exchange of views may be helpful particularly where the Consultant has adversely commented upon a project proposal.

# BRIEF OVERVIEW ON THE
# INTERNATIONAL LEAD AND ZINC STUDY GROUP
# AND THE LEAD AND ZINC MARKET[1]

## 1 THE ROLE OF LEAD AND ZINC

Zinc and lead are the most widely used non-ferrous metals after aluminium and copper and are vital materials in everyday life. They are mined and smelted in many countries in both the developed and developing world. An increasing proportion of the supply of both metals, over 50% for lead and nearly 30% for zinc, is being met by recycling. Consumption is predominantly in industrialised countries but is increasing rapidly in developing countries. Zinc's effectiveness in protecting steel against corrosion by galvanising is well recognised while the ability to die-cast complicated components makes zinc indispensable in a multitude of industry and household products. It also has important markets in the brass and construction industries and in chemicals and constitutes an essential nutritional element. The principal consumption of lead is for lead-acid batteries which are used in vehicles, in emergency systems (e.g. in hospitals) and in a range of other industrial and commercial applications. Lead is also used in compounds in the glass and plastics industries and for radiation shielding.

## 2 OBJECTIVES OF THE STUDY GROUP

The International Lead and Zinc Study Group was formed in 1959 by the United Nations as an autonomous intergovernmental organisation to:

- provide opportunities for regular intergovernmental consultations on international trade in lead and zinc;
- provide continuous information on the supply and demand position of lead and zinc and its probable development;

---

[1] Paper presented by the International Lead and Zinc Study Group (ILZSG).

- make special studies of the world situation in lead and zinc;
- consider possible solutions to any problems or difficulties which are unlikely to be resolved in the ordinary development of world trade.

The Study Group does not interfere with national economic policies on lead and zinc nor does it impose any restrictions on member countries.

## Membership

Membership of the Group is open to member countries of the United Nations or of its specialised agencies or of the GATT, which consider themselves substantially interested in the production or consumption of or trade in lead and/or zinc. Each member has one vote. The current membership is representative of producing and consuming countries, exporting and importing countries, market and centrally-planned economies and developed and developing countries. In addition, several intergovernmental and non-governmental organisations, all substantially interested in lead and zinc, are officially accredited Observers. The member countries of the Group represent about 90% of the world production and over 80% of the world consumption of both lead and zinc. The membership presently comprises 30 countries.

## Committees and advisory panel

The work of the Group is largely carried out by its three main committees: Standing, Economic and Statistical, in which all member countries are represented. Four sub-committees under the Economic Committee (Production; Consumption; National and Economic Policies; Environment and Regulations) and two under the Statistical Committee (New Mine and Smelter Projects; Recycling) are given specialised assignments. An Industry Advisory Panel, consisting of about 10 senior experts from the lead and zinc industry of member countries, provides to the Study Group a body for advice and consultation.

## Annual sessions and meetings

The Group meets in full session at least once a year, usually in October, at the United Nations in Geneva or Vienna, although there is a provision for meetings to be held in member countries. At its annual Sessions, in addition to receiving reports from its three main committees on their programmes of work and on administrative and financial matters, the Group makes an exhaustive review of the current lead and zinc market situation, including a short-term (one year ahead) forecast of expected trends. In this, it is assisted by a detailed report from the Statistical Committee and by national statements from member countries. Representatives from the lead and zinc industry participate in the Session as advisors to their government delegates. The market forecast is subsequently brought up-to-date at the regular Spring meeting of the Group's Standing Committee which, in addition to its responsibility for the permanent staff of the Secretariat and the financial affairs of the Group, has the responsibility for the general conduct of the affairs of the Group between the Sessions.

## Special meetings

In recognition of the importance of secondary recovery, in particular for the lead industry, the Study Group has organised Special Meetings on "Secondary Recovery of Lead and Zinc" in 1974, 1979, 1984, 1987, all held in Washington D.C., U.S.A., and in 1991 in Rome, Italy. These Special Meetings have been conducted under the auspices of the Sub-Committee on Scrap and later the Sub-Committee on Recycling. In February 1991 the Study Group held, for the first time, a regional meeting in Latin America on "Lead and Zinc in the 1990's - World and Latin America". These Special Meetings have been met with great interest by industry and government. The proceedings are published.

## Studies and publications

To facilitate the attainment of its dual objectives of intergovernmental consultation and maximum market transparency, the Group, since its inception, has published a monthly statistical bulletin providing up-to-date information on lead and zinc production, consumption, stocks, trade, prices, end uses, secondary metal recovery and world supply and demand. A consistent effort has been and continues to be made to improve both the timeliness and quality of the data collected and published, on the basis of internationally agreed and accepted definitions.

In the attainment of the two principal objectives, an important contribution is made by the special studies carried out by the Group's six sub-committees. An annual survey, looking five years ahead, is made of new mine and smelter projects or expansions planned throughout the world, in the field of lead and zinc. Surveys are regularly made of principal uses, world trade and economic trends and their impact on lead and zinc. Periodic studies are made of joint production of lead and zinc; trends in production and consumption; environmental and health control legislation and regulations.

World directories of lead and zinc mines and primary metallurgical works as well as secondary lead and zinc plants are maintained. Two general studies, one on the market situation for zinc, the other on the market situation for lead, have been published. Studies on other subjects vital to lead and zinc consumption and production, including secondary production, and trade are continuously undertaken.

### 3  ROLE OF DEVELOPING COUNTRIES

The role of developing countries in the Study Group is exemplified in the case of zinc.

### Demand for Zinc

Demand for zinc in industrial countries expanded very quickly over 1960-73 in Western Europe, US/Canada and Japan, leading to peak levels in 1973 prior to the onset of the first energy crisis (Figure 3). Thereafter, growth has been more restricted, and consumption in industrial countries could not increase much beyond the pre-oil crisis peak even during the recovery of the 1980s. Zinc consumption in US/Canada in 1991 was in fact a little lower than in 1973, while demand in Western Europe and Japan was only slightly higher than the 1973 level.

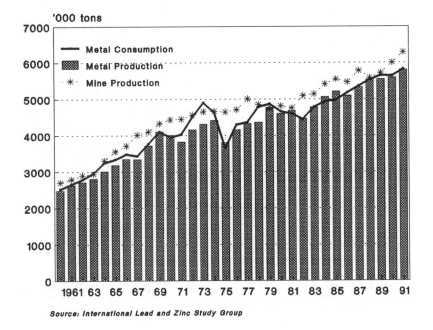

*Figure 1:*    Total zinc consumption and production in industrial and developing countries

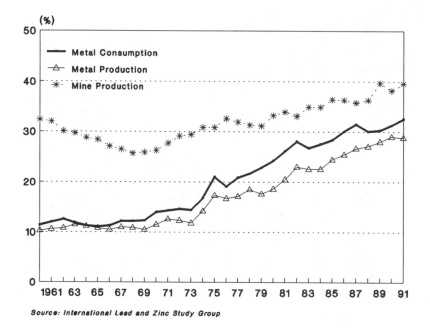

Source: International Lead and Zinc Study Group

*Figure 2:*    Zinc consumption and production in developing countries as a
              percentage of total

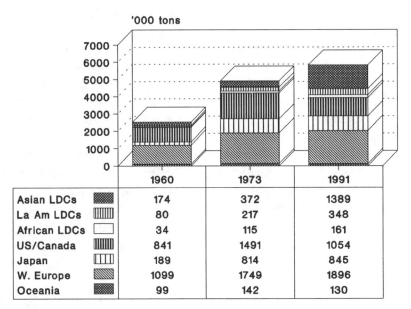

| | 1960 | 1973 | 1991 |
|---|---|---|---|
| Asian LDCs | 174 | 372 | 1389 |
| La Am LDCs | 80 | 217 | 348 |
| African LDCs | 34 | 115 | 161 |
| US/Canada | 841 | 1491 | 1054 |
| Japan | 189 | 814 | 845 |
| W. Europe | 1099 | 1749 | 1896 |
| Oceania | 99 | 142 | 130 |

Source: International Lead and Zinc Study Group

*Figure 3:* Total zinc metal consumption in industrial and developing countries

By contrast to industrial countries, demand increased rapidly in develping countries between 1973 and 1991, consolidating on a period of steady expansion over 1960-73 (Figure 3). The rise was especially rapid in Asia, but slower in Latin America and Africa. As a result, the share of developing countries in world consumption of zinc rose from 11.5% in 1960 to 14% in 1973 and further to 33% in 1991. The Asian region accounted for 24% of consumption in 1991, while Latin America and Africa were lower at 6% and 3% respectively.

The trends in the developing countries reflect developments in economic growth and industrial production. Significantly, increase in zinc consumption stemming from economic growth was sufficient to more than overcome any dampening effects from technology changes towards "thinning down" or miniaturisation. As developing countries begin to industrialise and create employment in the manufacturing sector away from agricultural activities, the use of zinc should expand further particularly in transportation, infrastructure and building activities.

The example of South Korea is illustrative. Over 1965 to 1991, zinc consumption rose from 4,000 tonnes to 269,000 tonnes, as iron and steel, shipbuilding, automobile and other metal intensive industries expanded. This was accompanied by an increase in zinc metal production from nil tonnes in 1965 to 232,000 tonnes in 1991. A significant portion of the consumption went into export goods. At the same time, real per capita GDP (1985 prices) increased from $560 in 1965 to $3250 in 1991.

**Supply of Zinc**

*Mining of zinc* has grown strongly over 1960-91, and is geographically fairly well distributed across industrialised and developing regions of the world (Figure 4). Zinc mining output expanded in industrial countries between 1960 and 1991, especially in North America before 1973 and in Australia after 1973, although the share of industrial countries came down by about 10%. By contrast, the share of developing countries rose from 30% in 1960 to 40% in 1991. The expansion occurred both in Asia (16% share in 1991), a relatively small mining area before 1973, and in Latin America (21% share in 1991) already an important mining region in 1960. In Africa, however, production fell back due to depletion of ore reserves in Zaire and Zambia.

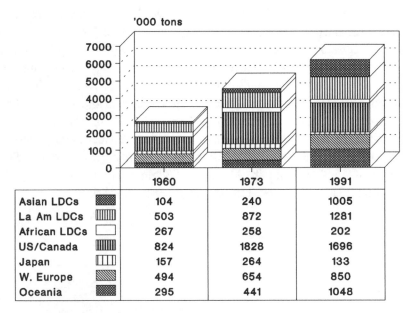

| '000 tons | | | |
|---|---|---|---|
| | **1960** | **1973** | **1991** |
| Asian LDCs | 104 | 240 | 1005 |
| La Am LDCs | 503 | 872 | 1281 |
| African LDCs | 267 | 258 | 202 |
| US/Canada | 824 | 1828 | 1696 |
| Japan | 157 | 264 | 133 |
| W. Europe | 494 | 654 | 850 |
| Oceania | 295 | 441 | 1048 |

*Source: International Lead and Zinc Study Group*

*Figure 4:* Total zinc mine production in industrial and developing countries (metal content of concentrate)

LDCs important in zinc mining are Argentina, Brazil, Bolivia, Mexico and Peru in Latin America; China, India, Iran and Thailand in Asia; and Algeria, Morocco, Namibia, Tunisia, South Africa, Zaire and Zambia in Africa. The Study Group's survey of New Mines and Smelter Projects shows that in 1992 zinc mine capacity increased by 267,000 tonnes, of which LDCs accounted for 165,000 tonnes (62%) principally in Mexico (68,000 tonnes), Morocco (55,000 tonnes), Iran (24,000 tonnes), Bolivia (9,500 tonnes) and Peru (7,500 tonnes). Projects expected to be completed by 1997 indicate a potential capacity expansion of 764,000 tonnes. Of this, the developing countries share is expected to be 444,000 tonnes (58%), primarily in Brazil (108,000 tonnes), China (98,000 tonnes), India (70,000 tonnes), Peru (55,000 tonnes), Tunisia (40,000 tonnes) and Turkey (35,000 tonnes). Other projects are planned in Algeria, Burkina Faso, Nigeria and Zimbabwe in Africa; China, India, Iran and Nepal in Asi

Between 1960 and 1973, expansion in world *zinc metal production* occurred primarily in industrial countries, especially in Japan and Western Europe (Figure 5). Developing countries only accounted for about 10-12% of output, with Latin American and African LDCs producing more than those in Asia. After 1973, there was a rapid growth in zinc metal output particularly in Asia and in Latin America, and the share of developing countries increased to about 29% in 1991 (Asia 19%, Latin America 9% & Africa 3%). The LDCs involved in zinc metal production are Argentina, Brazil, Mexico and Peru in Latin America; Algeria, South Africa, Zaire and Zambia in Africa; and China, India, Indonesia, Iran, South Korea, Taiwan China, Thailand and Turkey in Asia.

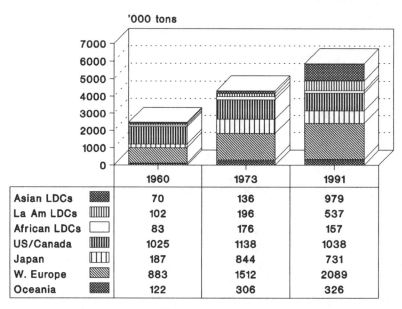

'000 tons

| | 1960 | 1973 | 1991 |
|---|---|---|---|
| Asian LDCs | 70 | 136 | 979 |
| La Am LDCs | 102 | 196 | 537 |
| African LDCs | 83 | 176 | 157 |
| US/Canada | 1025 | 1138 | 1038 |
| Japan | 187 | 844 | 731 |
| W. Europe | 883 | 1512 | 2089 |
| Oceania | 122 | 306 | 326 |

*Source: International Lead and Zinc Study Group*

*Figure 5:*    Total zinc metal production in industrial and developing countries

Smelter projects planned for completion by 1997 may lead to additional capacity of 563,000 tonnes in industrial and developing countries. The LDCs share is 413,000 tonnes (73%), of which China (160,000 tonnes), Iran (88,000 tonnes), Thailand (80,000 tonnes), Brazil (75,000 tonnes) and India (10,000 tonnes). Feasibility studies are under way for other projects in China, India, Mexico and Turkey. With expanding zinc metal production in developing countries and capacity increases continuing during the 1990s, the case for zinc producing LDCs to vertically diversify into zinc die castings and galvanized products, the two principal uses of zinc, becomes even stronger.

## Issues Ahead

Developing countries often face the disadvantages of their deposits being in remote locations with no or little infrastructure. Frequently the country is only partly geologically surveyed. Cheaper prospecting and exploration techniques would certainly be of advantage to developing countries. While some developing countries have expanded vertically into smelting and refining, only the more advanced developing countries have, to some extent, processing industries to produce semi-finished and finished products. Some of the products may also need to be adapted to the special conditions of developing countries.

# THE INTERNATIONAL RUBBER ORGANISATION AND THE RUBBER MARKET[1]

## 1 PRESENT SITUATION

The area planted to rubber in developing countries in the humid tropics is over 9 million hectares. Small farmers typically with holdings of 2 hectares or less account for an estimated 80% of the rubber acreage, the remaining rubber being grown mainly on large plantations. Thus many millions of people in developing countries are dependent on rubber production for their livelihood as either estate workers or small growers.

World rubber production in 1991 was 5.3 million tonnes compared to 3.3 million tonnes in 1975 and only 1.9 million tonnes in 1950. Rubber is grown in almost all countries where the climatic conditions are suitable, production, however, is concentrated in Indonesia, Malaysia and Thailand which account for over 70% of global output. Other important producers are India which is basically self-sufficient and China which is major importer of raw rubber. Countries in West and Central Africa at present account for 6% of production while this figure is expected to increase to about 10% by the early years of next century. Table 1 shows natural rubber production in 1991.

---

[1] Presentation by the International Natural Rubber Organization (INRO)

*Table 1:* World natural rubber production 1991

| Producer | 1000 tonnes |
|----------|-------------|
| Thailand | 1341 |
| Indonesia | 1284 |
| Malaysia | 1257 |
| India | 360 |
| China | 270 |
| Philippines | 201 |
| Sri Lanka | 104 |
| Africa | 307 |
| Others | 196 |
|  | 5320 |

*Source:* IRSG Rubber Statistical Bulletin March 1993

The consumption of natural rubber which is an essential industrial raw material in 1991 was 5.2 million tonnes. This figure is expected to rise to about 6.75 million tonnes by the year 2000. However, new developments in tyre technology may increase demand while the introduction of an open market economy in Eastern Europe and the former USSR may result in the substitution of natural rubber for synthetic rubber in those countries so that total demand could exceed 7.5 million tonnes by the early years of the next century. Approximately 70% of natural rubber is consumed by the tyre manufacturing sector which tends to be concentrated in a number of multinational companies with worldwide operations. The most important geographical area for rubber consumption is the Asia/Pacific rim which now accounts for 44% of the market. Figure 1 shows the regional consumption of natural rubber during 1991.

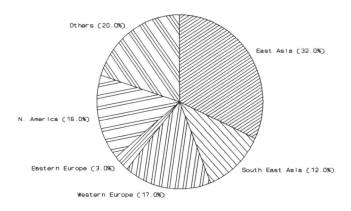

*Source:* IRSG Rubber Statistical Bulletin March 1993

*Figure 1:* Regional distribution of natural rubber consumption (1991)

## 2 MAJOR PROBLEM

For the past decade, the producers of natural rubber, the majority of whom are small farmers in developing countries, have been facing a problem which is common to the producers of most tropical commodities: prices are inadequate to provide a reasonable and rising standard of living. Table 2, which is based on a comparison of the INRO average daily market indicator prices since the establishment of the organization in 1980, shows that the price of natural rubber has been stagnant since 1981. Figure 2 shows the monthly, average daily indicator prices against the long term trend from 1980 to 1992. It should be noted that the price received takes no account of inflationary pressures which in some developing countries have been severe. A problem is that if the price received by farmers is not remunerative they will replant their rubber with other more profitable crops which may lead to supply difficulties in future years. The increases in total rubber production over past years are as a

result of investment decisions made ten and more years ago because of the
long production cycle (some thirty years from planting to replanting) of
rubber trees.

*Table 2* Price index (1980 = 100)

| 1980 | 100 | 1985 | 61 | 1989 | 74 |
|------|-----|------|----|----- |----|
| 1981 | 80  | 1986 | 65 | 1990 | 65 |
| 1982 | 63  | 1987 | 77 | 1991 | 63 |
| 1983 | 80  | 1988 | 91 | 1992 | 62 |
| 1984 | 73  |      |    |      |    |

# Monthly Average
## DMIP:1980-1992 / Price Index: 1980-1992

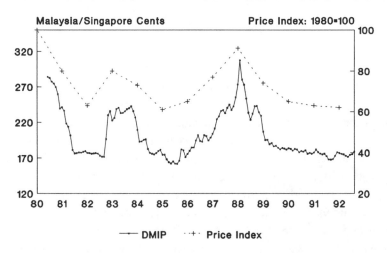

*Source:* INRO

*Figure 2*

## 3 SEMINAR TOPICS REGARDING NATURAL RUBBER

### Productivity improvements

Plant breeders working over the years have developed high yielding varieties of rubber that can give commercial yields of over 2 tonnes of dry rubber per hectare per year. In most producing countries smallholder yields remain undesirably low because the majority of smallholders use low-yielding seedling material. Major problems associated with small growers accepting improved production technologies are concerned with difficulties of technology transfer to small farmers and the provision of finance to support the farm families over the long gestation period before the trees come into tapping.

### Commercial utilization of waste and by-products

The use of rubber wood as a source of timber after the latex-bearing years are over has developed rapidly over the past ten years. The market for rubber wood is probably in excess of US$500 million, while its potential as a utility timber is immense and still largely untapped. The use of rubberwood for furniture, kitchen utensils and chipboard is most developed in Malaysia and Thailand. Several countries in Asia, particularly China, India, Indonesia, Sri Lanka and Vietnam are actively developing their rubber wood industries.

The primary processing of rubber results in the production of large quantities of highly polluting effluent. The International Rubber Research and Development Board has identified effluent disposal from rubber processing factories as a priority problem for the natural rubber industry. A project costed at US$3 million using enclosed anaerobic reactors that produce methane, a fuel gas, and algal animal foodstuff has been submitted to an international financing agency for external funding. In a recent development new techniques have been developed for producing solid fertilizer from latex-concentrate factory effluent.

### Increased processing in developing commodity producing countries

As shown in Figure 1 the producing countries of South East Asia together with Singapore now account for 12% of world rubber consumption compared to a negligible figure in 1950. In 1991 17% of production in Malaysia; 8% in Indonesia; and 6% in Thailand was consumed locally. The rubber manufacturing sector is expanding rapidly in all three countries as they industrialize so that the proportion of rubber consumed in their domestic industries is forecast to substantially increase. India and China have large rubber manufacturing industries and consume all the natural rubber they produce. In Africa only Nigeria has a significant rubber manufacturing sector.

## Problems affecting quality and regularity of supply

The globalization of quality standards, the imposition of Just-in-Time supply of rubber components and the automation of rubber manufacturing operations place increasing demands on producers to supply a consistent quality raw rubber with predicable processing and performance behaviour. The major manufacturers require consistent behaviour between batches and between deliveries irrespective of the origin of the raw material. These requirements have encouraged the development of direct trading links between large consumers and chosen suppliers who can produce to the customers' specifications. Rubber processing factories are increasingly adopting the ISO 9000 quality management system to guarantee the consistency and quality of their raw rubber. A recent initiative by the Professional Association for Natural Rubber in Africa (ANRA) specifically addresses the issue of improving the quality of African rubber.

## Search for new applications and/or new consumers; and

## Defence against competing products and better marketing.

Natural rubber currently accounts for 36% of the world rubber market compared to over 60% for synthetic elastomers. There is a need to develop new markets for natural rubber in the face of continuing competition from the synthetic rubbers. Developments to increase the market share of natural rubber have been funded both by national rubber development organizations and international funding agencies. Some examples of recent work to produce new materials and expand the market are as follows:

- *New forms of rubber:* Liquid natural rubber. Powdered natural rubber. Epoxydized natural rubber.
- *New materials:* Thermoplastic natural rubber. Blends of natural rubber with nitrile/butadiene and ethylene/propylene synthetic rubbers. Natural/epoxydized blended rubber.
- *New applications/markets:* Winter tyres. Truck retreads. Earthquake bearings for buildings.

## Domestic marketing

Over capacity in processing factories in the major producing countries ensures keen competition for smallholder raw material. The radio services in these countries broadcast daily local prices and in some cases the Singapore international prices. The market is, therefore, transparent and farm gate prices closely reflect prices in the international market place. In countries where rubber is a new crop the development of small farm rubber is generally through the nucleus estate system. The farmers are contracted to sell to a central factory and receive a price calculated from the current international market price with deductions for processing and loan repayments.

## International marketing

It is estimated that between 60-70% of exports of rubber are traded direct between large integrated producers or processing factories, and the multinational tyre manufacturers. The other 30-40% of exports is traded through the international rubber market. The main exchanges are Singapore and Kuala Lumpur in the producing region; and Tokyo, Kobe, London and New York in consuming countries. The increase in direct trading links in the past ten years has led to a decline in the number of rubber traders particularly in the London and New York markets. The most important international exchange which deals in both physical and paper rubber is in Singapore where all the major tyre manufacturers and commodity trading firms have buying offices. The Rubber Association of Singapore Commodity Exchange has three internationally recognized contracts. RSS 1 in Singapore Dollars; RSS 3 in US Dollars; TSR 20 in Singapore Dollars, and is open for trading Monday to Friday at the following hours:

10.00 - 13.00 (Asian time zone)
15.30 - 18.00 (European time zone)
21.30 - 00.30 (American time zone)

# THE INTERNATIONAL RUBBER STUDY GROUP AND THE RUBBER MARKET[1]

## 1 THE ROLE OF THE INTERNATIONAL RUBBER STUDY GROUP

The International Rubber Study Group (IRSG) comprises 23 member countries who collectively account for nearly 80% of the world's natural (NR) and synthetic rubber (SR) industry activity, with its NR producing members contributing over 85% of world output. In its unique position to take an overview of the entire elastomer industry the Group is well placed to identify the key factors that will influence longer-term development. It is also better able to consider issues relating to individual areas such as the globalisation of tyre manufacture or the marketing of NR. Its role has expanded significantly from its original function as a purely statistical organisation to one that now also seeks to address the wide range of issues that challenge the global industry.

The stated objectives of the Group are the collection and dissemination of statistical and economic information and the development of appropriate methodologies to aid analysis of industry trends. Through its annual Forums and the Secretariat Work Programme, the Secretariat also monitors trends in production/consumption, changing technology, pricing/markets and evolving trends in rubber manufacturing. These activities assist the IRSG to fulfil its primary objective, to encourage 'the orderly growth of the world elastomer industry'. Two advisory panels, drawn from industry experts, advise the Secretariat on economic and statistical research work.

In addition to its routine activities, over the last five years the IRSG has identified three priority areas meriting special attention: meeting the raw rubber quality and processing consistency requirements of manufacturers; remedying deficiencies in the NR price determining mechanism and promoting the concept of the symbiosis of NR and SR. Foremost is the quality of raw rubbers. Rubber manufacturers, both tyre and GRP, are

---

[1] Background review from the International Rubber Study Group (IRSG)

constantly seeking improved quality and consistency in raw material. Two aspects were identified by the Group: firstly, the question of NR quality, specifically the elimination of foreign matter contamination including the use of non-timber packaging for NR and secondly, to respond to manufacturers' requirement for processing consistency of raw rubbers. The Group mandated the Secretary General to address these issues. Assisted by relevant industry experts, the IRSG formulated a programme to assist producers to eliminate external contamination of their rubber at field and processing stages. The Group also sponsored a Common Fund for Commodities financed project by RAPRA Technology Ltd (UK) to design a timber-free packaging system for Technically Specified Rubber (TSR), now the major form of dry rubber. This project has succeeded in developing a stacking tray packaging system, now undergoing trial shipment. On processability, the IRSG has submitted a project proposal to the Common Fund for Commodities which aims to develop the knowledge and equipment which will enable NR producers to take the necessary steps at the field and processing stages such that their rubber will process in a consistent manner.

## 2  BACKGROUND INFORMATION ON NATURAL RUBBER

### Hevea Brasiliensis

Natural rubber is extracted from the Hevea brasiliensis tree, which when 'tapped' yields a milky liquid containing around 30% rubber and other solids suspended in an aqueous solution. The latex is then processed either into a liquid latex concentrate (>60% dry rubber content/drc) or into a form of dry rubber (>99% drc) such as Ribbed Smoked Sheet(RSS) or Technically Specified Rubber (TSR) of crumb blocks. Today shares by type are approximately 10-12% in latex concentrate, 50-52% TSR, 32-33% RSS, with the remainder in other forms of dry rubber such as crepes, speciality rubbers etc.

Hevea is a tropical, perennial tree crop, with an immaturity period of 5-7 years before it is ready for latex extraction which continues for 25 years. It is considered quite a 'hardy' crop in that it can be grown on slopes, can tolerate a reasonable variation from its ideal growing conditions in terms of temperature, rainfall, wind etc. and does not require undue attention in terms of maintenance. A wide range of bud-grafted clonal planting materials with different physical and productive features are now in use: while essentially similar, the latex from different clones exhibit slight variations in certain characteristics such as rubber content, non- rubber materials, degree of hardness or modulus, viscosity etc.

Latex can be extracted throughout the year (apart from a seasonal downturn at time of refoliage known as 'wintering' depending on climatic conditions). When the tree is productive, maintenance and extraction (i.e. tapping/collection) does not occupy the entire day, enabling the cultivator to attend to other activities. For such reasons it is an ideal smallholder crop. Rubber cultivation is frequently a family business and tappers are often women. Furthermore, NR is often cultivated in remote rural areas which may not as readily support other means of livelihood. For example, NR is now successfully established in Kalimantan through Indonesia's transmigration programme while Thailand has extended NR plantations to the North-East of the country which is economically depressed.

**Planted area, production and exports**

Total planted area of NR has close to doubled since 1960, from just under 5 million ha. to over 9 million ha. in 1990 (Table 1). The three major SE Asian producing countries: Indonesia, Malaysia and Thailand account for about 72% of NR area and the remaining 2.5 million ha. is in other Asian countries (19%), Africa (6%) and Latin America (3%). The geographical distribution of NR production is similarly dependent on the three major producers, but their share is now edging down in response to expansion at existing producers in Asia and Africa as well as a number of smaller producing countries (Table 2) where NR has been established on a commercial scale since the mid 1960s to diversify export earnings (i.e. Côte d'Ivoire, Guatemala, Papua New Guinea) or to supply domestic manufacturing industry (China PR, Philippines) as well as on social welfare grounds for rural livelihood.

NR is now very much a smallholder crop. These small farmers typically tend plots of about 2-3 ha. in size, although smallholdings are officially defined as being less than 40 ha. 80% of area and 76% of global production is from this sector as Tables 1 and 3 detail. Smallholders are particularly important in all the major Asian rubber producers as well as in Nigeria and Brazil. Therefore the socio-economic importance of the NR industry is considerable and underlies producing countries' efforts to improve production efficiency, price received and secure long term markets.

Turning now to the market for raw rubber. Of the 5.6 million tonnes now produced, about 4 million tonnes are internationally traded. Available statistics are for net exports, as there is a flow of raw rubber for reprocessing/shipment to Malaysia and Singapore from Asian and African producing countries. About 1.4 million tonnes are now consumed in the country of production. Two groups can be identified: the net importing NR producing countries of Brazil, China, India (the latter has occasionally exported NR) and the net-exporting NR producers, particularly Malaysia and other Asian countries who are rapidly increasing domestic rubber manufacturing of both latex and dry rubber goods. NR consumption at both groups of NR producing countries has expanded strongly in the last five years, in sharp contrast to the more modest increase in global offtake in a recessionary world. Since 1990 around a quarter of global NR output has been used in the country of production.

*Table 1:* Estimates of Natural Rubber Planted Area, 1960 and 1990
(1000 ha.)

| | 1960 | 1990 | Country Share (%) 1990 | Share Small-holders[1] (%) |
|---|---|---|---|---|
| Bangladesh | ... | 47.0 | 0.5 | ... |
| Cambodia | 40.0 | 52.3 | 0.6 | ... |
| China | 15.0 | 600.0 | 6.5 | 21 |
| India | 123.0 | 451.0 | 4.9 | 83 |
| Indonesia | 1936.0 | 3040.0 | 32.8 | 83 |
| Malaysia | 1555.0 | 1832.0 | 19.7 | 81 |
| Myanmar | 55.0 | 76.0 | 0.8 | 59 |
| Papua New Guinea | 10.0 | 15.0 | 0.2 | 80 |
| Philippines | 8.0 | 86.0 | 0.9 | 41 |
| Sri Lanka | 270.8 | 230.0 | 2.5 | 56 |
| Thailand | 482.0 | 1860.0 | 20.0 | 95 |
| Vietnam | 105.0 | 200.0 | 2.2 | ... |
| Other Asia | 5.0 | 3.0 | ... | ... |
| **Total Asia** | **4604.8** | **8492.3** | **91.6** | **79** |
| Cameroon | 10.0 | 41.0 | 0.4 | 6 |
| C.A.R. | ... | 1.0 | ... | ... |
| Côte d'Ivoire | 5.0 | 67.0 | 0.7 | 29 |
| Gabon | ... | 10.0 | 0.1 | 4 |
| Ghana | 6.0 | 12.0 | 0.1 | 33 |
| Liberia | 53.0 | 110.0 | 1.2 | 50 |
| Nigeria | 117.0 | 260.0 | 2.8 | 81 |
| Zaire | 93.0 | 40.0 | 0.4 | ... |
| Other Africa | 10.0 | 5.0 | 0.1 | ... |
| **Total Africa** | **296.0** | **546.0** | **5.8** | **50** |
| Brazil | 17.0 | 197.0 | 2.1 | 69 |
| Guatemala | ... | 28.0 | 0.3 | ... |
| Mexico | 4.0 | 8.0 | 0.1 | ... |
| Other Latin America | 10.0 | 10.0 | 0.1 | ... |
| **Total Latin America** | **31.0** | **243.0** | **2.6** | **60** |
| **WORLD** | **4931.8** | **9281.3** | **100.0** | **80** |

*Notes:* [1] Estimated in recent years

*Sources:* IRSG.

*Table 2:* NR Production by country, 1960-92 (1000 tonnes)[1]

|            | 1960 | 1980 | 1990 | 1992 | Country share (%) 1960 | Country share (%) 1992 | Growth (%pa) '60-'92 |
|------------|------|------|------|------|------|------|------|
| Cambodia   | 37   | 0    | 32   | 39   | 1.8  | 0.7  | 0.2  |
| China      | 3    | 113  | 264  | 310  | 0.1  | 5.6  | 15.6 |
| India      | 25   | 155  | 324  | 383  | 1.2  | 6.9  | 8.9  |
| Indonesia  | 620  | 1020 | 1262 | 1387 | 30.4 | 24.9 | 2.5  |
| Malaysia   | 764  | 1530 | 1291 | 1218 | 37.5 | 21.8 | 1.5  |
| Myanmar    | 11   | 16   | 15   | 15   | 0.5  | 0.3  | 1.0  |
| PNG        | 4    | 4    | 3    | 5    | 0.2  | 0.1  | 0.7  |
| Phil       | 3    | 70   | 185  | 205  | 0.1  | 3.7  | 14.1 |
| Sri Lanka  | 99   | 133  | 113  | 104  | 4.9  | 1.9  | 0.2  |
| Thailand   | 171  | 501  | 1271 | 1481 | 8.4  | 26.5 | 7.0  |
| Vietnam    | 77   | 46   | 52   | 77   | 3.8  | 1.4  | 0.0  |
| **Asia**   | **1814** | **3588** | **4812** | **5224** | **88.9** | **93.6** | **3.4** |
| Cameroon   | 5    | 17   | 38   | 44   | 0.2  | 0.8  | 7.0  |
| Cote d' Ivoire | ... | 23 | 69   | 72   | ...  | 1.3  | ...  |
| Ghana      | ...  | 4    | 4    | 6    | ...  | 0.1  | ...  |
| Liberia    | 48   | 78   | 40   | 32   | 2.4  | 0.6  | -1.3 |
| Nigeria    | 60   | 47   | 152  | 129  | 2.9  | 2.3  | 2.4  |
| Zaire      | 36   | 25   | 15   | 8    | 1.8  | 0.1  | -4.6 |
| Other Africa |    | 0    | 1    | 2    | ...  | 0.0  | ...  |
| **Africa** | **149** | **194** | **319** | **293** | **7.3** | **5.3** | **2.1** |
| Brazil     | 24   | 28   | 30   | 30   | 1.2  | 0.5  | 0.7  |
| Guate-mala | 0    | 9    | 18   | 19   | 0.0  | 0.3  | ...  |
| Other L America | 7 | 11  | 8    | 10   | 0.3  | 0.2  | 1.1  |
| **Latin America** | **31** | **48** | **56** | **59** | **1.5** | **1.1** | **2.0** |
| Unclassified[2] | 46 | 20 | 23   | 4    | 2.3  | 0.1  | ...  |
| **TOTAL**  | **2040** | **3850** | **5210** | **5580** | **100** | **100** | **3.2** |

*Notes:*   [1] All totals rounded.
          [2] Including statistical discrepancies.

*Sources:* Rubber Statistical Bulletin, IRSG.

*Table 3a:* Production of Natural Rubber, 1960-92 (1000 tonnes)

| Year | Estates[1] | Small-holding[1] | Total | Small-Holdings (%) |
|---|---|---|---|---|
| 1960 | ... | ... | 2040 | |
| 1970 | 1275 | 1865 | 3140 | 59.4 |
| 1971 | 1325 | 1810 | 3135 | 57.7 |
| 1972 | 1300 | 1860 | 3160 | 58.9 |
| 1973 | 1350 | 2195 | 3545 | 61.9 |
| 1974 | 1375 | 2095 | 3470 | 60.4 |
| 1975 | 1300 | 2060 | 3360 | 61.3 |
| 1976 | 1400 | 2225 | 3625 | 61.4 |
| 1977 | 1425 | 2230 | 3655 | 61.0 |
| 1978 | 1450 | 2320 | 3770 | 61.5 |
| 1979 | 1475 | 2395 | 3870 | 61.9 |
| 1980 | 1425 | 2425 | 3850 | 63.0 |
| 1981 | 1425 | 2275 | 3700 | 61.5 |
| 1982 | 1440 | 2310 | 3750 | 61.6 |
| 1983 | 1465 | 2565 | 4030 | 63.6 |
| 1984 | 1485 | 2770 | 4255 | 65.1 |
| 1985 | 1515 | 2885 | 4400 | 65.6 |
| 1986 | 1565 | 2925 | 4490 | 65.1 |
| 1987 | 1590 | 3250 | 4840 | 67.1 |
| 1988 | 1590 | 3530 | 5120 | 68.9 |
| 1989 | 1610 | 3600 | 5210 | 69.1 |
| 1990 | 1560 | 3650 | 5210 | 70.1 |
| 1991 | 1430 | 3920 | 5350 | 73.3 |
| 1992 | 1310 | 4270 | 5580 | 76.5 |

*Notes:* [1] The division between estates and smallholdings had been made on incomplete data.

*Source:* Rubber Statistical Bulletin (IRSG).

*Table 3b:*   Consumption of Natural Rubber, 1960-92

| Year | Total Consumption | Local Consumption in NR producing Countries | | Consumption in Brazil, China and India[1] | |
|------|------|------|------|------|------|
|      | 1000t | 1000t | % | 1000t | % |
| 1960 | 2080 | 39 | 1.9 | 193 | 9.3 |
| 1970 | 3090 | 100 | 3.2 | 373 | 12.1 |
| 1971 | 3120 | 117 | 3.8 | 395 | 12.7 |
| 1972 | 3240 | 140 | 4.3 | 395 | 12.2 |
| 1973 | 3460 | 156 | 4.5 | 429 | 12.4 |
| 1974 | 3600 | 166 | 4.6 | 437 | 12.1 |
| 1975 | 3400 | 180 | 5.3 | 458 | 13.5 |
| 1976 | 3570 | 203 | 5.7 | 480 | 13.4 |
| 1977 | 3740 | 211 | 5.6 | 534 | 14.3 |
| 1978 | 3750 | 228 | 6.1 | 555 | 14.8 |
| 1979 | 3870 | 252 | 6.5 | 589 | 15.2 |
| 1980 | 3780 | 257 | 6.8 | 592 | 15.7 |
| 1981 | 3720 | 278 | 7.5 | 531 | 14.3 |
| 1982 | 3670 | 295 | 8.0 | 570 | 15.5 |
| 1983 | 4020 | 319 | 7.9 | 640 | 15.9 |
| 1984 | 4290 | 333 | 7.8 | 703 | 16.4 |
| 1985 | 4420 | 351 | 7.9 | 746 | 16.9 |
| 1986 | 4460 | 387 | 8.7 | 807 | 18.1 |
| 1987 | 4790 | 428 | 8.9 | 948 | 19.8 |
| 1988 | 5190 | 482 | 9.3 | 1096 | 21.1 |
| 1989 | 5300 | 533 | 10.1 | 1133 | 21.4 |
| 1990 | 5280 | 637 | 12.1 | 1080 | 20.4 |
| 1991 | 5220 | 726 | 13.9 | 1111 | 21.3 |
| 1992 | 5470 | 752 | 13.7 | 1149 | 21.0 |

*Notes:*   [1] Total NR used by these 3 countries who are traditionally net importers of NR to supplement local NR production.

*Source:* Rubber Statistical Bulletin.

## International trading and markets

Despite the increasing tonnages expected from the net importing producer group and local consumption at other NR producers, the bulk of NR will continue to be traded for the foreseeable future. Much effort has therefore been devoted to improving all aspects of the international trading of NR. The TSR scheme includes a quality control system for exports and specified packaging and labelling procedures and building on this the packing, shipping and overall handling of NR exports has improved significantly in the last decades. Freight and shipping facilities however do continue to pose problems for some smaller producers and West African NR exporters.

On the international marketing front, INRA (International Natural Rubber Agreement) has provided reasonable price stability since its inception in 1981. A less welcome feature however has been the weakening of official markets. The trend to increased direct, producer-consumer trade in TSRs, particularly between the larger suppliers and the tyre makers, by-passes official markets which raises questions on the accuracy of the price determining mechanism reflecting market fundamentals. This area has been extensively discussed in recent years, and among the problems identified were the lack of a successful futures market, insufficient liquidity of existing markets, the impact of direct trade on smaller producer-consumers and the role of international traders. A central, global market such as the recently opened Rubber Association of Singapore Commodity Exchange (RASCE) could revitalise the international marketplace for NR.

Many of the difficulties surrounding the global market place for NR reflect the many changes in the composition and structure of NR consumption and changing practices at its main end-using industries.

## Consumption and end-use markets

Natural rubber shares the 'elastomer market' with a family of synthetic rubbers, and at present it accounts for 37% of this market but this share is considered to be constrained by production rather than by technical or economic limitations. As dry natural rubber is increasingly used in combination with either general purpose (such as Styrene Butadiene Rubber (SBR) or Polybutadiene Rubber (BR)) or more specialised synthetics, the two types of rubbers are more complementary than competing. The better 'tack' and 'green strength' (which enables products to be 'built-up' prior to vulcanisation) makes NR the material of choice for vehicle tyres, particularly larger commercial vehicle tyres where resistance to heat build-up is important. Hence over 65% of NR is destined to the tyre sector, around 10-12% is used in latex form and the remainder in the dry rubber based General Rubber Product sector.

The rapid industrialisation and economic success of Asian NICs, China PR and India together with Japan's growing intake of raw rubber for her auto/tyre sectors has led to Asia becoming the focal point for growth in total, and natural rubber in particular. Table 4 illustrates that the developing world in L America, Africa and Asia together use close to 50% of NR and 30% of total rubber. These non-OECD Asian economies account for 40% of world NR consumption, which is likely to increase to 40-45% by the end of this decade, as rapid growth in offtake is anticipated in China, India and ASEAN. The market liberalisation of the former USSR and Eastern European countries also represents an increasing market for NR, albeit in the much longer-term given the region's economic and political problems at present. In the former USSR, rubber usage was characterised by a minimal use of dry natural rubber, which was substituted by synthetic cis poly-isoprene for reasons of self-sufficiency. Hence the raw material mix in the former East European region's rubber industry used a very low percentage of NR: 15% in the 1980s compared to world average use of 33%. As the production and use of this type of SR is not commercially viable in a market-economy, its use of NR can be expected to increase substantially in the next century.

There have also been substantial changes within rubber's main end-use sectors. In the vehicle tyre sector, the largest end-use for NR, the commercial introduction of the more NR-intensive radial tyre greatly expanded NR's market potential. While radialisation in passenger car tyres is now virtually complete in OECD economies, NR demand will continue to benefit as this extends to developing countries as well as commercial vehicle tyres. The importance of the tyre sector to NR consumption is likely to continue to increase. The emphasis in modern tyre manufacturing is on efficiency through automation and quality. Globalisation has led to mergers and acquisitions resulting in an increasingly concentrated market with just six companies providing over 80% of world tyre activity by 1990.

The dry rubber based General Rubber Product (GRP) sector includes footwear, engineering products and other (non-tyre) automotive uses. NR's market share in this sector is on a declining trend due to a combination of the greater usage of NR in tyres and the development of 'special-purpose' synthetic materials for niche GRP applications. Much effort is being devoted to identifying and developing non-tyre markets to lessen its dependence on the tyre sector. To this end, speciality NR grades and blends have been developed and novel uses such as its use in road surfacing, earthquake protection etc. have been successfully promoted by NR producing countries led by Malaysia. Latex-based manufacturing has however expanded significantly since the mid-80s AIDS-inspired demand boost. Latex is used for thin-walled rubber goods made by dipping (gloves, condoms), extruding (thread) or foaming (mattresses, carpet underlay).

*Table 4*: Consumption of Natural, Synthetic and Total Rubber, 1992

| | NR<br>1000t | SR<br>1000t | Total<br>1000t | SR<br>% | Shares by Country<br>NR<br>% | SR<br>% | Total<br>% |
|---|---|---|---|---|---|---|---|
| Canada | 87 | 198 | 285 | 70 | 1.6 | 2.2 | 1.9 |
| U.S.A. | 911 | 1981 | 2892 | 69 | 16.6 | 21.6 | 19.7 |
| **Total N.**<br>**America** | **997** | **2179** | **3176** | **69** | **18.2** | **23.8** | **21.7** |
| | | | | | | | |
| **EEC, of**<br>**which:** | **818** | **1708** | **2525** | **68** | **14.9** | **18.6** | **17.2** |
| France | 174 | 365 | 539 | 68 | 3.2 | 4.0 | 3.7 |
| Germany | 211 | 472 | 683 | 69 | 3.8 | 5.1 | 4.7 |
| Italy | 119 | 300 | 419 | 72 | 2.2 | 3.3 | 2.9 |
| Spain | 107 | 155 | 262 | 59 | 2.0 | 1.7 | 1.8 |
| UK | 125 | 210 | 335 | 63 | 2.3 | 2.3 | 2.3 |
| | | | | | | | |
| **Oth.Eur.**<br>**of which** | **287** | **2186** | **2473** | **88** | **5.2** | **23.8** | **16.9** |
| USSR | 100 | 1730 | 1830 | 95 | 1.8 | 18.9 | 12.5 |
| Poland | 20 | 78 | 98 | 80 | 0.4 | 0.9 | 0.7 |
| Romania | 18 | 40 | 58 | 69 | 0.3 | 0.4 | 0.4 |
| Turkey | 68 | 71 | 139 | 51 | 1.2 | 0.8 | 0.9 |
| | | | | | | | |
| **Total**<br>**Europe** | **1105** | **3893** | **4998** | **78** | **20.2** | **42.4** | **34.1** |
| | | | | | | | |
| Brazil | 134 | 267 | 401 | 67 | 2.4 | 2.9 | 2.7 |
| Mexico | 72 | 117 | 189 | 62 | 1.3 | 1.3 | 1.3 |
| Other L<br>America | 117 | 165 | 282 | 59 | 2.1 | 1.8 | 1.9 |
| **Total L**<br>**America** | **323** | **549** | **872** | **63** | **5.9** | **6.0** | **6.0** |

N.B. Totals may not add up due to rounding.

*Source:* Rubber Statistical Bulletin.

*Table 4 (Continued):* Consumption of Natural, Synthetic and Total Rubber, 1992 (000t)

| | NR 1000t | SR 1000t | Total 1000t | SR % | Shares by Country NR % | SR % | Total % |
|---|---|---|---|---|---|---|---|
| South Africa | 40 | 48 | 88 | 55 | 0.7 | 0.5 | 0.6 |
| Other Africa | 91 | 55 | 146 | 38 | 1.7 | 0.6 | 1.0 |
| **Total Africa** | **131** | **103** | **234** | **44** | **2.4** | **1.1** | **1.6** |
| | | | | | | | |
| Australia | 37 | 53 | 90 | 59 | 0.7 | 0.6 | 0.6 |
| Japan | 685 | 1081 | 1766 | 61 | 12.5 | 11.8 | 12.1 |
| *Sub-total Asia 1* | 722 | 1134 | 1856 | 61 | 13.2 | 12.4 | 12.7 |
| | | | | | | | |
| Rep. of Korea | 273 | 280 | 553 | 51 | 5.0 | 3.1 | 3.8 |
| Taiwan | 111 | 196 | 307 | 64 | 2.0 | 2.1 | 2.1 |
| *Sub-total Asia 2* | 384 | 476 | 860 | 55 | 7.0 | 5.2 | 5.9 |
| | | | | | | | |
| China | 610 | 500 | 1110 | 45 | 11.1 | 5.4 | 7.6 |
| India | 405 | 112 | 517 | 22 | 7.4 | 1.2 | 3.5 |
| Indonesia | 116 | 52 | 168 | 31 | 2.1 | 0.6 | 1.1 |
| Malaysia | 249 | 20 | 268 | 7 | 4.5 | 0.2 | 1.8 |
| Thailand | 69 | 36 | 105 | 34 | 1.3 | 0.4 | 0.7 |
| *Sub-total Asia 3* | 1448 | 720 | 2167 | 33 | 26.5 | 7.8 | 14.8 |
| | | | | | | | |
| Other Asia | 363 | 121 | 484 | 25 | 6.6 | 1.3 | 3.3 |
| **Total Asia/ Pacific** | **2917** | **2450** | **5367** | **46** | **53.3** | **26.7** | **36.6** |
| **World Total** | **5470** | **9170** | **14640** | **63** | **100.0** | **100.0** | **100.0** |

N.B. Totals may not add up due to rounding.

*Source:* Rubber Statistical Bulletin.

## 3 STRATEGY FOR THE NATURAL RUBBER SECTOR

The overall aim of strategy planners is to increase the price received by the smallholders for their rubber - both through a higher share of farm-gate to final fob price and efforts to increase the international price level while seeking to widen cost-price differential through greater productivity. As a commodity where over 70% is used in the competitive global automotive sector: the world's largest manufacturing industry, NR must both maintain this market by meeting tyre-makers' requirements while striving to expand usage in both GRP and latex sectors. As a raw material used by industries often at the forefront of technology, the practices and aims of modern manufacturing, whether cost efficiency, reliability, quality and quality controls, after-sales service etc. is increasingly demanded by NR consumers. Equally important now are environmental aspects: while NR cultivation promotes conservation as well as yielding a valuable rubber-wood resource, attention must also be paid to HSE (Health, Safety and Environment) aspects in processing and manufacture of rubber goods in terms of additives, effluent disposal, energy use and recyclability and disposal of final rubber goods.

### Improving economic viability of NR cultivation and production

This is primarily through transfer of known technology from the traditional producers to both the small farm sector and other producing areas. Overall, the accent has been on boosting productivity through developing stronger, disease resistant trees capable of yielding more rubber. At present, commercial yields of over 2000 kg/ha/yr are achievable. Therefore replanting of rubber with high-yielding clones replacing unselected seedlings is a priority for the longer-established NR producing countries, particularly those where smallholders predominate. A variety of schemes have been developed: at its simplest and some would say one of the most successful in terms of cost-benefit, a new and re-planting grant or financial assistance as administered by the traditional Asian producers. More 'controlled' group schemes are also in operation, such as the Nucleus Estate Scheme or Outgrower type schemes or the Malaysian models run by FELDA (Federal Land Development Authority). While normally administered by RRIs (national Rubber Research Institutes or their equivalents), multilateral international agencies have also been very active in this field, providing financial assistance to establish Hevea cultivation (Côte d'Ivoire, Cameroon, Bangladesh) or rehabilitate smallholder sectors

(Sri Lanka, Thailand, Indonesia, Myanmar) as well as projects to improve domestic marketing/preliminary processing facilities. Côte d'Ivoire for example, whose Hevea plantations were established as crop-diversification measure with assistance from international agencies, boasts the highest national average yield at 1750 kg/ha/yr in the form of high quality latex Technically Specified Rubbers. This compares with national average yields of 500-900 kg/ha/yr at traditional producing countries such as Nigeria, Sri Lanka, Indonesia and Thailand.

Attention is also being paid to improving labour productivity through the development of novel tapping instruments and techniques, automated tapping and/or collection, the use of ethrel stimulation to enable maintenance of production with less frequent tapping etc. Such programmes help to secure NR's longer term competitiveness and income generating potential. While the labour intensity of NR cultivation is a positive factor in many cases where it provides rural income generation, the worldwide trend to urbanisation and the alternative employment opportunities etc. necessitate continuous attention to improving all aspects of NR productivity and cost efficiency.

Preliminary processing and domestic marketing of smallholder rubber is yet another area which has received considerable attention in recent years. The traditional two or three level dealer network often resulted in a low smallholder farmgate price in terms of share of final fob price. Solutions include Group smallholder schemes where smallholder rubber is processed by the nucleus estate, co-operatively owned smokehouses for smallholders and other Group processing centres, private or state-owned central processing crumb rubber factories collecting smallholder latex and field coagula such as MARDEC in Malaysia. Such schemes have resulted in a steady increase in farmgate prices received to as high as over 80% of final fob price in some cases.

The NR industry is fortunate in having a relatively well developed network for the transfer and exchange of information internationally through producing associations such as the ANRPC (Association of Natural Rubber Producing Countries) and the IRRDB (International Rubber Research and Development Board). Measures to boost productivity and cost efficiency at the cultivation, production and preliminary processing stages are a regular feature at many countries. These can include:

- Investigation of Rubberwood harvesting to yield additional income;
- Intercropping to generate cash while NR immaturity (cash/food crops, livestock);
- Widen genetic base, with particular reference to SALB (South American Leaf Blight) resistance;
- Extension services for transfer of technology, availability of planting materials, chemical inputs;
- Improving smallholder rubber marketing.
- Improving and extending the NR cultivation base outside the three major producing areas. Many countries have identified large tracts of land suitable for NR cultivation (i.e. Vietnam, Guatemala, Brazil, Mexico) while R&D has enabled Hevea to be grown in 'hostile' environments of low temperature, less rainfall etc. as exemplified by plantations in China and North East Thailand.

**Types and grades of NR, price markets and international trade**

Although all Hevea latex is essentially the same, variations can and do occur in line with different planting stock as much as subsequent handling/mishandling of the latex from tree to rubber manufacturing factory. The only significant difference in raw materials can be said to be that between deliberately coagulated latex i.e. tapped and collected and latex that auto-coagulates, known as field latex of cup-lumps, tree lace etc. The start of the TSR scheme in the mid 1960s allowed the entire crop to be converted into quality rubber, with smallholder material and field latex converted to TSR 20 grade, which is now the major grade of rubber used.

At present there are perhaps 30 different 'grades' of NR within the broad types of RSS, TSR, Crepes and specialities, with attendant scheme of pricing discounts. RSS1 is often used as the basic indicator price but this grade of rubber now accounts for perhaps 4% of trade. The volume tyre rubbers are now RSS 3, TSR 10 and TSR 20, which typically sell at a discount to both RSS1 and latex-grade TSR. Although field-grade materials are the specified source for TSR10 and TSR 20 grades, many producers include higher quality latex in these grades to secure tyre markets. Three possibilities are available with regard to type/grade mix.

- Upgrading grade-mix of TSR production from TSR10/20 to TSR 5 or equivalent could be economically attractive. It is arguable that the absolute level of price paid for NR is not as important to tyre customers, provided that it is competitive with that paid by their competitors: NR constitutes a very small percentage of tyre production costs.

- Working towards standardisation of types and grades between producing countries. At present national specifications vary slightly while other countries follow ISO standards with added specifications. The commanding market power held by tyre makers means that their requirements for volume, quality, reliability etc, often on a direct contract with large suppliers, makes it difficult for smaller or newer producers /producing countries to secure their custom at a similar price. For these reasons, it is felt that were producers able to standardise specifications and work toward interchangeability of TSR grades, pricing and marketing would benefit. An added complication is the continuation of RSS grades which are preferred by certain consumers who claim greater consistency and cleanliness (i.e. lack of foreign contamination).
- Cooperative effort to identify a 'tyre-grade' rubber, using a mixture of latex and field latex materials which would allow the entire crop to be used. This could then be sold at a price higher than TSR 20 and if produced in sufficient volume by a number of producers, simplify and improve processing and marketing costs. Such a rubber is available (Malaysian SMR GP, using 60% latex/sheet and 40% field materials) but this has not been a commercial success.

**Quality**

In this area, the pre-requisites for NR are a product free from contamination, the use of non-timber packaging for shipment and the development of the parameters and tools necessary to assess the true quality of their rubber. IRSG activities were described earlier. National and internationally co-ordinated efforts have been made to reduce external contamination of NR both in Asia and Africa.

The global drive to TQM, Total Quality Management, systems in the rubber sector has seen the adoption of process controls at many NR producers and now the accreditation of ISO 9000 standards to rubber factories in Malaysia. In addition to confirming the quality and specifications under existing TSR schemes however, consumers are increasingly demanding processing consistency: i.e. the ability to predict how a rubber will process and thus assist final product consistency and reduce wastage at manufacturing centres. Once the knowledge is developed, it is likely that some form of 'consistency' indicator will form part of the specifications of NR produced and sold in the future. It is important that NR producers are involved in the research and development of such an indicator or else it may well be that manufacturers' or SR producers' derived concepts are imposed on the NR producing sector.

### Pattern of consumption, expanding local manufacturing of rubber

A combination of factors have assisted in greatly expanding potential for manufacturing of locally produced rubber, offering the interesting idea of production- manufacturing complexes; perhaps with smallholder scheme plantation, rubber processing and manufacturing and also wood processing facilities together on one site. While most producers are looking to export rubber products, domestic and regional markets in Asia for example offer supplementary outlets.

The co-inciding of industrialisation in NR producing countries with (a) the globalisation of rubber manufacturing and subsequent interest in siting facilities close to new and emerging markets and (b)the trend to re-locating certain product manufacture away from OECD and NIC countries for cost reasons and (c) the current climate of joint ventures, technology and franchise agreements have resulted in the establishment and expansion of rubber manufacturing in many NR producer/exporting countries in Asia. Rubber product manufacturing in NR exporting countries is at present dominated by latex goods, particularly of dipped goods, typified by Malaysia. While this group now accounts for 14% of total NR consumption, the share of world latex consumption is much higher at close to 30%.

Latex manufacturing is likely to be the start of local processing for many countries: gloves, condoms, other dipped goods and foam products are likely to have a domestic/ regional market as well as export potential. Smaller volume GRP products are also a possibility while the global tyre makers are providing technology to most tyre facilities outside OECD economies. While the Malaysian rubber manufacturing industry is the most advanced among producing countries, the success of many Indian and Chinese tyres and other products on the world market testify to the existing potential. The globalisation of the auto and tyre industries together with economic regional integration groupings in Asia and America offers the potential for significant expansion of tyre and other dry rubber products in Asian countries.

Two areas are likely to require investigation.
- The first is market identification of suitable products for manufacture. International organisations have been involved in this area. An ADB (Asian Development Bank) sponsored study for the ANRPC addressed

this subject while more recently, an ITC/GATT project has assisted selected product manufacturers in Asian countries to develop and expand their market base.
- Installing SR production capacity in NR producing countries. Installation of local or preferably regional general purpose SR capacity on a suitable scale to ensure viability is likely to be needed in the Asian region if NR producers intend to be global competitors in the world tyre and GRP markets. This is likely to spur research into the symbiosis of NR and SR.

**Environmental factors**

Harvesting rubber-wood as a valuable by-product of NR latex extraction has been practised for many years. However, in the light of forest depletion and the need for tropical timber the developing of NR latex/rubber wood co-products is now topical. ITC/GATT are undertaking a detailed investigation of this subject.

The cultivation of NR is certainly environment friendly, as it conserves forest cover and timber resources. However, it must be borne in mind that, apart from thin walled latex dipped goods, most rubber products are a chemical composite, typically comprising more than one type of elastomer, a variety of chemicals, carbon- blacks, oils etc. Once vulcanised, products such as tyres cannot easily be decomposed/recycled. The use of reclaim rubber has dwindled due to its high cost but this is an area that could be re-examined in line with the international interest in tyre recycling and safe disposal.

**Conclusion**

In conclusion therefore, in addition to the routine objectives of productivity and production increases to meet market requirements which are expected to increase by another 1 to 1.5 million tonnes by 2000, the NR producing sector must devote effort to improving quality and consistency of its product, developing the right product mix to maximise earnings and thereby seek to improve the final price received. In this context, a fair and equitable price level would assist producer and consumer alike through guaranteeing security of market/supply while a pricing mechanism which better reflects market fundamentals is also necessary. In order to secure its longer term future, it is necessary to maintain its existing base in the tyre market while developing new markets, if necessary by designing new blends or special grades of NR.

# THE IOOC: ITS ROLE IN IMPROVING QUALITY AND RAISING PRODUCTIVITY IN OLIVE OIL[1]

## 1. INTERNATIONAL OLIVE OIL COUNCIL

The International Olive Oil Council (IOOC) was created in 1959 under the auspices of the United Nations Conference on Trade and Development (UNCTAD). Ever since then this intergovernmental organisation has been responsible for administering the succession of international agreements that have been concluded on olive oil. The Agreement is one of the current world commodity agreements and the only one so far in the fats and oils sector. Its main objective is to bring together producers and consumers to solve the problems existing within the sector by implementing measures to achieve greater market transparency, better production, especially from the point of view of quality, higher consumption and other goals.

The International Olive Oil Agreement was negotiated a few years after the end of the Second World War. The first one dates back to 1956, the second, which was extended and amended on several occasions, was concluded in 1963. A third Agreement followed in 1979, and the current fourth one, now enlarged to include table olives, in 1986. More recently, on 10 March 1993 to be precise during the United Nations Geneva Conference on Olive Oil and Table Olives, it was decided to prolong the 1986 Agreement. Although mainly involving the Mediterranean countries, the Agreement also aims to defend the 'olive civilisation' which has outgrown its Mediterranean confines to spread throughout the world.

## 2. IMPORTANT ISSUES

A review of developments in the international market is presented in the Figures at the end of this presentation. One fundamental feature of olive

---

[1] Paper presented by the International Olive Oil Council (IOOC)

production is the irregularity and cyclical nature of olive harvests and market supply, which results in fluctuations in the value of production, instability in prices and export earnings and large swings in producers' income. The answers to these problems often transcend national frontiers and call for international action in different areas:

- *international cooperation* is needed to achieve the integrated development of the olive economy and to coordinate production, industrialisation and trading policies on olive oils and table olives;
- action is needed to *modernise olive cultivation and olive oil processing*, the aim being to improve quality and cut cost prices, while bearing in mind environmental requirements;
- *media and consumer education* is required to inform people on the nutritional and health properties of olive oil and to circulate scientific findings;
- *international trade needs to be expanded* and action has to be taken to improve market access and to stabilise supplies;
- *international trade also has to be regularised* to strike a balance between production and consumption, to harmonise domestic regulations, to reduce the fluctuations in market supplies and to improve data collection processes.

These are the tasks the Council has been entrusted as an instrument for bringing about improvements in the sector, thereby enabling its Members to produce and market a quality product.

To help it fulfil these tasks, the international agreements that have succeeded each other since 1956 have focused on regularising the international olive oil market by bringing into play non-interventionist technical and economic measures. These measures involve *regularising* and *drawing up rules for international trade* in order to afford legal guarantees and ensure fair competition in commerce, as well as to achieve economic stability (by coordinating national policies in the sector to avoid fluctuations and to balance supply and demand) and to safeguard product quality. Other measures are designed to *modernise production factors*. The objective here is to encourage research and development on olive farming and the olive products industry in addition to stimulating a flow of technology from the industrialised world to the developing countries and to training senior personnel in countries needing this sort of assistance. Yet another set of measures is directed at *promoting the products of the olive tree* and finding new markets to maintain the balance between supply and demand. In this area the Council's action basically revolves around distributing scientific knowledge on the health-related properties of olive oil and carrying out generic promotion. Another promotional tool it uses is its international product guarantee label.

Raising productivity, where possible, and improving quality in every case is extremely important to the developing olive-growing nations. In the Southern and Eastern Mediterranean countries large sections of the rural population are virtually dependent on olive production for a living. Because of its economic and social significance in this region, olive cultivation had been calling for some time for a programme to select and adapt the best suited olive varieties to natural local conditions in order to raise productivity.

Productivity is alarmingly low at present in the developing world where, in the majority of cases, olive farming is based on a single predominant cultivar. The chief reason for this poor productivity is that unsuitable varieties are grown, most of which are the result of past indiscriminate transplanting from one geographical area to another. This has prompted marked changes in the physiological behaviour of the olives and in the majority of cases has caused varietal mutations with negative implications. Thanks to the support of the Common Fund for Commodities, the developing olive-growing countries will be benefiting in the very near future from the results of a genetic breeding programme applied to their varieties.

When it comes to commodity quality, the problem is basically one of technological training. Its solution depends to a large extent on the amount of action or programmes implemented to transfer know-how to the developing countries in the Southern and Eastern Mediterranean where barely 10% of all the olive oil produced is quality virgin oil. The structure of the olive oil processing industry has seen little modernisation. There are natural, sometimes exceptional conditions, under which good oil is obtained. However, a high proportion of the oils produced have defects and are not fit for consumption unless they are refined beforehand. The fact that mill operators and supervisors do not have sufficient technological grounding plainly results in low quality oil. Several factors attributable to human error during the production process have frequently had a negative impact on quality. This is why it is essential to eliminate staff shortcomings through an intensive training scheme.

Restructuring and modernising processing plants means simultaneously updating the technological expertise of the personnel in charge. Before any switch from traditional to continuous-process facilities, processors have to be equipped with the latest expertise.

Poor quality impairs product competitiveness on the market. It is also detrimental to the international promotion campaigns run by the Council and its Members. We must remember that the extra virgin olive oil sold on the world market does not represent even 6% of all the olive oils marketed. Clearly, it is essential to improve quality if olive oil is to gain and hold on to a prestige image. It also has to be improved if we want a sound olive economy. This is especially true when the world market offers such promising opportunities for growth in quality olive oils.

Overall, IOOC action is geared towards upgrading the quality of all the olive oils produced. The object is to boost the supply of top-rate virgin olive oils since this is what consumers seem to be turning to more and more on the markets on which the IOOC is operating.

It is important for international and national agencies alike to realise how essential it is to implement a scheme for a North-South transfer of technology if developing countries are to be equipped with the specific know-how to raise commodity quality.

# Olive Oil Exports
## World Trend

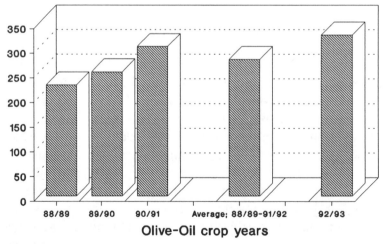

Olive-Oil crop years

Thousand Tonnes

# Olive Oil Product. & Consumpt.
## World Trend

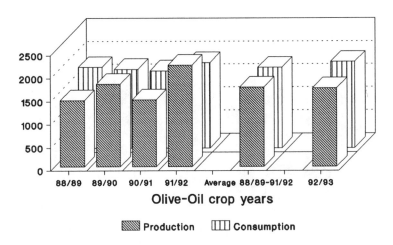

Olive-Oil crop years

Production    Consumption

**Thousand Tonnes**

# Olive Oil Production
## World Trend

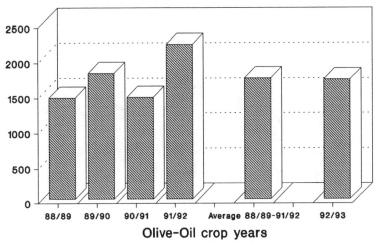

Olive-Oil crop years

**Thousand Tonnes**

# Table Olive Production
## World Trend

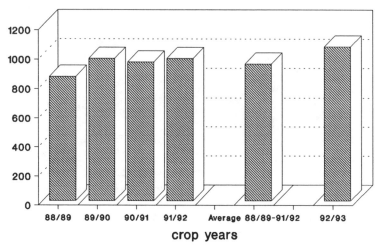

Thousand Tonnes

# Table Olive Prod. & Consum.
## World Trend

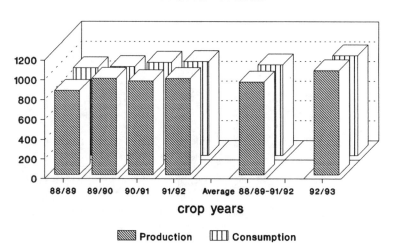

Thousand Tonnes

# THE SITUATION IN THE WORLD SUGAR MARKET[1]

## 1 CHARACTERISTICS OF THE MARKET

Historically, the world sugar market has been one of the most volatile of all commodity markets, characterized by short, sharp price peaks followed by long, low troughs. This cyclical pattern has tended to repeat itself around every seven years. Consequently, the market has been more often over-supplied - the high prices of deficit years leading to a surge in production which takes up to five years to adjust due to the characteristics of sugar production and the market itself. For example, in the 30 years since 1962 only 11 deficits of world production, compared to world consumption, have been recorded.

Sugar faces the structural problem of asymmetric supply and demand responses and additionally production is subject to large swings caused by weather and other natural phenomena. Typically, the global supply response of sugar is more mobile in the upward than in the downward direction (cf Figure 1). There is normally sufficient spare capacity to expand output quickly in response to rising prices. However, falling and even unremunerative prices do not cause a commensurate contraction in supply. One explanation is that sugar production requires a particularly heavy investment in field, factory, storage and handling. This asset fixity is particularly marked for sugar cane because it is a perennial crop. In the short term the volume and the fixity of the assets committed, plus the problem of finding an alternative use for the land, can lead to the maintenance or even an increase in output as prices fall. Thus a pattern emerges of high prices causing a surge in production, leading to falling prices but not immediately falling production, so that surpluses are built up. As production gradually adjusts downwards towards consumption, while surpluses are cleared, prices remain low. Consumption, on the other hand, tends to increase steadily from year to year (averaging around 2% growth) except when prices are very high. The structural problems associated with the asymmetric responses of supply and demand, plus the

---

[1] Background paper by the International Sugar Organization (ISO)

vulnerability of supply to weather, are exacerbated by the nature of the world sugar market, which has often been characterized as a 'residual' market. Only around 25% of world sugar production enters the market. Thus a relatively small surplus of production can represent a significant increase in market supply, depressing prices. The market is further marginalized by the existence of 'special arrangements' - sugar traded at prices outside the world market, often set at government level, and usually, except for the price peak years, higher than the world market price. Until the break-up of the USSR around 30% of world sugar trade came under this heading. Not only did this diminish further the size of the clearing, price setting market, but those countries with a special arrangement component in their exports are able to offset losses in the free market with the revenue from special arrangements. Finally, the second largest sugar exporter, the EEC, has an internal system which guarantees prices which are normally higher than free market prices for a substantial part of its exports. All these factors reinforce the tendency for sugar to be over supplied except when a coincidence of bad weather and low stocks occurs.

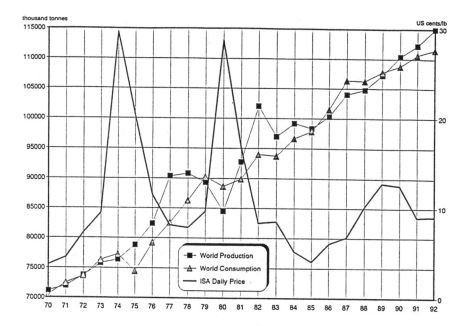

*Figure 1:*  World sugar production and consumption and raw sugar prices, 1970-1992

## 2  EVOLUTION OF THE MARKET

Without changing its cyclical nature there has been a major structural change in the world sugar market over the past two decades which has had a fundamental effect on the price formation process. The watershed was the 1973/74 sugar price boom, when sugar prices reached unprecedented levels which had a profound effect on both the supply and demand for sugar. At that time, two thirds of demand came from price insensitive developed countries, particularly the US and Japan. The price levels attained encouraged the development in the US, and to a lesser extent Japan, of industries producing a corn based alternative to liquid sugar (HFCS - High Fructose Corn Syrup or Isoglucose) which rapidly penetrated the soft-drinks industry. High world prices in 1980 gave a fresh impetus to this process, so that by the mid 1980s sugar consumption in the US had fallen by 30% and imports from around 5 million tonnes to around 1 million tonnes. In 1981 this drastic adjustment was embodied in an import quota system to limit imports to the difference between domestic supply and the at that time falling consumption. Meanwhile, from 1974 onwards, imports by developing countries increased, led by sugar imports from oil exporting developing countries benefiting from the first and second oil price shocks. The generally very low world sugar prices between 1982 and 1989 encouraged further growth in developing country imports. The result of the decline in developed country imports and the rise in developing country imports has been a complete reversal of the market structure since the mid 1970s. By 1990 two thirds of the world sugar imports were accounted for by developing countries. This fundamental change has been reflected in world sugar price behaviour (cf Figure 2). The domination of the market by price sensitive developing countries has increased the stability of the world sugar price. Since 1988 the world sugar price has ranged between 8.97 cents/lb and 12.82 cents/lb (annual averages). By comparison, over the 5 years 1980-85 the world sugar price fluctuated between 4.06 cents/lb and 28.69 cents/lb (annual average).

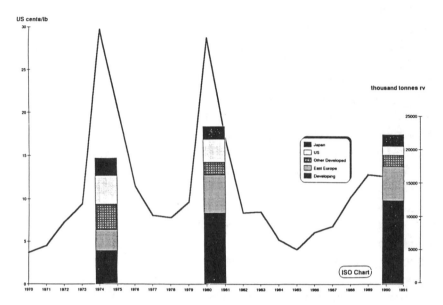

*Figure 2:* World sugar prices and the composition of imports

## 3 THE CURRENT SITUATION

Structural change continues in the world sugar market. The situation in 1991 is reviewed in Table 1, showing the top ten producers, consumers, net exporters and net importers. The most recent development has been the break-up of the Soviet Union, which has had two effects: i) The Soviet Union was the world's largest net importer of sugar, importing 4-5.5 million tonnes annually (18-24% of the market) in the 1980s. The main source was Cuba with 3-4 million tonnes under preferential terms. In the free market, the Soviet Union was relatively price insensitive, topping up its purchases from Cuba according to need with little regard to the price. (For example, in 1980 when the world price peaked, averaging 28.69 cents/lb for the year, the USSR purchased 2.2 million tonnes from the free market, thus making a significant contribution to the price rise). Now that the preferential trade has ended and given the severe shortage of hard currency in the former USSR, Russia and the other importing republics are behaving much more like developing countries. ii) The loss of the preferential markets in the former USSR has caused severe structural problems in Cuba and caused a sharp decline in output in 1992/93. The shortages of raw materials, fuel and fertilizer are likely to continue.

The 1992/93 crop cycle began with the prospects of a considerable surplus after a surplus of 2.2 million tonnes in 1991/92. The demand side was expected to be relatively weak because of the financial problems of Russia and because China, after record output in 1991/92, had become a net exporter of more than 1 million tonnes after having been a net importer of almost 4 million tonnes as recently as 1988. India had also had a record crop in 1991/92 and had built up carry-over stocks of around 4 million tonnes. Thailand, which had increased output significantly in a contra-cyclical expansion begun in the mid-1980s was expected to have another record crop. Prices reflected this rather dismal scenario, falling as low as 8 cents/lb in December 1992. However, poorer crops than expected were announced in India and China, and Thailand had a significantly lower crop due to drought (3.8 million tonnes compared to expected 5 million tonnes plus). Around March 1993 bad weather and worse structural problems than expected made it clear that production in Cuba would be significantly less than anticipated. Consequently, the world price began to rise sharply from mid-February. Having been again slightly below 8 cents/lb on 9 February the price reached 12.5 cents/lb by end-April.

It is now clear that 1992/93 will be a deficit year, perhaps in the region of 2-3 million tonnes. However lack of offtake in the demand side and adequate carryover from the previous crop cycle has meant that prices have not been sustained at the high achieved in April. Prices are currently at around 11 cents/lb.

Thus, the world sugar market is currently in deficit with prices at the upper end of the range established since 1988. The current crop cycle is a foreshortened example of the product of the new structure of the market - when a surplus was expected, prices did not fall below 8 cents/lb; when it became clear that there would be a deficit prices rose but demand was choked off at above 12.5 cents/lb.

*Table 1:* Top ten producers, consumers, net exporters and
net importers in 1991

| Top Ten Producers | | Top Ten Consumers | |
|---|---|---|---|
| EEC | 15989 | EEC | 13166 |
| India | 13113 | USSR | 1300 |
| Brazil | 9342 | India | 12056 |
| Cuba | 7233 | U.S.A. | 7994 |
| USSR | 7000 | Brazil | 17276 |
| China | 6950 | China | 7100 |
| U.S.A. | 6562 | Mexico | 4200 |
| Thailand | 4248 | Japan | 2846 |
| Mexico | 3744 | Pakistan | 2662 |
| Australia | 3195 | Indonesia | 2629 |
| **World** | 112220 | **World** | 110670 |

| Top Ten Net Exporters | | Top Ten Net Importers | |
|---|---|---|---|
| Cuba | 6767 | USSR | 4777 |
| EEC | 3150 | Japan | 1893 |
| Australia | 2441 | U.S.A. | 1063 |
| Brazil | 1614 | Canada | 916 |
| S. Africa | 841 | Algeria | 909 |
| Guatemala | 699 | Korea Rep. | 851 |
| Mauritius | 584 | China | 785 |
| Swaziland | 492 | Egypt | 736 |
| Poland | 372 | Iran | 672 |
| Fiji | 369 | Mexico | 646 |
| **World** | 22857 | **World** | 21555 |

## 4 THE FUTURE

FAO/ISO recently published a joint study on the world sugar market to the year 2000[2]. The general conclusion was that structural change would continue, in particular with the prospect of higher production from the low yielding run-down sugar industries of the former Soviet Union and the possible consequences for the Cuban sugar industry. However, it was stressed that supplies of sugar to the market were likely to remain adequate with the possibility of expansion in Thailand and Australia particularly. The world sugar import market is expected to expand over the decade to reach 25.5 million tonnes by 2000, 3.9 million tonnes (18%) higher than 1990. Virtually all the increase in world market size is expected to come from the price sensitive developing countries. However, although this scenario is reasonably promising for exporters the most likely price scenario that accompanied this increase in the market size was for prices to fall to a mid-decade low of 7.5 cents/lb (1990 terms) in 1995 as a result of the production increase brought about by the higher prices in the early 1990s, and rise thereafter to a decade high of just over 10 cents/lb (1990 terms) by 2000. Therefore the conclusion of the study was that the price range established since the late 1980s will largely apply for the decade of the 1990s.

## 5 STRATEGY FOR DEVELOPMENT

The results of the FAO/ISO study suggest that world prices are likely to remain on average, in the 7-10 cents price range in real terms. Sensitivity analysis, taking into account the effect of random (weather) supply stocks, gave a range of 4.24 cents/lb to 15.86 cents/lb. Very little information is available about the cost of production of sugar. It is generally accepted that the most efficient exporters (e.g. Australia, Thailand) require at least 10 cents/lb to make money. Clearly, therefore, the prospects are for a sugar market that will grow but will probably be adequately supplied, with prices at the lower limit of what could be viewed as remunerative. Within this perspective, two primary goals for the development of sugar suggest themselves: 1) Lowering the cost of production through improvements in productivity, 2) Broadening the financial base of the industry through vertical diversification.

---

[2] The World Suger Market - Prospect for the Nineties, FAO, Rome, 1992.

# RECENT TRENDS AND MEDIUM-TERM PROSPECTS FOR TROPICAL TIMBER[1]

## 1 INTRODUCTION

The International Tropical Timber Organization annually surveys its fifty Members through a 'Forecasting and Statistical Enquiry', and, utilising this and other relevant information, it prepares an Annual Review and Assessment of the World Tropical Timber Situation. This year, for the first time, the Annual Review also compiled Members' reports on their progress towards the Organization's 'Target 2000' - a common understanding that by the year 2000 all internationally-traded tropical timber shall originate from sustainably managed resources.

However, it is important to note that the International Tropical Timber Agreement, 1983, defines 'tropical timber' as essentially *solid hardwood* logs or products, and thus excludes coniferous wood (except where it is part of the lay-up of hardwood plywood), pulp, paper, and reconstituted panels (except plywood). Furthermore, 'Producer' Members must have part of their territory between the Tropics of Cancer and Capricorn, and Members qualifying for both categories must opt for one upon joining. Thus, there are minor but significant tropical forest areas in 'Consumer' Members such as Australia and China, and there are 'Producer' Members who are net importers of tropical timber, such as Thailand and Togo. Finally, although the territory of ITTO's producer Members holds over 80% of the closed tropical moist forest of the world, and the consumer Members account for nearly 90% of global tropical timber trade, there are regionally some significant non-Member producers such as Myanmar and Solomon Islands who export mainly to ITTO Members.

---

[1] Paper presented by the International Tropical Timber Organization (ITTO)

## 2  COMMODITY FOCUS

Whilst, in the long run, all primary resources are non-renewable when viewed in the context of the entropy inevitably produced by all economic activity, nevertheless, on the human scale, we are accustomed to view commodities as non-renewable e.g. minerals and metals, or as renewable e.g. seasonal agricultural crops such as cotton and bananas. For both categories conservation strategies can be devised, in the former class through exploration, stocking, recycling, and pricing, in the latter through extending planted areas, improving growth and preserving genetic gains, and in both through greater processing efficiency and reduction of wastage in use.

In the past, tropical timber has displayed aspects of both groups. It is widely believed that sustainable i.e. perpetually renewable production of tropical timber is technically feasible in all areas where soils are not too fragile or slopes and climates extreme, but a widely publicised survey commissioned by ITTO showed that only a small fraction of the world's tropical rainforests were demonstrably under sustainable management, strictly defined. In other words, tropical timber was being managed much like a non-renewable commodity.

The reasons for this state of affairs lie largely outside the commodity market itself. To successfully manage tropical forests in a manner which maintains a healthy and fruitful ecosystem requires the existence of a permanent forest estate, delineated both legally and upon the ground, and protected against those other land-use claims which cannot co-exist with the intact forest. Within this permanent estate, there must be good control of all forestry operations, especially harvesting, and the essential prerequisite for such control is sound inventory and continuous monitoring of growth through sample plots to make yield predictions precise. Finally, it is necessary that the economic agents in the process of establishment, growth, processing, and distribution, in other words, all forestry sector operators, should be able to make reasonable profits from their enterprise.

The International Tropical Timber Organization has placed its weight firmly behind the wheel of progress towards sustainable management of tropical forests. In support of its Target 2000 defined in the introduction to this paper, it has developed guidelines for the sustainable management of both *natural* and *planted* tropical forests, published criteria to enable the assessment of levels of sustainability, and will shortly publish guidelines on conservation of biological diversity in tropical production forests. Furthermore, the ITTO is preparing guidelines on sustainable development of forest industries and protection of tropical forests against fire. It has conducted successive investigations and encouraged debate among its Members on the role of the trade in promoting sustainable development of tropical forests.

Many of ITTO's Producer Members have adopted policies designed to ensure the long-term economic security of their forestry sectors. These include log export bans, quotas, and taxes to encourage domestic processing. A nation must be prepared to view such policies as investments, since during the initial years total income will fall until the infant processing industry is able to recoup the loss through export of higher value-added products. Often such policies discriminate between species and those countries who have advanced further down this track such as Indonesia have imposed selective taxation of products still considered to be insufficiently processed before export e.g. rough sawn timber. A variety of policies and associated regulations have been tested by different countries on the ground with mixed results. For example, long-term success of log export bans demands *inter alia* other methods to prevent indirect subsidies of log prices for local processors leading to inefficiencies and over-capacity.

Technological improvements such as plantation development with fast-growing and high-value species in the growing segment and expansion of kiln-drying capacity in the milling segment are also part of these developments. Reform of royalty and taxation systems to ensure tax neutrality and rational economic signals to growers and processors alike is also likely to be more in evidence in the future.

Probably the most significant and wide-ranging development, however, has been the response of the Sarawak Government to the ITTO Mission in 1990. Progressive harvest reductions which entail significant employment and income loss for the State in the short-term have been implemented for the years leading up to 1995 and already the import markets of East Asia have been profoundly affected by the Sarawak Government's move to bring its permanent forest estate onto a sustainable basis of management, in fact well before the 2000 Target set by the ITTO.

In addition to these movements which, by reducing the flow of tropical wood into international trade, tend to increase prices to the extent that competitively priced temperate wood or non-wood substitutes are not available, there have been strong pressures from several consumer countries to reduce or halt the market acceptance of tropical timber. By curtailing demand, such movements tend to force down prices and make sustainable management of tropical forests a less economic proposition. Nevertheless, unilateral import bans or selective certification schemes by city and provincial governments, and last year by one national government, have been introduced, despite protests from producer governments that such measures are discriminatory in the context of GATT.

Since there are strong competing land-uses for most tropical forest areas, a fall in forest values is a serious issue. In fact only one-sixth of all tropical timber cut or otherwise cleared is destined to be industrial wood, since much forest is burnt to provide land for subsistence agriculture by populations increasingly displaced from the poorest stratum of the cash economy. Once sustainable, shifting cultivation is no longer so when fallow cycles have sharply decreased in duration. Beyond this, more than half the world's wood harvest is still for firewood, which furnishes heat for cooking, night warmth, cottage ceramics manufacture, smoke for curing fish, tobacco, and other crops, and lighting. Firewood cutting is still practised unsustainably, with the cost paid in human transport to more remote sources, and, as always, in higher urban prices.

Of the industrial wood harvested, less than one-third is exported in round or product form, so that in fact only about 6% of the total tropical non-coniferous harvest is traded internationally. This percentage appears to have been declining by about 2% per decade. In future declining log exports will barely be offset, quantitatively, by increased product exports. The latter still face, in many import markets, higher tariff barriers than their unprocessed predecessors. Again, many former producers have become importers of tropical timber, and this South-to-South trade can be expected to expand further.

Whilst it is not possible to simulate all the potential results of the various environment-related influences now acting on the international trade in tropical timber at present, it has been essential to preface this report with a brief description of the forces at work. The trade has now reached the stage where it would be impossible to understand the current status of this commodity in trade by simply examining the market elements of supply, demand, and price. Every analysis must now take seriously the effects (including, in the case of import bans, the threat of unrealised fears) of policies now being adopted and implemented by producers and consumers alike.

The momentum gained by the sustainable management choice originates in the tandem effect of environmental awareness in consumer countries of the benefits of tropical forests *in situ* (climate amelioration, carbon sink, non-timber products, livelihood of people in and around the forest) and the commercial awareness in producer countries that profits from their processing industries will decline through decreased raw material supply unless sustainable management is introduced. This observation does not imply there is no commercial awareness in consumer countries or environmental awareness in producer countries, but logically these apparent opposites will also gravitate to the same goal.

Since tropical forests are classic multiple-use resources, perhaps rivalled only by the world's oceans in this respect, it is really necessary to seek a universal methodology for *quantifying* the various kinds of values in use, and to examine which uses are more or less compatible with minimum trade-offs, and which are mutually exclusive, such as complete clearance and total preservation.

## 3 MARKET OVERVIEW

The following sketch is derived from ITTO's Annual Review, prepared in April of each year. A few graphs are presented at the end of this Section. The Review's most up-to-date Members' Reports generally cover the calendar year two years earlier although partial data is available for the previous year. In considering the trade in tropical timber, it should also be recalled that the total value of trade in this commodity, US$7.5 billion in 1991, is still less than 10% of the total world trade in all forest products.

In 1992 log exports from ITTO Producer countries declined by 10% (5.7% in 1991), but the increased value of exports of veneer and plywood, primarily from Indonesia and Malaysia, enabled the nominal value of primary timber products to rise by 2.6% to US$7.51 billion in 1991. However, as producers are experiencing a colossal fall of perhaps 25% in log exports (down to 15.7 million m³) for the current year, 1993, a decline in total value seems certain to be registered.

In 1991, ITTO Members' production of tropical saw and veneer logs fell by 11% from 1990 figures to 122.5 million m³. In Latin America virtually all such logs are utilised domestically; in Asia 81%, and in Africa 61%, although both the latter regions are seeking to increase this percentage. Sawnwood production also declined by 16.5% from 1990 levels to 32.9 million m³ in 1991. Both the sawlog and sawtimber decreases are largely accounted for by the report submitted by one country, Indonesia, but 1992 statistics show a complete recovery in aggregate.

However, in 1991 tropical veneer production increased by 12.7% from 1990 to reach 1.5 million m$^3$, and plywood production by 3.7% to 12.8 million m$^3$. The former increase was due to new plant capacity in Malaysia, and the latter to both Malaysia and Indonesia. Rates of expansion of capacity are now faster in Malaysia as she brings on stream new plants in Sabah and Sarawak, whereas Indonesia, already endowed with high capacity, is tailoring permits for new plants to annual allowable cut considerations.

The Consumer countries of ITTO also produced significant quantities of tropical timber products during 1991, including 2.4 million m$^3$ of sawnwood, almost 0.6 million m$^3$ of veneer, and nearly 8.5 million m$^3$ of plywood. Since virtually all this production is from imported tropical logs, it dwindled during 1992 as a result of constraints on supply.

Malaysia generated 81% of the 23.9 million m$^3$ of logs exported by ITTO producers in 1991, but nevertheless this is a marked reduction from the 86.7% recorded for 1990, and further decreases can be anticipated as the Sarawak Government's policy takes stronger effect. Sawnwood exports were steady at 7.3 million m$^3$ in 1991, with an increase of 7.6% in 1992, but a return to the earlier level during 1993. Malaysia accounted for 67% of the total in 1991, but Indonesian exports, now stable, may increase as producers adapt to the new export taxes imposed in 1989-90.

Veneer exports, primarily from Malaysia, increased by 23% on 1990 levels to almost 0.83 million m$^3$, and plywood exports, of which Malaysia and Indonesia account for 95%, increased by 7.5% from 1990 to 1991, reaching 10.5 million m$^3$.

There was a significant trade in Europe of tropical timber exports and re-exports, of which plywood accounted for 0.49 million m$^3$. Again, a 1993 decline in this trade is occurring.

In 1991, ITTO Members imported 26.5 million m$^3$, of which 'Consumers' imported 22.9 million m$^3$ and 'Producers' 3.6 million m$^3$. Since the total figure is 2.5 million m$^3$ greater than that reported as exported by ITTO Members, it can be inferred that the difference (beyond any statistical error) is accounted for by non-ITTO suppliers, in particular Myanmar, Laos, Vietnam, Solomon Islands, Fiji, and some relatively minor African log exporters. However, this figure is probably the maximum these non-ITTO exporters can provide, so the widening estimated shortfalls for 1992 (5.2 million m$^3$) and 1993 (9.8 million m$^3$) must be supplied by substitute materials, mainly temperate softwoods.

Japan is still the largest importer of tropical logs among consumer countries, but the proportion is expected to progressively decrease; in

1990 it was 53%, in 1991 45%. China (including Taiwan Province) is the only ITTO consumer country expected to record increased tropical log imports in 1992-3, but producer countries such as Thailand and the Philippines also predict increasing imports for this period.

Japan's tropical sawnwood imports fell by 26% from 1990 to the 1991 figure of 1.0 million m$^3$, the previous years of 1989-90 having registered a similar percentage decrease. Although she was still the largest importer out of the ITTO consumer Member total of 5.5 million m$^3$ in 1991, nevertheless Thailand imported 1.5 million m$^3$ in the same year, and the latter imports are projected to reach 1.8 million m$^3$ in 1993. By way of contrast, all ITTO consumer Members except for the Republic of Korea predict declining imports of tropical sawnwood in 1993. European importers' share has shown a steady decline.

Japan was again the dominant tropical hardwood veneer importer in 1991, absorbing 677,000 m$^3$ which comprised 57% of all consumer imports. Her revised figures suggest continued growth this year. Japan's plywood imports also rose 5% from 1990 to 2.9 million m$^3$ in 1991. In fact, this commodity is experiencing growth in all consuming countries, with a 1991 total of 8.1 million m$^3$.

Secondary processed wood products (SPWP) are not explicitly included in the definition of 'tropical timber' made by the International Tropical Timber Agreement, 1983, but their importance is quite clear from the emphasis in the ITTA on further processing in producer countries, also an objective of the ITTO Action Plan. The UNSO Comtrade database monitors markets for these products in OECD countries.

The U.S.A. is still the largest importer of SPWP among OECD countries, with 47% of the total 1991 value of US$4.4 billion imported from developing countries and China. The major ten importers, all ITTO Members, accounted for 95% of total imports. Only the U.S.A., Japan, and Australia obtain a high proportion of these products from developing economies. European importers still acquire SPWP largely from each other.

Wooden furniture is the most important category, with 72% of OECD imports, but the list includes builder's woodwork, especially mouldings and dowels, packaging, and tools. However, developing countries only accounted for 17% of the value of OECD furniture imports. Formerly, the entrepôt group of Taiwan Province, Hong Kong, Singapore, and the Republic of Korea were the main exporters, but now Malaysia and Thailand are significant contributors to the trade, both relying heavily on the rubberwood resource, made possible by technological progress in drying and chemical protection. Indeed, Indonesia is now the largest ITTO exporter of SPWP, with rattan a vital raw material, and, as China also makes rapid progress with her SPWP industries, she will look to further imports of the raw materials needed to sustain these industries. In contrast, the Philippines and Brazil have seen little growth with these exports.

ITTO sponsors a bi-weekly Market News Service (MNS) produced by the UNCTAD/GATT International Trade Centre (ITC) in Geneva, which closely monitors prices and markets. Prices have been constant for Latin American exporters, and have firmed for Asian producers. However, African exporters suffered a slight price decline. At the end of 1992 tighter supply gave rise to significant increases in Asian log and sawn-wood prices, a trend expected to intensify during 1993. Of course, there were also fluctuations during 1991-2 due to exchange rate movements, consumer stockpiling, and the global economic situation.

## 5  PROSPECT TO 2000

ITTO has scheduled a mid-term review of progress towards Target 2000 for 1995. By this time, major effects of the process should already be apparent in the world markets for tropical timber, in particular as a result of the phased 1.5 million $m^3$/annum reduction in the Sarawak harvest, whose effects will spill out from the Pacific as major importers such as Japan and Korea seek alternative sources in Africa and temperate substitutes. Their industries must re-tool for material of different dimensions and workability. Indeed, a minor example of this flow-on effect can already be seen, as Japanese importers, seeking tropical log substitutes, have bid up the export price of temperate logs from smaller suppliers such as Chile and New Zealand, leading to a shortage of domestic housing material in the latter country, as private forest owners seek the more lucrative export market.

Owing to the substitutability of many tropical timber products, the move to sustainable management is not likely to produce any dramatic price-rises, except for short-term movements. Of course, higher prices can help to fund the costs of sustainable forests management, and estimates submitted by some ITTO Producer Members for the total costs of meeting Target 2000 vary greatly. A resources working group has also made estimates of these financial needs, but figures still range from US$1.5 billion per annum until 2000 for all ITTO Producers to national estimates exceeding US$1 billion per country for the remaining part of the century. But, however welcome price rises might be, the perception of price instability might have a negative effect, as operators may be tempted to earn temporary superprofits which the forest cannot sustain.

Recent exchange rate trends show that some major consumers will be able to enjoy the benefits of strong currencies for purchasing tropical timber with US$, but, of course, the U.S.A. herself will be the major exception to this windfall.

The possibility of using plantations to reduce pressure on natural forests has not developed as rapidly or as widely in the tropics as in temperate zones, since the investment costs are high. Exceptions like Fiji and Zimbabwe where softwoods have been developed for this purpose are not ITTO Members, and among ITTO Members plantation efforts have been specifically for pulpwood, as in Brazil, or using slow-growing species, such as teak on Java, whose productivity is not high enough to supplement more than a minor proportion of domestic and export demand. Nevertheless, planted forests continue to hold promise where the investment can be made at concessionary interest rates, and technology can be employed to improve and standardise the export product.

The development of rubberwood in Peninsular Malaysia as a major timber species was unforeseen by a major FAO/UNDP mission which prepared twenty year projections at the beginning of the seventies, and forecast lower national incomes based on continuing log exports of native species. The rise to pre-eminence of Indonesia as the world's major tropical plywood exporter was also predicted by few commentators. These kinds of unanticipated events, the results of a judicious combination of policy reform, and product research and development, cannot be ruled out when attempting to glimpse the pattern of tropical timber trade in 2000 and thereafter.

The move to further processing can be expected to continue, with Asian exporters leading the way, and breaking into markets formerly the preserve of African exporters, such a Spain. Larger populations and growing economies in Latin America and Asia will force earlier switches to domestic markets and the desirability of more specialised niches for Africa's high quality timber will become increasingly clear.

ITTO Members are currently negotiating a successor agreement to the International Tropical Timber Agreement, 1983, which expires at the end of March 1994. Producers desire an extension of the commodity coverage to *all* timber and a restriction of project activity to trade and market matters. In their eyes, the pressure by consumer countries to demand sustainable management of tropical forests without submitting their own, largely temperate or boreal forests, to the same dictum is evidence of a double standard. Consumers, on the other hand, believe that such an extension would detract from the project funds available to be used solely for the benefit of *tropical* forests, and would like to see the Target 2000 as an integral part of the new Agreement. It remains to be seen what will finally emerge, but it is clear that tropical timber, whilst modest in value terms, will continue to be an commodity of international trade that attracts much global interest and concern.

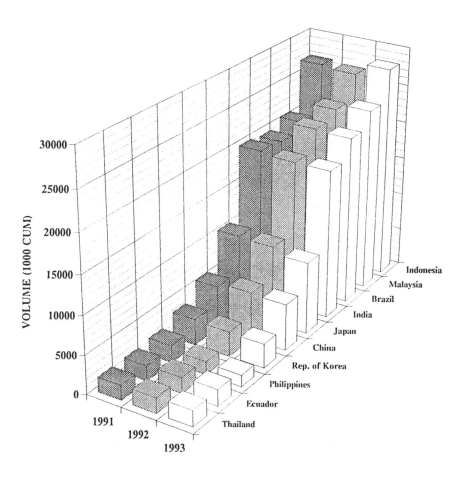

*Figure 1:* Major Tropical Log Consumers

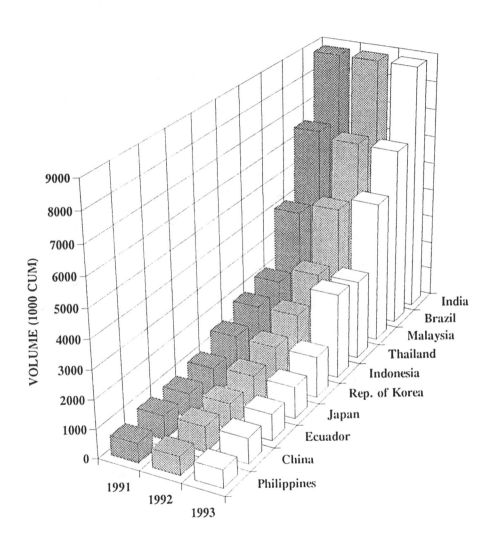

*Figure 2:* Major Tropical Sawnwood Consumers

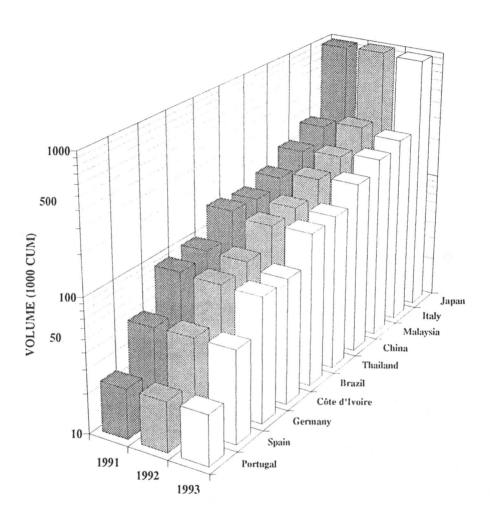

*Figure 3:* Major Tropical Veneer Consumers

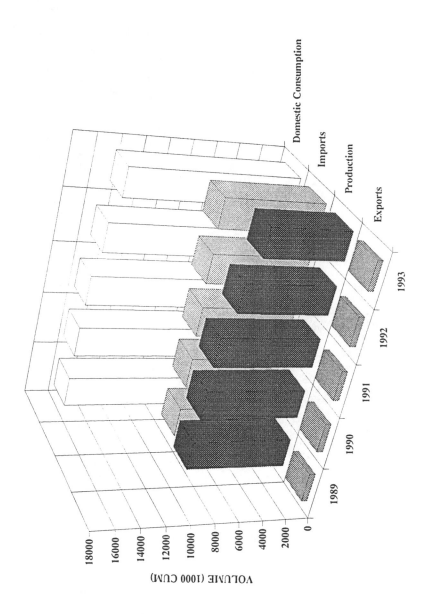

*Figure 4:* Consumers' Production, Trade and Consumption of Tropical Plywood

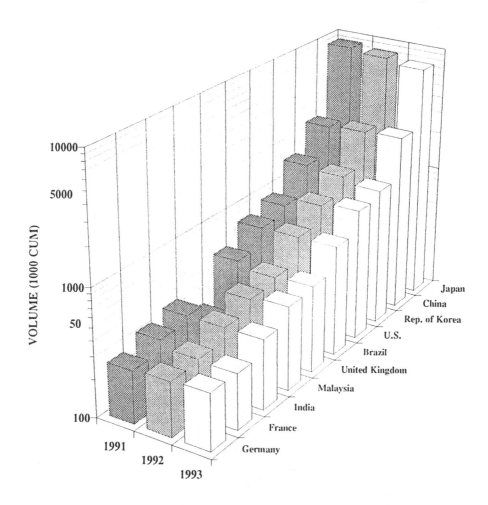

*Figure 5:* Major Tropical Plywood Consumers

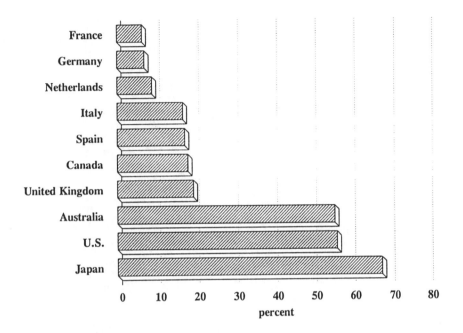

*Figure 6:*   Developing Countries' Share of Major Markets for Secondary Processed Wood Products (SPWP) in 1991

# THE CURRENT SITUATION IN THE TUNGSTEN MARKET[1]

## 1 INTRODUCTION

This paper will examine the current situation with regard to the core problems which have been recently faced by the tungsten market. It will look at the origins of these problems and provide in the conclusions some ideas regarding project proposals which could be useful components of an international strategy for tungsten within the objectives of the Second Account of the Common Fund.

## 2 IDENTIFICATION OF THE PROBLEMS

The main problems which have been at the centre of discussions on tungsten in UNCTAD are the deterioration of world demand, the abundant availability of tungsten materials, a price destabilizing competition between supplies of tungsten concentrates and intermediate products in a buyers' market, the large scale closure of tungsten mines, an increasing overhang of idle capacities and an absence of significant developments in new applications for tungsten.

### Decreasing world demand for tungsten

In recent years, all commodities with few exceptions have suffered from poor demand conditions, largely as a result of the weakness of the world economy. The recessions/slowdowns in the periods of 1982-1983, 1985-1986 and 1990-1993 were marked by sharp falls in tungsten consumption (see Figure 1). The decline in the latter period was particularly severe due not only to the recession affecting the world industry but also to sharp falls of demand in the former U.S.S.R. resulting from economic reform and restructuring. Between 1979 and 1992, world consumption of tung-

---

[1] Paper presented by the Intergovernmental Group of Experts on Tungsten (IGET), UNCTAD. The views of the author do not neccessarily reflect those of UNCTAD.

sten achieved significant increases only in 1984 and 1988, when the world economy attained its highest growth rates during the period. Consumption was stagnant if not decreasing in the other years even in 1985, 1987 and 1989 when world economic growth rates were over 3%.

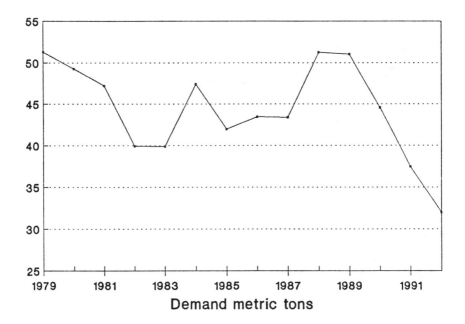

*Figure 1:* World Tungsten Demand

In comparison with other commodities, one particular economic factor which has strongly affected the tungsten market perhaps more than any other metal is the fact that the recent economic slowdowns have been felt more severely by sectors which are major tungsten consumers. These sectors include metal products and machinery and equipment, heavy manufacturing, petroleum and gas, and mining, which together account for over 80% of world tungsten consumption. Their performance in recent years has been either stagnant or declining, a situation quite opposite to what it was in the 1970s. The metal products, machinery and equipment sector and the heavy manufacturing sector were among the fastest growing sectors in the 1970s but they have become among the slowest recently. Even the petroleum and gas sector, which has recently experienced the best growth performance among the four sectors, was enjoying higher growth rate in the 1970s. As regards the mining sector, its performance has been in decline and compares poorly with the period 1970-1979 when higher profitability, lower interest rates and greater investment incentives led to substantial growth rates (see Figure 2). Recent trends and forecasts provide no indications of substantial improvements in the performance of the world economy or the major tungsten-consuming sectors, at least in the foreseeable future. With growing emphasis on quality rather than quantity of growth, the performance of these sectors would continue most likely to fall behind the other sectors even in the event of an improved performance of the world economy.

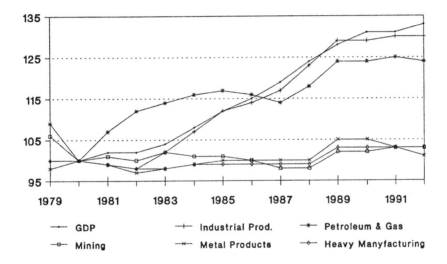

*Figure 2:* Major Tungsten-consuming sectors in world economy, 1979-1992

## Substitution, tool coatings and other technological changes

During the late 1970s and the early 1980s, high prices (see Figure 3) provided substantial incentives to substitute tungsten by other materials with a view to reducing production costs as well as the dependence on international supplies. The areas of consumption most affected are applications which account for the larger proportions of tungsten consumption, steel tools, drills, cutting tools and wear parts, and heavy alloys. In these applications, the main substitutes for tungsten include products, such as molybdenum steel tools, ceramics and cermets, and depleted uranium. The substitution of tungsten by other materials in other applications also exists but it is much more limited, particularly where tungsten constitutes only a fraction of the total production cost as, for example, in electric bulbs.

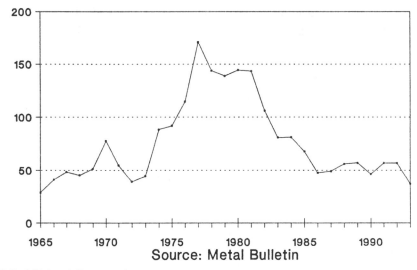

Source: Metal Bulletin

United States dollar per m.t.u.

*Figure 3:*  Annual average price 1970-1993 Tungsten Concentrates

The inroad made by substitutes into the tungsten market during the period of high tungsten prices is still being felt despite the substantial decreases in tungsten prices and the abundant availability of supply in recent years. Following the price collapse of 1985-1986, when the price of tungsten fell to below US$ 40 per m.t.u., it has seldom been higher than US$ 60 per m.t.u., compared to US$ 179 per m.t.u. in 1979 and an average which stayed above US$ 100 per m.t.u. in the early 1980s (see Figure 3). There has been some reversal in the substitution process in favour of tungsten in order to benefit from the new market situation but tungsten has not regained all the ground lost to rival products. In some areas of application, it faces even more competition as new products are put on the market.

The reversal of the negative effect of substitution on tungsten have proved to be particularly difficult where the substitution was not based on price considerations alone. Many of the substitutes adopted or developed proved to improve efficiency as well as productivity. The reversal of the latter type of substitution is more difficult. For example, the use of cermets is of this type and the progress made by cermets in the market may have slowed down recently but not stopped.

World demand for tungsten has also been negatively influenced to a significant extent by technological changes. These include mainly improvements in coating technology, improved tool geometry, the advent of near-net-shape techniques, downsizing and the increasing use of composite materials at the expense of metallics in industry.

The use of coatings allows improvement in the performance of various tools by giving more hardness to the tool surface. Productivity gains are made through an increase in the tool life, in many operations by as much as a factor of 2 to 10 times, and by the increased speed in operation which is made possible. The negative influence on consumption due to improved tool geometry, near-net-shape techniques and downsizing was accentuated in the wake of rising material costs and the shocks of the oil crises of the 1970s. It is estimated that the tungsten economies achieved through technological changes from 1980 to 1986 amounted to 2,500 metric tonnes per year. Of these economies, about 50% are due to improvements in tool coating, about 25% due to tool geometry, and about 10% each due to near-net-shape techniques and downsizing. However, progress in these fields has been more limited in recent years since there are limits to the economies that can be achieved by improved tool geometry, near-net-shape techniques and downsizing.

Perhaps a far more important development affecting demand of tungsten in the future is the increasing use of composite and non-metallic materials for many structural and engineering applications in industry. The advantages of these materials consist mainly of their lighter weight and lower prices compared to metallics. Recently, a great effort has been made through research and development to increase their mechanical and structural strength. Tungsten tool demand is affected by such substitution to the extent that it leads to reduced or different tool requirements.

### Supply and demand imbalance

Owing to the weak demand situation, the tungsten market has recently faced large supply surpluses, an abundant availability of tungsten materials and painful adjustments through substantial supply cutbacks (see Figure 4). The burden of supply cutbacks has fallen most heavily on the developed market economy countries with their mine production down by more than three-fourths from 13,776 metric tonnes to 3,200 metric tonnes between 1979 and 1992. The economic recession of 1982-1983, the price collapse of 1985-1986, and the more recent economic recession of 1991-1992 were marked by painful cutbacks in their mine production while the improved economic conditions in the periods of 1984-1985 and 1988-1989 brought little relief to the tungsten industry in these countries. Between 1979 and 1992, their mine production as a proportion of total world supply fell from 28% to 8%.

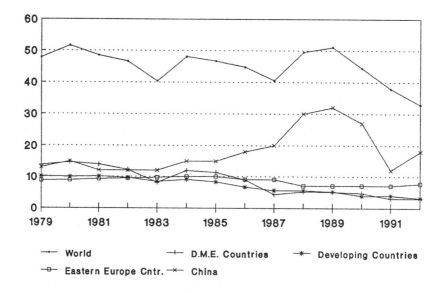

Metric Tons

*Figure 4:* World supply of Tungsten

In the developing countries, the burden of supply cutbacks was also heavily felt although to a somewhat lesser degree. The market situation between 1979 and 1992 reduced mine production in these countries by two-thirds, down from 10,166 metric tonnes to 3,100 metric tonnes. To some extent, their production cutbacks were cushioned by factors such as the depreciation of local currencies, the negative effect on supply elasticity due to deficits in the balance of their foreign trade and the consequent need for foreign exchange, and the social costs of closure. It may be noted that the decline of mining operations in some developing countries had already started in the 1970s in the face of rising production costs particularly energy, spare parts and other imported inputs in those years. The recent difficulties have only aggravated the decline. Between 1979 and 1992, the supply of tungsten from these countries as a proportion of total world supply fell from 21% to 10%.

As regards China, its supply changed greatly in volume and composition during the period under review. Tungsten supply in China also fell during the recession of 1982-1983. But as from 1984, both its mining and processing capacities experienced substantial expansion which coincided with a new phase of its policy of economic reform and opening. Changes took place which affected both production and marketing of its tungsten materials. With its large tungsten reserves and the relative high labour intensity of tungsten mining, China was a relatively low-cost producing country. Largely under-exploited in the past, tungsten mining in China expanded in both the 1970s and 1980s, although, the expansion in the latter period took place in a much difficult market situation. China's supply, which had fallen to 12,000 metric tonnes from 15,000 metric tonnes during the recession of 1982-1983, surged to reach 32,000 metric tonnes in 1989, most of it as export material in the form of intermediate products. There was plentiful of tungsten materials competing for buyers, and this competition greatly intensified during 1985 and 1986. During the substantial demand upturn in 1988, the international market was able to secure the tungsten supplies it needed without any substantial increase in tungsten prices. However, the severe recession in 1991-1992 and the sharp decline of imports by the former U.S.S.R. under trade protocols forced China also to cut back its supply, which was estimated at 18,000 metric tonnes in 1992. As a proportion of world mine production, China's share increased from 27% in 1979 to 55% in 1992.

The former U.S.S.R. accounts for most of the supply of countries of Eastern Europe, where consumption has recently been drastically reduced as a result of the on-going economic reform and restructuring. However, the cutbacks in consumption are assumed to have affected mostly imported materials. The domestic supply in the former U.S.S.R. was estimated at around 9,000 to 10,000 metric tonnes per year between 1979 and 1987. The estimates were recently revised downward to 7,000 metric tonnes per year as industrial production fell, particularly in the mining, steel and energy industries. Despite the cutbacks, the proportion of the former U.S.S.R. mine production in total world supply rose from 18% in 1979 to 22% in 1992. It may be noted that the supply from the former U.S.S.R. does not usually enter the international market and therefore, it does not have the same market effect as supplies which are exported. Whether the situation will remain the same or not in the future remains to be seen.

**Idle mine capacities**

The supply cutbacks have led to large-scale mine closures and a substantial increase of idle mine capacities in the world tungsten industry, particularly in the developed market economy countries. The number of mines in operation, which had been 59 in the developed market economy countries and 69 in the developing countries at the peak of world supply in 1980, was reduced to only 5 and 25 respectively by 1992. Mines in developed market economy countries are often among the most vulnerable partly because, as noted earlier, tungsten mining is a relatively labour intensive industry and the high labour costs make it difficult to operate such mines in times of depressed prices. As examples, Canadian Tungsten was among the first hit by the depressed prices of 1982-1983, as were some Australian and United States mines which were opened in the middle or later part of the 1970s. However, the largest number of mine closures occurred in 1985-1986 with the collapse of tungsten prices.

Many closed-down mines have been put on care and maintenance. While the capacity of these mines has been withdrawn from production, their overhang effect on the market remains as they could be re-opened if market conditions improved. As a result of these idle capacities, the tungsten industry currently suffers from a problem of capacity under-utilisation. On the basis of the ratio of mine production to mine capacity, it is estimated that the rate of capacity utilization in the tungsten mining industry has dropped to below 60% recently compared to above 95% in 1979 when the world was facing supply shortages.

## 3 CONCLUSIONS

From the foregoing examination, the image which emerges of tungsten is that of a commodity in distress. The present situation in the tungsten market does not lead to optimism. On the basis of recent trends and forecasts, there are still no indications of an imminent demand recovery in the tungsten market through a substantial growth of the world economy. Any economic growth seems to be likely to be modest at least in the near future, and the growth in the major consuming sectors would be even more modest as the recent experience has shown. The slowdowns experienced by these sectors look likely to be difficult to reverse in the light of changing priorities in major world economies, which tend to put greater emphasis on quality rather than quantity of economic growth.

In this difficult market situation, the world tungsten industry faces a number of challenges which it must meet in order to gain new markets as well as to defend its market share vis-à-vis rival materials. In the past, high tungsten prices and the image of a commodity with a problem of supply security considerably handicapped the use of tungsten *vis-à-vis* rival materials in the market. This situation has greatly affected investments in research and development for developing new applications of tungsten. The need to find significant new uses for tungsten remains a challenge up to these days. Another challenge is related to the emerging market conditions. As noted earlier, tungsten faces significant competition from rival materials in major applications. Tungsten products must meet new market requirements if they are to stand successfully against competition from rival products.

Since there exists no international agreement which covers tungsten, measures which are provided under the First Account of the Common Fund are excluded from consideration in the development of an international strategy for tungsten. However, some possibilities exist under the Second Account although they might not be entirely adequate for providing a solution to all the problems currently facing tungsten. Such possibilities include *inter alia* efforts to enhance the international image of tungsten as a commodity environmentally sound and reliable in supply, to diversify horizontally by developing new grades of tungsten materials and vertically by developing new applications for tungsten, and to strengthen research and development for benefiting the commodity by assisting national or international R and D programmes.

# WHEAT MARKET PROBLEMS
# AND NECESSARY MEASURES[1]


Major economic problems facing developing countries exist in the areas of production incentives, credit availability, market access, foreign exchange reserves, and consumer buying power.

For wheat and other grains, agricultural policies of some developed countries tend to result in surplus production within those countries, which is frequently exported to world markets at subsidised prices that are often lower than the cost of production. The resulting negative effect on the value of indigenous production in developing countries discourages an expansion of production in those countries. Some argue that these practices benefit those developing countries that are deficit producers of these commodities, for they lower the cost of fulfilling import requirements. But most agree the negative effects of these policies on the overall growth of agricultural economies of developing countries outweigh any perceived, selective advantage, even recognizing that global markets for these commodities continue to expand.

Protectionist policies in developed countries create import barriers on a wide range of commodities and commodity products that are difficult for developing countries to penetrate. This lack of market access creates disincentives for product improvement, new product development, and the creation of competitive efficiencies and actions. Elimination of these barriers would facilitate the generation of foreign exchange by developing countries as they could increase their exports. This in turn would generate more consumer buying power in developing countries and more rapid economic growth in those countries. These and other questions are being addressed in the GATT Uruguay Round negotiations. It is difficult to overstate the importance of these negotiations.

In the grains area there is an ongoing need to improve productivity via better seed stock, better farming practices, and more effective and efficient post-harvest practices. The latter include storage, processing and distribution activities. Strengthening agricultural education and extension

---

[1] Paper presented by the International Wheat Council (IWC).

capabilities within developing countries could accomplish much in these areas, assuming adequate funding and credit are available and a more liberalised trading climate ensues as a result of GATT agreements.

As, and if, foreign exchange reserves increase in developing countries and markets in developed countries expand for developing country products, new processing opportunities will develop. In the food area, quality control and quality reliability will be key determinants whether new markets, once developed, can be maintained. The best defence against competing products for developing countries' exports will be cost efficiencies, quality reliability and regular, dependable supply availability.

Global markets are forever changing, as the profiles of consumers change, as buying power changes, as dietary patterns change, as preferences change, as new or substitute products emerge, and as consumer and industrial needs change. A principal function of International Commodity Bodies such as the International Wheat Council is to keep countries apprised of the ever-changing market so that, where necessary, country strategies can be altered, new product development efforts accelerated, etc. Employment of the Second Account for projects that help developing countries identify and understand global markets and operate in them effectively can be of lasting benefit.

# REVIEW OF THE WORLD COMMODITY
# SITUATION AND OUTLOOK[1]

## 1 INTRODUCTION

This document reviews recent developments in the world commodity situation and assesses the short term market outlook. It is drawn from the more detailed review contained in the *FAO Commodity Review and Outlook 1992-93*.

## 2 SUMMARY

Prominent features of the markets for agricultural products in 1991 and 1992 included:

- Declines in the *prices* of many agricultural commodities relative to 1990 especially in prices that affect the export earnings of the developing countries. The UN index of commodity export prices for the agriculture, forestry and fishery products of the developing countries was estimated to have fallen in real terms by 6% between 1990 and 1992. By contrast, there has been virtually no change in that for the developed countries;
- Commodities with particularly large decreases in price between 1990 and 1992 include: cotton, coffee, cocoa, sugar, pepper, groundnut oil, cattle hides, jute, sisal and wool. Some of the large changes in price reflected cyclical patterns of production expansion and contraction such as in cotton and pepper. In other commodities stocks accumulated over a number of years and were high relative to requirements, as in coffee, cocoa, natural rubber and sugar with real prices in 1992 only half those in 1979-81. However, the greater permanence of productive capacity in these crops may only have deferred problems of alternation between surplus and shortage;

---

[1] Paper presented by the FAO

- *Export earnings* of agricultural products were estimated to have increased slightly in 1991 and 1992, but for the developing countries the slight increase in 1991 was estimated to have been reversed in 1992. Expansion of agricultural exports and imports has been strongest in the Far East while those from Latin America and the Caribbean, and Africa have contracted in purchasing power;
- The purchasing power of the major agricultural commodity exports of the developing countries was no higher in 1991 than in 1979-81 reflecting a decline in real prices that offset the strong growth in export volume;
- Commodities with a decline in export earnings greater than 20% between 1990 and 1992 included: coffee, sugar, pepper, cotton, jute, sisal, natural rubber and hides and skins. Increases in export earnings of more than 20% over the two years were obtained for skim milk powder and tobacco leaf;
- Exports of agricultural products other than the major commodities have grown in their contribution to export earnings. These diverse products accounted for 42% of world agricultural exports in 1991, compared with 28% in 1979-81. Included in these diverse products are: roots; tubers; pulses; many horticultural products; nuts; spices and miscellaneous food and feed products;
- *Imports* of food by the developing countries declined in 1991 from the relatively high level of 1990; for Africa, however, there was an increase in the region's net imports, reflecting the reduction in food exports. Further increases in Africa's net food imports were anticipated for 1992 and 1993;
- *Prospects* of progress in reducing structural imbalance in some markets and increased growth in demand with recovery for economies in recession would tend to lighten the generally sombre outlook for agricultural product exporters.

## 3  DEPRESSED GLOBAL ECONOMIC CONDITIONS AND SLOW GROWTH IN DEMAND FOR COMMODITIES

Depressed rates of growth in the global economy have continued to inhibit expansion of agricultural trade. The global economy was estimated to grow by only 1.1% in 1992 and by 3.1% in 1993 according to the IMF in October 1992[2]. The developing countries were anticipated to have higher rates of economic growth than the developed countries where it remained slow and uneven and where uncertainty continued to prevail over the magnitude and timing of recovery. Growth in the industrial countries, excluding Eastern Europe and the former USSR, was anticipated to be 1.7% in 1992 and 2.9% in 1993 although, as pointed out by the IMF, the balance of risks remained on the downside.

Countries in Eastern Europe and the former USSR have confronted grave economic and social difficulties in the early phases of their economic transformation process. After a slight decline in 1990, output in this group of former centrally planned economies fell 10% in 1991 and further, by an estimated 17%, in 1992. However, while the decline was expected to continue in the former USSR, the Eastern European economies were forecast to expand by 2.4% in 1993, the first growth since 1988.

In contrast with the lacklustre performances and prospects of the developed countries, the economic situation and outlook has improved significantly in much of the developing world. This is remarkable considering the increasing globalisation of economic influences. Income in the developing countries as a whole rose 3.2% in 1991 and was expected to expand by over 6% in both 1992 and 1993. Regional forecasts for 1992-93 were: continuing economic expansion in most Asian countries at a somewhat stronger pace than in the previous three years; significant recovery in Latin America and the Caribbean where, for the first time since 1987, per caput GDP rose in 1991, a performance that should be repeated in 1992 and more so in 1993; and considerable progress in the Near East associated with reconstruction and the normalization of trade, financial, and labour flows following the conflict in the Persian Gulf area. However, on the negative side, acute economic problems continued to affect Africa, where per caput GDP was expected to fall again in 1992 and increase only slightly in 1993. The economic outlook appeared particularly gloomy in countries of southern and eastern Africa affected by severe drought and civil strife.

The fact that many of the developing countries have been able to overcome the effects of the adverse external environment reflects to a large extent successful reform policies. For many countries the long-

---

[2] Unless otherwise indicated, estimates and forecasts in this section are from IMF World Economic Outlook, October 1992.

awaited rewards from stabilization and structural adjustment efforts appeared to be finally forthcoming. The IMF reported that 35 countries, accounting for over half of the total output of the developing countries, can now be characterized as successful adjusters, even though the reforms have not yet been completed in all cases. Many of these countries are also benefiting from a return of investors' confidence, a reversal of capital flight and significant capital inflows. A number of indebted countries, particularly highly indebted middle-income economies, are also benefiting from stronger export growth, lower interest rates and debt-reduction operations.

The decline in rates of economic growth, especially in the developed countries, depressed demand for commodities since 1990. Some commodities were particularly affected, such as natural rubber and other agricultural raw materials as well as animal feeds.

## 4  DEPRESSED MARKETS FOR MANY COMMODITIES FROM DEVELOPING COUNTRIES

### Slight rise in export prices in 1992 negated by inflation

Export prices for agricultural, fisheries and forestry commodities increased 2% in dollar terms in 1992. The estimated increase in the UN export price indices in 1992 reflected higher prices for commodities largely exported by the developed countries (see Table 2). Cereal prices were up by 11% with a sharp rise in wheat prices partly offset by a decline in those of rice and coarse grain. Dairy product prices rose 8% including a 25% rise for skim milk powder, while butter prices continued to decline. However, cotton prices collapsed reflecting the increased size of crops and stocks as well as lower levels of demand growth. The Cotlook 'A' index price went as low as 52 cents/lb in October 1992 while it had averaged 81 cents per lb in 1990. Wool prices also fell during the year. Fine wool fell as low as 413 cents/kg in November compared with its 1990 average of 808 cents/kg prior to the withdrawal of support buying by Australia and New Zealand.

The overall export price index for the developing countries declined slightly in 1992. For coffee and cocoa it was another year of still lower prices. On average, the International Coffee Agreement composite indicator price was 21% down and that reported under the International Cocoa Agreement was 8% down with relatively large stocks of both commodities. Tea prices increased by 9% even though the effects on the market of a drought-reduced crop were partly offset by a sharp contraction in buying by the republics of the former USSR. Natural rubber prices started to increase but were still below the levels of the late 1980s.

The barter terms of trade between the agricultural, fishery and forestry commodities and the group of manufactured goods and crude petroleum declined further in 1992. Manufactured goods were traded at increased prices and their unit value in dollars increased by 5%. This was partly offset by a 4% decrease in the average price of crude petroleum making the weighted increase 3%. For agricultural, fishery and forestry products this turned estimates of a slight increase in nominal prices into a slight decrease in their barter terms or real price. This decline was estimated to be 4% for the developing countries.

## The decline in real prices since 1979-81

The level of real export prices of agricultural, fishery and forestry products in 1992 was estimated to be 25% below that at the start of the 1980s. Relative to average prices over the years 1979 to 1981 the index of real prices for exports of developing countries was down by 38% and for that for developed countries down by 18%. Commodities with very large declines in real prices over this period included: coffee and cocoa, 70% down; sugar, nearly 60% down; and cotton and rubber nearly 50% down. Coffee for example had an average price of 134 cents/kg in 1979-81 and this fell to 53 cents/lb in 1992 as shown by the ICA composite indicator price. In the meantime, the index for manufactures and crude petroleum had risen 28% indicating a real price for coffee in 1992 of only 41 cents/lb. Unlike coffee, some of the agricultural commodities in Table 2 had nominal price increases but these increases since the 1979-81 period were in all cases less than that in the index for manufactures and crude petroleum indicating a decline in the real prices of all these commodities.

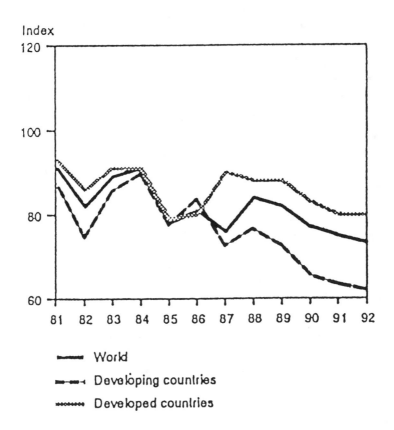

*Figure 1:* Real export price indices agricultural, fishery and forestry products (1979 = 100).

The decline in real prices reflected several factors. For many commodities a major change was the technologically driven increase in yields.[3] Over the years to 1991 the percentage increase in output per hectare of many of

---

[3] An initial examination of aspects of the decline in the terms of trade of agricultural commodities was provided for the FAO Council at its 102nd session (Document CL 102/2-Sup. 1). The commodities examined globally were: coffee; cocoa; tea; natural rubber; and for the developing countries as well as globally for: cotton, sugar, soybeans, rice, wheat and maize.

the commodities was over 20%. Further, increases in production exceeded increases in yield for each of the commodities except cotton. Most of the increases in production exceeded 25%, there was a 46% increase for cocoa and a 93% increase in soybean production in developing countries. Demand, however, grew at a slower rate. The major markets for many of these commodities in the developed countries had a population growth of only 0.7% a year. The growth in income in these markets, 3% a year, added little to the level of demand that was near satiety as reflected in low income elasticities of demand. Further, there was a negative impact on demand for some commodities stemming from changes in manufacturing technology as in the sweetener and rubber industries. Exacerbating the decline in prices was the characteristic unresponsiveness or inelasticity of consumption to price. At the level of producers' markets for primary products the price decline was further amplified by the small share of raw material costs in the price paid by consumers. Protectionism by a number of industrialized countries also contributed to the weakness of several agricultural commodity prices.

The decline in real prices for all these commodities was so large that it exceeded the increase in yields, thus by 1991 the value of output per hectare had a lower purchasing power than in 1979-81. That is to say there had been a decline in the single factor terms of trade. Coffee and cocoa were particularly affected with a decline in purchasing power per hectare of some 50% for both commodities.

Explanations of the persistence of production in these circumstances included: (i) the durability of productive capacity and thus the slowness of response to declines in the incentives for production; (ii) cost reducing changes on the supply side over and above those stemming from yield increases; (iii) distortions in the relationship between production incentives at the farm level, prices quoted on markets of international significance and those paid by consumers.

**Export earnings increased slightly since 1990**

Data for 1991, the latest year for which detailed statistics are available, show global export earnings from agricultural, fishery and forestry products slightly above those in the previous year despite the dollar price decline between the two years. For 1992 the estimate was of a further slight increase but not for exports of the developing countries. For agricultural products the slight increase in 1991 comprised a decline in the earnings of the major commodities, listed in Table 5, and an increase in the other agricultural products. Earnings from agricultural commodity exports declined as the decrease in prices exceeded the increase in the volume of exports (see Table 3). Commodities with a decline in export earnings close to 20% included: sugar; natural rubber; hides and skins; and hard fibres. The decline for tea; jute; wheat and coarse grains exceeded 8%. Gains were obtained in the livestock products and tobacco leaf. For 1992 serious declines were anticipated in the export earnings of: coffee; pepper; butter; the fibres and hides and skins. By contrast, earnings increased considerably for wheat, skim milk powder and cheese.

In real terms there was a 5% gain in the purchasing power of agricultural, fishery and forestry exports in 1991 reflecting a 5% decline in the index of the dollar price of manufactures and crude petroleum (see Table 4). However, the deflator almost reverted to its 1990 value in 1992 and a decline in the purchasing power of around 2% was indicated for these exports.

### Increase since 1979-81 in purchasing power of exports except for agricultural commodities from developing countries

Compared with 1979-81 the purchasing power of agricultural, fishery and forestry product exports in 1991 was up by 30%. The increase for the developing countries was 19% and that for the developed countries was 34%. However, for agricultural products alone, that is excluding fishery and forestry, the increase was 18% and the developing countries had only a 4% gain in the purchasing power of these exports. However, within the agricultural product aggregate there was a decline for the major commodities (as listed in Table 5). For coffee and jute the decline was close to 50%, other commodities with losses exceeding 30% were cocoa, sugar, wheat, natural rubber, and hides and skins. In contrast, large increases in purchasing power were obtained for exports of: meat, milk powder and bananas. For the developing countries the 45% increase in the volume of the major agricultural commodity exports was offset by the fall in their real unit value. The result was a slight decrease in the purchasing power of major export items. For the developed countries a volume increase of 14% for major commodities was accompanied by a slight rise in their real unit value reflecting some expansion of demand over the period.

Diversification away from export of the major commodities is reflected in the relatively high rate of growth of exports of agricultural products other than the major commodities. At $138,000 million in 1991 (see Table 5, last row) the purchasing power of these diverse exports had grown by 79% since 1979-81. Their share of the agricultural product total grew from 28% to 42% over the period with expansion for both the developing and developed countries.

Development of natural resource based industries has not only reduced the importance of the major commodities in agricultural product exports but has increased the proportion of output going to factories and then exported under headings such as textile and leather merchandise. Thus the overall contribution of agriculture, fisheries and forestry to total exports exceeds the $456,000 million shown in Table 6.

Regional differences in the growth of export earnings from agriculture, fisheries and forestry have been greater than that between developing and developed countries. Of the developing countries those in the Far East achieved the highest growth in 1991 and since 1979-81, even as measured by exports of agricultural, fishery and forestry products (see Table 6). In contrast, earnings from these exports contracted in Latin America and the Caribbean, and Africa in 1991 and, in purchasing power, since 1979-81 as well. The rate of decline in agricultural product exports was greatest in Africa.

## Imports: expansion in the developing countries

Expansion in the dollar value of imports of agricultural, fishery and forestry products in 1991 was limited to the developing countries, mainly in the Far East (see Table 7). Imports of agricultural raw materials in the Far East increased notably relative to both 1990 and to 1979-81. In contrast, spending on imports of food fell in all regions from the high level of 1990. Africa's food imports fell 7% to $8,400 million and that of all the low-income food-deficit countries by 8% to $21,600 million. However, food imports exceeded exports for the developing countries as a whole. The proportionate excess of imports over exports was even larger in Africa and a further increase in the region's net food imports was anticipated for 1992 and 1993.

## 5 COMMODITY MARKETS IN SUMMARY

### Beverages, sugar, bananas and pepper: general downward pressure on prices

World *coffee* production in 1992/93 was estimated to decrease from the level of the previous year. Output in most of the major producing countries was forecast to decline, except in Colombia where a larger harvest was expected. However, the large stocks that had accumulated in producing countries in earlier seasons were not expected to be significantly reduced in 1992/93. Stocks held by traders in importing countries have also accumulated to unprecedented levels and were expected to dampen import demand. Prices and export revenues would thus continue to be depressed, especially if no breakthrough occurs in negotiations for a new International Coffee Agreement with economic provisions.

World *cocoa* production during 1992/93, at 2.4 million tonnes, was expected to be 4% above the relatively low level of 1991/92. However, the anticipated increase in world cocoa grindings was likely to exceed that in production and a stock draw-down of approximately 20,000 tonnes was likely to occur by end 1992/93. In the previous season there had also been a stock draw-down of approximately 72,000 tonnes. Such a succession of draw-downs had not occurred since 1983/84. However, during the first half of 1992 prices decreased steadily. New factors contributing to the decline were: the larger than expected 1991/92 crop in Côte d'Ivoire; the continued absence of the former USSR from the market; expectations of increased production for 1992/93; and reduced consumption of chocolate in major markets. However, in the second half of the year, less favourable weather in West Africa and sizeable buying for manufacturing, started to support prices but only to a limited extent due to the excessively high level of stocks.

Global *tea* production in 1991 rose slightly to a new record of 2.5 million tonnes. However, there was a notable contraction of imports by Eastern Europe and those of the former USSR fell drastically. There was a corresponding contraction in exports from India, Sri Lanka and especially China and Latin America, which more than offset increased exports from East Africa. In 1992 global tea production was expected to decline significantly as smaller crops in India, Sri Lanka and East Africa were not offset by increased production in Bangladesh. In spite of the reduced production, world export availabilities and import requirements were expected to be roughly matched during 1992, due to a continuing reduction in shipments to the former USSR. Tea prices, expressed in US dollars, remained depressed during most of 1992 but were expected to rise moderately in early 1993.

World *sugar* production was forecast to increase slightly to a record 117 million tonnes in 1992/93, following a one per cent increase in the previous year. Most of the increase would come from a recovery in output in the EC, the former USSR and Australia. Global consumption was put at 114 million tonnes for 1993, one per cent above the previous year. World stocks were likely to increase again and would be at the highest level since 1986/87. These stocks would amount to 35% of annual apparent consumption. The value of exports in 1991 was 22% down at $10,600 million with prices on the world market 28% below those of 1990. Little change in export earnings was expected in 1992 as the effect of a slight lift in prices would probably be offset by the lower volume shipped.

World *banana* exports during 1991 rose by 9% to reach a record 10.3 million tonnes. Expansion was considerable in Ecuador, Colombia, Costa Rica and the Philippines. Import growth was strong in Germany, the Republic of Korea, Turkey and the United States. During the first half of 1991, prices stayed at the previous year's levels, but declined in the second half of the year due to a large increase in the volume of exports. This downward pressure on prices continued during 1992 and was expected to last well into 1993 due to the ample supplies of bananas and bumper crops of other fruit in Europe.

The world *pepper* market continued to be heavily supplied during 1991 and 1992 with production, especially in 1991, well above the average level of the years 1987 to 1989. Pepper prices continued to fall under the weight of abundant supplies. Export earnings of major exporters also fell despite an increased volume of sales. The short-term outlook for the pepper market remained one of abundant supplies and downward pressure on prices.

### Cereals: recovery in levels of production in 1992/93

*Wheat* production declined more than utilization in 1991/92, especially in the developed countries. As a result, carryover stocks were drawn down and world wheat prices rose during 1991/92, partly recovering from a sharp decline in 1990/91. However, it was expected that global supply and utilization would remain relatively closely balanced in 1992/93. World imports were expected to decline, reflecting the higher prices and prospective production increases, especially among developed importing countries. Imports by the developing countries were also expected to fall from their record level in 1991/92. World wheat stocks were expected to recover somewhat, prices to tend downwards and export competition to remain strong.

Global *coarse grain* supplies shrank during 1991/92 as less was produced in the developed countries, especially of barley and rye. Carryover stocks were reduced to their lowest levels since 1984/85. World trade expanded slightly with larger imports by both developing and developed countries. These factors contributed to a rise in coarse grain prices during 1991/92.

The forecast for 1992/93 was of some increases in production and utilization. Most of the production increases were forecast for maize and sorghum. Trade was expected to continue to expand mainly in response to the increased import needs of drought-stricken African countries. Some rebuilding of carryover stocks and downward pressure on international prices were also expected.

The volume of global trade in *rice* expanded by 9% to about 13 million tonnes in 1992. As the year progressed competition among exporters intensified and export prices fell on expectations of a rise in world output of paddy, estimated at 526 million tonnes. A substantial rise in import demand coming from Indonesia, the former USSR and the Near East provided an early boost to trade. Major increases in exports, of 1.2 million tonnes, were obtained by Thailand and Viet Nam, while exports from the United States fell. Expectations for 1993 were for export supplies to rise relative to import demand, exerting downward pressure on prices. The volume of world trade was expected to fall slightly below the 1992 level.

World *cassava* production rose significantly in 1992 with higher output in Africa and Asia. Global trade also recovered from the depressed level of 1991 reflecting bigger shipments to both EC and non-EC destinations. The early outlook for 1993 is for a continuing expansion in global production, while trade might contract, particularly during the second half of the year, after the implementation of the first year of reforms in the EC's Common Agricultural Policy, which could make cereals more competitive in the EC.

By contrast, world production of *pulses* fell in 1992, largely on account of a reduced output in Africa and the Far East. Global utilization also dropped, mainly reflecting a reduction in the use of pulses as feed in the former USSR. World trade reached a record level in 1992, reflecting a rise in imports by countries in Africa and Asia. Exports, from both developing and developed countries increased appreciably. Prices declined in the first nine months of 1992 and then increased sharply. The prospect for 1993 was for a decrease in global trade, resulting from reduced import demand in several developing countries and lower export availabilities in some developed countries.

## Oilseeds, oils and fats, oilcakes and oilmeals: consumption expansion slows

The rate of growth in world consumption of *oils and fats* slowed in 1992 reflecting, in part, another year of sluggish expansion in the global economy. For *oilmeals*, the rate of growth was significantly higher as consumption was boosted by the robust worldwide expansion in the high oilmeal-consuming poultry sector.

World production of oils and fats and oilmeals in 1992 recovered after the stagnation of the previous year. For oils and fats the increase was largely the result of considerably greater output of rapeseed. For oilmeals, the increase mainly reflected the recovery in the soybean harvest. For the developing countries, oils and fats production increased by 2.7% and oilmeal production by 4.6%. In the developed countries, oils and fats production increased by 3.5% while oilmeal was 2.7% higher.

The volume of world trade in 1992 for oilseeds and products was estimated to have increased. In 1991 the only growth was in oilmeals and this was slight. International market prices in dollars were also higher in 1992 and the total value of trade in oilseeds and products went up, possibly reaching the 1988 record of $36,800 million.

In 1993, world production of oils and fats and oilmeals was expected to increase mainly due to expanded output of soybeans and palm products. However, decreases were expected in rapeseed, due to unfavourable weather in the main producing countries and in cottonseed due to reduced plantings by the main producers.

The forecast production levels of oils and fats in 1993 were considered adequate to meet foreseeable consumption requirements with a modest replenishment of stocks likely. For oilmeals, the outlook was for consumption growth to slow down, mainly due to a contraction in livestock numbers and poultry production in the former USSR and Eastern Europe. Nevertheless, some draw-down in stocks was anticipated and this would be expected to exert some upward pressure on prices. There could thus be an incentive to increased production in the Southern Hemisphere, where crops would become available in the first half of 1993.

### Meat: expansion mainly in poultry

*Meat* production was estimated to have increased slightly in 1992, as larger poultry and pork output outweighed the reduced output of bovine and ovine meat. As in 1991, world trade in meat was sustained by large concessional sales, which outweighed the effects of low income growth and shortages of foreign exchange. As a result only a slight contraction in trade was expected in 1992. A number of countries continued to resort to limitations on trade through the negotiation of Voluntary Restraint Agreements and imposition of higher barriers against cheap imports, although market access improved in countries such as Japan, the Republic of Korea and Egypt. The outlook for 1993 was for faster growth in world meat production and trade. However, there was considerable uncertainty about the impact of policies in the major exporting countries notably connected with the mid-1993 implementation of the CAP reform in the EC.

### Milk: some lessening of surpluses

World *milk* production was estimated to have fallen two per cent in 1992, following a similar fall in the previous year. Amongst the developed countries, production dropped in Europe and the former USSR, while it increased in North America, Oceania and Japan. In the developing countries, milk production increased in Latin America and Asia, but drought heavily curtailed production in southern Africa. International prices for most dairy products rose, although reduced demand for butter meant that its price remained depressed. Expansion of demand for milk powder in importing countries, coupled with lower production in some exporting countries, led to a notable increase in prices and decreases in public stocks in the EC and the United States. The volume of world trade rose further in 1992 but a sizeable proportion continued to be shipped at specially reduced prices or as food aid.

### Raw materials: serious decline in many prices

World *cotton* production rose 9% in 1991/92 under the continuing influence of the remunerative prices of previous years. Consumption rose only fractionally and the accumulation of stocks steadily pushed prices to their lowest levels for five years by late 1992. A further small decline in trade volume coupled with depressed prices resulted in an 18% drop in the value of exports in 1991/92. Production was expected to contract in 1992/93 while consumption was likely to expand, bringing convergence of world output and use, and stability in stock levels. The volume of trade was likely to decline, and, with some upward pressure on prices, no major change in the value of exports was foreseen.

World supplies of *jute* fibre were expected to remain ample in 1992/93, despite an exceptionally low level of production as a result of relatively large carryover stocks from 1991/92 and weak demand due to recessionary economic conditions. Imports of products fell to a record low in 1991, and import demand for fibre remained at a relatively low level. Prices of jute fibre and products declined in 1991/92, but those of *kenaf* increased due to scarcity of supplies of this fibre in Thailand. In 1992/93, prices of jute were expected to remain stable at relatively low levels.

Export earnings of all *hard fibres* and their manufactures declined by 7% in 1991 and 1992 and the downward trend could continue in 1993. International market prices for sisal fibre fell to their lowest levels in decades in 1992 and prices of sisal harvest twine also declined. At the same time world production of sisal and henequen declined by 5% underlining the continued contraction in demand. A further, though small, contraction in world output was expected in 1993. By contrast, abaca prices strengthened markedly in 1991 and 1992, but efforts in the Philippines to supply more fibre may prompt prices to return to more competitive levels in 1993. The global volume of abaca stripped in 1992 remained at around the level of 1991, following drought in the Philippines in the first part of the year. Prices of brown coir and of coir yarn firmed in 1992 and coir yarn prices could rise further due to increased demand for coir geotextiles. Global extraction of brown coir fibre stabilized in 1992, but coir yarn production continued to expand.

Prices of *natural rubber* were at very low levels in 1992. World production of natural rubber rose further and despite some recovery in demand, exceeded global utilization. World stocks by end-year were expected to increase for the second consecutive year. Export earnings from natural rubber declined slightly in 1991. Earnings were estimated to fall more sharply in 1992 due to a decline in both export volume and prices.

Early forecasts indicated that expansion of demand for natural rubber could accelerate in 1993, while production was anticipated to decline following the period of depressed prices. In these circumstances, global consumption could exceed production and prices would be likely to rise.

The stagnant global demand for *hides and skins* in 1992 reflected the standstill in expenditure on leather manufactures in the major consuming countries affected by economic recession. There was also a slight contraction in production of bovine hides and skins, sheepskins and goatskins. The outcome was that average prices at all processing levels fell below the 1991 levels, and foreign exchange earnings of those developing countries which are prominent exporters of leather and leather products rose at a slower pace in 1992 and 1991 than in previous years, to slightly exceed $13,000 million. Minor changes in bovine hide output were expected in 1993. With no indications of vigorous sustained recovery in demand, prices of most types of hides and skins were unlikely to show any significant rise in the short-term.

## Citrus: expanding production

*Citrus* production was buoyant in 1992/93 following an excellent harvest in 1991/92. Much of the additional orange crop would be used for the production of frozen concentrated orange juice (FCOJ) and its price declined during late 1992. Trade in 1992/93 was expected to remain similar to that of the previous year as additional competition will stem from the very large supplies of deciduous fruit. Prices of fresh fruit may decline during the early part of the season.

## Wine: lower qualities in surplus

Global *wine* production recovered in 1992/93 following improved vintages in the three major producing countries in Western Europe. The volume of trade in 1992 is expected to be broadly similar to that in 1991, with some possible increase in values. However, ample supplies in 1993, with little prospect of any substantial increase in consumer demand, could put downward pressure on prices of table wines. Nevertheless, stronger demand for quality wines will probably increase the premium they obtain.

## Tobacco: sustained expansion

*Tobacco* production continued to increase and was slightly higher than utilization in 1992 with a consequent small rise in stocks. Recent vigour in output has stemmed from the developing countries, which have also been the principal beneficiaries of increases in exports. Output in China, nearly all of it for domestic consumption, was over three million tonnes for the second year in succession and now forms 40% of the world total. Production of the largest exporter, the United States, has remained stable for the past three years. Prices in 1992 have remained virtually the same as 1991 when expressed in local currency. However, dollar values have fallen and the purchasing power of exports from the developing countries was probably lower.

*Table 1a:* Selected indicators of agricultural commodity trade

| | 1987-1989 Average | 1990 | 1991 | 1990-91 change |
|---|---|---|---|---|
| | | | | *Percent* |
| **AGRICULTURE, FISHERY AND FORESTRY PRODUCTS** | | | | |
| **Total exports** | *'000 million $* | | | |
| World | 397 | 462 | 465 | 1 |
| Developing countries | 109 | 120 | 122 | 2 |
| Developed countries | 288 | 341 | 343 | - |
| | *percent of all merchandise* | | | |
| **Share of world trade** [1] | 14 | 13 | 13 | |
| **Export price indices:** | *Index: 1979-1981 = 100* | | | |
| **Current prices** [2] | | | | |
| World | 93 | 99 | 94 | -5 |
| Developing countries | 85 | 84 | 80 | -6 |
| Developed countries | 98 | 106 | 102 | -4 |
| **Real prices** [3] | | | | |
| World | 81 | 77 | 76 | -1 |
| Developing countries | 74 | 66 | 64 | -2 |
| Developed countries | 85 | 83 | 82 | - |

*Notes:*

1. World exports of agricultural fishery and forestry products as a percentage of all products.
2. Derived from the UN indices entered as Group I and Group II in Table 2.
3. Values at current prices deflated by the rise in prices of manufactured exports and crude petroleum since 1979-81 as shown in Table 2.

*Sources:* FAO, Statistics Division and Commodities and Trade Division.

*Table 1b:* Selected indicators of agricultural commodity trade

| | | 1987-1989 | 1990 | 1991 | 1990-91 |
|---|---|---|---|---|---|
| | | Average | | | change |
| | | | | | Percent |
| AGRICULTURAL PRODUCTS | | | '000 million $ | | |
| Total exports | World | 281 | 327 | 329 | 3 |
| | Developing countries | 82 | 91 | 91 | - |
| | Developed countries | 199 | 236 | 238 | 1 |
| | | Index: 1979-1981 = 100 | | | |
| Volume of commodity exports | World | 117 | 119 | 123 | 3 |
| | Developing countries | 130 | 139 | 145 | 5 |
| | Developed countries | 112 | 111 | 114 | 2 |
| | | | '000 million $ | | |
| Total imports | Developing countries | 75 | 86 | 86 | - |
| | Developed countries | 232 | 267 | 266 | - |

*Table 1c:* Selected indicators of agricultural commodity trade

| | 1987-1989 Average | 1990 | 1991 | 1990-91 change % |
|---|---|---|---|---|
| **FOOD PRODUCTS** [4] | | | | |
| **Total exports** | | | | |
| Developing countries | 60 | 68 | 54 | -21 |
| Developed countries | 151 | 179 | 165 | -8 |
| **Total imports** | | | | |
| Developing countries | 56 | 65 | 59 | -9 |
| Low-Income Food-Deficit Countries [5] | 21 | 23 | 22 | -8 |
| Food aid | 3 | 2.9 | 3 | 5 |
| Developed countries | 175 | 207 | 180 | -13 |
| | *Index: 1979-1981 = 100* | | | |
| **Export price indices:** | | | | |
| Current prices [6] World | 91 | 96 | 93 | -3 |
| Real prices [3] World | 79 | 75 | 75 | 1 |

*Notes:*

3 Values at current prices deflated by the rise in prices of manufactured exports and crude petroleum since 1979-81 as shown in Table 2.

4 The food products group includes cocoa and oil crops for human consumption but excludes fish.

5 Low-income Food-Deficit Countries (with per caput GNP of $ 1 195 or less in 1991 and net imports of cereals).

6 UN Index for Group I in Table 2.

*Sources:* FAO, Statistics Division and Commodities and Trade Division.

*Table 1d:*  Selected indicators of agricultural commodity trade

| | | 1987-1989 Average | 1990 | 1991 | 1990-91 change |
|---|---|---|---|---|---|
| | | | | | % |
| **BEVERAGE CROPS** [7] | | | | | |
| **Total exports** | World | *'000 million $* | | | |
| | | 16 | 15 | 13 | -12 |
| **Export price indices:** | | *Index: 1979-1981 = 100* | | | |
| Current prices | World | 84 | 57 | 53 | -7 |
| Real prices [3] | World | 73 | 45 | 43 | -4 |
| | | | | | |
| **RAW MATERIALS** [8] | | | | | |
| **Total exports** | | *'000 million $* | | | |
| | Developing countries | 18 | 20 | 20 | -2 |
| | Developed countries | 37 | 43 | 40 | -6 |
| | | | | | |
| **Total imports** | | *Index: 1979-1981 = 100* | | | |
| | Developing countries | 16 | 18 | 19 | 6 |
| | Developed countries | 42 | 44 | 42 | -5 |
| | | | | | |
| **Export price indices:** | | | | | |
| Current prices [9] | World | 98 | 104 | 97 | -7 |
| Real prices [3] | World | 86 | 81 | 78 | -3 |

*Notes:*   [3]  Values at current prices deflated by the rise in prices of manufactured exports and crude petroleum since 1979-81 as shown in Table 2.

[7]  Coffee, tea, cocoa and products.

[8]  Agricultural raw materials excludes fishery products.

[9]  UN index for Group II in Table 2.

*Sources:* FAO, Statistics Division and Commodities and Trade Division.

*Table 2:*   UN export price

| | 1987-89 Average | 1990 | 1991 | 1992 |
|---|---|---|---|---|
| | *Indices 1979-81 = 100* | | | |
| **Agricultural fishery and forestry commodities** [1] | | | | |
| World | 93 | 99 | 94 | 97 |
| Developing countries | 85 | 84 | 80 | 79 |
| Developed countries | 98 | 106 | 102 | 105 |
| **Group I** | | | | |
| World | 91 | 96 | 93 | 97 |
| Developing countries | 81 | 78 | 73 | 72 |
| Developed countries | 95 | 105 | 102 | 109 |
| Beverage crops | 71 | 57 | 53 | 49 |
| Sugar | 55 | 69 | 51 | 52 |
| Cereals | 81 | 88 | 91 | 101 |
| Meat | 102 | 115 | 111 | 113 |
| Dairy products | 109 | 117 | 112 | 121 |
| Fish | 116 | 121 | 126 | 128 |

| | 1987-89 Average | 1990 | 1991 | 1992 |
|---|---|---|---|---|
| | *Indices 1979-81 = 100* | | | |
| **Group II** | | | | |
| World | 98 | 104 | 97 | 95 |
| Developing countries | 92 | 94 | 89 | 90 |
| Developed countries | 103 | 109 | 101 | 98 |
| Oilseeds | 80 | 77 | 76 | 76 |
| Textile fibres | 96 | 101 | 89 | 72 |
| Natural rubber | 82 | 68 | 65 | 68 |
| Hides and skins | 167 | 162 | 126 | 120 |
| Forestry products | 110 | 124 | 115 | 117 |
| **Other** | | | | |
| Crude petroleum | 63 | 76 | 61 | 59 |
| Manufactures | 124 | 138 | 137 | 144 |
| Manufactures and crude petroleum [2] | 115 | 129 | 124 | 128 |

*Notes:*    1   The index for agricultural, fishery and forestry commodities was derived from the UN indices entered as Group I and II.

2   The indexs for manufactures and crude petroleum was derived from the indices for these products with weights adjusted by changes in their volumes traded internationally.

*Source of data:* UN Monthly Bulletin of Statistics.

Table 3: Export indices: main agricultural commodities

| | 1987-89 Average | 1990 | 1991 | 1990-91 change |
|---|---|---|---|---|
| | Indices 1979-81 = 100 | | | Percent |
| **Value of exports** | | | | |
| World | 120 | 137 | 136 | - |
| Developing countries | 113 | 123 | 123 | - |
| Developed countries | 123 | 144 | 143 | - |
| **Volume of exports** | | | | |
| World | 117 | 119 | 123 | 3 |
| Developing countries | 130 | 139 | 145 | 5 |
| Developed countries | 112 | 111 | 114 | 2 |
| **Unit value of exports** | | | | |
| World | 102 | 115 | 111 | -3 |
| Developing countries | 87 | 88 | 84 | -5 |
| Developed countries | 109 | 129 | 126 | -3 |

Sources: FAO Statistics Division.

Table 4: Exports of Agricultural, fishery and forestry products by value

| | 1987-89 Average | 1990 | 1991 | 1990-91 change |
|---|---|---|---|---|
| | '000 million $ | | | Percent |
| **At current prices** | | | | |
| World | 397 | 462 | 465 | 1 |
| Developing countries | 109 | 120 | 122 | 2 |
| Developed countries | 288 | 341 | 343 | - |
| **At real prices[1]** | '000 million $ (1979-81) | | | |
| World | 346 | 358 | 376 | 5 |
| Developing countries | 95 | 93 | 99 | 6 |
| Developed countries | 251 | 265 | 277 | 4 |

Notes: 1 Values at current prices deflated by the rise in prices of manufactured exports and crude petroleum since 1979-81 as shown in Table 2.

Sources: FAO, Statistics Division and Commodities and Trade Division.

*Table 5a:*  Exports of agricultural, fishery and forestry products by value

| | World | | | Developing countries | | | Developed countries | | |
|---|---|---|---|---|---|---|---|---|---|
| | 1990 | 1991 | 1990-91 change | 1990 | 1991 | 1990-91 change | 1990 | 1991 | 1990-91 change |
| | '000 million $ | | Percent | '000 million $ | | Percent | '000 million $ | | Percent |
| **Total** | **461.8** | **465.1** | **1** | **120.4** | **122.3** | **2** | **341.3** | **342.8** | **-** |
| Fishery products | 36.4 | 38.6 | 6 | 16.2 | 17.3 | 7 | 20.2 | 21.2 | 5 |
| Forestry products | 98.7 | 98.0 | -1 | 13.8 | 14.4 | 4 | 84.8 | 83.6 | -1 |
| Agricultural products | 326.7 | 328.5 | 1 | 90.4 | 90.6 | - | 236.3 | 237.9 | 1 |
| **Beverages, sugar and other products** | **30.4** | **26.7** | **-12** | **22.5** | **19.8** | **-12** | **6.9** | **6.3** | **-9** |
| Coffee | 7.1 | 6.9 | -4 | 6.6 | 6.4 | 13 | 0.5 | 0.4 | -16 |
| Cocoa[1] | 4.1 | 3.9 | -5 | 2.0 | 2.1 | 7 | 1.2 | 1.1 | -7 |
| Tea[2] | 2.3 | 2.0 | -14 | 2.3 | 2.0 | -14 | - | - | - |
| Sugar | 13.6 | 10.6 | -22 | 8.8 | 6.2 | -29 | 4.8 | 4.3 | -10 |
| Bananas | 2.7 | 2.9 | 8 | 2.4 | 2.6 | 9 | 0.3 | 0.3 | 20 |
| Pepper[3] | 0.6 | 0.5 | 1 | 0.5 | 0.4 | -5 | 0.1 | 0.1 | -8 |
| **Oilseeds, fats and products** | **30.0** | **30.4** | **1** | **13.3** | **13.7** | **2** | **16.7** | **16.7** | **-** |
| Oilseeds | 10.4 | 10.1 | -3 | 3.3 | 3.1 | -6 | 7.1 | 7.0 | -1 |
| Oils and fats[4] | 12.8 | 13.4 | 4 | 6.0 | 6.4 | 7 | 6.9 | 7.0 | 2 |
| Oilseed cake and meal[5] | 6.8 | 6.9 | 2 | 4.0 | 4.2 | 3 | 2.7 | 2.7 | -1 |

*Notes:*

1  Including cocoa products.
2  Net exporting countries.
3  Including pimento, capsicum, and chillies.
4  Excluding butter (shown separately) and marine oils (included in fishery products).
5  Excluding fishmeal (included in fishery products).

*Source:* FAO, Statistics Division and Commodities and Trade Division.

*Table 5b:* Exports of agricultural, fishery and forestry products by value

| | World | | | Developing countries | | | Developed countries | | |
|---|---|---|---|---|---|---|---|---|---|
| | 1990 | 1991 | 1990-91 change | 1990 | 1991 | 1990-91 change | 1990 | 1991 | 1990-91 change |
| | '000 million $ | | Percent | '000 million $ | | Percent | '000 million $ | | Percent |
| Cereals | 36.4 | 33.8 | -7 | 5.1 | 6.0 | 17 | 31.3 | 27.9 | -11 |
| Rice | 4.1 | 4.3 | 7 | 2.4 | 2.6 | 10 | 1.7 | 1.7 | 2 |
| Wheat | 17.7 | 16.2 | -9 | 1.3 | 1.5 | 8 | 16.4 | 14.7 | -10 |
| Coarse grains | 14.6 | 13.3 | -9 | 1.4 | 1.9 | 36 | 13.2 | 11.4 | -13 |
| Meat | 42.5 | 44.8 | 5 | 6.5 | 7.1 | 8 | 36.0 | 37.8 | 5 |
| Beef and bovines | 18.9 | 20.0 | 6 | 2.9 | 3.0 | 1 | 16.0 | 17.1 | 6 |
| Sheepmeat and ovines | 3.0 | 3.0 | -1 | 0.9 | 0.7 | -16 | 2.1 | 2.3 | 5 |
| Pigmeat and swine | 13.0 | 13.5 | 4 | 1.5 | 2.0 | 26 | 11.4 | 11.5 | 1 |
| Poultry meat and poultry | 4.4 | 5.1 | 15 | 0.9 | 1.2 | 25 | 3.5 | 4.0 | 13 |
| Other meat | 3.2 | 3.2 | 2 | 0.3 | 0.3 | - | 2.9 | 2.9 | 2 |
| Milk and milk products | 19.9 | 20.6 | 3 | 0.5 | 0.5 | -3 | 19.4 | 20.1 | 3 |
| Butter | 3.1 | 3.4 | 8 | 0.1 | 0.1 | -10 | 3.1 | 3.3 | 8 |
| Cheese and curd | 8.0 | 8.2 | 2 | 0.1 | 0.1 | -20 | 7.9 | 8.1 | 2 |
| Powder and other products | 8.8 | 9.0 | 3 | 0.3 | 0.3 | 4 | 8.4 | 8.7 | 3 |

*Source:* FAO, Statistics Division and Commodities and Trade Division.

*Table 5c:* Exports of agricultural, fishery and forestry products by value

| | World | | | Developing countries | | | Developed countries | | |
|---|---|---|---|---|---|---|---|---|---|
| | 1990 | 1991 | 1990-91 change | 1990 | 1991 | 1990-91 change | 1990 | 1991 | 1990-91 change |
| | '000 million $ | | Percent | '000 million $ | | Percent | '000 million $ | | Percent |
| **Raw materials** | **18.1** | **16.0** | **-11** | **8.8** | **7.8** | **-12** | **9.3** | **8.3** | **-11** |
| Cotton lint | 8.4 | 8.1 | -4 | 3.8 | 3.7 | -2 | 4.6 | 4.4 | -5 |
| Jute, and allied fibres | 0.2 | 0.1 | -13 | 0.1 | 0.1 | -13 | - | - | - |
| Hard fibres[6] | 0.1 | 0.1 | -20 | 0.1 | 0.1 | -20 | ... | ... | ... |
| Natural rubber | 4.4 | 3.4 | -21 | 4.2 | 3.3 | -22 | 0.1 | 0.1 | 8 |
| Hides and skins | 5.1 | 4.3 | -16 | 0.5 | 0.5 | -2 | 4.6 | 3.7 | -18 |
| **Other commodities** | **17.0** | **18.0** | **6** | **3.3** | **3.6** | **8** | **13.7** | **13.9** | **2** |
| Citrus fruit | 3.6 | 3.9 | 9 | 0.9 | 0.9 | 1 | 2.7 | 3.0 | 11 |
| Wine, vermouths, etc. | 8.5 | 8.3 | -2 | 0.1 | 0.2 | 5 | 8.3 | 8.2 | -2 |
| Tobacco leaf | 4.9 | 5.7 | 17 | 2.3 | 2.6 | 10 | 2.6 | 2.7 | 4 |
| **Other agricultural products** | **132.3** | **138.1** | **4** | **30.2** | **32.2** | **6** | **103.0** | **107.1** | **4** |

*Notes:* 6 From fibre producing countries only.

*Source:* FAO, Statistics Division and Commodities and Trade Division.

*Table 6:* Exports of all merchandise and agricultural, fishery and forestry products

| | All merchandise | | | Agricultural, fishery and forestry products | | | | | |
| | | | | Total value | | | Percentage of all | | |
| | 1987-89 Average | 1990 | 1991 | 1987-89 Average | 1990 | 1991 | 1987-89 Average | 1990 | 1991 |
| | '000 million $ | | | '000 million $ | | | Percentage | | |
|---|---|---|---|---|---|---|---|---|---|
| World total | 2 817 | 3 486 | 3 527 | 397 | 462 | 456 | 14 | 13 | 13 |
| Developing countries | 622 | 799 | 846 | 109 | 120 | 122 | 18 | 15 | 14 |
| Latin America | 110 | 134 | 132 | 37 | 42 | 40 | 33 | 31 | 29 |
| Africa | 47 | 62 | 60 | 12 | 12 | 12 | 25 | 20 | 20 |
| Near East | 106 | 148 | 134 | 7 | 7 | 8 | 6 | 5 | 6 |
| Far East | 356 | 452 | 515 | 53 | 58 | 61 | 15 | 13 | 12 |
| Low-Income Food-Deficit[1] | 204 | 252 | 274 | 44 | 46 | 47 | 22 | 18 | 17 |
| Oil importers | 467 | 578 | 637 | 96 | 107 | 106 | 21 | 18 | 17 |
| Developed countries | 2 196 | 2 688 | 2 681 | 288 | 341 | 343 | 13 | 13 | 13 |

*Notes:* 1 Low-Income Food-Deficit Countries (with per caput GNP of 1,195 or less in 1991 and net imports of cereals).
*Source:* FAO Statistics Division.

*Table 7:* Imports of all merchandise and agricultural, fishery and forestry products

| | All merchandise | | | Agricultural, fishery and forestry products | | | | | |
| | | | | Total value | | | Percentage of all | | |
| | 1987-89 Average | 1990 | 1991 | 1987-89 Average | 1990 | 1991 | 1987-89 Average | 1990 | 1991 |
| | '000 million $ | | | '000 million $ | | | Percentage | | |
| World total | 2 891 | 3 609 | 3 669 | 433 | 502 | 491 | 15 | 14 | 13 |
| Developing countries | 477 | 779 | 873 | 95 | 110 | 111 | 20 | 14 | 13 |
| Latin America | 91 | 118 | 135 | 14 | 17 | 18 | 16 | 15 | 13 |
| Africa | 53 | 63 | 64 | 11 | 12 | 12 | 21 | 20 | 19 |
| Near East | 128 | 127 | 133 | 23 | 27 | 24 | 18 | 21 | 18 |
| Far East | 201 | 466 | 534 | 46 | 53 | 56 | 23 | 11 | 10 |
| Low-Income Food-Deficit[1] | 217 | 253 | 279 | 36 | 40 | 40 | 17 | 16 | 14 |
| Oil importers | 487 | 623 | 694 | 71 | 84 | 86 | 15 | 13 | 12 |
| Developed countries | 2 283 | 2 830 | 2 797 | 338 | 391 | 380 | 15 | 14 | 14 |

*Notes:* 1 Low-Income Food-Deficit Countries (with per caput GNP of $ 1,195 or less in 1991 and net imports of cereals).
*Source:* FAO Statistics Division.

# MEDIUM-TERM PROSPECTS FOR AGRICULTURAL COMMODITIES: AGRICULTURAL COMMODITY PROJECTIONS TO 2000[1]

## 1 INTRODUCTION

This document summarizes FAO's medium-term projections to 2000 of production, demand, trade and prices for major agricultural commodities or groups of commodities for almost all countries. The full results, to be issued later in 1993, will also include analyses of different scenarios and cover other issues such as the food security implications of these projections. Assumptions regarding economic and population growth, technological change, normal weather and unchanged agricultural policies (as of end 1992) were used to prepare a 'central' scenario for individual commodity production, demand and trade projections. It should be stressed that the projection results are indicative of what would happen under specified macro-economic, demographic and commodity-specific assumptions, all of which are subject to uncertainty.

The methods used in the present study are summarized in Annex II[2]. The projections for the cereal-feed-livestock-fats and oil complex were generated using the FAO World Food Model, a price-equilibrium recursive model. The projections for the other commodities used techniques ranging from econometric single-commodity models to constant-price/constant-policy projections of supply and demand. In each case, judgements of commodity specialists, nutrition and agricultural experts, shaped the final results.

---

[1] Paper presented by the FAO.

[2] For further details see also FAO, *FAO Agricultural Commodity Projections to 1990*. Economic and Social Development Paper No. 62. Rome, 1989, reprint.

## 2  GENERAL REVIEW

### Population and income assumptions

Global demand for many commodities is crucially linked to economic and population growth and, especially in developing countries, to population shifts from rural to urban areas. Commodity projections to 2000 are based on the United Nations' medium variant, which estimates that world population will expand by 1.7% annually in the nineties[3]. In the developing countries, population is projected to expand by 2% annually; in the developed countries by 0.5% (Table 1a).

*Table 1a:*  Assumptions on population and GDP growths, 1970 to 1990
            actual and 1990 to 2000 projected

POPULATION

| Region | 1970 | 1980 | 1990 | 2000 | Growth rates | | |
| --- | --- | --- | --- | --- | --- | --- | --- |
| | ................... Actual ................... | | | Projected | 1970−80 1980−90 Actual | | 1990− 2000 |
| | ......................... million ......................... | | | | .......... per cent per year ......... | | |
| WORLD | 3698 | 4448 | 5294 | 6263 | 1.9 | 1.8 | 1.7 |
| Developing Countries | 2624 | 3280 | 4046 | 4948 | 2.3 | 2.1 | 2.0 |
| Developed Countries | 1074 | 1169 | 1248 | 1315 | 0.8 | 0.7 | 0.5 |

---

[3] By convention, "nineties" encompasses the period from the base year of the projections, the average of production, consumption and trade during the 1987-89 period. "Eighties" covers the period from 1978 to 1988, where "1978" is the 1977-79 average.

*Table 1b:* Assumptions on population and GDP growths, 1970 to 1990 actual and 1990 to 2000 projected

TOTAL GDP at 1980 prices

| Region | 1970 | 1980 | 1990 | 2000 | Growth rates | | |
|---|---|---|---|---|---|---|---|
| | .................. Actual .................. | | | Projected | 1970–80 | 1980–90 | 1990– |
| | | | | | Actual | | 2000 |
| | .................. billions of US $ ..................... | | | | .......... per cent per year ......... | | |
| WORLD | 7945 | 11562 | 15415 | 20816 | 3.8 | 2.9 | 3.0 |
| Developing Countries | 1438 | 2467 | 3500 | 5670 | 5.5 | 3.6 | 4.9 |
| Developed Countries | 6507 | 9095 | 11914 | 15146 | 3.4 | 2.7 | 2.4 |

PER CAPUT GDP at 1980 prices

| Region | 1970 | 1980 | 1990 | 2000 | Growth rates | | |
|---|---|---|---|---|---|---|---|
| | .................. Actual .................. | | | | 1970–80 | 1980–90 | 1990– |
| | | | | | Actual | | 2000 |
| | ........................... US $ ........................... | | | | .......... per cent per year ......... | | |
| WORLD | 2148 | 2599 | 2912 | 3324 | 1.9 | 1.1 | 1.3 |
| Developing Countries | 548 | 752 | 865 | 1146 | 3.2 | 1.4 | 2.9 |
| Developed Countries | 6057 | 7783 | 9544 | 11519 | 2.5 | 2.1 | 1.9 |

World gross domestic product (GDP) in 1980 prices is projected by the World Bank to increase by 3% per year, more slowly initially but increasing to 3.5% annually for the second half of the decade. World per caput GDP in 1980 prices is expected to increase by 1.3% annually during the decade compared with 1.1% annually in the eighties. In the developing countries, it should rise by 2.9% annually. Per caput GDP in the Far East region is projected to grow most rapidly, 4.3% per year. By contrast, African per caput GDP is expected to lag, rising only 0.8% per year. Per caput income in the developed countries is expected to expand by 1.9% annually.

**Global agricultural projections**

The nineties are expected to be characterized by aggregate growth rates
for the production, demand and trade of food and agricultural commodities covered by this study substantially lower than during the eighties,
and at or below projected rates of population increase (Table 2a, b, c).
World demand for food and agricultural commodities (for all uses) is
expected to grow by only 1.6% annually, slightly below the rate of
population growth and below the 2% annual increase in the eighties. By
contrast, the rate of growth of production is projected to decline only
slightly, from 1.8% annually in the eighties to 1.7% annually in the
nineties, with some commodity groups, such as livestock, fats and oils
and tropical beverages, slightly below the trend. The fact that consumption growth exceeded that of production in the eighties reflected the large
drawdown of stocks of a number of agricultural commodities. Overall
supplies are projected to be sufficient to meet global effective demand.
The growth in food and agricultural commodity trade is projected to
decline from 2.9% annually in the eighties to 1.4% annually in the
nineties, well below projected growth rates for merchandise trade in
general. Thus, agricultural commodity trade will decline in proportion to
total trade. Trade growth for all agricultural commodity sectors, except
fruit and wine, share in the decline; trade in staple foods would be
particularly affected, declining from 3.1% annual growth in the 1980s to
0.3% in the 1990s.

Table 2a:  Growth of world agricultural production, demand and trade, past and projected

| Commodity Groups | Production | | Demand | | Trade 1/ | |
|---|---|---|---|---|---|---|
| | 1978*−88* | 1988*−2000 | 1978*−88* | 1988*−2000 | 1978*−88* | 1988*−2000 |
| | ............ percent per year ............ | | | | | |
| All Commodities covered | 1.8 | 1.7 | 2.0 | 1.6 | 2.9 | 1.4 |
| Foodstuffs | 1.8 | 1.7 | 1.9 | 1.6 | 3.0 | 1.2 |
| Staple Foods | 1.3 | 1.6 | 1.6 | 1.5 | 3.1 | 0.3 |
| Cereals | 1.8 | 1.8 | 2.1 | 1.6 | 2.4 | 0.8 |
| Roots and Tubers | 0.1 | 1.0 | 0.2 | 1.0 | 5.5 | −3.0 |
| Pulses | 2.5 | 1.7 | 2.5 | 1.6 | 10.0 | 2.1 |
| Livestock Products | 2.2 | 1.6 | 2.2 | 1.6 | 2.9 | 1.3 |
| Fats and Oils | 3.6 | 2.9 | 3.8 | 2.7 | 3.9 | 2.5 |
| Sugar 2/ | 1.7 | 1.6 | 2.4 | 1.5 | −1.1 | 0.8 |
| Fruit and Wine 2/ | 0.3 | 1.7 | 0.2 | 1.6 | 1.7 | 1.5 |
| Tropical Beverages | 2.5 | 1.7 | 2.8 | 2.1 | 2.7 | 1.3 |
| Agricultural Raw Materials | 1.9 | 2.3 | 2.5 | 2.0 | 2.7 | 2.4 |

Notes:  1978* signifies 1977 to 1979 average, 1988* signifies 1987 to 1989 average.
1 Gross.
2 net imports and exports for sugar, citrus and wine.

*Table 2b:* Developed countries: growth of world agricultural production, demand and trade, past and projected

| Commodity Groups | Production | | Demand | | Imports 1/ | | Exports 1/ | |
|---|---|---|---|---|---|---|---|---|
| | 1978*–88* | 1988*–2000 | 1978*–88* | 1988*–2000 | 1978*–88* | 1988*–2000 | 1978*–88* | 1988*–2000 |
| | ........................................................ percent per year ........................................................ | | | | | | | |
| All Commodities covered | 0.8 | 0.7 | 1.0 | 0.5 | 2.3 | 0.3 | 2.7 | 0.9 |
| Foodstuffs | 0.8 | 0.7 | 1.0 | 0.5 | 2.4 | 0.3 | 2.8 | 0.8 |
| Staple Foods | 0.0 | 0.9 | 0.4 | 0.2 | 1.9 | -2.0 | 2.9 | 0.3 |
| Cereals | 0.3 | 1.1 | 0.7 | 0.3 | 0.3 | -1.9 | 2.4 | 0.3 |
| Roots and Tubers | -1.5 | 0.4 | -0.7 | -0.2 | 4.8 | -3.3 | 6.0 | 0.2 |
| Pulses | 6.5 | 0.7 | 5.9 | 0.3 | 9.8 | 0.2 | 13.0 | 2.2 |
| Livestock Products | 1.3 | 0.4 | 1.2 | 0.3 | 2.6 | 0.7 | 3.2 | 0.7 |
| Fats and Oils | 2.0 | 1.7 | 2.7 | 1.5 | 2.2 | 1.0 | 1.0 | 0.8 |
| Sugar 2/ | 1.3 | 0.6 | 0.4 | 0.2 | -5.1 | -2.6 | -1.7 | -0.9 |
| Fruit and Wine 2/ | -0.4 | 1.3 | -0.1 | 1.2 | 2.4 | 0.9 | 2.4 | 2.9 |
| Tropical Beverages | – | – | 2.7 | 1.4 | 3.0 | 1.3 | – | – |
| Raw Materials | 0.7 | 1.6 | 1.2 | 0.5 | -0.6 | 0.9 | -0.3 | 3.4 |

*Notes:*    1978* signifies 1977 to 1979 average, 1988* signifies 1987 to 1989 average
1 gross
2 net imports and exports for sugar, citrus and wine

*Table 2c:* Developing countries: growth of world agricultural production, demand and trade, past and projected

| Commodity Groups | Production | | Demand | | Imports 1/ | | Exports 1/ | |
|---|---|---|---|---|---|---|---|---|
| | 1978*–88* | 1988*–2000 | 1978*–88* | 1988*–2000 | 1978*–88* | 1988*–2000 | 1978*–88* | 1988*–2000 |
| | ....................................................................... percent per year ....................................................................... | | | | | | | |
| All Commodities covered | 3.2 | 2.8 | 3.3 | 2.9 | 4.7 | 3.3 | 3.9 | 2.1 |
| Foodstuffs | 3.2 | 2.8 | 3.3 | 2.9 | 4.6 | 3.2 | 3.8 | 2.2 |
| Staple Foods | 2.2 | 2.0 | 2.4 | 2.2 | 4.9 | 2.5 | 3.6 | -0.2 |
| Cereals | 2.9 | 2.5 | 3.3 | 2.5 | 4.8 | 2.6 | 0.7 | 2.0 |
| Roots and Tubers | 1.0 | 1.3 | 0.8 | 1.6 | 14.2 | -1.2 | 6.3 | -4.4 |
| Pulses | 0.8 | 2.1 | 1.0 | 2.3 | 9.8 | 4.5 | 6.7 | 1.3 |
| Livestock Products | 4.3 | 3.5 | 4.4 | 3.5 | 3.8 | 3.4 | 2.2 | 3.7 |
| Fats and Oils | 5.5 | 4.0 | 5.4 | 4.0 | 7.0 | 4.2 | 6.9 | 4.2 |
| Sugar 2/ | 2.1 | 2.2 | 4.4 | 2.5 | 3.9 | 2.8 | -0.9 | 0.9 |
| Fruit and Wine 2/ | 2.0 | 2.9 | 1.6 | 3.2 | -2.2 | 5.8 | 3.7 | 2.1 |
| Tropical Beverages | 2.5 | 1.7 | 2.9 | 3.4 | 2.4 | 2.6 | 3.0 | 1.6 |
| Raw Materials | 2.8 | 2.7 | 3.7 | 3.0 | 5.6 | 3.4 | 4.3 | 1.4 |

*Notes:* 1978* signifies 1977 to 1979 average, 1988* signifies 1987 to 1989 average
1 gross
2 net imports and exports for sugar, citrus and wine

Factors in the slowdown of world demand include a reduced growth in population and per caput income and, in some cases, increasing competition by synthetics. Aggregate figures for some categories, such as wines, tea and coffee, mask significant changes in consumer preferences, for instance for high quality wines, $CTC^4$ teas and mild coffees. Aggregate production growth rates, which are not projected to decrease significantly, reflect factors such as declining rates of expansion in yields; changes in agricultural support programmes, such as the European Community's (EC) reform of its Common Agricultural Programme (CAP); and closer linkage to demand conditions, it being expected that in general excess stocks will not accumulate again because of policies to curb excess production. Trade in many commodities will be particularly affected by developments in the former USSR, a major importer of a number of commodities in the past, and China, where increasing domestic production is expected to reduce imports and, in some cases, make China a net exporter. Other factors affecting trade include the tendency in some commodities, including tea and agricultural raw materials, toward increased consumption or processing in the producing country.

The developing countries will account for much of the growth in overall commodity demand because of their comparatively buoyant per caput GDP expansion, twice the rate of the eighties (but less than in the seventies), and the greater responsiveness of demand to income growth. By contrast a slow growth in demand is foreseen for the developed countries, because high current consumption and saturated markets are expected to limit the demand growth rate for many commodities. Agricultural production in the developing countries is projected to increase by 2.8% annually in the nineties; i.e. slower than the 3.2% annual rate of the eighties, but still allowing for increasing per caput production. By contrast, the developed countries are projected to raise their production by 0.7% annually. The aggregate gross imports of the developing countries are expected to rise by 3.3% annually in the nineties, increasing their share of world imports, from 34% for the 1987-89 average to 42% in 2000; and aggregate gross exports are projected to grow by 2.1%. Thus, owing to the greater growth of imports than exports, by 2000 the developing countries are projected to be net importers compared to the end of the eighties, when they were net exporters of the commodities covered in the projections. Both import and export growth rates for the developed

---

[4] Processed according to "Crash, Tire and Curling" method.

countries are expected to decline sharply in the nineties relative to the eighties.

International markets for agricultural commodities should be in fairly close balance providing weather conditions are normal. Overall, by 2000, real prices are projected to be around 1988 levels, ignoring year-to-year fluctuations, although with significant exceptions. For instance, livestock product prices are projected to be generally higher in 2000, while relatively ample supplies projected for tea, oranges and wheat, could lead to some downward pressure on prices for these commodities. Competition for shares of slowly-expanding export markets, especially wheat, could lead to an increase in trade tensions and exacerbate downward pressure on prices.

**Key sector review**

World *staple food crop*[5] production is expected to increase by 1.6% annually, slightly faster than during the eighties which was characterized by a significant drawdown in stocks. In the developing countries, production is estimated to grow by 2.0% annually, almost the same as during the eighties. While crop yields in the developing countries are projected to grow more slowly than in the eighties, this will be offset by area growth (Table 3). In developed countries production should rise slightly faster than during the eighties. Global demand (for all uses) is projected to grow by only 1.5% annually, less than in the eighties and less than the growth in population. The volume of staple food trade is projected to decline sharply to 0.3% annually during the nineties from 3.1% in the eighties.

In the staple food sector, the growth of world *cereals* production is projected to stay at 1.8% annually, the same rate as in the eighties. Total trade is expected to grow by only 0.8%, compared with 2.4% annual growth of the eighties. However, developing country import demand for cereals will continue to increase sharply, resulting in a projected net trade deficit of 123 million tonnes in 2000 (up from the 89 million tonne 1987-89 average) and gross imports of 161 million tonnes (119 million tonnes in 1987-89). World wheat trade growth is expected to slow down from 3.7% annually in the eighties to only 0.2% in the nineties, reflecting sharply reduced imports by China and the former USSR. This is likely to increase export competition, although changes in policy in the developed countries may reduce surplus production. Real international prices of

---

[5] Cereals, roots and tubers, pulses.

cereals during the nineties are projected to be generally above the 1988 level, except for wheat prices which could decline somewhat because of the drop in the growth of trade.

The growth of the world *livestock* economy is projected to decline, even though poultry and pigmeat sectors are likely to remain fast-growing, while the expansion in developing countries should exceed the rate of growth in the developed countries. World trade growth for these commodities is also expected to slow down. Reflecting the slowdown in the livestock sector, world *feed*[6] demand is projected to grow by 1.2% annually during the nineties compared with 1.5% in the eighties; agricultural policy reform, particularly in the EC, is expected to have an important impact on feed imports, as reductions in domestic cereal prices are expected to reduce imports of cassava and pulses and to curb the growth for oilmeals. Sharp declines in the livestock sector in eastern Europe and the former USSR are expected to contribute significantly to the slow growth in feed demand and trade. Much consumption growth for coarse grains, especially maize and oilmeals, is foreseen to come from the developing countries, where the demand for feed is expected to be particularly strong.

---

[6] Feed uses of cereals (wheat, maize, other grains), roots and tubers, pulses and oilmeal proteins.

*Table 3a:* Staple foods: area, yield and production, past and projected

| Commodity/ Region | 1987–89 Average | | | 2000 Projected | | | Growth rates | | | | | |
|---|---|---|---|---|---|---|---|---|---|---|---|---|
| | | | | | | | Area | | Yield | | Production | |
| | | | | | | | 1978*– 1988 | 1988*– 2000 | 1978*– 1988 | 1988*– 2000 | 1978*– 1988 | 1988*– 2000 |
| | Area | Yield | Production | Area | Yield | Production | ............ percent per year ............ | | | | | |
| | million ha | 100 kg/ ha | million tons | million ha | 100 kg/ ha | million tons | | | | | | |
| **WHEAT** | | | | | | | | | | | | |
| WORLD | 221.6 | 23.5 | 521.2 | 230.8 | 27.7 | 640.1 | -0.3 | 0.3 | 2.4 | 1.4 | 2.1 | 1.7 |
| Developing countries 1/ | 99.0 | 22.0 | 217.6 | 106.3 | 28.0 | 297.5 | 0.5 | 0.6 | 3.8 | 2.0 | 4.3 | 2.6 |
| Developed countries | 122.6 | 24.8 | 303.6 | 124.5 | 27.5 | 342.6 | -0.9 | 0.1 | 1.8 | 0.9 | 0.9 | 1.0 |
| **RICE, MILLED** | | | | | | | | | | | | |
| WORLD | 145.1 | 22.4 | 324.9 | 146.8 | 27.9 | 409.4 | 0.1 | 0.1 | 2.5 | 1.8 | 2.6 | 1.9 |
| Developing countries 1/ | 140.7 | 21.8 | 307.2 | 142.6 | 27.4 | 390.1 | 0.2 | 0.1 | 2.6 | 1.9 | 2.8 | 2.0 |
| Developed countries | 4.4 | 40.4 | 17.7 | 4.2 | 45.8 | 19.3 | -0.7 | -0.4 | 0.4 | 1.1 | -0.4 | 0.7 |
| **COARSE GRAINS** | | | | | | | | | | | | |
| WORLD | 334.6 | 23.8 | 794.9 | 341.2 | 28.6 | 977.7 | -0.3 | 0.2 | 1.0 | 1.5 | 0.7 | 1.7 |
| Developing countries 1/ | 181.5 | 16.0 | 290.9 | 195.2 | 20.7 | 404.2 | 0.4 | 0.6 | 1.8 | 2.2 | 2.2 | 2.8 |
| Developed countries | 153.1 | 32.9 | 504.0 | 146.0 | 39.3 | 573.5 | -1.0 | -0.4 | 0.9 | 1.5 | -0.0 | 1.1 |

*Notes:* [1] Including other developing countries in Oceania.

*Table 3b*: Staple foods: area, yield and production, past and projected

| Commodity/ Region | 1987–89 Average | | | 2000 Projected | | | Growth rates (percent per year) | | | | | |
|---|---|---|---|---|---|---|---|---|---|---|---|---|
| | Area | Yield | Production | Area | Yield | Production | Area | | Yield | | Production | |
| | | | | | | | 1978*–1988 | 1988*–2000 | 1978*–1988 | 1988*–2000 | 1978*–1988 | 1988*–2000 |
| | million ha | 100 kg/ ha | million tons | million ha | 100 kg/ ha | million tons | | | | | | |
| **ROOTS AND TUBERS** | | | | | | | | | | | | |
| WORLD | 47.1 | 125.0 | 590.1 | 47.9 | 139.0 | 667.1 | -0.4 | 0.1 | 0.5 | 0.9 | 0.1 | 1.0 |
| Developing countries 1/ | 35.0 | 111.0 | 388.3 | 37.0 | 123.0 | 455.4 | 0.0 | 0.5 | 1.0 | 0.9 | 1.0 | 1.3 |
| Developed countries | 12.1 | 167.0 | 201.8 | 10.9 | 193.0 | 211.7 | -1.6 | -0.9 | 0.1 | 1.2 | -1.5 | 0.4 |
| **PULSES** | | | | | | | | | | | | |
| WORLD | 67.2 | 8.1 | 54.2 | 72.8 | 9.1 | 66.0 | 1.0 | 0.7 | 1.5 | 1.0 | 2.5 | 1.7 |
| Developing countries 1/ | 55.9 | 6.3 | 35.1 | 61.5 | 7.4 | 45.2 | 0.6 | 0.8 | 0.2 | 1.4 | 0.9 | 2.1 |
| Developed countries | 11.3 | 17.0 | 19.1 | 11.3 | 18.3 | 20.8 | 2.9 | 0.0 | 3.5 | 0.6 | 6.4 | 0.7 |
| **TOTAL STAPLE FOODS 2/** | | | | | | | | | | | | |
| WORLD | 815.6 | 28.0 | 2285.3 | 839.5 | 32.9 | 2760.3 | -0.1 | 0.2 | 1.3 | 1.3 | 1.1 | 1.6 |
| Developing countries 1/ | 512.1 | 24.2 | 1239.1 | 542.6 | 29.3 | 1592.4 | 0.3 | 0.5 | 1.9 | 1.6 | 2.2 | 2.1 |
| Developed countries | 303.5 | 34.5 | 1046.2 | 296.9 | 39.3 | 1167.9 | -0.8 | -0.2 | 0.8 | 1.1 | -0.0 | 0.9 |

*Notes:*   1 Including other developing countries in Oceania.
          2 In product weight.

*Tropical beverage crops* are projected to continue to experience difficulties in the nineties, with their markets near saturation in the major developed countries that account for over 80% of demand for coffee and cocoa. World demand is expected to grow at 2.1% annually during the nineties, substantially below the growth experienced in the eighties. Much of the growth in demand is projected to occur in producing developing countries. Coffee and cocoa markets are expected to be roughly in balance. Production, consumption and trade in tea is expected to be more dynamic; even though a moderate tea export surplus is projected for 2000 with some risk of downward pressure on prices.

Growth in aggregate world demand for *agricultural raw materials* is expected to slow down to 2% annually, from 2.5% in the eighties. Competition from synthetics, particularly in developed country markets, will continue to constrain demand and trade in virtually all agricultural raw materials. However environmental considerations and the development of markets for non-traditional products could result in improved prospects for some agricultural raw materials. Increased consumption in producing developing countries reflects declining trade opportunities for some raw or semi-processed materials and, in some instances, increased processing in the producing countries.

## 3 PROJECTIONS BY COMMODITY

### Staple foods

#### Rice

By 2000, global rice output is projected to reach 409 million tonnes of milled rice. Rising by 1.9% annually, growth is expected to be slower than in the previous decade. Yield improvements due to advances in plant technology are expected to account for most of the growth; area under rice is projected to show only minor increases, mainly in Africa. In Latin America, production is expected to grow faster than elsewhere but slower than in the previous decade. In the United States and the EC, some increase in output is also likely to occur.

World rice demand is projected to grow to 408 million tonnes, or two percent annually, about the same rate as production. Ninety percent of the demand is for food. Feed-use, representing less than 2% of total demand, is projected to rise slightly faster, mainly in China, where significant quantities are being fed to pigs.

World rice trade is projected to increase by 2.9% annually to 17.1 million tonnes (in milled terms) by 2000, faster than the 1.9% annual growth achieved in the eighties. By 2000, increased output in some Far Eastern importing countries would enable them to become exporters. In most other regions, demand for rice is projected to continue to exceed domestic production, stimulating a rise in global imports. With export supplies projected to grow at a slightly slower pace than import demand, international rice prices in real terms in 2000 are likely to be moderately above the 1987-89 average. Global rice stocks are projected to rise by 2.5% per annum to 68.5 million tonnes, to represent 17% of projected consumption requirements.

*Wheat*

During the nineties, growth of global wheat production is projected to slow to 1.7% annually, reaching 640 million tonnes in 2000. Production growth in the developed countries is expected to remain almost unchanged at one percent annually; thus, the decline in overall growth rates is expected to be due entirely to slower production growth in the developing countries, especially in Latin America and the Far East. Falling wheat prices, relative to those for coarse grains, are expected to account for some of the slower growth. In the developed countries, reform of the Common Agricultural Policy (CAP) is expected to reduce production in the EC while production is expected to accelerate in the United States and the former USSR.

Global wheat consumption in the nineties is expected to reach 639 million tonnes in 2000. The growth rate of 1.5% per year, slower than in the eighties, reflects in part wheat market maturity at relatively high levels of per caput food consumption in several developing countries, especially in North Africa and the Near East. In the EC, Japan and Australia, per caput consumption is projected to decline. Feed use of wheat is also expected to grow more slowly during the nineties as domestic policies discourage feeding wheat and because of structural adjustments, such as in the former USSR, where livestock numbers are expected to recover only slowly.

World wheat trade is projected to grow by only 3 million tonnes to 117 million tonnes in 2000, which could lead to intensified export competition and declining real prices. Primary causes include an expected reduction in import requirements by China and the former USSR, the world's largest importers. By contrast, high import demand is foreseen for sub-Saharan Africa and Latin America. For Latin America, the NAFTA and MERCO-

SUR trade agreements are expected to generate larger wheat imports by Mexico and Brazil.

## Coarse Grains

Coarse grains production is forecast to grow to 978 million tonnes in 2000, or 1.7% annually, more than double the growth rate of the eighties. Growth above the global average rate is projected for sub-Saharan Africa, Brazil, Algeria, the Islamic Republic of Iran, Saudi Arabia and China. Coarse grain production in the developed countries is also expected to recover from the stagnant levels of the eighties, except in the EC, where CAP reform is likely to constrain production, and the former USSR and eastern Europe, where sectoral reform is expected to inhibit production growth.

In the nineties, global coarse grains demand is projected to continue to increase by 1.4% annually, reaching 976 million tonnes in 2000. Total food and feed uses are expected to increase, although per caput food use is likely to decline. Most consumption growth is foreseen to come from the developing countries, especially in Asia and sub-Saharan Africa, driven by feed demand. Coarse grains demand is projected to remain weak in the developed countries due to slower livestock expansion. Feed demand in the former USSR, where livestock output has dropped dramatically, is projected to recover slowly.

International coarse grain trade is projected to continue to grow sluggishly, increasing by ten% over the entire projection period to reach 120 million tonnes in 2000. Developing country imports are expected to grow by 3.6% annually, half the rate prevailing during the eighties. Strong import growth is expected to continue in Latin America and in the Near East. China is likely to become a larger net importer as more of its domestic coarse grain production is used for its expanding livestock sector. By contrast, imports by the developed countries, especially the former USSR, are projected to decline further.

## Roots and Tubers

World production of roots and tubers in 2000 is projected to increase to 667 million tonnes, or 1.0% annually, the growth being primarily in the developing countries. In the developed countries, production is projected to reverse the declines of the eighties and grow by 0.4% a year to 211 million tonnes in 2000. Production growth, stemming from yield improvements, is projected to be particularly strong for potatoes, sweet potatoes and cassava. Area devoted to roots and tubers is likely to increase modestly in Africa; in eastern Europe and the former USSR area is likely to be reduced.

World demand by 2000 is projected to increase to 667 million tonnes, or one percent annually, faster than during the previous decade. Food demand is projected to expand by 1.4% a year to 378 million tonnes, reflecting primarily growing consumption in the developing countries. Overall demand for feed is projected to decline, mainly due to falling potato and cassava feed use in Europe, particularly in the EC. By contrast, developing countries' demand for feed is expected to expand, but more slowly than in the eighties, and would continue to be concentrated in Brazil (cassava) and China (sweet potatoes).

By 2000, global roots and tubers trade is expected to decline to 29 million tonnes, as EC CAP reform reduces cassava feed imports. Nevertheless, cassava, imported for feed, is projected to account for over half of world roots and tubers trade. Developed countries are expected to account for more than 90% of cassava imports.

*Pulses*

At 1.7% annually, world pulse production in the nineties is expected to expand at a lower rate than in the eighties. Global output in 2000 is projected at 66 million tonnes with most of the expansion occurring in the developing countries where significant improvements in yields are expected. Policies to support pulse production are likely to be strengthened in several developing countries, reflecting growing government concern over periodic supply shortages with their adverse effect on nutritional standards. In the developed countries, production growth is projected to slow appreciably due to falling domestic food and feed demand and slow export market growth.

As food use accelerates and feed use slackens, world demand in the nineties for pulses for food is projected to reach 41 million tonnes in 2000, rising 2.2% annually. For feed use, world demand in 2000 is expected to reach 17 million tonnes, up only 0.4% annually, reflecting greater competition from grains in the EC following CAP reform. During the nineties, per caput consumption is expected to increase, mostly in the developing countries and notably in the Far East.

Pulses trade is expected to reach 7 million tonnes in 2000, growing by 2% per year compared with 10% in the eighties, when import demand for feed pulses by developed countries stimulated trade. Growth rates in the nineties reflect primarily the developing countries' expected rise in demand for food pulses. Exports by both the developing and the developed countries are projected to grow by about 2% per year, compared to 7% and 14% respectively in the eighties. The overall net trade position of the developing countries is projected to deteriorate further.

**Oilseeds, oils and oilmeals**

The world oilseeds, oils and oilmeals economy is projected to continue to expand in the nineties but, at 3% annually, slower than in the past. In 2000, production is expected to reach 108 million tonnes for fats and oils and 71 million tonnes for oilmeals[7], reflecting increases in area and, increasingly, productivity. Developing countries will have the fastest growth rates in both oils and fats and in oilmeals and thus have increased market shares in both sectors in the nineties.

Annual demand growth, at 2.7% for both fats and oils and for oilmeals is relatively dynamic but slower than the 3.8% and 3.7%, respectively, growth rates in the eighties. In 2000, world demand is expected to reach 108 million tonnes for fats and oils and 71 million tonnes for oilmeals. Developing countries are expected to increase their consumption significantly. Increasing substitution of petroleum-based products with more environmentally-friendly oleochemicals in the manufacture of, *inter alia*, detergents as well as in fuel, is expected to stimulate demand.

World trade is projected to reach 37 million tonnes for fats and oils, growing at 2.6% annually, and 32 million tonnes, or 2.1% annually, for oilmeals. The slower growth in trade than in the 80s is expected to be accompanied by intensified competition between developing and developed country exporters and some downward pressure on oil prices compared with the levels of the late eighties. Imports and exports of developing countries are expected to expand substantially, enhancing opportunities for increased trade between developing countries.

**Livestock products**

*Meat*

In 2000, world meat production is projected to reach 216 million tonnes, with growth (2.3% annually), considerably slower than in the eighties. Global poultry and pigmeat production is likely to grow rapidly, reflecting the expansion in intensive animal raising practices particularly near urban areas. The developing countries are anticipated to expand meat production

---

[7] All oilmeal data are given on a 100 percent protein basis.

faster than the developed countries, where expansion is projected to slow further due to modest growth in domestic and international markets, the implementation of policies to reduce surpluses and environmental concerns.

Global meat demand is expected to increase to 216 million tonnes in 2000, only 2.4% annually and slower than in the eighties. Poultry demand, stimulated by relatively low prices, is anticipated to grow most rapidly. Developing countries are expected to account for most of the expansion, particularly in the Far East. However, meat consumption in the developed countries is projected to remain considerably higher than in the developing countries.

Meat trade is projected to reach 17.6 million tonnes in 2000, rising 2.0% annually. Although trade growth would be slower than in the eighties, real prices are projected to increase significantly and export earnings should rise considerably. However, developing countries' net imports are projected to reach 1.4 million tonnes in 2000. Bovine meat exports are expected to grow slowest, reflecting continuing competition from other meats. Developing countries are projected to account for most of the 1.1% annual expansion in pigmeat trade. Sheep and goat meat trade is expected to recover from the depressed levels of the eighties. Developing countries are expected to gain a larger share of the rapidly expanding world poultry meat export market and to considerably reduce their net import requirements.

*Milk*

In 2000, milk production and demand are projected to rise to 565 million tonnes, or 0.6% annually, compared with the 1.5% annual increase of the eighties. Production is projected to grow most where consumption also increases. India is likely to experience the greatest expansion; China and other countries in Asia should also raise milk production rapidly. Lower output is projected for Europe, the former USSR and Canada; however, continued growth is projected in Oceania, the United States and Japan. For the developed countries overall, a slight reduction in consumption is projected.

World trade in dairy products is projected to increase to 60 million tonnes (milk equivalent) in 2000, at a rate much slower than in the eighties. Overall, developing countries are expected to increase their net imports to 23 million tonnes in 2000, up from 20 million tonnes annually in 1987-89. During the nineties, Japan is projected to become the biggest net importer; most requirements will be met by New Zealand and Australia, whose exports are projected to increase significantly. In spite of decreasing production, the European Community is expected to continue to be the world's largest exporter. As milk output in northern hemisphere developed countries in excess of effective demand is expected to decline, real prices are projected to recover from the depressed levels prevailing at the end of the eighties.

**Tropical beverages, sugar, fruit and wine**

*Coffee*

World coffee production is projected to reach 7 million tonnes by 2000, growing at 1.3% annually, half the growth rate of the eighties. In Latin America and the Caribbean annual growth is projected at 1.1% annually, resulting in production of 4.4 million tonnes, still 61% of world production.

World coffee demand is projected to grow by only 1.8% annually, from 5.7 million tonnes in 1987-89 to 7.1 million tonnes by the year 2000, a significant decrease from the growth rate of the eighties. A major factor is market saturation in western Europe and North America. By contrast, demand in the developing countries is projected to grow by 3% annually, to account for 34% of global coffee demand in 2000 mainly due to increased consumption in producing countries.

In 2000 the global coffee export availability and import requirements, rising 1.3% yearly, are projected to be in balance at 5.1 million tonnes, and at real prices around the average 1987-89 levels. It should be noted, however, that producers held 2.5 million tonnes of stocks at the end of the 1991/92 coffee year. Latin America and the Caribbean with a 63% export share in 2000 is expected to remain the leading coffee exporting region; developed countries are expected to absorb 93% of world imports. Firmer prices could result from a new International Coffee Agreement, currently being negotiated, if it constrained coffee output by major producers and regulated world exports and prices.

*Cocoa*

World cocoa production is projected to reach 2.8 million tonnes, growing by 1.8% annually compared with 4.3% annually in the eighties. In Latin America and the Caribbean, production is projected to decrease by 14% over the period to 2000. By contrast, Far Eastern cocoa output is anticipated to increase sharply, based on high-yielding hybrid material and ample land availability. In Africa production is expected to remain stagnant during the nineties, but Côte d'Ivoire is expected to remain the world's leading cocoa producer.

In 2000, world demand for cocoa is projected to grow at 2.3% annually to reach 2.7 million tonnes, of which 2.2 million tonnes will be consumed in the developed countries. Developing countries' cocoa demand is projected to grow by 4.3% annually to reach 504,000 tonnes. Latin America would remain the largest consuming region, accounting for 52% of the cocoa consumed in developing countries.

By 2000 the world cocoa market, mainly in the form of beans, is expected to be roughly in balance. World net export availabilities are expected to reach 2.36 million tonnes, growing by 1.3% annually, slightly faster than projected world import demand. Cocoa import demand in the developed countries is expected to grow 1.1% annually. Western Europe would continue to be the main market. Price volatility, which results mainly from the lag in production response to price changes and is an inherent problem for most tree crops, remains a major concern. However, efforts to negotiate an international cocoa agreement capable of stabilizing trade and prices have not been successful to date, but are being continued.

*Tea*

Projections to 2000 indicate that production of black tea is expected to be relatively buoyant, with total output increasing by 2.6% annually, from 1.9 million tonnes in 1987-1989 to 2.6 million tonnes in 2000. CTC teas are projected to account for 53% of production in 2000. The increase will come from a rise in tea plantings, particularly in India, the largest consumer, and yield improvements. However, Africa, where there is more scope for yield improvement, is expected to register the fastest production growth rates.

Global tea demand, strongly linked to population and income growth, is projected to grow 2.8% annually to reach over 2.5 million tonnes by 2000. The developing countries are expected to account for most of the increase in demand, now estimated at around 4% annually. Over 70% of the demand growth in developing countries is projected to occur within producing countries. Annual demand growth in the developed countries is projected at only 1%.

Black tea net export availabilities, projected to reach 1.3 million tonnes by 2000, with an annual growth of 2.5%, would surpass import demand, particularly for orthodox teas. Africa, with production expanding more rapidly than its still-small domestic markets, will account for the greatest percentage increase in export availabilities. Sri Lanka, China and Indonesia will also have significantly increased black tea export availabilities. Developing countries are likely to account for most of the import growth, their total imports rising by 52% over 1990. Reflecting the slow growth of demand in most developed countries, the volume of imports is projected to increase by only 9%. Overall, an 8% gap between export availabilities and import requirements is projected, which could lead to oversupply, particularly for orthodox teas, and continuing pressure on international prices. These estimates would be affected if low prices led to production curtailments or if agreed higher international quality standards reduced quantities reaching international markets.

*Sugar*

Projected to grow at only 1.6% from 1987-89 to 2000, world sugar production would reach 127 million tonnes by 2000. Thailand's dramatic expansion and India's production growth are expected to slow; nevertheless, Asian production would increase by 3% per year and reach 33% of world production by 2000. Production growth in sugar deficit countries is expected to continue to be strong in the nineties. European Community production is projected to be stable and United States output to increase, reflecting consumption growth and the reaching of the substitution limit for high fructose corn syrup (HFCS).

Annual consumption is projected to reach 128 million tonnes in 2000, growing at 1.5% annually, somewhat slower than in the eighties. By comparison with 1990, however, growth would amount to 1.8% annually[8]. Over 90% of the growth is expected to be in the developing countries, continuing the trend established in the eighties. Asia is expected to account for more than half of the projected increase in world consumption - 12.9 million tonnes out of the total increase of about 21 million tonnes.

World net imports are expected to grow at an annual rate of 0.8%, reversing the downward trend of the previous decade. The large decline in developed countries' imports is projected to be more than offset by increases in developing country imports, whose share of total imports should rise from 57% in 1990 to 65% in 2000. By 2000, total export availabilities, reflecting declines expected in the EC and Brazil, are projected to fall short of import demand by one million tonnes. As a

---

[8] The figures given in this paper differ from those presented in the FAO/ISO joint study 'The World Sugar Market. Prospects for the Nineties', due to different base-periods used.

result, prices could improve, although year-to-year sugar prices have been historically volatile. The trade impact of restructuring eastern Europe and the former USSR (which used to account for 12% of production, 16% of consumption and 20% of imports) is expected to be the dominant issue in 1990's world sugar markets[9].

*Bananas*

World production of bananas for export is projected to grow from 8.1 million tonnes in 1987-89 to 12.4 million tonnes in 2000, or 3.7% annually compared with 1.4% in the eighties. Between 1987-89 and 2000, export availabilities are expected to grow most rapidly in Latin American and the Caribbean. Ecuador, the world's leading banana exporter, is expected to expand its exportable banana production by 5.2% annually. Strong production growth is also expected in the Caribbean, Colombia and Costa Rica. Export availabilities in the Far East are expected to increase by only 0.4% annually and, while growing rapidly, Africa's share of world banana trade is projected to be only 2.5% in 2000.

World import demand for bananas is projected to rise from 7.8 million tonnes in 1987-89 to 10.9 million tonnes in 2000, or 2.8% annually. This increase is the result of import liberalization by both developed and developing countries. EC demand is projected to grow by 3.2% annually, and more rapidly in eastern Europe and the former USSR, which by 2000 projected to have resumed steady economic growth. Banana demand in North America and Japan is projected to expand moderately. Developing country import demand is projected to grow by 7% annually to 2000 and their total share in world markets is expected to increase to 13%.

For 2000, based in part on marketing expectations of exporting countries, global import requirements are projected at 10.9 million tonnes and global export availabilities at 12.4 million tonnes, resulting in a hypothetical 1.5 million tonnes surplus. In practice, however, production expansion programmes would likely be adjusted to bring them into line with market realities.

---

[9] The 'baseline' scenario assumed that sugar production in the former USSR will increase 'moderately' and that income increases will be 'medium'. See Food and Agriculture Organization/International Sugar Organization. 'The World Sugar Market. Prospects for the nineties.' FAO/ESC/M/92/3, Rome 1992

## Citrus Fruit

Based on projections made in 1989, world citrus fruit production is projected to reach 85 million tonnes by 2000, growing by 2.8% annually. Orange production is expected to grow most rapidly, 3.3% annually. Developed countries' production is expected to grow 2.6% annually, mainly in the United States and in some Mediterranean countries. Developing countries' growth is estimated at 3.0% and they would account for 60% of total output in 2000. Productivity improvements and area increases are expected to stimulate production, particularly strongly in the United States, China and Brazil. Tangerine, lemon/lime and grapefruit production is expected to increase more slowly.

World demand for fresh and processed citrus in 2000 is projected to increase to 79 million tonnes, or 2.6% per year. Developed country demand is expected to increase less rapidly, 2.1% annually. Oranges, especially processed, which account for about 73% of total demand, and grapefruit are projected to have the greatest rates of growth. Per caput consumption is expected to remain highest in producing countries, such as Cyprus, Israel and the United States, but further per caput increases are expected for the high-income importing countries of Western Europe.

In 2000, world net trade in fresh and processed citrus appears likely to reach 18.0 million tonnes but to grow at a slower rate than in the eighties, reflecting primarily sharply reduced imports by the United States, which is expected to increase production strongly, and slower import growth in Western Europe. Total net export availabilities would rise at about 2.0% annually, below historic rates, to reach 24 million tonnes. For 2000, citrus fruit export availabilities are therefore expected to exceed import requirements, particularly for oranges and tangerines. Thus, the world citrus economy may have to confront the need to adjust to surplus production, primarily in oranges, and to suffer periodic pressures on prices.

## Wine

By 2000, global wine production is projected to reach 338 million hectolitres, growing at 0.8% annually. Developing countries, mainly in Latin America, are expected to achieve relatively significant output increases; however, developing countries will continue to account for only about 10% of world production. Output is expected to stabilize in the EC as a result of restructuring in the industry and the continuing conversion to quality wine production, reflecting changes in consumption patterns. By contrast, production increases are projected for eastern Europe, North America and Oceania.

Global demand for wine is projected to reach 331 million hectolitres by 2000, a 0.8% annual growth rate. Direct consumption would account for about 80% of total demand. Developed country consumption is projected to increase by 0.75% annually due to slackening per caput consumption growth in non-traditional markets and lower or stagnant consumption in traditional Western European markets. Latin America and the Caribbean, the major developing country wine consuming region, is expected to increase consumption to raise total developing country consumption by almost 2% annually. Future consumption will be affected by changing social attitudes toward alcohol consumption, health concerns and changing life-styles.

World net import requirements are projected to reach 42 million hectolitres by 2000, growing by 1.6% annually. Western Europe and, to a lesser extent, North America are expected to absorb most of the increase. Global export availabilities, mainly in the developed countries, are projected to expand to over 49 million hectolitres; the very large surplus projected would be concentrated in lower quality table wines, which thus face depressed trade and price prospects. By contrast, quality wines will continue to experience rising demand and favourable prices to the year 2000.

**Agricultural raw materials**

*Cotton*

By 2000, world cotton production is projected to increase to 24.7 million tonnes, or 2.9% annually. Production expansion, mostly as a result of yield improvements, is expected to be concentrated in the developing countries, especially in Asia. However, virtually all cotton producing countries, developing and developed, are expected to increase their production during the nineties, although prospects in the former USSR are uncertain.

Cotton consumption, buoyed by increasing world population and income, is projected to continue its strong growth (2.5% annually) to reach over 24 million tonnes in 2000. Globally, final cotton consumption is projected to expand to almost 4 kilograms per caput in 2000, largely due to improved consumer income. Fibre consumption in Asia is expected to grow strongly. However, cotton is expected to lose market share to other fibres, especially synthetics, in most countries. The projections show strong growth in mill consumption continuing to 2000 in the Far East and, to a lesser extent, in other developing regions; in the developed countries, little growth in mill consumption is expected in the nineties.

Raw cotton trade in 2000 is projected to reach 7.2 million tonnes, growing at 3.2% annually. Exports from Africa, the United States and Australia are expected to expand further while those from the former USSR are expected to increase as production recovers during the second half of the decade. Developing countries, especially Far Eastern textile exporters, are expected to increase exports of cotton manufactures to the developed countries and, in turn, increase imports of cotton fibre. By contrast, European imports are projected to expand little, reflecting slow growth in end-use demand and only limited increases in processing. In other developed countries, imports of cotton manufactures are expected to increase. Real prices for raw cotton are expected to continue to decline slowly.

*Jute, kenaf and allied fibres*

Although weather conditions can lead to wide fluctuations, world production of jute[10] is projected to reach to 3.6 million tonnes in 2000, up 1.2% annually from the 1987-89 average but exactly the same as in 1990. Higher yields resulting from improved agronomic techniques and inputs will be offset by expected declines in the total area devoted to jute cultivation. Among the major producing countries, only India's output would expand, reflecting primarily the strength of the domestic market for packaging materials. Elsewhere, production is expected to decline as farmers switch to more remunerative crops.

Jute consumption is projected at 3.5 million tonnes in the year 2000 compared to the average of 3.7 million tonnes in 1985-90, reflecting a continuing shift to synthetics and the extension of bulk handling facilities. Producing countries will become proportionally even greater consuming countries. In India, demand should continue to rise, despite inroads by domestically-produced synthetics, in part because of administrative regulations mandating the use of jute in certain applications. Synthetic sacking capacity expansion in China is expected to reduce growth in apparent consumption there.

World trade in jute fibre and products could amount to about 1 million tonnes in 2000, down by 2.7% annually. The decline is expected to be

---

[10] 'Jute' refers to true jute, kenaf, mesta and allied fibres.

particularly marked for raw jute, as importing countries opt increasingly for imported products or install production equipment for synthetics. The trend of real prices is expected to continue to decline, although year to year prices will continue to be strongly influenced by annual crop fluctuations. Exports of higher valued jute products should account for an increasing proportion of world jute trade.

### Hard Fibres

Sisal production is projected to fall to 370,000 tonnes in 2000, declining by 0.7% annually. Contracting production by the major producers, i.e. Brazil, Mexico and Africa, reflecting weakening demand, may be partially offset by increases in China. Abaca output should expand to 82,000 tonnes, due partly to productivity increases in the Philippines. Based on unlimited supplies of raw material, coir production is projected to grow to 395,000 tonnes, an increase of 2% annually. India, the major consumer, is projected to expand processing to meet domestic consumption growth; however, white fibre output is likely to be constrained for environmental reasons in favour of mechanically extracted brown fibres.

Demand for sisal and henequen, used largely for agricultural twines, is projected to continue to decline, by 0.7% annually in the nineties, due to competition from synthetics and harvesting techniques using less or no twine, particularly in the United States and Europe. Economic recovery in eastern Europe and the former USSR is likely to reverse recent declines in sisal and henequen consumption there. A technological breakthrough in the use of sisal as reinforcement for recycled paper pulp could have a considerable demand impact. In the nineties, abaca consumption is projected to increase by 1.1% annually, although cordage use will continue to decline, and coir consumption is expected to expand by 2% annually.

In the absence of successful large-scale promotion of sisal harvest twine or a major expansion of sisal use in papermaking, sisal exports are projected to contract to 215,000 tonnes in 2000. The decline, 1.3% annually, would be, however, slower than the 4.7% annual decline during the eighties. By contrast, abaca exports, primarily from the Philippines, are expected to increase to 69,000 tonnes, or one percent annually, to meet pulp demand in developed countries. Global coir exports are projected to increase to 112,000 tonnes, or 0.3% annually, although exports to the developed countries are expected to decline. Yarn and products are likely to constitute an increasing proportion of shipments.

*Hides and Skins*

By 2000, production of hides and skins, produced primarily as by-products from livestock industries, should reach 6.2 million tonnes, growing at 0.7% annually. Output of cattle hides and calfskins will be influenced by slower growth of bovine slaughtering, particularly in the developed countries, as result of increased competition from poultry and pigmeat. Sheep and goatskin production is expected to reflect a recovery in the wool sector but, with 1.6% annual growth, is projected to expand more slowly than in the eighties.

Influenced by growing income and population, world demand should reach 6.2 million tonnes, or 0.8% annually, balancing production. However, consumption is likely to be constrained by the supply available, which could lead to some firming of prices over the period. The proportion of leather used in footwear may decline because of the increased demand for leather in other products, such as upholstery. Demand for leather and leather goods in developing countries, particularly in the Far East, is projected to expand at a higher rate than in developed countries.

World trade in hides and skins is projected to reflect the strong growth in tanning and manufacturing in some developing countries, notably India, Republic of Korea, China (Province of Taiwan) and Bangladesh, and the decline in developed countries' leather industries. This trend, and expanded tanning capabilities in China and other low-cost Asian countries, is expected to generate increased import requirements for high quality cattle hides. Developing countries' exports of leather products, primarily to developed country markets, are also projected to expand. Developing countries overall would remain net exporters of sheep and goat skins, but the rate of expansion would decline because of increased domestic processing.

## 4 CONCLUSIONS

The slowdown in world trade of the agricultural commodities covered in these projections to the year 2000 is likely to cause some significant adjustment problems for the exporting countries. Firstly, even during the eighties when the growth of agricultural trade was stronger it was not enough to stall the rise in protectionism and the fierce competition for markets that took place. There are some signs of the intention to reverse the protectionist trend in world agricultural markets through the Uruguay Round as well as through autonomous moves towards liberalization by many developing countries and formerly centrally planned economies in Eastern Europe and the former USSR. However, the trading system could be put under considerable strain by the slow growth of world markets for the main agricultural commodities, particularly cereals. It is much easier to liberalize when markets are expanding and when competition for market shares is less aggressive. If these prospects materialize, therefore, the Committee will need to keep the development of export competition under close scrutiny and be vigilant against new forms of protectionism that could be engendered in response to a rather difficult market situation. Needless to say a widespread recourse to such approaches could cause agricultural commodity prices to be weaker than currently foreseen.

Secondly, at the same time that agricultural commodity markets are likely to be growing slowly, the net agricultural trade situation of the developing countries is projected to deteriorate significantly. If these projections materialize, the developing countries could turn from net exporters of the main primary agricultural commodities at present to net importers by the year 2000. While to some extent this turnaround reflects an increased processing of certain agricultural raw materials, the overall outcome would be a blow to those developing countries who continue to rely heavily on agricultural commodity exports for an important sources of export earnings to pay for their other vitally needed imports. This underlines the vital importance of a successful Uruguay Round that would facilitate an expansion in their export earnings. Moreover, this finding together with the fact that nearly one-half of the export earnings from agriculture are now accounted for by non-traditional, processed or semi-processed agricultural commodities, points to the importance to the developing countries of the expansion in the newer, more dynamic agricultural export markets, including horticulture, processed products and certain feedstuffs.

Thirdly, the net cereal import gap of the developing countries is projected to grow from 89 million tonnes in 1987-89 to 123 million tonnes by the year 2000. At the same time, the gross cereal imports of the developing countries are projected to rise to 161 million tonnes from 119 million tonnes over the same period. This is another steep increase that will put an additional burden on the developing countries. The danger is that even at constant prices this will lead to a large rise in their import bill. Moreover, the national level of food security of these countries is more vulnerable to the instability of the world food market and to possible increases in prices stemming from the move to a more liberalized trading system. It will be important for the international community to make sure that the developing countries, especially the low-income, food-deficit countries, are in a position to import these volumes, otherwise the hoped for, and indeed projected, rise in per caput consumption and improved nutrition would be put in jeopardy.

# ANNEX I

*Annex Table 1a:* World production by major commodity group

| Commodity or commodity group | 1977–79 average | 1987–89 average | 1990 actual | 2000 projected | Growth rates 1978*–1988* | Growth rates 1988*–2000 |
|---|---|---|---|---|---|---|
| | ······ million metric tons ······ | | | | percent per year | |
| Cereals | 1413.2 | 1640.9 | 1793.2 | 2027.2 | 1.5 | 1.8 |
| Wheat | 422.0 | 521.2 | 598.5 | 640.1 | 2.1 | 1.7 |
| Rice, milled | 250.5 | 324.9 | 349.9 | 409.4 | 2.6 | 1.9 |
| Coarse grains | 740.7 | 794.8 | 844.8 | 977.7 | 0.7 | 1.7 |
| Maize | 395.5 | 442.2 | 478.0 | 583.8 | 1.1 | 2.3 |
| Millet and sorghum | 92.9 | 91.6 | 85.4 | 112.6 | −0.1 | 1.7 |
| Other coarse grains n.e.s. | 252.3 | 261.0 | 281.4 | 281.3 | 0.3 | 0.6 |
| Roots and tubers | 585.8 | 590.1 | 599.5 | 666.5 | 0.1 | 1.0 |
| Pulses | 42.5 | 54.2 | 57.9 | 66.0 | 2.5 | 1.7 |

*Notes:*  1978* signifies 1977 to 1979 average, 1988* signifies 1987 to 1989 average.

*Annex Table 1b:* World production by major commodity group

| Commodity or commodity group | 1977–79 average | 1987–89 average | 1990 actual | 2000 projected | Growth rates 1978*–1988* 1988*–2000 | |
|---|---|---|---|---|---|---|
| | ......... million metric tons ......... | | | | ......... percent per year ......... | |
| Meat | 123.6 | 164.4 | 172.4 | 216.4 | 2.9 | 2.3 |
| Bovine meat | 47.5 | 52.4 | 53.7 | 60.9 | 1.0 | 1.3 |
| Sheepmeat and goatmeat | 7.1 | 9.0 | 9.5 | 11.6 | 2.4 | 2.1 |
| Pigmeat | 45.9 | 66.1 | 69.6 | 85.9 | 3.7 | 2.2 |
| Poultry meat | 23.1 | 36.9 | 39.6 | 58.0 | 4.8 | 3.8 |
| Whole milk | 449.5 | 523.1 | 530.5 | 565.3 | 1.5 | 0.6 |
| Fats and oils | 53.6 | 76.5 | 81.5 | 107.7 | 3.6 | 2.9 |
| Oilmeal protein | 35.3 | 50.2 | 53.2 | 71.3 | 3.6 | 3.0 |
| Sugar | 88.8 | 105.5 | 108.4 | 127.3 | 1.7 | 1.6 |
| Bananas 1/ | 7.0 | 8.1 | 9.4 | 12.4 | 1.4 | 3.7 |
| Citrus fruit | 49.3 | 61.0 | 74.7 | 85.0 | 2.2 | 2.8 |

*Notes:* 1978* signifies 1977 to 1979 average, 1988* signifies 1987 to 1989 average.
 1 Production for export.

*Annex Table 1c:* World production by major commodity group

| Commodity or commodity group | 1977–79 average | 1987–89 average | 1990 actual | 2000 projected | Growth rates 1978*–1988* | 1988*–2000 |
|---|---|---|---|---|---|---|
| | ........ million metric tons ........ | | | | ........ percent per year ........ | |
| Wine 2/ | 321.7 3/ | 300.9 4/ | 289.4 | 338.1 | –0.7 5/ | 0.8 5/ |
| Coffee | 4.7 | 6.1 | 6.3 | 7.2 | 2.6 | 1.3 |
| Cocoa | 1.5 | 2.2 | 2.4 | 2.8 | 4.3 | 1.8 |
| Tea 6/ | 1.8 | 1.9 | 1.9 | 2.6 | 0.5 | 2.6 |
| Cotton, raw | 13.6 | 17.4 | 20.8 | 24.7 | 2.5 | 2.9 |
| Jute, kenaf and allied fibres | 3.7 | 3.1 | 3.6 | 3.6 | –1.7 | 1.2 |
| Hard fibres | 0.9 | 0.8 | 0.8 | 0.8 | –0.9 | 0.6 |
| Sisal and henequen | 0.5 | 0.4 | 0.4 | 0.4 | –2.0 | –0.7 |
| Abaca | 0.1 | 0.1 | 0.1 | 0.1 | –2.4 | 1.1 |
| Coir | 0.3 | 0.3 | 0.3 | 0.4 | 1.2 | 2.0 |
| Hides and skins | 5.2 | 5.7 | 6.2 | 6.2 | 0.9 | 0.7 |
| Bovine | 4.8 | 5.2 | 5.6 | 5.6 | 0.8 | 0.6 |
| Sheep and goat | 0.4 | 0.5 | 0.6 | 0.6 | 2.3 | 1.6 |

*Notes:*   1978* signifies 1977 to 1979 average, 1988* signifies 1987 to 1989 average.

1 Production for export.    4 1985-87 average.
2 Million hectolitres.    5 between periods shown.
3 1975-77 average.    6 black tea

*Annex Table 2a:* World total demand by major commodity groups

| Commodity or commodity group | 1977–79 average | 1987–89 average | 2000 projected | Growth rates 1978*–1988* | 1988*–2000 |
|---|---|---|---|---|---|
| | ·········· million metric tons ·············· | | | ······ percent per year ········ | |
| Cereals | 1384.5 | 1684.6 | 2022.6 | 2.0 | 1.5 |
| Wheat | 419.4 | 536.5 | 638.9 | 2.5 | 1.5 |
| Rice, milled | 248.0 | 321.7 | 407.9 | 2.6 | 2.0 |
| Coarse grains | 717.1 | 826.4 | 975.8 | 1.4 | 1.4 |
| Maize | 377.9 | 467.2 | 582.2 | 2.1 | 1.9 |
| Millet and sorghum | 90.8 | 96.1 | 112.7 | 0.6 | 1.3 |
| Other coarse grains n.e.s. | 248.4 | 263.1 | 280.9 | 0.6 | 0.5 |
| Roots and tubers | 584.8 | 595.0 | 667.1 | 0.2 | 1.0 |
| Pulses | 42.7 | 54.4 | 66.0 | 2.5 | 1.6 |

*Notes:*   1978* signifies 1977 to 1979 average, 1988* signifies 1987 to 1989 average.

*Annex Table 2b:* World total demand by major commodity groups

| Commodity or commodity group | 1977–79 average | 1987–89 average | 2000 projected | Growth rates 1978*–1988* | 1988*–2000 |
|---|---|---|---|---|---|
| | ......... million metric tons ......... | | | ...... percent per year ...... | |
| Meat | 123.1 | 163.5 | 216.4 | 2.9 | 2.4 |
| Bovine meat | 47.0 | 52.0 | 60.9 | 1.0 | 1.3 |
| Sheepmeat and goatmeat | 7.0 | 9.0 | 11.6 | 2.5 | 2.1 |
| Pigmeat | 46.0 | 65.6 | 85.9 | 3.6 | 2.3 |
| Poultry meat | 23.1 | 36.9 | 58.0 | 4.8 | 3.8 |
| Whole milk | 449.0 | 528.6 | 565.4 | 1.6 | 0.6 |
| Fats and oils | 53.4 | 77.7 | 107.5 | 3.8 | 2.7 |
| Oilmeal protein | 35.8 | 51.6 | 71.2 | 3.7 | 2.7 |
| Sugar | 84.6 | 106.8 | 128.3 | 2.4 | 1.5 |
| Bananas 1/ | 6.9 | 8.3 | 11.2 | 1.9 | 2.5 |
| Citrus fruit | 47.1 | 58.0 | 79.3 | 2.1 | 2.6 |

*Notes:* 1978* signifies 1977 to 1979 average, 1988* signifies 1987 to 1989 average.
1 Production for export.

*Annex Table 2c:* World total demand by major commodity groups

| Commodity or commodity group | 1977–79 average | 1987–89 average | 2000 projected | Growth rates 1978*–1988* | 1988*–2000 |
|---|---|---|---|---|---|
| | ..... million metric tons ..... | | | ..... percent per year ..... | |
| Wine 2/ | 318.9 3/ | 294.7 4/ | 331.3 | −0.8 5/ | 0.8 5/ |
| Coffee | 4.5 | 5.7 | 7.1 | 2.3 | 1.8 |
| Cocoa | 1.4 | 2.1 | 2.7 | 3.8 | 2.3 |
| Tea 6/ | 1.3 | 1.8 | 2.5 | 3.3 | 2.8 |
| Cotton, raw | 13.7 | 18.3 | 24.7 | 3.0 | 2.5 |
| Jute, kenaf and allied fibres | 3.3 | 3.4 | 3.5 | 0.2 | 0.4 |
| Hard fibres | 0.9 | 0.8 | 0.8 | −0.9 | 0.6 |
| Sisal and henequen | 0.5 | 0.4 | 0.4 | −2.0 | −0.7 |
| Abaca | 0.1 | 0.1 | 0.1 | −2.4 | 1.1 |
| Coir | 0.3 | 0.3 | 0.4 | 1.2 | 2.0 |
| Hides and skins | 4.7 | 5.6 | 6.2 | 1.8 | 0.8 |
| Bovine | 4.3 | 5.1 | 5.6 | 1.7 | 0.7 |
| Sheep and goat | 0.4 | 0.5 | 0.6 | 2.3 | 1.6 |

*Notes:*  1978* signifies 1977 to 1979 average, 1988* signifies 1987 to 1989 average.
1 Production for export.
2 Million hectolitres.
3 1975-77 average.
4 1985-87 average.
5 between periods shown.
6 black tea

*Annex Table 3a:* World international trade, actual and projected

| Commodity or commodity group | 1977-79 average | 1987-89 average | 2000 projected | Growth Rates 1978*-1988* | Growth Rates 1988*-2000 |
|---|---|---|---|---|---|
| | ........... million metric tons ........... | | | per cent per year | |
| Cereals | 187.7 | 235.6 | 254.3 | 2.3 | 0.6 |
| Wheat | 79.4 | 114.3 | 117.4 | 3.7 | 0.2 |
| Rice, milled | 10.0 | 12.1 | 17.1 | 1.9 | 2.9 |
| Coarse grains | 98.3 | 109.2 | 119.8 | 1.1 | 0.8 |
| Maize | 67.1 | 71.1 | 76.3 | 0.6 | 0.6 |
| Millet and sorghum | 10.8 | 9.5 | 11.4 | -1.3 | 1.5 |
| Other coarse grains n.e.s. | 20.4 | 28.6 | 32.1 | 3.4 | 1.0 |
| Roots and tubers | 24.7 | 42.3 | 29.5 | 5.5 | -3.0 |
| Pulses | 2.2 | 5.6 | 7.2 | 10.0 | 2.1 |

*Notes:*     1978* signifies 1977 to 1979 average, 1988* signifies 1987 to 1989 average.

*Annex Table 3b:* World international trade, actual and projected

| Commodity or commodity group | 1977–79 average | 1987–89 average | 2000 projected | Growth Rates 1978*–1988* | Growth Rates 1988*–2000 |
|---|---|---|---|---|---|
| | ......... million metric tons ............ | | | per cent per year | |
| Meat | 9.9 | 13.9 | 17.6 | 3.5 | 2.0 |
| Bovine meat | 4.8 | 6.0 | 7.3 | 2.1 | 1.7 |
| Sheepmeat and goatmeat | 0.9 | 1.1 | 1.5 | 2.0 | 2.5 |
| Pigmeat | 2.9 | 4.5 | 5.1 | 4.3 | 1.1 |
| Poultry meat | 1.2 | 2.4 | 3.7 | 6.9 | 3.8 |
| Whole milk | 43.5 | 56.3 | 60.3 | 2.6 | 0.6 |
| Fats and oils | 18.2 | 26.8 | 36.5 | 4.0 | 2.6 |
| Oilmeal protein | 17.5 | 24.9 | 32.1 | 3.6 | 2.1 |
| Sugar 1/ | 25.8 | 23.1 | 25.5 | –1.1 | 0.8 |
| Bananas | 6.9 | 7.8 | 10.9 | 1.3 | 2.8 |
| Citrus fruit 1/ | 11.7 | 16.3 | 18.0 | 3.4 | 0.8 |

*Notes:* 1978* signifies 1977 to 1979 average, 1988* signifies 1987 to 1989 average.
    1 Net imports.

*Annex Table 3c:* World international trade, actual and projected

| Commodity or commodity group | 1977–79 average | 1987–89 average | 2000 projected | Growth Rates | |
|---|---|---|---|---|---|
| | | | | 1978*–1988* | 1988*–2000 |
| | ......... million metric tons ......... | | | per cent per year | |
| Wine 1/ 2/ | 34.2 | 33.7 | 41.8 | -0.1 | 1.6 |
| Coffee | 3.4 | 4.3 | 5.0 | 2.5 | 1.3 |
| Cocoa | 1.3 | 2.0 | 2.3 | 4.5 | 1.1 |
| Tea 3/ | 0.9 | 1.0 | 1.2 | 1.1 | 1.5 |
| Cotton, raw | 4.6 | 5.4 | 7.2 | 1.8 | 2.4 |
| Jute, kenaf and allied fibres | 1.6 | 1.3 | 1.0 | -2.2 | -2.7 |
| Hard fibres | 0.6 | 0.4 | 0.4 | -3.9 | -0.5 |
| Sisal and henequen | 0.4 | 0.3 | 0.2 | -4.7 | -1.3 |
| Abaca | 0.1 | 0.1 | 0.1 | -1.2 | 1.0 |
| Coir | 0.1 | 0.1 | 0.1 | -3.0 | 0.3 |
| Hides and skins | 3.4 | 5.2 | 7.0 | 4.4 | 2.5 |
| Bovine | 3.1 | 4.9 | 6.5 | 4.5 | 2.5 |
| Sheep and goat | 0.3 | 0.4 | 0.5 | 2.2 | 3.0 |

*Notes:*     1978* signifies 1977 to 1979 average, 1988* signifies 1987 to 1989 average.
             1 Net imports.     2 Million hectolitres.     3 black tea.

Annex Table 4a: Developing countries: international trade, actual and projected

| Commodity or commodity group | Gross imports | | | Gross exports | | | Net trade | | |
|---|---|---|---|---|---|---|---|---|---|
| | 1977–79 average | 1987–89 average | 2000 projected | 1977–79 average | 1987–89 average | 2000 projected | 1977–79 average | 1987–89 average | 2000 projected |
| | million metric tons | | | | | | | | |
| Cereals | 74.4 | 119.2 | 161.4 | 28.4 | 30.4 | 38.7 | 46.0 | 88.8 | 122.7 |
| Wheat | 45.6 | 68.4 | 84.9 | 6.2 | 8.4 | 9.4 | 39.4 | 60.0 | 75.5 |
| Rice, milled | 8.0 | 9.1 | 13.3 | 7.2 | 9.0 | 13.2 | 0.8 | 0.1 | 0.1 |
| Coarse grains | 20.8 | 41.7 | 63.2 | 15.0 | 13.0 | 16.1 | 5.8 | 28.7 | 47.1 |
| Maize | 13.9 | 26.6 | 40.3 | 9.2 | 9.8 | 11.0 | 4.7 | 16.8 | 29.3 |
| Millet and sorghum | 2.4 | 3.6 | 5.9 | 4.8 | 2.0 | 3.2 | −2.4 | 1.6 | 2.7 |
| Other coarse grains n.e.s. | 4.5 | 11.5 | 17.0 | 1.0 | 1.2 | 1.9 | 3.5 | 10.3 | 15.1 |
| Roots and tubers | 1.4 | 5.3 | 4.6 | 15.7 | 28.8 | 16.7 | −14.2 | −23.6 | −12.2 |
| Pulses | 0.9 | 2.3 | 3.9 | 1.2 | 2.3 | 2.7 | −0.3 | 0.0 | 1.2 |
| Meat | 2.1 | 3.4 | 5.8 | 2.1 | 2.8 | 4.4 | 0.0 | 0.6 | 1.4 |
| Bovine meat | 0.9 | 1.3 | 2.2 | 1.6 | 1.5 | 1.6 | −0.7 | −0.2 | 0.6 |
| Sheepmeat and goatmeat | 0.3 | 0.5 | 0.8 | 0.1 | 0.2 | 0.2 | 0.2 | 0.3 | 0.6 |
| Pigmeat | 0.3 | 0.5 | 1.6 | 0.3 | 0.6 | 1.5 | 0.0 | −0.1 | 0.1 |
| Poultry meat | 0.6 | 1.1 | 1.2 | 0.1 | 0.5 | 1.1 | 0.5 | 0.6 | 0.1 |
| Whole milk | 15.3 | 20.8 | 25.9 | 0.6 | 1.2 | 2.8 | 14.7 | 19.6 | 23.1 |
| Fats and oils | 6.8 | 12.8 | 20.0 | 7.0 | 13.1 | 21.7 | −0.2 | −0.3 | −1.7 |
| Oilmeal protein | 2.0 | 5.5 | 11.6 | 6.4 | 13.8 | 21.5 | −4.4 | −8.3 | −9.9 |

*Annex Table 4b:* Developing countries: international trade, actual and projected

| Commodity or commodity group | Gross imports | | | Gross exports | | | Net trade | | |
|---|---|---|---|---|---|---|---|---|---|
| | 1977–79 average | 1987–89 average | 2000 projected | 1977–79 average | 1987–89 average | 2000 projected | 1977–79 average | 1987–89 average | 2000 projected |
| | million metric tons | | | | | | | | |
| Sugar 1/ | 8.9 | 13.1 | 18.2 | 18.8 | 17.2 | 19.2 | −9.9 | −4.1 | −1.0 |
| Bananas | 0.6 | 0.6 | 1.4 | 6.3 | 7.3 | 11.5 | −5.7 | −6.7 | −10.1 |
| Citrus fruit 1/ | 1.3 | 0.9 | 1.7 | 6.4 | 12.6 | 15.1 | −5.1 | −11.8 | −13.4 |
| Wine 1/2/ | 2.4 | 2.3 | 4.2 | 5.9 | 1.9 | 1.8 | −3.5 | 0.4 | 2.4 |
| Coffee | 0.2 | 0.3 | 0.4 | 3.4 | 4.3 | 5.1 | −3.1 | −4.1 | −4.7 |
| Cocoa | 0.1 | 0.1 | 0.1 | 1.3 | 2.0 | 2.4 | −1.2 | −1.9 | −2.3 |
| Tea 3/ | 0.3 | 0.4 | 0.6 | 0.7 | 0.9 | 1.3 | −0.4 | −0.5 | −0.7 |
| Cotton, raw | 1.9 | 2.6 | 4.5 | 2.0 | 2.6 | 2.9 | −0.1 | 0.0 | 1.5 |
| Jute, kenaf and allied fibres | 0.6 | 0.6 | 0.5 | 1.6 | 1.4 | 1.0 | −1.0 | −0.8 | −0.5 |
| Hard fibres | 0.1 | 0.1 | 0.0 | 0.6 | 0.4 | 0.4 | −0.6 | −0.4 | −0.4 |
| Sisal and henequen | 0.1 | 0.0 | 0.0 | 0.4 | 0.3 | 0.2 | −0.4 | −0.2 | −0.2 |
| Abaca | 0.0 | 0.0 | 0.0 | 0.1 | 0.1 | 0.1 | −0.1 | −0.1 | −0.1 |
| Coir | 0.0 | 0.0 | 0.0 | 0.1 | 0.1 | 0.1 | −0.1 | −0.1 | −0.1 |
| Hides and skins | 0.7 | 1.7 | 2.2 | 0.8 | 1.9 | 2.8 | −0.1 | −0.2 | −0.6 |
| Bovine | 0.7 | 1.6 | 2.1 | 0.7 | 1.7 | 2.7 | − | −0.1 | −0.6 |
| Sheep and goat | − | 0.1 | 0.1 | 0.1 | 0.2 | 0.1 | −0.1 | −0.1 | 0.0 |

*Notes:*    1 Net imports.         2 Million hectolitres.         3 black tea.

# ANNEX II

## *Methodology and main assumptions*

FAO's last commodity projections were made in 1985, covering the period to 1990. The current projections were carried out mainly in 1992 and early 1993.

### Demographic and macroeconomic assumptions

The 'baseline' scenario used United Nations Population Division's 1990 'medium variant' for country population growth. United Nations data was also used for estimating the level and growth of urban and rural population, for projecting the impact of urbanization on changing consumption patterns, especially in developing countries. The Gross Domestic Product (GDP) growth assumptions for the nineties were based mainly on World Bank long-term economic forecasts supplemented where necessary with data from other sources.

### Commodity and country coverage

Like the 1985 projections, the current work has been undertaken utilizing the FAO's World Food Model, which covers simultaneously the cereal/livestock/fats and oil complex. Commodities covered outside the World Food Model include roots and tubers, pulses, sugar, tropical beverages, fruit, wine and agricultural raw materials.

The projections, whether or not using the World Food Model, have a worldwide coverage. The World Food Model framework provides projections for 137 individual countries and for 10 country aggregates grouping all others, generally small countries and territories. Aggregate data for EC relates to the 12 member States, including the new German Länder. The Republics of the former USSR are treated as a group for lack of disaggregated data.

### The framework of the World Food Model

The World Food Model is interactive (i.e., it allows for the simultaneous determination of commodity supply, demand, trade, stock levels and prices) and dynamic (i.e., it allows for the outcome of one year or a sequence of years to influence the outcome of future years). Fundamentally it is a price equilibrium model, which means that commodity price is determined at the level where world supply is equal to world demand and all variables are simultaneously determined.

The model consists of a set of demand, supply and stock equations for each commodity and for each country with the levels of production and demand determined by factors including population and income growth rates, income elasticities, own and cross-price demand and supply elasticities, demand and supply shift variables and various assumptions about economic trends and policies. However, price assumes a central role in the model, as price enters in the determination of all supply and demand equations for all countries and all commodities. Domestic prices are linked to world prices which in turn are determined by world demand and supply. In equilibrium, the difference between supply and demand for each country or country group represents net trade, while the world total of such differences is by definition equal to zero. The model incorporates resource constraints and provides for changes in fertilizer prices, crop conditions and livestock and crop farming technologies, as well as expert judgement.

Basic foodstuffs production scenarios largely assumed continuation of trends in areas, livestock numbers and crop and animal yields, as modified by the interaction of prices generated through a market clearing mechanism and checked for technical feasibility. It assumes, with some exceptions, a continuation of current national and international policies affecting production, consumption and trade. It also assumes 'normal weather'; that is, the absence of any particular climatic condition, either favourable or unfavourable, which could affect yield or harvested area.

Elasticities and parameters used in the equations are mainly from estimates made by FAO, supplemented by the elasticity database of the United States Department of Agriculture's SWOPSIM model and the Organisation for Economic Cooperation and Development's MTM model. All parameters are held constant during the projection period.

The projections for the commodities not included in the World Food Model, namely some staple foods (pulses, roots and tubers), sugar, the tropical beverages, fruits, wine and the agricultural raw materials were made using methodologies, ranging from detailed econometric commodity models, for sugar and cotton, to demand and supply projections based on past trends supplemented by expert judgements of commodity specialists. In a number of cases, the projections were prepared jointly or in cooperation with international commodity bodies, universities and other international organizations.

# BRIEFING NOTE ON FISHERY COMMODITIES[1]

## 1 STRATEGY

The FAO Conference on Fisheries Management and Development held in 1984 adopted a strategy document which in relation to international trade in fish and fishery products reads as follows:

> *"Training programmes must provide for instruction in the best fishing techniques for catching existing species and for the distribution of fishing charts indicating the location of fishing grounds. Top priority in training should be accorded to fishing communities. Training should be adjusted to the renewal of the fleet and to the characteristics of the new types of vessels, so as to improve both yields and safety and ensure a rational utilization of the exclusive economic zones.*
>
> *The developing countries should plan their aquaculture bearing in mind their national potential and opportunities for the exchange of programmes, knowledge, experience, technical assistance and training, through the mechanisms of regional cooperation."*

## 2 CURRENT SITUATION

### World fish production

In 1991, world fish production declined for the second consecutive year to 97 million tonnes. Estimates for 1992, however, indicated a reversal of the downward trend and forecast a return to the 1990 level of 98 million tonnes. The reasons behind the 1991 decline include the problems encountered by the former USSR and the effect of 'El Niño'. China is now the top producer with some 13 million tonnes. The importance of aquaculture continues to expand, but the growth rates of both shrimp and salmon culture seem to be levelling off.

---

[1] Presented by the Sub-Committee on Fish Trade, FAO.

*Table 1a:*   World fish production and trade

|  |  | 1986 | 1987 | 1988 | 1989 | 1990 | 1991 | 1992 |
|---|---|---|---|---|---|---|---|---|
| World fish production | million t | 92.8 | 94.4 | 99.0 | 100.2 | 97.4 | 96.9 | 96.9 |
| Growth over previous year | % | | 1.7 | 4.7 | 1.2 | -2.8 | -0.5 | 0 |
| Exports of fishery products | '000 million US$ | 22.9 | 27.9 | 31.8 | 32.2 | 35.8 | 39.4 | |
| Growth over previous year | % | | 21.8 | 13.9 | 1.2 | 11.2 | 10.1 | |
| Developed countries | '000 million US$ | 12.6 | 15.3 | 17.3 | 17.3 | 20.2 | 22.4 | |
| Growth over previous year | % | | 21.8 | 12.8 | 0.5 | 16.3 | 11.3 | |
| Developing countries | '000 million US$ | 10.4 | 12.6 | 14.5 | 14.8 | 15.6 | 16.9 | |
| Growth over previous year | % | | 21.8 | 15.3 | 2.1 | 5.3 | 8.5 | |

*Table 1b:* World fish production and trade

| | | 1986 | 1987 | 1988 | 1989 | 1990 | 1991 |
|---|---|---|---|---|---|---|---|
| Imports of fishery products | '000 million US$ | 24.3 | 30.5 | 35.3 | 36.0 | 39.6 | 43.3 |
| Growth over previous year | % | | 25.7 | 15.7 | 2.1 | 9.8 | 9.5 |
| Developed countries | '000 million US$ | 21.2 | 26.8 | 30.6 | 31.0 | 34.4 | 37.4 |
| Growth over previous year | % | | 26.5 | 14.2 | 1.2 | 11.0 | 8.6 |
| Developing countries | '000 million US$ | 3.1 | 3.7 | 4.7 | 5.0 | 5.2 | 6.0 |
| Growth over previous year | % | | 20.1 | 26.8 | 7.7 | 2.6 | 15.4 |
| Developing countries' surplus exports over imports | '000 million US$ | 7.3 | 8.9 | 9.8 | 9.8 | 10.4 | 10.9 |
| Growth over previous year | % | | 21.9 | 10.1 | 0 | 6.1 | 4.8 |
| Developed countries' net imports | '000 million US$ | 8.6 | 11.5 | 13.4 | 13.7 | 14.2 | 15.0 |
| Growth over previous year | % | | 33.7 | 16.5 | 2.2 | 3.6 | 5.6 |

## World fish trade[2]

*Exports*

The increased volume of international trade in fishery products in 1991 was associated with lower prices for some key commodities such as salmon and shrimp. The result was that the value of exports increased less than the volume to US$ 39,400 million. First indications for 1992 were for an increase in the value of fishery products traded, due to higher prices. Thailand is now the top exporter of fishery products among developing countries, accounting for about 8% of total world fish exports.

*Imports*

Developed countries accounted for about 90% of total fish imports in 1991. Japan was again the biggest importer of fishery products, accounting for some 28% of the global total. The EEC further increased its dependency on import for its fish supply. The USA, besides being the world's leading exporting country, was also the second biggest importer. In 1992, fish imports by Japan and the EEC have increased, while the market for foreign fish products in the USA seemed to have contracted further.

The increase in net receipts of foreign exchange by developing countries - deducting their imports from the total value of their exports - is impressive, rising from US$ 5,200 million in 1985 to US$ 10,900 million in 1991. For many developing nations, fish trade represents a significant source of hard currency earnings.

## Major Commodities

*Shrimp*

The economic crises in Japan and the USA had a surprisingly limited impact on shrimp consumption in the two countries. Demand for shrimp was generally strong and prices went up in the course of 1992. On the European market, plentiful supplies of coldwater shrimp led to a decline in prices of this species. Imports of shrimp into France, the UK and the USA reached record levels, while Japanese shrimp imports declined for the first time after eight years of continuous expansion.

---

[2] It should be noted that the analysis and forecasts given in this section are based on the information available in April 1993.

The world shrimp market was strong in the opening months of 1993, with steady demand and an increase in prices. The supply situation seemed to become difficult, with cultured production no longer growing and with the shrimp catch declining. The US policy to have the Turtle Exclusion Device (TED) installed on Latin American and US vessels might lead to a reduction of wild shrimp supplies to their markets. The European market is expected to be rather bleak in 1993, due to the difficult economic situation in the main consuming countries combined with a devaluation of their currencies.

## Tuna

The decision by most canned tuna consuming countries to use only tuna caught with 'dolphin-friendly' methods (these are methods avoiding the deaths of dolphins while catching tuna) created a major uproar on the market. The tuna fleets of Mexico, Venezuela and Ecuador were hit by this decision, and their market outlets were reduced to only a few countries. Prices of yellowfin declined sharply in 1992, as Latin American countries were trying to sell as much tuna as possible before the start of the import ban in Italy and Spain.

Since 1 January 1993, canned tuna imports into the EEC, excluding ACP countries, have been subject to an import quota. For 1993, this quota has been fixed at 74,000 tonnes. The quota was calculated based on 1990 and 1991 'true' tuna imports of each EEC country, that is, excluding bonito (sarda). For a country like Germany where 80% of its tuna imports were bonito, the quota system means a substantial reduction of imports. The Philippines and Thailand are severely hit by this measure. These two countries were trying to sell at rather low prices in early 1993, just before the quota was filled. The main beneficiaries of this move were canneries in ACP countries (Lomé conventions), that is Côte d'Ivoire, Fiji, Senegal and the Seychelles. The majority of these canneries are French-owned and were very able to defend their interests: on the one hand with the quota system they protected their market from cheap canned tuna from Southeast Asia, and on the other they forced other European countries to buy from their subsidiaries in ACP countries.

## Groundfish

Mid-1992 will be remembered as one of the worst periods for the groundfish fisheries worldwide. Canada announced a two-year moratorium on northern cod and, almost at the same time, Iceland decided on a heavy cut in its cod quota. At the end of August 1992, China, Japan, the Republic of Korea, Poland, the Russian Federation and the USA decided to close the Alaska pollack fisheries in the 'Donut Hole', an international zone outside the American and Russian waters, for two years.

In the opening months of 1993, the European market was flooded by cheap cod, mainly coming from Russian catches. Reportedly, Russian vessels were landing cod directly in Icelandic and Norwegian harbours at prices below US$ 1/kg, while the 'normal' price is about double or triple. These low-priced imports created major problems for EEC fishermen, with the French fishermen feeling the stress more heavily. At the end of February 1993, the EEC decided on minimum import prices for cod and haddock, a measure which however failed to stop cheap imports. In comparison, the US cod market was calm, with some recovery experienced in the Lent season.

*Small pelagics*

In 1992, all major frozen mackerel exporters - Norway, the Netherlands, the UK and Ireland - experienced grave problems. Prices declined sharply, as the main markets were reluctant to buy. The situation is expected to normalize in the course of 1993. The lack of hard currency in Russian and Eastern Europe led to a glut of herring in Western Europe in 1992. In the UK, sales to klondykers dropped drastically while herring landings increased strongly in 1992. There was a marked price drop in the major markets in the course of that year. The herring resource in the North Atlantic seems to have recovered and catch forecasts are very optimistic.

The canned small pelagic industry has continued to change, and uncertainty of supplies lifted canned sardine prices. In South America, the El Niño current has struck again reducing Chile and Peru's harvest of pilchard to very low levels. Producers in Asia have only been slightly affected by supply problems in the production of canned small pelagics. Thailand stands out as a growing supplier of sardines, taking market shares from Japan for which the rise in the value of the yen has been a handicap.

In 1992, Europe reported good catches of sardines after years of relatively bleak supplies, and Portugal was able to recover its share in the European market. In 1993, the situation was expected to change due to the new duty arrangement for Moroccan sardines: under this, Moroccan canned sardines will only be subject to an 8% tariff, compared to 25% for other non-EEC countries.

## Cephalopods

Prices on the octopus market in Japan fell sharply between June 1992 and December 1992 due to large supplies. Las Palmas producers, who normally sell all their octopus to Japan, tried to reopen their own domestic market. Japan's squid catch on the high seas was reduced in the 1991-92 season. As a result of lower domestic production, squid imports increased in 1992 by 15%. Due to a shortage of Argentine *illex* squid, prices moved up and *loligo* squid prices were also somewhat above those in 1991. However, cuttlefish prices did not follow the downward movement of octopus prices and a large-sized cuttlefish is now selling for more than the same sized octopus. A further reduction of squid supplies on the world market was anticipated for 1993 as a result of the ban on driftnet fisheries. Price increases for squid, especially in the lower quality bracket were thus foreseen. The octopus market was expected to return to average levels after a period of excess supplies in 1992. The cuttlefish market was forecasted to stay firm.

## Salmon

Both the farmed and wild salmon supply to the world market declined in 1992. Of the wild salmon, pink salmon catches were lower, while sockeye landings increased substantially in Alaska. Norway reduced its farmed salmon output. As a result of lower supplies, prices increased substantially in the first part of 1992. Since August 1992, however, a continuous decline of farmed salmon prices was experienced, indicating acute oversupply. Sockeye prices declined worldwide as a result of good catches and heavy inventories in Japan.

Norway's production is not likely to match the 1990 record before 1995, and 1993 figures could be down. Nevertheless, Norwegian salmon prices continued to decline and no end to the downward spiral is in sight. The Chilean salmon industry is rapidly coming to the fore as a world producer and is a major supplier to Japan and the USA. A record 1993 harvest is forecasted for wild salmon.

## Fishmeal

In 1992, production of fishmeal in the major exporting countries was 3.2 million tonnes, an 8% increase. Practically all countries reported a higher output. On the other hand, Japan -where fishmeal production is mainly consumed domestically - reported a considerable decline in production. Peruvian fish catch was abundant in the closing months of 1992. The good production in the last quarter of the year made Peru again the main world fishmeal producer with some 1.28 million tonnes. Chile is a close second with 1.26 million tonnes, a 9% increase over 1991. Scandinavian countries, too, reported a strong increase in fishmeal production. Some 800,000 tonnes came from this region, 200,000 tonnes more than the 1991 output.

## 3 ACTION REQUIRED

The task is that developing countries increase their exports of value-added consumer products in all categories, as has happened with canned tuna in recent times, and thus enhance their participation in international trade. However, the wide variety of products results in a very complex market situation which complicates market research, trade promotion, and the provision of trade support services. In this connection, reducing fluctuations and increasing reliability and predictability of trade leading to reduced risks are important requirements for trade development.

As to trade between developing countries there are increasing possibilities to replace the traditional exports from developed countries of lower and medium valued products, such as canned small pelagics and cured fish, for which processing costs are becoming increasingly prohibitive in the industrialized world. These and other opportunities may be realized through regional cooperation activities in fish processing and marketing, including exchange of technical and market information, standardization of products and quality inspection methods, as well as preferential arrangements through customs unions or regional free trade associations. The establishment of trade connections will be a very important prerequisite for increased trade between developing countries.

The core requirement for successful exports to industrialized countries will be the compliance with consumer expectations, including quality and presentation. Diversification of product and markets will increase total trade and combined with increased manufacture of net value-added products, preferably in the exporting countries, holds the strongest potential for developing countries. To realize this option will necessitate substantial technology transfer, training and creation of forward and backward links and close cooperation with industry and trade in the importing countries. Due to the perishability of the product, suitable handling and preservation techniques will have to be applied which have to rely on the informed participation of primary producers. A number of flexible adaptations by small-scale operators in the field of aquaculture shows that this is feasible.

A number of obstacles prevent developing countries from reaping full benefits from international trade in fish and fishery products. These impediments can be divided into tariff and non-tariff members, which are the result of governmental actions, and into commercial constraints which are related to the characteristics of markets and to the fishery situation in developing countries. Frequently, the major obstacles to improving the participation and performance of developing countries in international fish trade are constraints of a commercial nature, which could be overcome by appropriate action by the industry itself and collaborating institutions: typically, such constraints are related to product quality and quality control, market information, specific market characteristics and market access, including distribution channels, and shortcomings with regard to trade-related services. Consequently, training and technical assistance for industry and institutions concerned, exchange of experiences and technical and economic cooperation among developing countries, including joint action in the field of trade-related services, and cooperation and transfer of product and marketing technology, would be the principal areas where the efforts of developing fish exporting countries need to be supported.

## STATEMENT OF THE
## INTERNATIONAL NICKEL STUDY GROUP (INSG)

The International Nickel Study Group is a relatively new group, having been inaugurated three years ago and become operational in early 1991. The INSG was modelled after the International Lead and Zinc Study Group and has broadly similar objectives and activities. Its main focus is on market transparency. The International Copper Study Group, which is meeting this week in Lisbon, was likewise modelled after the Lead-Zinc and Nickel groups. The INSG currently has 15 members which together account for over 80% of world nickel production, but only a bit more than 60% of nickel consumption. A key priority is, therefore, to expand membership, but this has proved difficult under the current depressed market conditions in nickel. The group has not yet applied to the CFC for designation as an ICB, but it is likely to do so in the future.

From the nickel market viewpoint, the most important issue is the large increase in nickel exports from the USSR and its successors, principally the Russian Federation. The problem is not so much the resulting contribution to excess supply in western markets - although this is of concern - as western production is now not adequate to meet demand without CIS metal. Rather, the most significant problem is the *uncertainty* as to actual quantities of nickel supplies from the CIS, both currently and in the future, owing to the lack of reliable statistics and other information from the CIS. The INSG is seeking to resolve this by encouraging the Government of the Russian Federation to participate actively in the meetings and other activities of the Group.

A review of the international distribution of nickel mine production is given in Figure 1. Most nickel originates from countries like CIS and Canada, followed by New Caledonia, Indonesia and Australia. Production of primary nickel is shown in Figure 2. The major producer is the CIS, followed by Canada and Japan. New Caledonia only takes a small share, leaving the processing largely to other countries. The same applies to e.g. Indonesia. The major consumers are Japan, the Commonwealth of Independent States, the USA and Germany (see Figure 3).

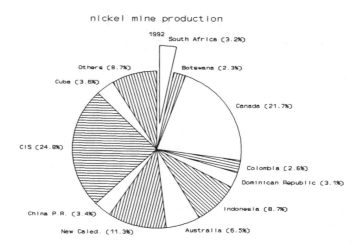

*Figure 1:*   The international distribution of nickel mine production

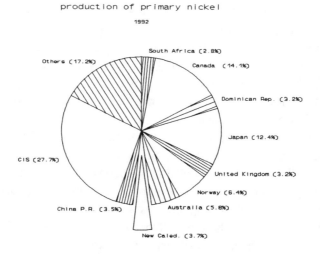

*Figure 2:*   The international distribution of primary nickel production

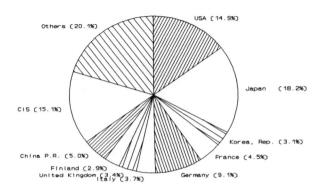

*Figure 3:* The international distribution of nickel consumption

# PART IV

---

## PRESENTATIONS

## BY GUEST SPEAKERS

# THE CHALLENGE OF FEEDING 100 MILLION
# MORE PEOPLE EVERY YEAR

DR. F.A. BERNARDO[1]

## 1  INTRODUCTION

About 90 million people are born every year. This population increase is expected to accelerate to over 100 million more mouths to feed annually, until it will begin to level off by the middle of the 21st century. Current trends in the balance of rural-to-urban population, particularly in Asia, are also changing rapidly. By the year 2020, more people are forecasted to live in cities than in the rural areas of Asia (Figure 1). Therefore, the cities will be under more pressure to meet the demand for affordable food. Add to this grim scenario the fact that more than 1.13 billion people now live below the poverty line (Figure 2). Indeed, we are working double-time against a time-bomb linked to food supply.

[1] Deputy Director General for International Programs, International Rice Research Institute (IRRI), Los Baños, Laguna, Philippines.

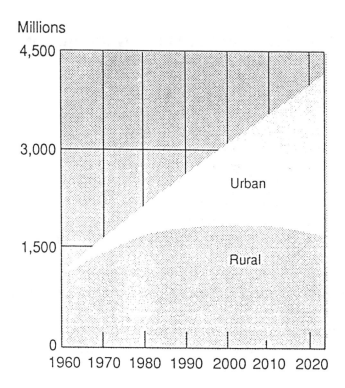

*Source:* World Bank, 1992

*Figure 1:*     The balance of rural-to-urban population in Asia is changing,
                and this means more pressure in the cities for affordable food

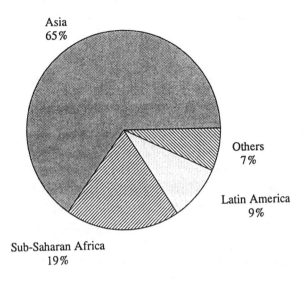

Asia
65%

Others
7%

Latin America
9%

Sub-Saharan Africa
19%

*Source:* World Bank, 1992

*Figure 1:*    Developing country population below the poverty line in 1990
              (1.13 billion). About two-thirds of the world's poor live in the
              developing countries of Asia

Rice is the basic food for half of the world. More than 90% of the world's rice is grown and consumed in Asia, home to almost two-thirds of the world's poorest and to more than 95% of total rice farmers. Only 4% of rice production is traded in the world market. The so-called Green Revolution in Asia, ushered in by high yielding rice varieties produced at the International Rice Research Institute (IRRI), resulted in unprecedented increase in annual rice supply, enough to feed the 600 million more people in the 1960s and 1970s. But this breakthrough in rice production had a price as indicated in IRRI's Medium Term Plan; there were unforeseen social and environmental costs. Nongovernment organizations and research groups initially alerted the world to adverse effects of reduced genetic diversity and pesticide misuse. While these issues are being addressed today, the need to increase further rice production to avert an impending famine should also be a great concern.

By 2020, the world must produce 350 million more tonnes of rice than it produced in 1992 to meet the needs of increasing populations and rising incomes. Since land to produce rice is limited - and is decreasing in many countries due to rapid urbanization and expansion of industrial areas - production increase must be achieved on less land, less water and less labour.

## 2 IRRI'S STRATEGIC PLAN: A MODEL FOR PRODUCTIVITY IMPROVEMENT OF COMMODITIES

IRRI has adopted a long-term strategic plan to address the rice supply problems in the 21st century. The goal is *'Improved well-being of present and future generations of rice producers and consumers, particularly those with low income'*. This strategic plan establishes the guiding principles and basic policies that focus on planning and implementation of research in rice and rice-based farming systems or other commodities grown in rice farms.

IRRI's plan for 1994-1998 focuses on meeting key challenges presented by the global food crisis: increasing productivity, achieving sustainability, protecting the environment, and addressing social equity. These plus new emerging concerns confront us all. The gigantic task of feeding about 100 million more mouths every year can only be matched by an ambitious long-term program designed to produce more scientific breakthroughs. IRRI's strategic plan could serve as a model plan in increasing production of commodities, particularly food.

IRRI's research program is now ecosystems-oriented, directed toward solving rice and rice-related production problems without degrading the natural resources in four major ecosystems (Figure 3):

- Irrigated rice ecosystem (81.4 million ha.);
- Rainfed lowland rice ecosystem (37.0 million ha.);
- Upland rice ecosystem (19.2 million ha.);
- Flood-prone ecosystem (10.7 ha.).

The irrigated rice ecosystem comprises about 55% of the world's rice area, and produces 71% of the world's rice supply while feeding people in most urban centers (Figure 4). Most of the rainfed lowland rice, and all the upland and flood-prone ecosystems are unfavourable rice environments, if not marginal areas. Rice production in these areas is low - only about 1-3 tonnes/ha. - and very unstable.

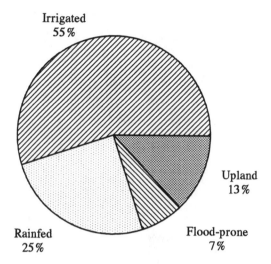

*World rice area harvested (148 million hectares)*

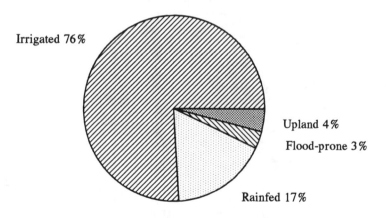

*World rice production (520 million tons)*

*Source:*    IRRI data base 1993. Production is estimated on the basis of farm household surveys and through consultation with national program scientists

*Figure 3:*    Harvested rice area and rice production in different ecosystems in 1991. Irrigated rice provides the major supply of urban consumers

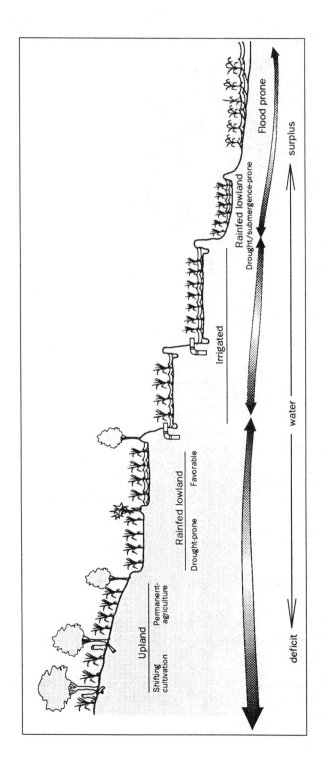

*For the description of the ecosystem see next page.*

*Figure 4:*    Rice ecosystem characteristics

## Description of the ecosystem

Rice ecosystems are characterized by the natural resources of water and land, and by the adaptation of the rice plant to them. Irrigated rice maybe found at any point in a toposequence if water delivery is available.

### Upland
Level to steeply sloping fields; rarely flooded, aerobic soil; rice direct seeded on plowed dry soil or dibbled in wet, nonpuddled soil.

### Rainfed Lowland
Level to slightly sloping, bunded field; noncontinuous flooding of variable depth and duration; submergence not exceeding 50 cm for more than 10 consecutive days; rice transplanted in puddled soil or direct seeded on puddled or plowed dry soil; alternating aerobic to anaerobic soil of variable frequency and duration.

### Irrigated
Leveled, bunded fields with water control; rice transplanted or direct seeded in puddled soil; shallow flooded with anaerobic soil during crop growth.

### Flood-prone
Level to slightly sloping or depressed fields; more than 10 consecutive days of medium to very deep flooding (50 to more than 300 cm) during crop growth; rice transplanted in puddled soil or direct seeded on plowed dry soil; aerobic to anaerobic soil; soil salinity or toxicity in tidal areas.

# Mega projects

To aggressively respond to the challenges facing rice research in the next decades, IRRI identified five important projects, called *Mega Projects*, where increased research investment would directly increase global food supply and ensure the permanency or sustainability of rice-based production systems. These projects are:

- *Raising the irrigated rice yield plateau*
  An ideotype of a new irrigated rice plant that is projected to give as much as 30% higher rice yields was designed by IRRI scientists. Among other characters, it would be low-tillering but with more grains. Research planned will seek to continue breeding to incorporate durable pest resistance into the rice plant, develop agronomic practices - planting method, nitrogen application, weed control - that will help the plant attain its full yield potential, and develop a rice plant that is much more efficient in its yield-related processes.

- *Reversing the trends in declining yield productivity in intensive
  irrigated rice*
  Data from 20 years of continuous cropping in IRRI's experiment station
  show declining productivity of rice (Fig. 5). Long-term experiments in
  India and Indonesia give similar results. We aim to identify the processes and mechanisms responsible for the declining productivity in
  intensively cropped soils. Emphasis will be on understanding the
  microbial and chemical factors that control organic matter decomposi-
  tion, humus formation, the nitrogen-supplying capacity of submerged
  soils, and the build-up of pests and disease in this kind of soil. After
  elucidating the cause of declining productivity, we will develop a
  feasible program to reverse the trend.

- *Improving rice-wheat cropping systems*
  This undertaking will involve collaboration with program scientists in
  Bangladesh, India, Nepal, and Pakistan, and CIMMYT and IRRI to
  work on the productivity and sustainability of rice-wheat systems,
  including an analysis of on-farm factor productivity and investigation of
  the biophysical as well as socioeconomic factors that constrain productivity.

- *Conserving rice genetic resources*
  This work would focus on ensuring the availability of genetic diversity
  as the basis of plant improvement through the continuous collection,
  conservation and evaluation of rice germplasm. Also, an analysis of
  genotype and environment interactions will be conducted, linking it
  with crop simulation and modelling to predict genotype performance in
  different environments. IRRI ensures unrestricted access to rice germplasm to all scientists worldwide.

- *Exploiting biodiversity for sustainable pest management*
  We are using molecular markers to identify rice genes resistant to key
  pests such as rice blast and bacterial blight. Work will include identifying genotypes that exhibit selective attraction to natural enemies of
  insect pests or those that emit substances toxic to insects.

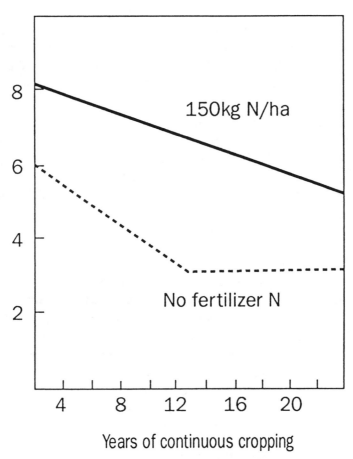

Grain yield (t/ha)

150kg N/ha

No fertilizer N

Years of continuous cropping

*Figure 5:* Response of continuously cropped rice to nitrogen is declining in IRRI's long-term experiment. This loss of factor productivity has important implications for increasing and sustaining intensive rice systems

## New frontier projects

*New Frontier Projects* are undertakings that go beyond known areas and currently accepted scientific boundaries. They present exciting opportunities for achieving scientific breakthroughs while not being constrained by concerns of failure. These projects, which await complementary donor funding, are:

- *Apomixis - ensuring equity in the use of hybrid rice*
  This research will initiate a systematic screening of rice germplasm for apomixis - a natural method of asexual seed reproduction that is seen to facilitate the wide diffusion of hybrid rice technology at affordable cost to rice farmers.
- *Assessing opportunities for nitrogen fixation in rice*
  Exploratory research will be conducted to improve the association between rice and nitrogen-fixing soil bacteria. If this is successful, we will aim to engineer a rice plant capable of nodulation and fixing nitrogen from the air. This could reduce the need to apply costly, inorganic fertilizer.
- *Managing weeds using less chemicals -- the role of allelopathy and biological control*
  Ways to manage the weeds more effectively through *allelopathy* - the direct or indirect effect of chemical compounds produced by one plant on another plant - and biological control methods will be explored. Ultimately, allelopathy is hoped to be integrated into improved cultivars through molecular marker selection.
- *Sustainable system for the uplands by developing a perennial rice plant*
  Through biotechnology, IRRI will work toward developing a perennial rice plant that would solve the problem of erosion in the upland rice ecosystem. A perennial rice crop is envisioned to provide permanent ground cover needed to prevent soil erosion.

## Strategies for risk management

About 77 million hectares, or about 45% of the total area planted to rice, are non-irrigated and subject to risks due to unreliable water supply as well as water-, soil-, and pest-related problems. To increase and stabilize rice production in these unfavourable rice environments, IRRI is developing technologies to minimize farmers' risks. The following comprise IRRI's risk management strategy:

- Development of varieties with tolerance for drought, flash flooding and submergence in deep stagnant water;
- Development of varieties with tolerance for salinity;
- Development of short duration varieties to escape unfavourable weather;
- Drought management through rainwater collection;
- Development of durable resistance to insect pests and disease;
- Development of low-input varieties and management practices to increase fertilizer use efficiency.

With these technologies we hope to increase yields in unfavourable rice environments by 30-50% without degrading the national resources or polluting the environment.

## 3 PARTNERSHIP - SHARING RESPONSIBILITIES IN FEEDING THE WORLD

World food problems can be solved more easily and in relatively less time through partnership and collaboration. IRRI works with national rice programs, advanced institutions and universities, sister agricultural research centres, nongovernment organizations (NGOs), and the private sector to seek knowledge and technologies on rice and rice-related crops for the ultimate use of the rice farmers in the world.

IRRI uses different modes of collaboration to improve the participation, competence and commitment of its partners.

### Research consortia

Under this form of collaboration, a group of selected institutions, including IRRI, mutually agree to accept different responsibilities to contribute to achieving a common objective. Division of responsibilities among consortia members take into account the comparative advantage of each and promote complementarity of roles and responsibilities.

As of May 1993, there are two rice research consortia with specific research foci as follows:

### Rainfed lowland rice research consortium

| Members | Research focus |
|---|---|
| Bangladesh Rice Research Institute | Drought and photoperiod sensitivity |
| Indian Council of Agricultural Research | Salinity and shallow flash flooding |
| Central Research Institute for Food Crops (Indonesia) | Potassium deficiency and direct seeding |
| International Rice Research Institute (Philippines) | Rainwater conservation and nutrient management |
| Department of Agriculture (Thailand) | Severe drought, phosphorus deficiency and blast disease |

### Upland rice research consortium

| Members | Research focus |
|---|---|
| Indian Council of Agricultural Research | Moderately acid soils, short rainy season |
| Central Research Institute for Food Crops (Indonesia) | Acid soils and slash-and-burn cropping |
| Philippine Rice Research Institute | Acid soils and weed control |
| Department of Agriculture (Thailand) | Moderately acid soils and slash-and-burn cropping |

Establishment of the third rice research consortium dealing with flood-prone rice ecosystems is still awaiting donor support.

## Research networks

Individual scientists from IRRI and other institutions organize themselves to conduct research driven by a predetermined theme or set of research tools. The important research networks are:

- *Asian Rice Biotechnology Network (ARBN)*
  This network, supported by the Asian Development Bank, complements the International Rice Biotechnology Program of the Rockefeller Foundation. It promotes exchange and use of modern tools and techniques to accelerate rice chromosome mapping, manipulation of genetic materials at the molecular level and transformation of promising varieties. The network uses rice species and nonrice as sources of genetic materials conferring resistance to pests or tolerance for abiotic stresses. Collaborating countries are India, Thailand, Indonesia, China, and the Philippines.

- *Systems Analysis and Simulation for Rice Production (SARP)*
  Initiated in 1986 with the assistance and support of the Netherlands Government through the Centre for Agrobiological Research, this research network trains interdisciplinary teams from participating countries. Computer modelling and field verification trials are conducted in:
  - Rice-based cropping patterns;
  - Water management;
  - Crop protection;
  - Rice production systems.

- *Integrated pest management network*
  This network focused on pest diagnosis workshops during its first two years of existence (1991-1992). It is now undertaking research on pest ecology and biological control of rice insect pests and diseases.
    The network has made initial successes in convincing farmers to reduce the frequency of chemical spraying from 3-4 times to 1 or no spraying at all. With little or no spraying of chemical pesticides, the balance between insect pests and insect parasites or predators is maintained.

## Technology evaluation networks

Technology evaluation networks promote the exchange of information and improved or emerging technologies among interested national programs. Membership is open to all interested research organizations, but rigorous technology evaluation activities are focused on a few selected key sites representing large targeted environments.

- *International Network for the Genetic Evaluation of Rice (INGER)*

  IRRI will continue to coordinate INGER which has facilitated the exchange and evaluation of promising varieties and elite breeding lines produced by IRRI, national programs and other international research centres. A study conducted by Dr. Robert Evenson of Yale University in 1992 showed that 390 modern rice varieties between 1965 and 1990 were borrowed -- developed in one country and released in another. IRRI provided 75% of the borrowed varieties through INGER.

  IRRI's share of ancestors delivered through INGER continues to grow: IRRI provided more than half the ancestors for varieties released in 1965-1974, nearly three-fourths the ancestors for varieties released in 1981-1990.

  The modern rice varieties being used in over 30 countries in Asia, Africa, and Latin America is estimated to be worth US$3.5 billion. Each modern variety is worth USD 2.5 million per year.

- *Crop and Resource Management Network (CREMNET)*

  This is a technology evaluation network presently being developed. It will facilitate exchange and evaluation of non-germplasm technologies. Emphasis will be on technologies that promote sustainable soil fertility and productivity, reduced use of chemical pesticides, improved well being of women farmers, more efficient use of labour, water and nutrients, and crop diversification.

  Rigorous testing of improved or emerging technologies in selected key sites and feedback to research programs will be an important responsibility of the network. It will also undertake *expost* impact studies of technologies.

  IRRI is seeking donor support for this network.

**Shuttle research**

Much of the expanding research in industrialized countries is relevant to IRRI's research agenda. We are building bridges with advanced research institutes in these countries to promote the application of advanced knowledge and research methodologies or techniques to help solve challenging rice production problems.

Shuttle research enables IRRI scientists to work with leading laboratories in key areas such as genetic mapping and genome manipulation (Cornell University, USA) and soil microbiology (Institute of Applied

Microbiology, Tokyo University, Japan). It also enables scientists form advanced institutions to come to IRRI to continue their field experiments on rice even during winter.

## 4 FACING THE CHALLENGE

IRRI is all geared up to do the utmost to contribute to making possible sustainable rice production that is profitable to the farmer and affordable to the consumer, in an environmentally secure world. But IRRI cannot do it alone. The strengths and resources of its partners - national rice research systems, donors and policymakers, institutions and universities, national governments, NGOs, other international agricultural research centres, and individual rice scientists - must be pooled and mobilized to face up to the challenge of feeding a growing world.

# ENVIRONMENT PROTECTION AS A PART OF A DEVELOPMENT STRATEGY FOR A COMMODITY: THE CASE OF WASTE RESIDUALS IN THE SUGAR CANE INDUSTRY

MR. JOSÉ A. CERRO[1]

## 1 INTRODUCTION

An evaluation of alternatives for solving problems pertaining to the environment, as generated by a specific economic activity, must be conducted within a comprehensive approach to said activity, considered as a whole. It is for this reason that we deem it of utmost importance to approach the topic with which we are concerned, within a comprehensive analysis of an economic activity with the features of the sugar industry. The first fact to be pointed out is the operation of the world sugar market, as an adequate framework for an analysis of the development of the industry, particularly as regards its repercussions on developing exporting countries. Following this overall analysis will proceed a study of this activity within its development and its potential, as a priority topic, regarding environmental problems.

The following subjects will be approached in this paper, for effects of this evaluation:

- the international sugar situation: analysis of its development;
- its impact on the economies of nations in the Latin American region;
- strategy for an effective, lasting solution;
- priority topics within said strategy;
- environmental protection, through specific projects;
- conclusions.

[1] Executive Secretary, Latin American and Caribbean Sugar Exporting Countries Group (GEPLACEA), Mexico City.

## 2 THE WORLD SUGAR SITUATION

The world sugar situation, described statistically in Tables 1 to 6 at the end of this paper, has been mainly characterized by the following factors.

- Sugar is produced from two raw materials: sugar cane, cultivated in tropical and subtropical climates, and sugar beet, grown in temperate climates. Thus a great majority of world production - over 80% - is consumed in the country where it is produced, with a relatively small portion of total output sold on the international market.
- Productivity varies widely, which is in turn reflected in significant differences in production costs among nations.
- Substitute sweeteners, such as corn derivatives and artificial sweeteners (as aspartame), have lowered consumption in some of the most important developed countries.
- A large part of the international market is regulated by special arrangements, which means that the so-called 'free market' becomes a residual market, where only the sugar that has not found a destination at better prices, or on domestic or preferential markets is sold.
- International prices on the so-called free market have been characterized by the following:
  - wide fluctuations;
  - below the production costs of even the most efficient producers most of the time;
  - a wide gap between international quotations and domestic prices.

All the aforegoing facts are the result of application of protectionist economic policy measures, chiefly by the more developed countries.

## 3 EFFECTS ON THE INDUSTRY IN LATIN AMERICA AND THE CARIBBEAN

The situation of the international sugar market has severely affected the development of our industries - of utmost importance in the economies of our nations. The Latin American and Caribbean region is the number one sugar-producing region in the world, with 66% of sugarcane output worldwide, nearly 30% of sugar production and 45% of international sugar exports. Further, the industry is an important source of employment, foreign exchange, energy and food for the region, which uses eight million hectares to produce 400 million tonnes of cane; which is then converted into 28 million tonnes of sugar and 13 billion litres of fuel alcohol. The region has over 600 sugar factories and 1000 plants producing derivatives and by-products, providing employment to over 2.5 million persons. Sugar is the third source of foreign exchange, following oil and coffee.

Productivity in the region is higher than the world average and production costs are lower, although this has been distorted by the aforementioned situation of the international market. Sugar production has remained virtually unchanged, while output worldwide has continued to grow. Our exports have fallen from 13 to 10 million tonnes, while our market share dropped from 55% to 45%, all since the mid-1970s. Since the beginning of the 1980s the value of exports to the so-called 'free market' fell from 7.2 billion dollars to 2.8 billion, while sales to the United States (traditionally our number one market) dropped from 1.4 billion dollars to 370 million.

This entire situation has led to an adjustment in the operations of our industries, with negative consequences in the economic, social and political spheres of our countries.

## 4  STRATEGY FOR A SOLUTION

The magnitude and variety of the problems outlined above call for an integral strategy that includes complementary action guidelines covering each and every aspect of sugar activity. In this respect, the Group of Latin American and Caribbean Sugar-Exporting Countries, *GEPLACEA*, an international organization founded in 1974 with the objective of undertaking actions aimed at consultation and co-ordination in all aspects pertaining to production, distribution and marketing of sugar, its derivatives and by-products, focuses its endeavours on four fundamental action guidelines as an effective response to the aforementioned problems:

- defense of markets and prices;
- an integral use of sugar cane to produce not only sugar but a variety of derivatives and by-products;
- modernization of the industry so as to raise productivity and efficiency and lower costs;
- analysis and planning of economic policy measures focused on an improved fulfilment of the aforementioned objectives.

Regarding point number one, the objective is to seek improved market conditions, both domestic and foreign, with quotations that reflect free play between supply and demand, in a steady movement toward a free international market, eliminating the current protectionist measures outlined above. With the foregoing, it would be comparative advantages rather than the financial capacity to subsidize that would determine the relative positions of exporting countries. The aim of point number two is the diversification of the sugar cane agro-industry, understood not as eliminating cane activity; but on the contrary, using cane integrally to produce not only sugar but derivatives and by-products as well. Thus diversification is presented as a long-term strategy for the sector, based on the potential for an integral use of the raw material, which constitutes an effective contribution by the cane agro-industry to the development of other production sectors. In the conviction that both the competitive presence on markets and diversification of the sugar industry are impossible under situations of inefficiency, the priority objective of point three is the modernization of activity, understood as any action involving improved efficiency and increased productivity, with consequent reductions in production costs.

In order for these objectives to be achieved, policies must be drafted for the sector making it possible to correct current distortions, improve the organization of the industry, create conditions for its modernization and implement a long-term integral strategy for the sustained development of this activity.

## 5 PRIORITY TOPICS FOR THIS STRATEGY

In line with the action guidelines mentioned above, the following noteworthy concrete activities might be mentioned as means of achieving these objectives:

a. *Actions for defense of markets and prices:*
   - research and monitoring of markets for sugar, by-products and derivatives, both domestic and international;
   - joint action in international fora, noteworthy examples of which include possibilities of the International Sugar Organization and talks for trade liberalization of agricultural products in the Uruguay Round of GATT;
   - training of traders in aspects pertaining to the market, negotiations, and the use of marketing alternatives, among others;
   - direct action before governments;
   - drafting of marketing strategies for domestic markets.

b. *Integral Use of Sugar Cane through Diversification:*
  - agricultural diversification, including crop rotation and inter-cropping;
  - industrial diversification, with intensive use of sugar cane, molasses and bagasse as raw material for products such as alcohol, paper, boards, plastics, animal feed, energy sources, etc;
  - diversification of sugar markets through production of special sugars, refined sugar and liquid sugar.

c. *Modernization of the Agro-industry:*
  - Within the agricultural sphere:
    ○ development and exchange of new sugar cane varieties;
    ○ pest and disease control;
    ○ improvement of cultivation and harvest tasks;
    ○ study and conservation of cane soils;
    ○ mechanization of agricultural tasks;
    ○ transfer of technology, training and agricultural extension pro-grammes.
  - Regarding industry:
    ○ increase in productivity at the plant;
    ○ mill maintenance;
    ○ improvement in energy generation and use;
    ○ development of electrical cogeneration;
    ○ research and application of biotechnology to the process;
    ○ environmental protection;
    ○ transfer of technology and training.

d. *Drafting and implementation of an economic policy for the sector*
  - At the international level:
    ○ monitoring of fora in which sugar issues are discussed;
    ○ establishment of conditions for liberalization of international markets.
  - At the national level:
    ○ relationship between the domestic market and the international market;
    ○ operation of domestic markets;
    ○ payment systems for the raw material;
    ○ organization of the industry;
    ○ financing systems;
    ○ organization of research and development tasks.

Within *GEPLACEA* there are two specialized Secretariats, Market and Technology, for the organization and implementation of the tasks aimed at the fulfilment of the aforementioned objectives, through a *Services Area* that drafts and puts into practice specific projects and programmes.

## 6  ENVIRONMENTAL PROTECTION THROUGH SPECIFIC PROJECTS

The environmental issue is a priority feature of this integral strategy, closely related to the objectives modernization and diversification. Our organization has approached a wide range of topics related to this activity, from various perspectives, including the following:

- the promotion of programs for the use of cane alcohol as a gasoline additive, based on the experience of countries in our region as leaders in this field. This also represents a renewable fuel alternative within an energy policy, as an ecological fuel as octane enhancer replacing lead in gasolines;
- substitution of systems calling for burning of cane fields for sugar cane harvest;
- integral pest handling programmes, thereby curbing the use of chemicals;.
- the application of energy cogeneration systems using bagasse, furthering the use of cleaner techniques;
- treatment of the residues generated by production of sugar and derivatives, underlining the possibility of using them to produce marketable goods.

The project for treatment of residues at alcohol distilleries is a noteworthy example of the this activity; using sugar cane molasses, recovery of *Saccharomyces* yeast and production of biogas. The programme also envisions construction of a pilot plant for this purpose, to be built with funding requested from the Common Fund for Commodities. This plant would be located within the 'Heriberto Duquesne' agroindustrial complex, in the Republic of Cuba, with the following aims and features:

- solve the problem created by a plant producing alcohol from molasses, which releases over 800 cubic metres of residues daily, with a polluting charge of 64 kgs/cubic metres plus the effluents from the sugar factory. The new plant would eliminate 17,500 kg daily of chemical demand for oxygen;

- recover *Saccharomyces* yeast for animal feed, obtain biogas as fuel to operate the factory and for fuel; and biological soil improvement mud, with 1,292,000 cubic metres annually for irrigation;
- obtain the following products in addition to current production (on annual bases):

|  | tonnes |
|---|---|
| Yeast | 954 |
| Biogas/furnace (fuel equivalent) | 2,370 |
| Methanol\Automobile (gas/oil equivalent) | 929 |
| Soil improvement mud | 13,000 |
| Irrigation water | 1,292,000 |
| Biogas for oxicorte | 244,000 |
| Biogas/population kerosene equivalent | 104 |

The principal advantages would be:

- the persons living in the region would benefit, due to environmental improvements;
- the utilization of the residues and effluents to produce fuel for use at the alcohol plant, with important effects on its energy balance;
- production of soil improvement mud and water for irrigation improves the situation of the cane fields surrounding the mill;
- production of animal feed improves the situation of this sector;
- benefits in the foreign sector as a result of increased exports or substitution of imports;
- considerable multiplier effect through dissemination of results and application of the project to other mills within and outside our region.

In short, the results would be as follows:

- reduction of the polluting source at the alcohol distillery;
- additional income from industrial utilization of the residues and effluents exceeding the costs of the project;

- production of yeast equalling 1035 tonnes of sunflower flour in demand for protein for animal feed;
- savings of approximately 26% of the fuel oil used in alcohol production;
- methane gas production to cover the fuel requirements of a truck fleet operating around the factory;
- biological soil improvement mud to fertilize 40 ha.;
- use of biogas for oxicorte and domestic use to substitute kerosene.

## 7  CONCLUSIONS

Projects related to environmental improvement, such as the specific case outlined above, are developed within an integral context, closely linked to the potential diversification of an industry, to improve its efficiency and as an effective response to structural problems of the market for its traditional products.

*Table 1:* Sugar prices, monthly average of free market

| Decade | Maximum | Minimum | Average |
|--------|---------|---------|---------|
| 1970\79 | 57.17 | 3.12 | 11.27 |
| 1980\89 | 41.09 | 2.74 | 10.80 |

*Source:* GEPLACEA

*Table 2:* Prices costs production ratio

| Year | Price | Cost Malawi | PR\ Cost | Average Cost | PR/ Cost |
|------|-------|-------------|----------|--------------|----------|
| 1980 | 29.01 | 8.48 | 342.10 | 14.23 | 203.87 |
| 1981 | 16.93 | 8.48 | 199.65 | 14.23 | 118.97 |
| 1982 | 8.55 | 8.48 | 100.83 | 14.23 | 60.08 |
| 1983 | 8.50 | 8.48 | 100.24 | 14.23 | 59.73 |
| 1984 | 5.18 | 8.48 | 61.08 | 14.23 | 36.40 |
| 1985 | 4.09 | 8.48 | 48.23 | 14.23 | 28.74 |
| 1986 | 6.07 | 8.48 | 71.58 | 14.23 | 42.66 |
| 1987 | 6.71 | 8.48 | 79.13 | 14.23 | 47.15 |
| 1988 | 10.18 | 8.48 | 120.05 | 14.23 | 71.54 |
| 1989 | 12.79 | 8.48 | 150.83 | 14.23 | 89.88 |
| 1990 | 12.56 | 8.48 | 148.11 | 14.23 | 88.26 |
| 1991 | 9.04 | 8.48 | 106.60 | 14.23 | 63.53 |

*Notes:*  Prices and costs are expressed in U.S. cents\lb.
Malawi is the country with minor costs.
Average refers to world average of cane raw sugar.
*Source:*  GEPLACEA, with figures from Landell Mills.

*Table 3:* World sugar situation (1000 MTRV) and the ratio between net imports and consumption(%)

| Year | Consumption | Net Imports | Net Imports/ Consumption |
|------|-------------|-------------|--------------------------|
| 1980/82 | 90840 | 24608 | 27.07 |
| 1989/90 | 107638 | 22849 | 21.23 |

*Source:*  GEPLACEA with figures from I.S.O.

*Table 4:* World sugar balance (1000 MTRV), September-August

|  | **1990/91** | **1991/92** | **1992/93** |
|---|---|---|---|
| Initial Stocks | 30392 | 33101 | 36918 |
| Production | 113903 | 115647 | 112358 |
| Availability | 144295 | 148748 | 149276 |
| Consumption | 110694 | 111330 | 113102 |
| Statistical Adjustment | 500 | 500 | 500 |
| Final Stocks | 33101 | 36918 | 35674 |
| Final Stocks as % of Consumption | 29.90 | 33.16 | 31.54 |

*Source:* GEPLACEA

*Table 5:* Productivity, average during the 1980s

| Group | Maximum | Minimum | Average |
|---|---|---|---|
| Cane | 12.83 Colombia | .80 Colombia | 5.13 |
| Beet | 9.35 France | 1.60 China | 4.21 |
| Total | 12.83 | .80 | 4.78 |
| Geplacea | 12.83 Colombia | .80 Haiti | 5.40 |
| EC | 9.35 France | 5.50 Spain | 7.61 |

*Source:* GEPLACEA with U.S.D.A. figures

*Table 6:* Average production costs during the 1980s (U.S. cents\lb)

| Group | Maximum | Minimum | Average |
|-------|---------|---------|---------|
| Cane[1] | 40.04<br>Uganda | 8.48<br>Malawi | 14.23 |
| Beet[2] | 43.84<br>Rumania | 13.51<br>Chile | 27.51 |

*Notes:* [1] Raw Sugar
[2] White Sugar

*Source:* GEPLACEA with figures from Landell Mills

# AGRICULTURAL COMMODITIES
# IN DEVELOPING COUNTRIES:
# WAYS OF ENHANCING THEIR LOCAL PROCESSING

### DR. G.D. KOUTHON[1]

## Abstract

The paper reviews trends in production, preservation, processing and marketing of agricultural commodities in the socio-economic development of countries in Africa, the Far East, Latin America and the Caribbean and the Near East.

Some degree of processing of agricultural commodities is already taking place in these countries. These will have to be strengthened in order to achieve a sustainable socio-economic development. However, a combination of political will, appropriate policies, technologies and supporting institutions capable of reaching all levels where processing activities take place, is deemed essential.

After a review of general considerations pertaining to the improvement of processing of agricultural commodities in developing countries, the paper provides some justifications for strengthening such processing. These relate to income generation, non-farm employment opportunities, scientific and technological upgrading of current technological practices, alleviation of rural poverty and value-addition to agricultural production.

Under the analysis of constraints to increased local processing of agricultural commodities, special reference is made to financial, poor technological and institutional supporting structures for research and development, lack of qualified personnel at all levels, poor transport infrastructures, irregular product quality and absence of a market information system. The important role played by women in the processing of agricultural commodities has been underlined.

---

[1] Senior Officer, Food Industries Group, Food and Agricultural Industries Service, Agricultural Services Division of the Food and Agriculture Organization of the United Nations. Paper is reproduced here by permission of that organization.

A set of corrective actions are proposed to be undertaken by government institutions, the private sector and the donor community. These will require the adoption of policies designed to establish essential links between R & D institutions, universities, the funding institutions, the manufacturing industry and the donor community.

I would like to thank the organizers of this Seminar for the invitation to address, in my personal capacity, the issue of enhancing the local processing of agricultural commodities in developing countries.

## 1  INTRODUCTION AND SCOPE OF THE PAPER

Poverty and shortage of basic foods are generally recognized as the main causes of hunger and malnutrition. This situation may be improved via an effective introduction of income generation activities and through people motivation for development. This would, in turn, help to increase and improve supply of food and other agricultural commodities and in addition generate further employment.

Traditional food and agro-processing technologies are often limited in their performance and cannot always provide a satisfactory answer to the increasing need for agricultural production and processing in developing countries.

Transfer of technology in the field of agro-processing is influenced by such major factors as security over control of information, degree of technical assistance, patents and trade marks, equipment and components, level of information exchange between the parties concerned and level of resources to be committed. Other constraints that are known are: access of developing countries to technology, capital management ability, tying of imports, export restrictions and the limitations on the use of technology after the contract.

In order to achieve their development policies, developing countries import of capital goods for which foreign exchange is required. Because their economies are largely based on agricultural production, they hope to acquire such resources from exportation of value-added products. This is another critical reason for acquiring new technologies, even though these may, at times, disrupt their socio-economic environments. Acquisition of new technologies has not always followed the same pattern nor reached the same degree of success in all developing regions.

In Asia and Latin America, for instance, over the past three decades many countries have successfully applied the results of research in the fields of agricultural production and preservation and processing of food and non-food agricultural produce. Innovative techniques have been applied in order to obtain higher yields in crop production, thereby increasing the quantity of available agricultural goods, without disrupting the people's habits in a dramatic manner.

In Africa, in particular, the gap between food production and market demand has been widening. Over the past two decades, the local food production has only increased by 0.7% per annum, whereas the rural population has risen at a rate of 2.1%. Improved technologies for rural preservation and processing of food and non-food commodities have not kept pace with the rise in population.

This paper reviews major requirements for local processing of agricultural commodities in developing countries. It also reviews technological and economic considerations which are in favour of this development. The paper should be seen in this context, for developing countries do not constitute an homogeneous block. Socio-cultural and economic factors have had beneficial impacts on some regions and less positive ones on others. Throughout this paper a focus has been maintained on small and medium scale agro-processing activities for high productivity and sustainable socio-economic development.

In 1988, FAO adopted the following definition of sustainability:

*"Sustainable development is the management and conservation of the natural resource base, and the orientation of technological and institutional change in such a manner as to ensure the attainment and continued satisfaction of human needs for present and future generations. Such sustainable development (in the agriculture, forestry and fisheries sectors) conserves land, water, plant and animal genetic resources, is environmentally non-degrading, technically appropriate, economically viable and socially acceptable"[2].*

## 2 MAIN CHARACTERISTICS OF AGRICULTURAL ACTIVITIES IN DEVELOPING COUNTRIES

Production, preservation, processing and marketing of agricultural commodities play a vital role in the socio-economic development of

---

[2] FAO Committee on World Food Security - 18th Session, Rome, 29 March-18 April 1993 - CFS: 93/3, February 1992.

countries in Africa, the Far East, Latin America and the Caribbean and the Near East. These countries share similar climatic conditions because of their geographical distribution in the Tropics. Other similarities may also be found in the predominance of agricultural rural population for 1990: 57.5% in the Far East, 66.0% in Africa, 26.4% in Latin America and the Caribbean and 37.5% in the Near East[3]. These are often characterized by a low level of literacy, malnutrition, low capital income, low agricultural inputs and yields, difficulty in transferring the findings from agricultural research as well as newly developed food and agro-processing techniques. Through the application of appropriate technologies for the processing of crop, livestock, fisheries and forest products, local processing industries can:

- improve food supplies and reduce imports;
- add value to raw material and increase export earnings;
- provide employment and reduce income gaps;
- assure better market opportunities and provide a stimulus to increase production;
- reduce population migration;
- improve standards of nutrition;
- increase opportunities for investment in rural areas.

Agricultural products constitute the major source of income to the farmers in these Regions. Utilization of agricultural products may be classified into different categories. First, commodities which are produced mainly to meet local demands and to fulfil the basic needs of the people. This is often difficult to achieve. It is not only the problem of producing enough food and other consumer goods, but also the ability to supply products of good quality and improved value. Furthermore, the price of the commodities must be taken into account as a priority because of the large number of people in low income groups. The second group of commodities are the ones which are meant for export. There are two major issues relevant to the export markets namely, quality and price. It is essential that the products should meet the various requirements set by the buyers. Prices in the international market are competitive.

Similarities also exist in the types of agricultural crops produced in the developing Regions of the world. The major food items are rice, maize,

---

[3] FAO Comprehensive Demographic Estimates and Projections (1950-2025).

cassava, groundnut, oil palm, coffee, cocoa, sugar cane and most fruits and vegetables, including spices. Patterns of animal husbandry, fishing techniques, and the exploitation of forestry products also have many common features. Infrastructures such as feeder roads (which are practicable all the year round), potable water supply, adequate means of transportation and energy supplies (such as electricity), are not always available to the population. Product marketing and distribution in developing countries have not always received adequate attention.

Inter-regional differences do exist. Some regions such as the Far East and Latin America and the Caribbean have achieved high level agricultural development thanks to the use of advanced irrigation techniques, improved crop varieties, appropriate processing technologies and functional marketing systems. In Africa, and some countries of the Far and Near East, however, development of a sustainable food and agro-industry will have to rely on a small to medium-scale industry approach. Labour intensive, rural-based small-scale enterprises represent an important source of non-farm employment and income for both women and the landless, and will result in the enhancement of current economic activities. Given the large number of marginal farmers in these Regions, agro-industry is seen as an important activity for adequate employment and income generation for the rural households. However, the combination of lack of access to raw materials, appropriate technology, machinery, skills and markets, have often limited the understanding of the importance of agro-industry in the development process of developing countries.

There is wide variation from one country to another on the degree of priority accorded to planning pattern, policies, programmes and resources devoted to the food industry. At one extreme are countries where agro-industries may have a low priority in the national development plans, while in others, the emphasis one of agro-industry as part of rural industries, with a clear priority on the need for restructuring the industrial sector. In another group of developing countries, the emphasis has traditionally been on large industries.

A major problem has been the lack of market outlets for many products obtainable from rural industries. The successful experience of three Far east countries (Taiwan, the Republic of Korea and China) could provide useful examples. The first factor in these cases was a high and sustained growth of both agriculture and industry. Secondly, in all these cases, rural land reforms had put more income into the hands of the poorer and middle-income groups, thus generating a demand for the products of rural industry.

A massive effort will be required if agro-industries are to serve as a major source of employment. It is also clear that industrialization of agro-processing *per se* will not guarantee labour absorption unless the strategy adopted explicitly acknowledges the employment objective. This calls for a combination of appropriate policies, technologies and supporting institutions capable of reaching the village and household levels.

Policies and technologies must support each other if the objective of meeting the food demand in all developing countries by or before the year 2000 is to be achieved. In many instances, experience suggests that policies are often in need of modification. A basic problem is often the absence of a clear identity for the sector and a tendency for it to fall between Ministries of Agriculture and Industry. Furthermore, because of the many disciplines involved in agro-industry, responsibilities tend to be spread over numerous other government ministries. A serious problem of inter-sectorial coordination, therefore, exists both at the stage of national policy planning and of policy implementation.

Adequate integration of national policies concerning agriculture and food industry must be based on a full appreciation of the role of technology. Traditional technologies are widely used and, especially given the need for small-scale production with minimal cash outlays, they will continue to be applied. These can often be improved. At the same time, major developments are taking place in industrial-scale processing.

## 3 IMPROVEMENT OF PROCESSING OF AGRICULTURAL COMMODITIES IN DEVELOPING COUNTRIES

The major changes foreseen in the developing countries with respect to income generation and urbanization call for an increasing share of total agricultural production which would necessarily have to be processed. In addition to handling a much larger volume and greater variety of products, agro-processing has to fulfil other roles related to socio-economic development objectives. The provision of increased rural non-agricultural income and employment is probably the most important of these objectives in many countries. Agro-industry also contributes to export earnings by providing export opportunities and increasing the value of exports.

Agro-processing transforms a wide range of food and agricultural materials into a form in which intermediate or final use takes place. Typical agro-processing is thus multi-disciplinary and, consequently, there is considerable diversity in both the scale of operation and of output.

- *Rural, small-scale agro-processing* is carried out at the village level using simple and traditional technologies for milling, sundrying of fruits and vegetables, salting and drying of fish, processing of hides and skins and animal by-products.
- *Medium-scale enterprises* are frequently mechanized to some extent and located in towns rather than in villages. They may be privately or publicly owned and they are usually subject to regulatory controls. On the food side they include canning, cereal milling, dairy processing and food freezing plants. On the non-food side there is a wide spectrum of activities for example timber sawing, animal skin tanning and cotton grinning.
- *Large-scale agro-industrial* operations usually apply modern technologies and a high degree of mechanization. They are normally subject to strict regulatory control. Examples include sugar and edible oils industries.

Many agro-processing technologies have been developed through long experience and have contributed to the improved processing of a very large percentage of agricultural commodities in developing countries. In the case of food commodities this can result in significant prevention of losses at the post-harvest level. These technologies and the products resultant have become an important part of the peoples' culture. With the changing socio-economic conditions, many of the traditional technologies have remained stagnant or have deteriorated, others have even disappeared. Where possible and desirable, they should be brought technically up-to-date and made economically viable, employment-generating, energy efficient and easily manageable by the people. This will enable them to contribute more effectively to socio-economic development and to the improvement of commodity supplies both quantitatively and qualitatively. This progress can be achieved through the promotion of human creativeness and productivity. A knowledge of the results of research and development and their economic achievements are particularly required. To this effect, key personnel should be provided with specialized training in related areas. Training programmes may be organized through special seminars, symposia, short courses and fellowships to build up capability in small-scale agro-processing plant development, operation and maintenance, as well as in research and management in this field.

The agro-industry sector in developing countries may be divided into two major groups. One group is characterized by large size processing units which are established to transform raw materials from estate plantations or from imported sources, using imported technologies. Examples of such units may be found in industries which process sugarcane, coffee, cocoa, palm oil and fruits. They are usually export market led. The other group is characterized by small scale units used to process indigenous raw materials for local consumption. Technologies are based on traditional practices with little or no scientific and technological support. Many of these may be improved if research and development efforts could be undertaken towards a better understanding of their underlining principles. The hygienic conditions under which such units operate is usually poor.

## 4  JUSTIFICATION FOR INCREASED LOCAL PROCESSING OF AGRICULTURAL COMMODITIES IN DEVELOPING COUNTRIES

Research and development in agro-processing require the mobilization of competent and pragmatic human resources to meet different needs, such as leadership in basic and technological research, consultancy service and extension, institution building and research management, training and education with a full awareness of the underlying socio-economic requisites.

### Income generation and economic considerations justifications

Rapid urbanization and overall population expansion are creating conditions for a potential market demand for processed agricultural products based on indigenous crops and animal and forestry products for local consumption. The aim should be to meet the demands through a practical and innovative technical approach. One example of this is in the field of the bakery industry where an attempt was made to introduce technological adaptations whereby some proportions of starchy sources may be used as substitutes for wheat. If successful commercially, it would make these materials more suitable for breadmaking and hence check mounting imports of wheat by poor countries. It would also improve local markets for their domestic producers of starch. Two emerging trends in attitudes in developing countries towards food and agricultural industries are of particular interest. One is the greater recognition of the competence of multi-national firms in this field; the other one is the potential advantages of entering into joint activities with them under equitable conditions.

According to the ILO, the non-agricultural labour force has grown faster than the agricultural labour force in all developing regions, indicating the growing importance of non-agricultural activities in the rural areas. Thus, in continental Latin America the annual growth-rate of the rural non-agricultural labour force between 1950 and 1980 was 2.6%, as against just 0.9% for the entire agricultural labour force. For the Near East the respective growth-rates were 4.6% for the rural non-agricultural labour force and 1.6% for the agricultural labour force, respectively. The corresponding figures for South Asia were 4.2% and 1.3%, and for South East Asia, 4.6% and 1.3%, respectively[4]. The importance of non-farm activities in the rural sector emerges also from the employment statistics. For a number of Asian countries, counting only those whose *primary* employment was in the non-farm sector, and including rural towns in the definition of 'rural', about 25-45% of the real labour force is occupied in the non-farm sector. Including secondary employment in the non-farm sector, between 35 and 65% of the rural labour force could be engaged in non-farm activities on a part-time or full-time basis. Even from the point of view of income, earnings from non-farm employment range from about 21% in Bangladesh and the Philippines to as much as 61% for Thailand. Thus, an expansion of rural non-farm activities can make an important contribution to the increase of rural incomes.

Wage labour is the most important category of employment. But more significant for the future are the deep transformations that have occurred in the structure of the rural labour force over the last 30 years, leading to an increasing integration of the rural agricultural and urban labour markets. The agricultural labour force has become more urbanized, while the rural labour force has been increasingly engaged in non-agricultural activities.

Non-farm activities are particularly important for those rural households with very small holdings or little or no land. In fact, there is an inverse relationship between non-farm employment and farm size. Available data show that this relationship holds good for the South Asian countries (Bangladesh, Sri Lanka, India and Pakistan), for Thailand and East Asia (Japan and South Korea), as well as for Nigeria and Sierra Leone in Africa, among others. Another important feature of non-farm employment is its counter-cyclical nature: typically, rural households seek non-farm employment in the slack agricultural season. As such, non-farm employment evens out the sharp drops in the monthly employment and income-earning patterns of rural households. This clearly helps in the reduction of

---

[4] Promotion of Employment and Incomes for the Rural Poor, including Rural Women, through Non-Farm Activity, ILO 1983.

inequalities in rural income distribution and in the alleviation of rural poverty, especially its seasonal fluctuations. In fact, the egalitarian effects of non-farm employment in a context of land inequality and scarcity have been noted in the successful Far East experience and is another incentive for developing countries to take overdue action in this very important field.

## Scientific and technological justification

Technologies developed and applied in industrialized countries usually undergo some adaptation when transplanted to developing countries as a consequence of the different factors such as costs, market sizes, financial and technical resources. Yet experience acquired through the operation of large-scale processing plants has led to frequent complaints about the lack of appropriateness of such transfers with regard to conditions prevailing in most developing countries. Because smaller-scale technologies may correspond better to the economic conditions of developing countries, they may be viewed as one of the better alternatives for transfer. This may also be justified on the ground that the technologies employed are, on average, relatively more labour intensive than those of larger enterprises, and also because they operate in an environment where capital requirements and production scales are relatively low.

## Socio-cultural justification

Productive work opportunities outside the rural sector will not be able to absorb more than a small percentage of growing rural population of working age in the coming decades. ILO's[5] labour force projections for 1990 suggested that the largely capital-intensive industrial sectors in developing economies would not be able to absorb more than one-fourth the expected additions to the labour force between 1973 and 1990. Hence, the number of openly unemployed would rise to 90 million, with a resultant unemployment rate of 8.2% in 1990, compared to the figure of 7% in 1983. Even labour-intensive agricultural development cannot ease the severe unemployment and under-employment of the landless and near-landless. The growing gap between the growth-rates of the rural population compared to the growth-rate of agricultural population in the period 1980-85 in the developing regions, has led to an increase of 28 million

---

[5] Promotion of Employment and Incomes for the Rural Poor, including Rural Women, through Non-Farm Activity, ILO, 1983.

people in the rural sector who are not employed in agriculture in this period alone (excluding the Asian centrally planned economies). *In this context, non-farm employment and rural industrialization become indispensable for alleviating rural poverty and for rural survival.* This is confirmed by the growing numbers of non-agricultural workers in the rural areas, who already constituted about 20% of the total rural labour force, a proportion which has doubled in 30 years (1950-80) in all the developing regions except the Near East[6].

## Other justifications

An emerging change is the general awareness at policy level of the need for agro-industry to be located in rural rather than in predominantly urban areas. Disadvantages of congestion and high land prices in large urban centres are becoming more evident to industry and government. The value of having a basic blueprint for the development of agro-industry in both rural and urban areas becomes clearer in these circumstances with attention being directed to specific determinants of optimum locations. Processed products for which refrigerated transport and storage are required and which have high value relative to bulk, e.g. town milk supplies or frozen foods, are best located nearer to major markets, while those which are based on raw materials which are bulky relative to value and more easily kept in simple storage, can be located in more distant rural areas, e.g. industries processing grains.

The industries based on agricultural products as raw materials comprise a wide group. They range from operations closely related to post-harvest handling, storage and primary processing to the production through varying scales, using traditional improved, modern, capital intensive methods of such articles as edible oils, margarine and soap. It is understood that national policy, in seeking to raise the socio-economic standards of the citizens, must consider all aspects of the food and agro-industrial problems, i.e., production, marketing and consumption, and the social and economic factors conditioning them.

It can be expected that informal groups and associations will be playing an increasing role in the future development of agro-industry. This is particularly relevant as far as groups of small agricultural producers are concerned who are expected to supply the agro-industries with agricultural

---

[6] Promotion of Employment and Incomes for the Rural Poor, including Rural Women, through Non-Farm Activity. ILO, 1983.

produce. It would therefore be important to determine the managerial capacity and capability of these groups and associations. Similarly, it is important to assess the training requirements and any assistance which may be necessary.

The majority of developing countries still have limited manufacturing capacity. Industrial activities initiated by foreign investors sometimes fail to meet the basic needs of the populations: many have not assisted economic integration, nor have they contributed to the modernization of the society in the developing world as a whole. In general, traditional agro-processing industry, especially for staple foods, is characterized by small economies of scale, high labour productivity and low capital investment.

In anticipation of an increase in agricultural production as a result of current strategies and activities, it is logical to promote the development of processing technology for preventing food wastage, increasing the potential and expanding markets for such products. A number of conservation and storage methods are practised, including physical, chemical and biological methods some of which have been in use for centuries. There is a need to improve existing methods including up-scaling and technical improvement of traditional methods, or to adopt new methods in order to provide simple and inexpensive techniques for product transformation which are suited to the conditions in developing countries.

## 5  CONSTRAINTS TO INCREASED LOCAL PROCESSING OF AGRICULTURAL COMMODITIES IN DEVELOPING COUNTRIES

There are a number of constraints limiting the promotion of local processing of agricultural commodities in developing countries. The following constraints have now been identified as major impediments to agro-industry development in developing countries:

- limited financial ability to purchase inputs, land tenure problems, lack of credit for seeds, fertilizers, implements and other inputs;
- inefficient links between industry, government and research institutions with the result that each sector is unaware of the activities of the other;
- limited technical knowledge, erratic labour availability and managerial skills;
- lack of road infrastructure and transport, inappropriate handling of containers and a neglect of food handling and packing in technical training and assistance programmes;

- poor facilities, lack of utilities, irregular supply of raw materials, and deficient quality control;
- insufficient product publicity, lack of market information and lack of retail opportunities and outlets; packaging materials used in most developing countries suffer from lack of attractiveness, and unsuitability to a good preservation of the products;
- irregular supply of products, short shelf-life, price fluctuations and lack of product quality assurance;
- lack of trained personnel, especially at the technical and managerial levels;
- lack of training facilities for middle level manpower required for technological activities, industrial extension services and maintenance and operation of machinery and for graduates in food and agricultural processing technology on practical experience;
- lack of extension facilities to convey research results to the users of technologies;
- lack of information in most institutions, as well as of coordination between various institutions working on similar activities at the national and regional levels;
- absence of national institutions involved in research and development and training in the field of food and agro-industries in some countries and lack of adequate facilities for these activities in other countries;
- absence of national institutions involved in product quality control to promote a safe and honestly presented supply, to protect consumers from products which are injurious to health, unfit for human consumption, adulterated or presented in a deceptive manner and to encourage the orderly development of food and agro-industries which can stimulate increased foreign earnings through the export of commodities which comply with acceptable standards.

Most nations seek to increase trade both domestically and with other nations. Expansion of the food and agricultural commodities trade at either level depends upon demand, which in turn, must be based on the confidence of purchasers which is best maintained when a strong inspection service insures compliance with standards. Without standards, purchasers have no assurance that the commodity will be of the expected composition, quality and purity levels.

An important constraint to the development of some agro-industries, especially in the medium and small-scale sectors in rural areas, is the availability of appropriate technologies. In many cases large-scale technologies available with larger corporations cannot be applied economically, while small-scale technologies which were in use in many advanced countries fifty years ago have become obsolete and are of little use until placed on a modern scientific basis. Specialized knowledge and experience are needed in selection, modification, development and utilization of appropriate technologies. This may not exist at present in many developing countries (or even at regional and international levels to which immediate reference can be made for advice) and will require priority attention.

Given the limited, though growing demand for highly processed products such as pastas, snack foods and breakfast cereals foods, indigenous foods are not yet being used as raw materials for such products. Where the processing operations cannot be mechanized, large enterprises are not usually interested. A number of food materials in developing countries could lend themselves to this growing market of exotic foods if suitable and economical processes could be designed for their use. In this connection, there is also need to upgrade the abilities of local entrepreneurs who will be called to apply the new technologies in agro-processing units. Appropriate training facilities already exist in some cases and should be complemented and strengthened to cover the identified needs in all aspects of management of such units.

The attainment of self-reliant and self-sustaining food industrialization implies the development of an effective industrial institutional infrastructure which, at present, is grossly inadequate in most developing countries. It is necessary to take action, especially at the national level, to develop new institutions or strengthen existing ones. The establishment of a national institute for food and agro-industry research may not be required in each country. Optimal use should be made of existing national and regional institutions whose mandate is related to the development of agro-industry. In this connection, particular attention should be accorded to institutions dealing with:

- the formulation and monitoring of industrial policies, plans and programmes;
- project identification, preparation and evaluation; development or upgrading of traditional technologies;
- standardization, testing and quality control; engineering and process design, industrial information;
- industrial and trade promotion;
- industrial training in finance and management.

Available information on the size of the raw material base for the development of processing industries is not always reliable. It should be noted that total production figures are not always good indicators of quantities available for processing. A great deal of the output is consumed fresh or requires no industrial treatment.

In summary, the constraints may be grouped into the following categories:

- economic and financial;
- scientific and technological;
- social and cultural;
- manpower qualification;
- structural and infrastructural;
- environmental.

## 6 ROLE OF WOMEN IN THE PROCESSING OF AGRICULTURAL COMMODITIES IN DEVELOPING COUNTRIES

In most developing countries women play a dominant role in both production and postharvest processing of crops through small-scale and largely unsophisticated agro-industries, particularly in supplying the basic staple foods and facilities for local communities by processing indigenous raw materials.

Women who fulfil such entrepreneurial roles face the normal difficulties of small-scale enterprises with access to credit facilities, lack of security, competition access to stable markets and limited managerial and technical capabilities. It would help if they were to benefit from the services of established industrial promotion agencies and technical support provided by governments. Thus far, women have largely been overlooked as users and agents of change in science and technology; women's needs as users, in such fields as labour-saving devices, technologies for human and basic needs and other quality-of-life improving means should be taken into account in designing industrial end-products or production processes. Women users should be involved in product testing and development.

Cooperative efforts in the purchase of raw materials and the marketing of products can strengthen the competitiveness of small producers isolated from the major market centres. In each case, however, special measures should be taken by the development agencies to extend their services to women entrepreneurs outside the main urban centres and to help them take advantage of the assistance provided.

## 7 FUTURE ACTION

The present review indicates that there are objective reasons for the promotion of the development of agro-industry in developing countries. A number of constraints have been identified which could be overcome by a coordinated effort, at the national, regional and international levels.

In the conditions of most developing countries, there is much to be said for greater attention to 'agro-oriented' industrialization. This could include enhanced use of indigenous food and agro-processing techniques and improved production of agricultural inputs. This would assure a higher level of production and better insure a steady and regular volume of supply of raw materials to these industries. It would aid off-farm employment and improve the level and distribution of income in rural areas.

Small-scale and large-scale agro-industry are frequently complementary. The choice of a scale of industrialization should take into account its socio-economic implications. In general, however, small-scale food industries are more adapted to the rural environment, even though they may not be more efficient in their use of resources.

For agro-industries aimed at food self-sufficiency, it should be recognized that the food production-processing-marketing system represents an integrated and inter-dependent relationship since no single sector can be developed in isolation. Viable food industries depend on steady supplies of raw materials of suitable quality and a steady demand for the final products. The inter-dependence inherent in this food 'system' means that several government ministries, agencies and other bodies including the private sector are involved, with the result that the system should be efficiently organized, as a single entity.

Governments may consider adapting policy measures designed to encourage national and regional institutions in their efforts to accelerate the implementation of programmes aimed at the promotion of the development of indigenous agro-industry. Such measures may include appropriate prices to producers, better identification and preparation of projects, improvement of institutional infrastructures for project implementation and monitoring, development and upgrading of local technologies for processing of local agricultural commodities, manpower development and marketing.

Government and international organizations may adopt policies to ensure maximum utilization of local expertise and acquisition of consultants' services. Attempts should be made to give priority to local consultants and their associations. Developing countries are encouraged to strengthen the link between R & D institutions, universities, manufacturers and their associations and users.

National Governments, international organizations and industrial associations should coordinate their actions to develop manpower development programmes capable of responding to the needs of agro-industrial development in product design, marketing and machinery repair and maintenance to ensure a more effective use of investments.

The key position of women in food and agro-processing at the domestic and small-scale levels as producers and processors is well understood. In developing a framework for food and agro-processing science and technology it will be necessary to take women's contribution into account. Current processes of change should be monitored so as to assess their impact on women, wherever their involvement in food processing is contemplated. Women themselves as full partners should be actively involved in planning and decision-making processes in food and agro-processing technology so as to ensure that they benefit from the available technologies, and that any adverse effects are minimized.

Because of the multi-disciplinary nature of agro-industries, a number of FAO's technical and economic units are involved in the planning and implementation of activities/projects in this area. Staff member specialized in technical and economic subjects are available to assist FAO Member Nations in the processing of agricultural commodities. The degree of intervention of the Organization varies, but a wide level of technical backstopping is provided. This includes assistance in project planning, recruiting experts, advising management of any technical or managerial aspects, reviewing periodically performance and problems, organizing and participation in expert meetings or workshops.

# ANNEX

*Global outlook on agricultural commodities:*
*share in production and processing between*
*developed and developing countries*[7]

In the FAO's medium-term projections towards the year 2000 for agricultural production, demand, trade and prices for major agricultural commodities or groups of commodities for almost all countries was summarized. These projections may lead to the following observation.

The 1990's are expected to be characterized by aggregate growth rates for the production, demand and trade of food and agricultural commodities substantially lower than during the 1980's and at or below projected rates of population increase (Tables 1a and 1b). World demand for food and agricultural commodities (for all uses) is expected to grow by only 1.6% annually, slightly below the rate of population growth and below the 2% annual increase in the 1980's. By contrast, the rate of growth of production is projected to decline only slightly, from 1.8% annually in the 1980's to 1.7% annually in the 1990's with some commodity groups, such as livestock, fats and oils and tropical beverages, slightly below the trend. The fact that consumption growth exceeded that of production in the 1980's reflected the large drawdown of stocks of a number of agricultural commodities. Overall supplies are projected to be sufficient to meet global effective demand. The growth in food and agricultural commodity trade is projected to decline from 2.9% annually in the 1980's to 1.4 in the 1990's below projected growth rates for merchandise trade in general. Thus agricultural commodity trade will decline in proportion to total trade. Trade growth for all agricultural commodity sectors, except fruit and wine, share in the decline; trade in staple foods would be particularly affected, declining from 3.1% annual growth in the 1980s to 0.3% in the 1990s.

---

[7] The information contained in this Annex has been abstracted from the Medium-Term Projects for Agricultural Commodities: Agricultural Commodity Projections to 2000 - DOC - CCP 93/18, March 1993.

*Table 1a:* Growth of world agricultural production, demand and trade, past and projected (per cent per year)

| Commodity Groups | Production | | Demand | | Trade[1] | |
|---|---|---|---|---|---|---|
| | 1978*-88* | 1988*-2000 | 1978*-88* | 1988*-2000 | 1978*-88* | 1988*-2000 |
| All commodities covered | 1.8 | 1.7 | 2.0 | 1.6 | 2.9 | 1.4 |
| Foodstuffs | 1.8 | 1.7 | 1.9 | 1.6 | 3.0 | 1.2 |
| Staple Foods | 1.3 | 1.6 | 1.6 | 1.5 | 3.1 | 0.3 |
| Cereals | 1.8 | 1.8 | 2.1 | 1.6 | 2.4 | 0.8 |
| Roots and Tubers | 0.1 | 1.0 | 0.2 | 1.0 | 5.5 | -3.0 |
| Pulses | 2.5 | 1.7 | 2.5 | 1.6 | 10.0 | 2.1 |
| Livestock Products | 2.2 | 1.6 | 2.2 | 1.6 | 2.9 | 1.3 |
| Fats and Oils | 3.6 | 2.9 | 3.8 | 2.7 | 3.9 | 2.5 |
| Sugar[2] | 1.7 | 1.6 | 2.4 | 1.5 | -1.1 | 0.8 |
| Fruit and Wine[2] | 0.3 | 1.7 | 0.2 | 1.6 | 1.7 | 1.5 |
| Tropical Beverages | 2.5 | 1.7 | 2.8 | 2.1 | 2.7 | 1.3 |
| Agricultural Raw Mat. | 1.9 | 2.3 | 2.5 | 2.0 | 2.7 | 2.4 |

*Notes:* 1978* signifies 1977 to 1979 average, 1988* signifies 1987 to 1989 average
[1] Gross.
[2] Net imports and exports for sugar, citrus and wine.

*Table 1b*: Developing countries: growth of agricultural production, demand and trade, past and projected (% per year)

| Commodity Groups | Production | | Demand | | Imports[1] | | Exports[1] | |
|---|---|---|---|---|---|---|---|---|
| | 1978*-88* | 1988*-2000 | 1978*-88* | 1988*-2000 | 1978*-88* | 1988*-2000 | 1978*-88* | 1988*-2000 |
| All commodities covered | 3.2 | 2.8 | 3.3 | 2.9 | 4.7 | 3.3 | 3.9 | 2.1 |
| Foodstuffs | 3.2 | 2.8 | 3.3 | 2.9 | 4.6 | 3.2 | 3.8 | 2.2 |
| Staple Foods | 2.2 | 2.0 | 2.4 | 2.2 | 4.9 | 2.5 | 3.6 | -0.2 |
| Cereals | 2.9 | 2.5 | 3.3 | 2.5 | 4.8 | 2.6 | 0.7 | 2.0 |
| Roots and Tubers | 1.0 | 1.3 | 0.8 | 1.6 | 14.2 | -1.2 | 6.3 | -4.4 |
| Pulses | 0.8 | 2.1 | 1.0 | 2.3 | 9.8 | 4.5 | 6.7 | 1.3 |
| Livestock Products | 4.3 | 3.5 | 4.4 | 3.5 | 3.8 | 3.4 | 2.2 | 3.7 |
| Fats and Oils | 5.5 | 4.0 | 5.4 | 4.0 | 7.0 | 4.2 | 6.9 | 4.2 |
| Sugar[2] | 2.1 | 2.2 | 4.4 | 2.5 | 3.9 | 2.8 | -0.9 | -0.9 |
| Fruit and Wine[2] | 2.0 | 2.9 | 1.6 | 3.2 | -2.2 | 5.8 | 3.7 | 2.1 |
| Tropical Beverages | 2.5 | 1.7 | 2.9 | 3.4 | 2.4 | 2.6 | 3.0 | 1.6 |
| Raw Materials | 2.8 | 2.7 | 3.7 | 3.0 | 5.6 | 3.4 | 4.3 | 1.4 |

*Notes:* 1978* signifies 1977 to 1979 average, 1988* signifies 1987 to 1989 average
[1] Gross.
[2] Net imports and exports for sugar, citrus and wine.

Factors in the slowdown of world demand include a reduced growth in population and per caput income and, in some cases, increasing competition by synthetics. Aggregate figures for some categories, such as wines, tea and coffee, mask significant changes in consumer preferences, for instance for high quality wines, CTC[8] teas and mild coffees. Aggregate production growth rates, which are not projected to decrease significantly, reflect factors such as declining rates of expansion in yields; changes in agricultural support programmes, such as the European Community's (EC) reform of its Common Agricultural Programme (CAP); and closer linkage to demand conditions, it being expected that in general excess stocks will not accumulate again because of policies to curb excess production. Trade in many commodities will be particularly affected by developments in the CIS (former USSR), a major importer of a number of commodities in the past, and china, where increasing domestic production is expected to reduce imports and, in some cases, make China a net exporter. Other factors affecting trade include the tendency in some commodities, including tea and agricultural raw materials, toward increased consumption of processing in the producing country.

The developing countries will account for much of the growth in overall commodity demand because of their comparatively buoyant per caput GDP expansion, twice the rate of the 1980's (but less than in the 1970's) and the greater responsiveness of demand to income growth. Agricultural production in the developing countries is projected to increase by 2.8% annually in the 1990's; i.e. slower than the 3.2% annual rate of the 1980's, but still allowing for increasing per caput production. By contrast, the developed countries are projected to raise their production by 0.7% annually. The aggregate gross imports of the developing countries are expected to rise by 3.3% annually in the 1990's, increasing their share of world imports, from 34% for the 1987-89 average to 42% in 2000; and aggregate gross exports are projected to grow by 2.1%.

## Key sector review

World *staple food crop* (cereals, roots and tubers, pulses) production is expected to increase by 1.6% annually, slightly faster than during the 1980's which were characterized by a significant drawdown in stocks. In the developing countries, production is estimated to grow by 2.0%

---

[8] Processed according to 'Crash, Tire and Curling' method.

annually, almost the same as during the 1980's. While crop yields in the developing countries are projected to grow more slowly than in the 1980's, this will be offset by area growth (Table 2). In developed countries production should rise slightly faster than during the 1980s. Global demand is projected to grow by only 1.5% annually, less than in the 1980's and less than the growth in population. The volume of staple food trade is projected to decline sharply to 0.3% annually during the 1990's from 3.1% in the 1980's.

In the staple food sector, the growth of world *cereals* production is projected to stay at 1.8% annually, the same rate as in the 1980's. Total trade is expected to grow by only 0.8%, compared with 2.4% annual growth of the 1980's. However, developing country import demand for cereals will continue to increase sharply, resulting in a projected net trade deficit of 123 million tonnes in 2000, (up from the 89 million tonne 1987-89 average), and gross imports and 161 million tonnes (119 million tonnes in 1987-89).

The growth of the world *livestock* economy is projected to decline, even though poultry and pigmeat sectors are likely to remain fast-growing, while the expansion in developing countries should exceed the rate of growth in the developed countries. World trade growth for these commodities is also expected to slow down. Reflecting the slowdown in the livestock sector, world feed, including demand for feed uses of cereals (wheat, maize, other grains), roots and tubers, pulses and oilmeal proteins is projected to grow by 1.2% annually during the 1990's compared with 1.5% in the 1980's; agricultural policy reform, particularly in the EC, is expected to have an important impact on feed imports, as reductions in domestic cereal prices are expected to reduce imports of cassava and pulses and to curb the growth for oilmeals. Much consumption growth for coarse grains, especially maize and oilmeals, is foreseen to come from the developing countries, where the demand for feed is expected to be particularly strong.

*Table 2a:* Staple foods: area, yield and production, past and projected

| Commodity/Region | 1987-89 Average | | | 2000 Projected | | |
|---|---|---|---|---|---|---|
| | Area million ha | Yield 100 kg/ha | Production million tons | Area million ha | Yield 100 kg/ha | Production million tons |
| **WHEAT** | | | | | | |
| World | 221.6 | 23.5 | 521.2 | 230.8 | 27.7 | 640.1 |
| Developing countries | 99.0 | 22.0 | 217.6 | 106.3 | 28.0 | 297.5 |
| Developed countries | 122.6 | 24.8 | 303.6 | 124.5 | 27.5 | 342.6 |
| **RICE, MILLED** | | | | | | |
| World | 145.1 | 22.4 | 324.9 | 146.8 | 27.9 | 409.4 |
| Developing countries[1] | 140.7 | 21.8 | 307.2 | 142.6 | 27.4 | 390.1 |
| Developed countries | 4.4 | 40.4 | 17.7 | 4.2 | 45.8 | 19.3 |
| **COARSE GRAINS** | | | | | | |
| World | 334.6 | 23.8 | 794.9 | 341.2 | 28.6 | 977.7 |
| Developing countries[1] | 181.5 | 16.0 | 290.9 | 195.2 | 20.7 | 404.2 |
| Developed countries | 153.1 | 32.9 | 504.0 | 146.0 | 39.3 | 573.5 |

*Notes:*　[1] Including other developing countries in Oceania.

*Table 2b:* Staple foods: area, yield and production, past and projected

| Commodity/Region | 1987-89 Average | | | 2000 Projected | | |
|---|---|---|---|---|---|---|
| | Area million ha | Yield 100 kg/ha | Production million tons | Area million ha | Yield 100 kg/ha | Production million tons |
| **ROOTS AND TUBERS** | | | | | | |
| World | 47.1 | 125.0 | 590.1 | 47.9 | 139.0 | 667.1 |
| Developing countries[1] | 35.0 | 111.0 | 388.3 | 37.0 | 123.0 | 455.4 |
| Developed countries | 12.1 | 167.0 | 201.8 | 10.9 | 193.0 | 211.7 |
| **PULSES** | | | | | | |
| World | 67.2 | 8.1 | 54.2 | 72.8 | 9.1 | 66.0 |
| Developing countries[1] | 55.9 | 6.3 | 35.1 | 61.5 | 7.4 | 45.2 |
| Developed countries | 11.3 | 17.0 | 19.1 | 11.3 | 18.3 | 20.8 |
| **TOTAL STAPLE FOODS[2]** | | | | | | |
| World | 815.6 | 28.0 | 2285.3 | 839.5 | 32.9 | 2760.3 |
| Developing countries[1] | 512.1 | 24.2 | 1239.1 | 542.6 | 29.3 | 1592.4 |
| Developed countries | 303.5 | 34.5 | 1046.2 | 296.9 | 39.3 | 1167.9 |

*Notes:*    [1] Including other developing countries in Oceania.
            [2] In product weight.

*Table 2c:* Staple foods: area, yield and production, past and projected

| Commodity/Region | Growth Rates (per cent per year) | | | | | |
| --- | --- | --- | --- | --- | --- | --- |
| | Area | | Yield | | Production | |
| | 1978*-1988 | 1988*-2000 | 1978*-1988 | 1988*-2000 | 1978*-1988 | 1988*-2000 |
| **WHEAT** | | | | | | |
| World | -0.3 | 0.3 | 2.4 | 1.4 | 2.1 | 1.7 |
| Developing countries[1] | 0.5 | 0.6 | 3.8 | 2.0 | 4.3 | 2.6 |
| Developed countries | -0.9 | 0.1 | 1.8 | 0.9 | 0.9 | 1.0 |
| **RICE, MILLED** | | | | | | |
| World | 0.1 | 0.1 | 2.5 | 1.8 | 2.6 | 1.9 |
| Developing countries[1] | 0.2 | 0.1 | 2.6 | 1.9 | 2.8 | 2.0 |
| Developed countries | -0.7 | -0.4 | 0.4 | 1.1 | -0.4 | 0.7 |
| **COARSE GRAINS** | | | | | | |
| World | -0.3 | 0.2 | 1.0 | 1.5 | 0.7 | 1.7 |
| Developing countries[1] | 0.4 | 0.6 | 1.8 | 2.2 | 2.2 | 2.8 |
| Developed countries | -1.0 | -0.4 | 0.9 | 1.5 | -0.0 | 1.1 |

*Notes:*   [1] Including other developing countries in Oceania.

*Table 2d*: Staple foods: area, yield and production, past and projected

| Commodity/Region | Growth Rates (per cent per year) | | | | | |
|---|---|---|---|---|---|---|
| | Area | | Yield | | Production | |
| | 1978*-1988 | 1988*-2000 | 1978*-1988 | 1988*-2000 | 1978*-1988 | 1988*-2000 |
| ROOTS AND TUBERS | | | | | | |
| World | -0.4 | 0.1 | 5.0 | 0.9 | 0.1 | 1.0 |
| Developing countries[1] | 0.0 | 0.5 | 1.0 | 0.9 | 1.0 | 1.3 |
| Developed countries | -1.6 | -0.9 | 0.1 | 1.2 | -1.5 | 0.4 |
| PULSES | | | | | | |
| World | 1.0 | 0.7 | 1.5 | 1.0 | 2.5 | 1.7 |
| Developing countries[1] | 0.6 | 0.8 | 0.2 | 1.4 | 0.9 | 2.1 |
| Developed countries | 2.9 | 0.0 | 3.5 | 0.6 | 6.4 | 0.7 |
| TOTAL STAPLE FOODS[2] | | | | | | |
| World | -0.1 | 0.2 | 1.3 | 1.3 | 1.1 | 1.6 |
| Developing countries[1] | 0.3 | 0.5 | 1.9 | 1.6 | 2.2 | 2.1 |
| Developed countries | -0.8 | -0.2 | 0.8 | 1.1 | -0.0 | 0.9 |

*Notes:*  [1] Including other developing countries in Oceania.
[2] In product weight.

*Tropical beverage crops* are projected to continue to experience diffi-culties in the 1990's, with their markets near saturation in the major developed countries that account for over 80% of demand for coffee and cocoa. World demand is expected to grow at 2.1% annually during the 1990's, substantially below the growth experienced in the 1980's. Much of the growth in demand is projected to occur in producing developing countries. Coffee and cocoa markets are expected to be in balance. Production, consumption and trade in tea is expected to be more dynamic; even though a moderate tea export surplus is projected for 2000, with some risk of downward pressure on prices.

Growth in aggregate world demand for *agricultural raw materials* is expected to slow down to 2% annually, from 2.5% in the 1980's. Compe-tition from synthetics, particularly in developed country markets, will continue to constrain demand and trade in virtually all agricultural raw materials. However, environmental considerations and the development of markets for non-traditional products could result in improved prospects for some agricultural raw materials. Increased consumption in producing developing countries reflects declining trade opportunities for some raw or semi-processed materials and, in some instances, increased processing in the producing countries.

In *conclusion*, it may be said that the slowdown in world trade of the agricultural commodities covered in these projection to the year 2000 is likely to cause some significant adjustment problems for the exporting countries. Firstly, even during the 1980's when the growth of agricultural trade was stronger, it was not enough to stall the rise in protectionism and the fierce competition for markets that took place. There are some signs of the intention to reverse the protectionist trend in world agricultural markets through the Uruguay Round (GATT) as well as through auton-omous moves towards liberalization by many developing countries and the formerly centrally planned economies in Eastern Europe and the CIS (former USSR). However, the trading system could be put under con-siderable strain by the slow growth of world markets for the main agricul-tural commodities, particularly cereals.

At the same time that agricultural commodity markets are likely to be growing slowly, the net agricultural trade situation of the developing countries is projected to deteriorate significantly. If these projections materialize, the developing countries could turn from net exporters of the main primary agricultural commodities (as at present) to net importers by the year 2000. While to some extent this turnaround reflects an increased processing of certain agricultural raw materials, the overall outcome would be a blow to those developing countries who continue to rely heavily on agricultural commodity exports for an important source of export earnings to pay for their other vitally needed imports. This under-lines the vital importance of a successful Uruguay Round that would facilitate an expansion in their export earnings. Moreover, this finding together with the fact that nearly one-half of the export earnings from agriculture are now accounted for by non-traditional, processed or semi-processed agricultural commodities, points to the importance to the developing countries of the expansion in the newer, more dynamic agricultural export markets, including horticulture, processed products and certain feedstuffs.

The net cereal import gap of the developing countries is projected to grow from 89 million tonnes in 1987-89 to 123 million tonnes by the year 2000. At the same time, the gross cereal imports of the developing countries are projected to rise to 161 million tonnes from 119 million tonnes over the same period. This is another steep increase that will put an additional burden on the developing countries. The danger is that even at constant prices this will lead to a large rise in their import bill. More-over, the national level of food security of these countries is more vulner-able to the instability of the world food market and to possible increases in prices stemming from the move to a more liberalized trading system. It will be important for the international community to make sure that the developing countries, especially the low-income, food-deficit countries, are in a position to import these volumes, otherwise the hoped for rise in per caput consumption and improved nutrition would be put in jeopardy. Table 3 summarizes the situation of Developing Countries with regard to International Trade (actual and projected). The last column of that Table shows a generally negative trend in average net trade, during the periods under review.

*Table 3a:* Developing countries: international trade, actual and projected (in million metric tonnes)

| Commodity or Commodity group | Gross imports | | | Gross exports | | | Net trade | | |
|---|---|---|---|---|---|---|---|---|---|
| | 1977-79 average | 1987-89 average | 2000 proj. | 1977-79 average | 1987-89 average | 2000 proj. | 1977-79 average | 1987-89 average | 2000 proj. |
| **Cereals** | 74.4 | 119.2 | 161.4 | 28.4 | 30.4 | 38.7 | 46.0 | 88.8 | 122.7 |
| Wheat | 45.6 | 68.4 | 84.9 | 6.2 | 8.4 | 9.4 | 39.4 | 60.0 | 75.5 |
| Rice, milled | 8.0 | 9.1 | 13.3 | 7.2 | 9.0 | 13.2 | 0.8 | 0.1 | 0.1 |
| Coarse grains | 20.8 | 41.7 | 63.2 | 15.0 | 13.0 | 16.1 | 5.8 | 28.7 | 47.1 |
| Maize | 13.9 | 26.6 | 40.3 | 9.2 | 9.8 | 11.0 | 4.7 | 16.8 | 29.3 |
| Millet & sorghum | 2.4 | 3.6 | 5.9 | 4.8 | 2.0 | 3.2 | -2.4 | 1.6 | 2.7 |
| Other coarse grains n.e.s. | 4.5 | 11.5 | 17.0 | 1.0 | 1.2 | 1.9 | 3.5 | 10.3 | 15.1 |
| **Roots and Tubers** | 1.4 | 5.3 | 4.6 | 15.7 | 28.8 | 16.7 | -14.2 | -23.6 | -12.2 |
| **Pulses** | 0.9 | 2.3 | 3.9 | 1.2 | 2.3 | 2.7 | -0.3 | 0.0 | 1.2 |
| **Meat** | 2.1 | 3.4 | 5.8 | 2.1 | 2.8 | 4.4 | 0.0 | 0.6 | 1.4 |
| Bovine | 0.9 | 1.3 | 2.2 | 1.6 | 1.5 | 1.6 | -0.7 | -0.2 | 0.6 |
| Sheep and goat | 0.3 | 0.5 | 0.8 | 0.1 | 0.2 | 0.2 | 0.2 | 0.3 | 0.6 |
| Pig | 0.3 | 0.5 | 1.6 | 0.3 | 0.6 | 1.5 | 0.0 | -0.1 | 0.1 |
| Poultry | 0.6 | 1.1 | 1.2 | 0.1 | 0.5 | 1.1 | 0.5 | 0.6 | 0.1 |

*Table 3b:* Developing countries: international trade, actual and projected (in million metric tonnes)

| Commodity or Commodity group | Gross imports | | | Gross exports | | | Net trade | | |
|---|---|---|---|---|---|---|---|---|---|
| | 1977-79 average | 1987-89 average | 2000 proj. | 1977-79 average | 1987-89 average | 2000 proj. | 1977-79 average | 1987-89 average | 2000 proj. |
| **Whole milk** | 15.3 | 20.8 | 25.9 | 0.6 | 1.2 | 2.8 | 14.7 | 19.6 | 23.1 |
| **Fats and oils** | 6.8 | 12.8 | 20.0 | 7.0 | 13.1 | 21.7 | -0.2 | -0.3 | -1.7 |
| **Oilmeal protein** | 2.0 | 5.5 | 11.6 | 6.4 | 13.8 | 21.5 | -4.4 | -8.3 | -9.9 |
| **Sugar**[1] | 8.9 | 13.1 | 18.2 | 18.8 | 17.2 | 19.2 | -9.9 | -4.1 | -1.0 |
| **Bananas** | 0.6 | 0.6 | 1.4 | 6.3 | 7.3 | 11.5 | -5.7 | -6.7 | -10.1 |
| **Citrus fruit** | 1.3 | 0.9 | 1.7 | 6.4 | 12.6 | 15.1 | -5.1 | -11.8 | -13.4 |
| **Wine**[2] | 2.4 | 2.3 | 4.2 | 5.9 | 1.9 | 1.8 | -3.5 | 0.4 | 2.4 |
| **Coffee** | 0.2 | 0.3 | 0.4 | 3.4 | 4.3 | 5.1 | -3.1 | -4.1 | -4.7 |
| **Cocoa** | 0.1 | 0.1 | 0.1 | 1.3 | 2.0 | 2.4 | -1.2 | -1.9 | -2.3 |

*Notes:*   [1] Net imports and exports.
      [2] Million hectolitres.

*Table 3c:* Developing countries: international trade, actual and projected (in million metric tonnes)

| Commodity or Commodity group | Gross imports | | | Gross exports | | | Net trade | | |
|---|---|---|---|---|---|---|---|---|---|
| | 1977-79 average | 1987-89 average | 2000 proj. | 1977-79 average | 1987-89 average | 2000 proj. | 1977-79 average | 1987-89 average | 2000 proj. |
| Tea³ | 0.3 | 0.4 | 0.6 | 0.7 | 0.9 | 1.3 | -0.4 | -0.5 | -0.7 |
| **Cotton, raw** | 1.9 | 2.6 | 4.5 | 2.0 | 2.6 | 2.9 | -0.1 | 0.0 | 1.5 |
| **Jute, kenaf and allied fibres** | 0.6 | 0.6 | 0.5 | 1.6 | 1.4 | 1.0 | -1.0 | -0.8 | -0.5 |
| **Hard fibres** | 0.1 | 0.1 | 0.0 | 0.6 | 0.4 | 0.4 | -0.6 | -0.4 | -0.4 |
| Sisal and henequen | 0.1 | 0.0 | 0.0 | 0.4 | 0.3 | 0.2 | -0.4 | -0.2 | -0.2 |
| Abaca | 0.0 | 0.0 | 0.0 | 0.1 | 0.1 | 0.1 | -0.1 | -0.1 | -0.1 |
| Coir | 0.0 | 0.0 | 0.0 | 0.1 | 0.1 | 0.1 | -0.1 | -0.1 | -0.1 |
| **Hides and skins** | 0.7 | 1.7 | 2.2 | 0.8 | 1.9 | 2.8 | -0.1 | -0.2 | -0.6 |
| Bovine | 0.7 | 1.6 | 2.1 | 0.7 | 1.7 | 2.7 | --- | -0.1 | -0.6 |
| Sheep and goat | - | 0.1 | 0.1 | 0.1 | 0.2 | 0.1 | -0.1 | -0.1 | 0.0 |

*Notes:* ³ Black tea.

# THE GLOBAL ERA - QUALITY CONCEPTS

TAN SRI DR. B.C. SEKHAR[1]

## 1 INTRODUCTION

Quality is an essential and critical element in the market stability of industrial commodities. This concept has become crucial with the globalisation of the manufacturing sector. Standardisation of product quality irrespective of manufacturing location, has become a must for market acceptance and economic viability. It is perhaps in this context that there is universal acceptance for the need to implement fully the elements of the ISO 9000 Series of quality management principles. While these principles are accepted and the consequential revolution in quality management techniques have taken hold widely in industrial products and chemicals, agricultural commodities have lagged significantly behind. This paper discusses various issues relating to the natural rubber sector.

## 2 THE CONCEPT OF QUALITY

There are basically two distinctive parts in the concept of total quality. The first relates to intrinsic quality as defined by acceptable specification and the second arises from consistent quality through standardised application of quality management checks and balances. The ISO 9000 Series basically addresses the latter. In dealing with agricultural commodities in terms of quality, the overall status of the particular commodity should be taken into account. This is perhaps best exemplified by using natural rubber as one of the more advanced of the agricultural commodities on the 'quality ladder'.

[1] Secretary-General, International Rubber Study Group (IRSG), London.

## 3 DEVELOPMENTS IN THE NATURAL RUBBER SECTOR

One essential element which perhaps renders the NR story unique, is the fundamental fact that all large scale use of rubbers in industry evolved from the discovery and use of NR from *Hevea Brasiliensis* more than a century ago. Subsequent massive development of man made rubber through chemical synthesis in the latter part of this century required that the synthetic rubbers behaved in performance equal to or better than natural rubber in specific uses. In other words, in this part of the evolutionary cycle, NR was the standard for other elastomers to emulate in performance behaviour. This has historically inspired some 'distortions' in quality management principles. From the start, manufacturing processes were attuned to the vagaries, subjective practices and adventitious variations inherent in the *Hevea* plantation and smallholder industries. Improvements in quality standards were neither seriously sought by the consuming sector nor significantly attempted by the producing sector in the first 50 years of the elastomer development history. It was the advent of the massive SR sector as a consequence of the Second World War that brought about motivation on the part of producers.

In most industries, it is the 'consumer pull' that brings about quality and development changes and provides incentives for innovation. 'Producer push' in this context will fall on the wayside because market entry becomes inhibited and limiting. The NR story is a case in point. Traditionally, the bulk of NR was sold in the solid form, as sheets smoked or air dried, with quality assessed visually against light and shipped bareback in 4 foot cubic bales which were talc coated. The bales arrived distorted and distended in the consumers factory. Handling was difficult, stacking a problem and the rubber required an elaborate procedure of straining, premastication and pre-testing before fabrication and conversion into products. It is perhaps the native excellence of the polymer that *Hevea* provides, which has enabled the wheels of industry to keep rolling in spite of such imperfections in the handling of NR after its emergence from the trees.

It is a simple fact that the manufacturing sector, the most important of which is the tyre industry, was simply prepared to accept sheet rubber at the lowest price the commodity market was prepared to provide. Variations in characteristics, contamination with adventitious matter, etc., could be obviated by handling procedures in consumer factories. The all important competitive feature was 'price'. There was no incentive or demand associated with top quality volume sheet or NR in any form. Such high quality NR can only find limited use in specialised applications. The tyre sector, which consumed over 70% of the commodity was simply satisfied in obtaining NR at the lowest possible price as they had the requisite technology to handle the man-made inadequacies.

Two factors changed the situation. The first was the erosion of the NR market caused by fierce SR competition. Most tyre manufacturers were integrated with SR production facilities and only needed to use NR where it was imperative technologically. The second factor which has become manifest in more recent years is automation, with features such as statistical process control and computerised operations in the manufacturing process.

The first factor led NR producers to implement new processing methods, technical specifications, modern packaging and presentation and basic quality guarantees. Introduced in Malaysia in 1965, accepted by other producing environments in the late 1960s and 1970s, TSR (Technically Specified Rubbers) now represent about 60% of the world's dry NR. Clearly, therefore, even today a significant tonnage (40%) of dry rubber used is in traditional forms, mainly sheet. Table 1 presents exports by type at the three major Asian NR producers. Obviously, consumers would like to have higher quality, i.e. higher quality of the lower market grades of sheets. As the *Hevea* tree produces only one type of polymer, careful and quality conscious processing can result in one or two high grades of rubber. The commodity market demands, however, a multitude of grades. The problem is that tyre manufacturers compete with each other and while they are not overly concerned with the absolute level of price, they are seriously influenced by the level of price paid by their competitors. There is simply no strong message on quality and market preference on the part of manufacturers in a unified form conveyed to the producers directly or through the market. The message simply is that they require the same market grades with the quality improved. New processing methods were devised to improve quality and in so doing these rubbers enter the highest quality criterion of the TSR specifications. Without a ready market, wider use of quality enhancing innovations is impeded and the development which could have opened up avenues to impart greater consistency inhibited. The present NR commodity market operations and manufacturers approach to NR quality grades are not conducive to real quality upgradation in the NR industry.

## 4  FUTURE STRATEGIES FOR THE NATURAL RUBBER SECTOR

The developments sketches above are, of course, no excuse for the NR producers to jump off the 'quality ladder'. In this global age, the fine distinction between producer and manufacturer is disappearing. It has become universally necessary to meet a single world quality criteria. As long as producers market a spectrum of quality grades, it makes commercial sense for manufacturers to choose the lowest market grade that will satisfy the minimum quality element the manufacturing operation demands. As the tree only produces one type of NR and as processing methods are available to enhance quality in large volume, should this not be the approach at all the NR producing environments? Instead of seeking market premiums for quality, the philosophy should be 'quality is free'. Without a multiple choice of market grades, there will be less subjective competitive considerations among manufacturers and the market price would simply reflect the fundamentals of supply-demand and will not be exacerbated by consumer manipulations.

Production, manufacture and end use are all sequences of a quality chain and they are integral to progress nationally, regionally and globally. The consequence of the inexorable march of globalisation are only beginning to be understood not only in commodity producing countries but also in the consuming areas. With one 'foot' firmly in the 20th Century, the consumers are demanding the benefits of the 21st Century criteria. The producers of NR are demanding the benefits of the 21st Century features before they are prepared to step out of the 'shackles' binding them with 15th Century entrenched marketing approaches.

In the case of NR, the initiative to move towards a very few market grades of NR which are consistent in processing and performance criteria, packaged and presented in modern form and arriving at the consumer door retaining the native excellence of the polymer, is with the producing environment. 'Producer push' in the case of NR should receive enthusiastic welcome from the erstwhile reluctant or recalcitrant consumers. NR producers can ill afford to wait for the 'consumer pull'.

*Table 1a:*   Gross Exports of Natural Rubber by type, volume ('000t)

|  | 1988 | 1989 | 1990 | 1991 | 1992 |
|---|---|---|---|---|---|
| **MALAYSIA** | | | | | |
| Latex | 302 | 242 | 192 | 190 | 152 |
| RSS | 323 | 268 | 200 | 116 | 78 |
| TSR | 929 | 909 | 877 | 773 | 760 |
| Others | 42 | 59 | 22 | 53 | 45 |
| Sum | 1,596 | 1,478 | 1,291 | 1,132 | 1,035 |
| **INDONESIA** | | | | | |
| Latex | 50 | 34 | 34 | 59 | 39 |
| RSS | 130 | 151 | 124 | 124 | 121 |
| TSR | 940 | 959 | 915 | 1,030 | 1,103 |
| Others | 12 | 8 | 4 | 7 | 5 |
| Sum | 1,132 | 1,152 | 1,077 | 1,220 | 1,268 |
| **THAILAND** | | | | | |
| Latex | 53 | 26 | 46 | 61 | 69 |
| RSS | 692 | 909 | 938 | 977 | 1069 |
| TSR | 118 | 129 | 130 | 147 | 230 |
| Others | 43 | 37 | 37 | 47 | 45 |
| Sum | 906 | 1,101 | 1,151 | 1,232 | 1413 |
| **SUM** | | | | | |
| Latex | 405 | 302 | 272 | 310 | 260 |
| RSS | 1,145 | 1,328 | 1,262 | 1,217 | 1,268 |
| TSR | 1,987 | 1,997 | 1,922 | 1,950 | 2,093 |
| Others | 97 | 104 | 63 | 107 | 95 |
| Sum | 3,634 | 3,731 | 3,519 | 3,584 | 3,716 |

*Table 1b:*   Gross Exports of Natural Rubber by type, share (%)

|  | 1988 | 1989 | 1990 | 1991 | 1992 |
|---|---|---|---|---|---|
| **MALAYSIA** | | | | | |
| Latex | 18.9 | 16.4 | 14.9 | 16.8 | 14.7 |
| RSS | 20.2 | 18.1 | 15.5 | 10.2 | 7.5 |
| TSR | 58.2 | 61.5 | 67.9 | 68.3 | 73.4 |
| Others | 2.6 | 4.0 | 1.7 | 4.7 | 4.3 |
| Sum | 100.0 | 100.0 | 100.0 | 100.0 | 100.0 |
| | | | | | |
| **INDONESIA** | | | | | |
| Latex | 4.4 | 3.0 | 3.2 | 4.8 | 3.1 |
| RSS | 11.5 | 13.1 | 11.5 | 10.2 | 9.5 |
| TSR | 83.0 | 83.2 | 85.0 | 84.4 | 87.0 |
| Others | 1.1 | 0.7 | 0.4 | 0.6 | 0.4 |
| Sum | 100.0 | 100.0 | 100.0 | 100.0 | 100.0 |
| | | | | | |
| **THAILAND** | | | | | |
| Latex | 5.8 | 2.4 | 4.0 | 5.0 | 4.9 |
| RSS | 76.4 | 82.6 | 81.5 | 79.3 | 75.7 |
| TSR | 13.0 | 11.7 | 11.3 | 11.9 | 16.3 |
| Others | 4.7 | 3.4 | 3.2 | 3.8 | 3.2 |
| Sum | 100.0 | 100.0 | 100.0 | 100.0 | 100.0 |
| | | | | | |
| **SUM** | | | | | |
| Latex | 11.1 | 8.1 | 7.7 | 8.6 | 7.0 |
| RSS | 31.5 | 35.6 | 35.9 | 34.0 | 34.1 |
| TSR | 54.7 | 53.5 | 54.6 | 54.4 | 56.3 |
| Others | 2.7 | 2.8 | 1.8 | 3.0 | 2.6 |
| Sum | 100.0 | 100.0 | 100.0 | 100.0 | 100.0 |

# PROMOTING AND LIMITING FACTORS TO EXPAND DEMAND FOR COMMODITIES TOWARD THE 21ST CENTURY

DR. TAKAHIKO HASEYAMA[1]

## 1 NEW ISSUES IN PRIMARY COMMODITY STUDIES

After the first oil crisis in 1973, the demand supply conditions and prices of commodities have been affected, directly and indirectly, by the energy price in the international market. According to a study by Institute of Developing Economies, Tokyo, primary commodity issues were essentially country as well as commodity specific nature, but, there are certain aspects common to all primary commodity producing countries, in particular, the aspects related to development. The study pointed out that the study on primary commodity issues in development should incorporate the study of petroleum and gold as an integral part. This is partly evidenced by the fact that out of 25 low-income countries where data were available, 13 countries spent more than 30% of their export revenues for importing energy, mostly petroleum, even in the 1980s. In the case of middle-income countries, too, 16 out of 50 countries registered an energy import/merchandise export ratio exceeding 30%. Analyzing the increasing inter-linkage among markets for petroleum and various non-fuel primary commodities, it is concluded that price stabilization measures on a single commodity basis are no longer effective. Pooling information not only of a commodity specific nature but also on the global economy, and, pooling sufficient funds for necessary interventions, together with the formation of a higher decision making international body may be needed.

The proportion of developed countries in the world primary commodity export has been substantially higher than that of developing countries. Nevertheless, the potential trade expansion by and among developing countries is very big. Because income elasticities of many primary

---

[1] Professor, Faculty of Policy Studies, Chuo University, Hachiojishi, Tokyo.

commodities are still much higher in developing countries, the increase in domestic demand along with economic (income) growth and industrial development will be relatively faster in developing countries. The cost of substitutes is much higher than natural primary commodities in the South than in the North, and, to that extent, demand for primary commodities would be maintained. It is also forecast that industrial relocation or technology transfer to the developing countries of those industries generating demand for primary commodities will be accelerated in the future.

However, it is now most important for us to consider the new problems, in addition to the above, if we are to make a policy oriented study on primary commodities from a long-range viewpoint, in particular the issues and problems of the trade-off or the dilemma between 'Development and Environment'. This paper tries to study the expansion of demand for commodities from this viewpoint, and also attempts to introduce some cases of Japanese self help efforts to exploit the new market for her primary commodities.

## 2  CURRENT LIMITING FACTORS TO EXPAND DEMAND FOR PRIMARY AND RELATED COMMODITIES

According to a study by the Worldwatch Institute, Washington, D.C., the ups and downs of international demand for mineral resources are as summarized below: a similar reasoning will hold for other primary commodities. The consumption of eight vital types of minerals expanded at the annual growth rate of 2 to 9% from 1950 to 1974. However, it dropped to less than 2% on an average respectively. Now, the annual growth rate is close to zero. The global consumption of mineral resources has mostly been shared by only eight high-income industrialized countries. In recent years about two-third of the supply of aluminium, copper and lead, more than half of iron ore and three-fifth of tin, zinc, iron and steel, have been consumed by these high-income industrialized countries.

It is estimated that about 80 to more than 90% of metal supply was consumed by these high-income industrialized countries in the 1960s. The reasons for the consumption drop can be grouped as the following five, which seem to be closely linked with the structural change of the economy in major consuming countries.

- The economic slow-down or stagnation of the industrialized countries after the oil crisis in 1973.

- The structural change of industrialized economies, or, the shifting trends in terms of GDP share from the manufacturing sector to the service sector and to the high technology sector. Medical and electronic industries, for instance, are at present the highest growth industries, but, they are far less raw material and energy intensive than the traditional mining and manufacturing industry.
- The development of resources recycling has reduced the demand for these primary products. The recycling of such rare and expensive mineral resources as gold, silver, platinum and platinum related products has become substantially more relevant. Following the strict regulation on lead use because of its poisonous effect, the efficiency of lead recycling has improved significantly in high-income industrialized countries (64% in case of USA) and the efficiencies of other metal recycling have also improved steadily (59% of iron and steel in USA, 10% of iron and steel in the world, 30% of aluminum in the world, all as percentage of production).
- The competition in many industrial fields from primary products and new artificial materials such as plastics, ceramics, high technology synthetic materials, polyethylene, vinyl and glass fibre.
- In the high-income industrialized countries, the basic infrastructure of roads and buildings are now well equipped and new mineral products will be needed mainly for repairing and renewal of existing facilities only.

It is estimated that the rate of consumption expansion by developing countries has been higher than that of developed countries. This is particularly the case with Asian Newly Industrializing Economies (NIEs), India, Brazil and Mexico. In fact, it is estimated by the Worldwatch Institute that the growth rate of aluminum consumption by developing countries increased from 10% to 18%, and, that of zinc increased from 16% to 24%, during a decade from 1978 to 1988.

However, the expansion of demand for mining products as a consequence of the rapid economic growth of developing economies, has increased various types of pollution not only in the local areas but also globally in the form of abandoned scraps of mineral products. This is also the case with artificial materials. This problem will be studied more in detail later.

The long lasting stagnation of the developed economies has a negative impact on the demand for primary and related commodities. On the other hand, the on-going and the future growth of developing economies would have a strong positive impact on the expansion of international demand for primary and related products. This would undoubtedly be the case for such dynamically developing economies as the Asian NIEs, Malaysia, Thailand and China. However, it is most important for us to consider the limiting factors to the expanding demand for primary and related commodities toward the 21st century. In the long term both demand for and supply of primary commodities, including processed ones, would be managed by the possible strategy and response to the trade-off between growth and environment at the country and global level.

## 3 ECONOMIC GROWTH, INDUSTRIAL STRUCTURE AND ENERGY CONSUMPTION

### Correlation between energy resources consumption and industrial activity

The demand for commodities, both primary and manufactured, is correlated with the level of income per capita, which is closely correlated with the level of energy consumption per capita. The energy consumption per capita (kilograms of oil equivalent) displays a tremendous disparity among countries, just as is the case for income (See Tables annexed to the World Bank, World Development Report 1992). The annual average per capita energy consumption in low-income countries was 124 in 1965 and 339 in 1990 (the latest year for which data are available for international comparison). This was 3.4% and 6.5% of the level in OECD member countries in the respective years. The levels of the low middle-income countries were 15.9% and 19.8% of those of the OECD member countries in each year. The international disparities in energy consumption per capita were much greater, when compared with the USA: in 1965 and in 1987, the low- income country levels were 1.9% and 4.3% of the levels in the USA.

Although the level of per capita energy consumption is in general closely correlated with the level of per capita income, we should also consider the difference in climatic conditions of the countries or regions concerned. The countries in the north consume more energy for heating. The per capita energy consumption of oil exporters, therefore, is lower than that of middle-income countries (MICs): 61.7% in 1965 and 86.3% in 1990 of MICs. Even then, from a macro-economic viewpoint, per capita consumption levels of energy will show a close correlation with per capita income levels, because higher income countries are mostly more industrialized and will inevitably consume more energy per capita than less industrialized countries, as long as the industrial activities depend upon the conventional technologies. This is also the case with agriculture: the more modern technology we adopt for agriculture, the more energy we need as input. Most of the energy resources currently used by both consumers for daily life and producers for industrial activities are petroleum and related energy resources. The above factors mean that developing countries will consume more and more energy in future in order to develop and improve their economic standard of living.

## Trade-off between energy resources consumption and economic growth

Because of the close correlation between energy consumption and economic growth, the more economic development a country tries to achieve, the more energy consumption and the more emission of $CO^2$ would be inevitable under the present industrial technologies. According to our analysis, the volume of emission of $CO^2$ is closely correlated with (a) the rate of economic growth, and, (b) the degree of energy saving activities including efforts to switch from fossil fuel energy into non-fossil recyclable energy.

The Economic Planning Agency, Government of Japan, prepared a set of long term projections of Japanese economic growth, using a long-term multi-sector model, estimating the possible effects of restraining the emission of $CO^2$. According to the above projections, the annual growth rate of Japanese economy would be 3.75% in the 1990s, and, 2.75% in the 2000s, the lower level being mainly due to the increasing labour shortage. However, the volume of emission of $CO^2$ increases 1.4 times from 1990 to 2010, even if emission $CO^2$ restraining technology could be so well developed as currently planned by major Japanese enterprises for the coming decades. The United Nations accepted a resolution in 1991 to let all countries in the world make international joint efforts in order not to increase the volume of emission of $CO^2$ per capita beyond the levels of 1990. If we are to follow the U.N. resolution, the impact on the economic growth of the respective countries will depend upon the degree of development of energy saving technologies.

Restraining the emission of $CO^2$ in Japan will depend upon both the curtailment of industrial production and some drastic energy saving on the part of households. If only the industrial sector should make joint efforts to reduce the production to respond to the U.N. resolution, the annual growth rate of the Japanese economy would be around 1.25%, and, the total loss of GDP from 1990 to 2010 would be ¥2,100 trillions. The negative impacts on Japanese economy would be, then, unprecedentedly serious in the above case.

Under another assumption wherein the households are supposed to curtail their current average consumption of energy, including that of their motor cars, by about 50% of the past, and, the industrial sector is also expected to develop the emission of $CO^2$ restraining technologies almost at the same speed as seen from 1975 to 1986 when it achieved a remarkable reduction of emission $CO^2$ per unit of industrial products under the pressure of sharp rise of petroleum price, it would be possible to avoid the fall in economic growth by the above restraint of emission of $CO^2$.

In the case of Japan, however, the industrial sector has already been promoting some significant energy saving efforts, with successful achievements, and, therefore, a lot of further severe efforts would be needed to additionally realize the same kind of steady progress in energy saving (emission of $CO^2$ restraining) technologies as seen in the past. It should also be remembered, as another limiting factor, that the Japanese industrial sector should make an active investment in labour saving technologies and equipment toward and into the 21st century, in view of the increasing seriousness of the labour shortage, forecasted after 2000. It would, then, further increase the energy consumption, which might offset the possible favourable effects of the above energy saving efforts.

### Industrial structure and energy consumption - shifting to an energy saving industrial structure

In the case of Japan, the volume of emission of $CO^2$ per unit of manufactured products is, at present, about 50% of that in 1973 before the oil crisis. According to the analysis by Economic Planning Agency (EPA), Government of Japan, about 70% of the curtailment of emission of $CO^2$ is estimated to be due to energy savings and about 30% is due to change of industrial structure. EPA forecasts the change of industrial structure and energy consumption pattern as follows: (1) The energy saving technologies will be promoted and develop in such mass energy consuming industries as chemical, ceramic, cement, iron and steel industries. (2) The percentage share of manufacturing industry in the total industrial production will decline, and, the energy saving as well as the cleaning of the emission of $CO^2$ and other gas in the industry sector will be promoted. Also, the percentage share of the service industry in the total industrial production will steadily increase. As the energy consumption per unit production in the service industry is generally less than that in the manufacturing sector, substantial effects of energy saving through the above structural change of industries would be possible. On the other hand, the possible increase of demand for electric power in the service industry would at least partly offset the said energy saving fruits. EPA projections indicate the need for strengthening the energy saving efforts in the service sector too, along with current efforts in the industry sector.

The above policy oriented analysis indicates the need for and the direction of financial and related resources allocation toward and into the 21st century in order to promote the required structural change of industries and/or the switching of the present industrial structure into a more energy saving and emission of $CO^2$ restraining one.

The above has serious implications, because energy saving technological innovation and the related structural change of countries, particularly of the industrialized countries importing a large volume of primary commodities, would have a strong impact on the international demand for primary commodities, with a linked chain reaction into various directions. For example, the more the resource recycling technologies develop, the less the demand for primary resources will be. And, the more the energy saving technologies develop, the more favourable would be the impact on the international demand market for primary resources, due to a possible breakthrough for restraining $CO^2$ emission.

It is necessary, however, to make a more analytical study on the above promoting and limiting factors to the international demand for commodities in relation to the possible action for environmental preservation toward the 21st century.

## 4 ECONOMIC SCALE OF ASIAN AND PACIFIC COUNTRIES AND POTENTIAL IMPORT DEMAND FOR COMMODITIES

There is a great disparity regarding income (GNP) per capita and economic performances and scales even among Asian Pacific countries, which have shown a remarkably high growth after the 1960s. In order to reduce the disparities, less developed countries should further promote their economic growth, and, more developed countries should further extend their economic cooperation efficiently, according to the stages and conditions of economic development of the respective recipient countries. Japan, for example, is internationally requested to replace the USA as the demand absorber of exports particularly from developing countries in order to offset the possible impacts on international economies in case USA should launch the twin deficits curtailment policy through tight money policy and import curtailment.

Japan alone may still fall short in substituting her economic power for that of USA. But, if Asian NIEs and ASEAN countries would be combined, its economic capacity may well compete with Japan, though each country alone cannot compete at all with Japan in terms of economic indicators per capita. If Japan, Asian NIEs and ASEAN countries would be a combined economic group, then, the united Asian economic power is competitive and much bigger than the USA. Including China, that is now mobilizing its economic potential, and the developing countries in South Asia, now slowly but steadily developing under the open door policy, Asian countries would be able to sustain the favourable economic growth by promoting the interdependent linkage among the countries in the region, even without their so much traditional dependence upon USA as the world demand absorber.

On the basis of a series of economic projections by the Institute of Developing Economies, Tokyo, for which this author was responsible as executive director, the above Asian countries have a high growth potential toward the 21st century. In fact, high growth performances are needed for the developing countries to improve the tremendous disparity between developed and developing countries, which would require the increased input of primary commodities accordingly, unless more economical substituting materials should be exploited. In the past, the developed economies have been the major demand absorbers of primary commodities and the demand supply conditions of primary commodities have been influenced strongly by the economic conditions by the major and traditional demand absorbers. From a long-term viewpoint, however, the influence of developing economies on the international market of both primary and manufactured commodities will steadily increase as a result of their economic growth. The per capita consumption of primary commodities of developing countries is on an upward trend, and, in view of the percentage share of population of developing economies, about 76% of the world total, the aggregate demand for primary commodities or substituting materials would be enormous in future, when simply forecast on the basis of past trend and future potential, despite the recent bearish situation of primary commodity markets.

In summary, the demand for primary commodities and/or their substituting materials has a very big potential for the growing needs of developing countries in particular, but, whether and to what extent the potential demand could be effective demand in the long range, would very much depend upon the possibility of harmonizing 'growth and environment preservation'. From the viewpoint of traditional cost benefit criteria, some or many substituting materials may be more preferable. However, the abandoned scraps of artificial materials are causing and would further cause some serious environmental problems, and, some policy measures to respond to the problem may have to change the traditional economic criterion and the sense of value in a long term. As to the competition between primary commodities and substituting materials, therefore, the determinant would be which is more conducive to preserving the local, area and global environment in order to obtain a given production, and then, growth.

## 5 CASE STUDY OF CEREALS: HUGE POTENTIAL DEMAND FOR CEREALS FOR FEED USE

The daily calorie supply per capita of developing countries, as a whole, has improved fairly well since the 1960s. However, the nutrition level of 18 countries dropped between 1965 to 1989, mostly from a low subsistence level to malnutrition or an almost starvation level. It should also be noted that the nutrition levels of 24 countries are still below the requirements of 2200 calorie per day (some nutrition experts assert 2400 calorie as the requirements), in spite of the improvement after the 1960s. Almost all these countries facing the above unfavourable nutrition condition are low-income countries, and, following the DAC classification, they are mostly the absolute poverty countries (below US$370 per capita) in Africa. In addition, according to my estimate, the disparity of animal calorie consumption per capita between developed countries and developing countries is, on an average, around 7 (developed) to 1 (developing). It seems to me that the higher level of animal calorie consumption per capita is not always recommendable from a medical viewpoint. Even then, however, the animal calorie consumption per capita of developing countries has been rapidly increasing in recent years, in middle-income countries in particular, but, in China, too.

The income elasticities of demand for such livestock products as meat, milk and milk products, are as high as 0.5 to 2.0 in most developing countries, indicating a big potential demand for them, compared to cereals for which the income elasticities are mostly 0.1 to 0.4. Though the income elasticities of demand for cereals will be negative even at the level of middle-income countries (Figure 1), those for livestock products, meats, for example, will not be negative, even at the level of high-income countries (Figure 2). The sources of these Figures are:

- T. Haseyama, Original statistics are those of FAO and IFPRI. Income elasticities of demand are estimates by FAO studies. Some estimates by the author are included. The computer work is due to IFPRI's cooperation.
- T. Haseyama and S. Honobe, *New Issues of Economic Cooperation*, Chapt. 21, Global Adjustment and the Future of Asian Pacific Economics, Myohei Shinohara and Fu-chen Lo (eds.), Joint publication by the Institute of Developing Economies (IDE, Tokyo) and the Asian-Pacific Development Center (APDC, Kuala Lumpur), 1989, Tokyo.

Whether recommendable or not, the average per capita consumption of livestock products would naturally increase, following their economic growth. In order to produce one calorie of livestock products, the required feed grain calorie as indirect consumption ranges from 4.03 times (the case of fresh milk), 6.43 times (pork), 12.44 times (chicken broiler), 6.03 times (hen eggs) to 30.43 times (grain fed beef). From the viewpoint of efficiency of food resources utilization, the indirect consumption is much more wasteful than direct consumption of food grains as 'food grains' for human beings.

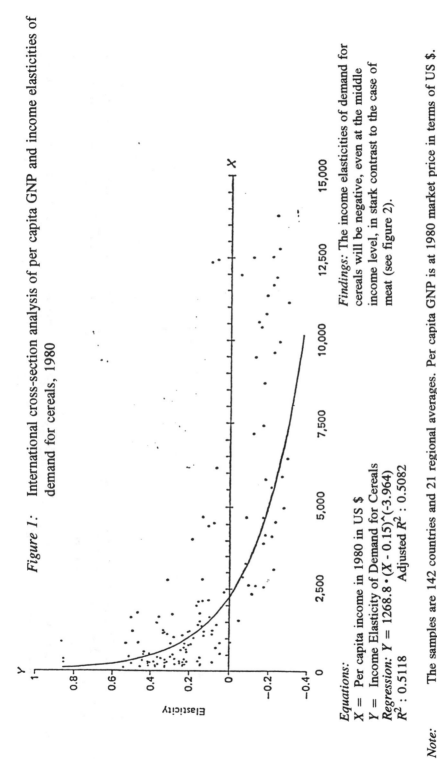

*Figure 1:* International cross-section analysis of per capita GNP and income elasticities of demand for cereals, 1980

*Equations:*
X = Per capita income in 1980 in US $
Y = Income Elasticity of Demand for Cereals
*Regression:* $Y = 1268.8 \cdot (X - 0.15)^{(-3.964)}$
$R^2$ : 0.5118        Adjusted $R^2$ : 0.5082

*Findings:* The income elasticities of demand for cereals will be negative, even at the middle income level, in stark contrast to the case of meat (see figure 2).

*Note:*    The samples are 142 countries and 21 regional averages. Per capita GNP is at 1980 market price in terms of US $.
*Source:*    Haseyama and Honobe (1989).

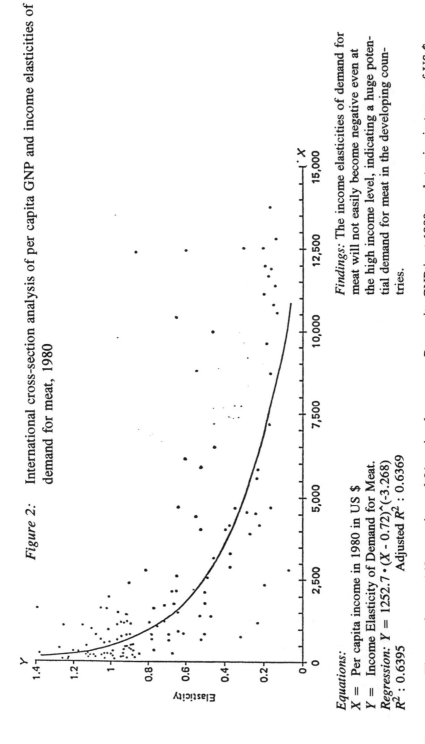

*Figure 2:* International cross-section analysis of per capita GNP and income elasticities of demand for meat, 1980

*Equations:*
X = Per capita income in 1980 in US $
Y = Income Elasticity of Demand for Meat.
*Regression:* $Y = 1252.7 \cdot (X - 0.72)^{\wedge}(-3.268)$
$R^2 : 0.6395$      Adjusted $R^2 : 0.6369$

*Findings:* The income elasticities of demand for meat will not easily become negative even at the high income level, indicating a huge potential demand for meat in the developing countries.

*Note:* The samples are 142 countries and 21 regional averages. Per capita GNP is at 1980 market price in terms of US $.

*Source:* Haseyama and Honobe (1989).

In case of direct consumption, about 200 kg cereals/year is considered to be sufficient to maintain our normal health. But, including indirect consumption, the cereals requirements will be much more. In the USA and the EC countries about 34 to 40% of daily calorie supply per capita (about 3000 to 3500) is animal calorie, consuming cereals annually at levels around 850 to 900 kg and 550 to 600 kg, respectively. The same can be said for other high-income countries. The developing countries, where about 10 to 15% of the daily calorie supply per capita (about 1800 to 2000) is animal calorie, consume less than 200 to 250 kg cereals per capita per year.

Cereals for feed use, or feed grains, are mostly coarse grains such as maize, sorghum, millet, barley, oat and rye, but, they are vital food grains as major calorie resource for low income population of many developing countries. The rapid increase in demand for livestock products in the developing countries occupying more than 76% of the population of the world, would need an enormous amount of feed grains, mostly cereals that could have been staple food for human beings. This has caused the inequality problems of food resource allocation, or, food/feed competition, international and domestic, among different income brackets.

Although the average per capita consumption of livestock products in the developed countries may be at the saturation point, their demand for such products and the required feed grains would further increase, following the increase in their population. The global demand for feed grains has a potential to increase steadily and/or fairly rapidly in future. Regarding Asian countries, however, only a few countries, probably only Thailand, Myanmar, and Vietnam, would have the production potential to be self-sufficient in view of the increasing demand for feed grains. The import demand for feed grains from the USA, Canada and other coarse grains surplus countries would increase in the long term.

Apart from the food/feed competition problems among respective income brackets, domestic and international, the increasing global dependence on the cereals production of some limited cereal exporting countries and the expanding livestock industry that has been encouraged in most developing countries will lead more seriously to problems of pollution, ecology and environment. This will also come to the fore as the dilemma between development and environment preservation.

6  CASE STUDY OF JAPANESE EFFORTS TO EXPLOIT THE OVERSEAS
   MARKET FOR PRIMARY COMMODITIES EFFORTS TO COVER HIGH PRICE
   BY QUALITY

It is generally believed that Japan is exclusively the giant exporter of manufactured commodities of high technology, soft and hard, and, at the same time, is one of the biggest importer of primary commodities. Indeed 98% of Japanese exports in 1990, for example, is manufactured exports. Japan has been forced by international pressure to liberalize agricultural products one by one and to open her traditionally closed market for some agricultural commodities. It is also generally believed that Japan is exclusively importer, so far as primary commodities are concerned.

It is important to know, however, that Japan has been making every effort to exploit the international demand for Japanese primary commodities, mostly agricultural products. It is useful to review some success stories of Japanese efforts and strategies on how to exploit the market for such more expensive products made in Japan.

### The Case of Japanese Mandarin Orange (MIKAN)

Japanese mandarin growers were very much afraid of possible serious damage, when the trade of oranges and other citrus fruits was to be liberalized. They then made every effort to exploit new markets, domestic and overseas, to compete with the inflow of foreign citrus fruits. They set up a propaganda campaign, for example, claiming that the Japanese MIKAN can be easily peeled by hand without using a knife. The 'handy MIKAN' has now become very popular in North America, particularly in Canada, as the 'Christmas Orange', because MIKAN is the only orange like fruit available in winter season. There is a record that Japan already exported MIKAN to the USA and Canada as far back as from 1887 to 1891, when Japan had no manufactured goods for export. In 1992, Japanese export of MIKAN was about 11,500 metric tons, all to North America (about 80% to Canada and 20% to the USA).

The MIKAN growers launched various campaigns to expand the - market, for example, by presenting the consumers with Japanese dolls in exchange for tickets enclosed in boxes of MIKAN. However, the sharp increase in price due to the recent appreciation of the Japanese yen (¥) is now a big limiting factor, as it almost doubled the price (from about US$3.-/kg to US$6.-/kg (fob) and about C$15.- per box of 4.2 kg, about three times higher than the 'local' orange. Therefore, the export of

MIKAN decreased very much, but the exporters are bullish, expecting the recovery of sales, in view of the favourable effects of a set of campaigns.

## The case of Japanese pears (NASHI) and apples

The Japanese pear or NASHI also succeeds in expanding the overseas market. According to a survey by the Federation of Agricultural Cooperatives of NASHI Growers, Japanese NASHI is obtaining popularity in the overseas market, due to the rich juiciness and the sweet taste, which are the fruits of long term efforts by the growers. About 7,000 tonnes of NASHI was exported in 1992, ranking only second to MIKAN. Through some intensive efforts by NASHI growers and exporters, the overseas market includes Europe, Australia, USA, Middle East and SouthEast Asia. The retail price of NASHI is about US$2.- to US$3.- a piece, much more expensive than many other local fruits. Even then, NASHI is supported by a deep rooted demand by NASHI lovers, and it has not been much adversely affected by the high appreciation of the Japanese (¥). It displays a good example of consumer's preference regarding the quality commodities.

The export of Japanese apples in 1992 was 1,500 tonnes. The major market is Southeast Asia where the new upper middle-income class is growing rapidly as a result of the steady high growth performances of the economies. This new growing purchasing power of middle-income countries will give new impacts to the demand for quality commodities, both primary and manufactured, along with the dynamic development of manufacturing industries.

## The case of Japanese beef

In terms of value, the largest imports of fresh food commodities in Japan are pork and beef. On the other hand, however, the All Japan Federation of Agricultural Cooperatives (ZENNO) is playing a core role in exporting Japanese beef mainly to the USA with some steady results. Japanese beef export is limited to the best quality one of indigenous beef cattle that is the most expensive in the world. In order to offset the handicap of the big price disparity in the international market, the Federation is trying to exploit the 'high quality' of Japanese beef by all means. The export campaign started in September 1990, when Japanese livestock farmers were anxious about the impact of liberalization of the beef trade to start in 1991, because foreign beef is much cheaper even in case of the high quality varieties. Then they tried to switch from defence to attack, exporting only the best quality beef, whereby they tried to participate in the beef market by competitive power in quality in order to cover the inferior competitive power in price. At the beginning, they tried to exploit the demand market for Japanese quality beef mostly into Japanese food restaurants and steakhouses in the USA and, for example, shops in New York and at the west coast, which sell 'WAGYU' (or Japanese beef) cooking. The export of WAGYU is not much yet: 4.4 tonnes in 1990/91, 4.9 tonnes in 1991/92 and 3.1 tonnes in 1992/93, because of the appreciation of the ¥. The Japanese quality beef has gained such qualifications as 'just like fine arts', 'melting taste', 'just the same as the highest quality caviar or wine', etc.

However, the biggest limiting factor is the high price. The retail price of A class WAGYU beef in Japan is about ¥2,000 per 100 grams, when American beef of the same class and variety is about ¥150 per 100 grams. WAGYU beef cannot compete at all in price with American beef, and, probably other quality beef. Even though the competitive power of WAGYU beef in quality and taste is outstanding, such an extremely big price disparity cannot stand in the market. Naturally, there should be a ceiling to the WAGYU price. Because of this inevitable price ceiling, the export business of WAGYU beef has more in deficit than in surplus so far, despite 'the slow but steady' expansion of demand for it. According to the All Japan Federation of Agricultural Cooperatives, however, the object of WAGYU exportation is to encourage the Japanese livestock farmers, letting them have a confidence in the quality of their WAGYU beef and further expanding the demand market for it in future.

### The Case of Japanese Vegetables

It is said that a foreign food culture needs about one to two decades for settling down in other countries. But, in Hong Kong and Singapore, only a few years were needed to change their traditional diet custom by introducing Japanese vegetables. The background is the high growth performances of these high-income NIEs in recent years, and, the efforts by Japanese exporting companies to exploit the new market based on the rapidly growing upper middle-income brackets in such upper middle-income economies as NIEs in Asia.

The Japanese exporters are exporting selected quality fresh vegetables mainly to the super markets in Hong Kong and Singapore. Now, the demand for Japanese expensive vegetables mostly by the well-to-do classes of these NIEs is gradually increasing. The price of Japanese vegetables is about two times higher than the domestic prices in Japan, due to marketing cost. But, the demand for Japanese vegetables is steadily increasing among the richer classes of NIEs, due to their preference for better quality, shape and delicate tastes suitable for fresh salads. For example, Japanese mushroom is appreciated, though more expensive, due to the better quality for chinese cooking.

The exports of Japanese vegetables, fresh, dried and frozen, are more than 10,000 tons in 1992. Though the absolute amount is not yet so much, the cases of vegetables, fruits and others have shown that in the long term the consumer have a preference for quality commodities, which is supported by the steady improvement in income level in the middle-income economies in Asia.

### In summary

It should be noted that the above cases of Japanese primary commodities export are based on some intensive or even desperate joint efforts by producers, exporters and such institutional bodies as cooperatives, so a joint effort from the sides of production, marketing and institution. Though the Japanese cases are rather of smaller scale, the same 'self help efforts' of similar strategies on the part of exporting countries of primary commodities would make some more favourable breakthrough in the demand market for their products.

**Major References:**

T. Haseyama, 'Ajia no keizai seicho to shokuryo anzen hosho' (Asian Economic Growth and Food Security), 1991, Taimeido Co., Ltd., Tokyo.

World Bank, World Development Report 1992.

World Watch Institute, State of the World 1992.

D.H. Meadows, D.L. Meadows and J. Randers, 'Beyond the Limits', 1992.
Economic Planning Agency, Gov. of Japan, 'Chikyu kankyo mondai, nihon keizai eno teigen' (World Environmental Problems and Proposal for Japanese Economy), 1992.

S. Hirashima and A. Kuchiki, 'Primary Commodity Issues in Development', Chapt. 13, *Global Adjustment and the Future of Asian Pacific Economy*, edited by M. Shinohara and Fu-chen Lo, IDE, 1989, Tokyo.

T. Haseyama and S. Honobe, 'New Issues of Economic Cooperation', Chapt. 21, *Global Adjustment and the Future of Asian Pacific Economy*, edited by M. Shinohara and Fu-chen Lo, IDE, 1989, Tokyo.

# PROMOTION OF DEMAND FOR COMMODITIES THROUGH MULTINATIONAL ACTION[1]

## MR. BJÖRN OLSEN[2]

## 1  INTRODUCTION

As is well known, developing countries continue to be highly dependent on commodity exports; excluding the petroleum sector, some 60 developing countries depend on only *three* commodities for more than 50% of their total exports. Most of the least developed, land-locked and island economies can be listed in this category. In many countries, the exports of only *one* basic commodity represent *more than half of total export earnings* and this scenario is not likely to change in the immediate future. Under such circumstances, it is clear that even a marginal improvement of the market situation for a commodity can have a substantial impact on the entire economy of a country.

For developing countries at Government level, the actions mainly consist of obtaining reductions of customs tariffs, restrictive import policies and other measures which represent obstacles for their commodity exports and entrance into the markets either of the basic commodity, or derivatives and manufactures of commodities. The attainment of a global objective of expansion of exports of commodities from the developing countries requires governmental and intergovernmental actions to achieve trade liberalization and improved market access. An important element is also the ability of developing commodity producing countries to mount imaginative marketing and promotional efforts for their produce to stimulate demand. It is however felt that this element has not been given adequate attention in the past.

---

[1] by permission of ITC (UNCTAD/GATT)

[2] Chief, Market Development Section for Commodities and Agro-based Products, Division of Product and Market Development, International Trade Centre UNCTAD/GATT, (ITC), Geneva.

In the UN system of organizations, ITC's mandate is to assist developing countries in their trade promotion efforts. In the case of commodities, ITC has been given a special mandate. It is in this context that this paper on promotion of demand through multinational action has been prepared.

## 2  DEMAND STIMULATION AND PROMOTION

### The need for demand stimulation

Stimulation of consumer demand and the promotion of consumption is in fact a highly important consideration for the entire range of the developing countries exporting commodities. The competitive position in the markets of commodities can of course be, and should be, enhanced by improvements in the quality of products offered for export, by developing new uses, by reducing their unit costs relative to competing products and in many other ways, but a very important factor, upon which the ultimate success of all other elements depend, is the establishment of channels of information and persuasion to facilitate a shift or maintenance of consumer preference in favour of the promoted commodity. In other words, promotional strategies have to be fully integrated with production and marketing strategies and vice versa, since no amount of promotion will overcome the disadvantages of an inferior product. Viewed in this perspective, promotional action plays a strategic role in marketing, and multinational action through generic promotion of a specific commodity.

### Brand or generic promotion

Promotion carried out by private companies are almost exclusively in direct support of their branded consumer-packed products derived from the basic commodities. Brand promotion aims at expanding a company's share of the market but also tends to influence the aggregate demand for the commodity. By far the largest part of commodity promotion is the promotion for branded consumer-packed products. In addition to brand promotion, there exist considerable collective promotional efforts undertaken by national organizations for specific commodities. Examples are: Colombian coffee, Swiss cheese, Swiss watches, French wine, New Zealand apples and kiwis, Danish bacon, etc. The next level of common action is multinational promotion where the financing derives from several countries and other sources. Over the years, there are numerous examples of multinational generic promotion actions, e.g. coffee, tea, cocoa, wool, sisal, linen, jute, olive oil, spices and tropical fruit.

As far as ITC is concerned, the Centre has been involved in the design and implementation of some of these multinational generic promotion activities which will be described in more detail later. Recent examples are sisal harvest twine and jute, silk and rubber products which all compete with synthetics. The Centre has also been involved in the design of tea, cocoa and spice promotion projects.

## Collaboration with trade and industry

A primary step in the development of generic promotion activities is that the export industries in developing countries must be able to identify options for stimulation of demand, in collaboration with their partners in the target markets. Also, the development and implementation of generic promotion strategies and plans must be done together with the trade and industry in the target market, and by experienced market communication agencies. Marketing strategies and business plans must be based on reliable market information and data. It should also be understood that there is not a miracle market promotion 'mixture' for the development of the demand for a commodity, and promotional actions should not be disassociated from the entire range of product and market development activities, which are required to improve the competitiveness of a commodity. Without active participation in the promotion action by the local trade and industry in a target market, the promotion action is not likely to be effective.

## 3  INTERNATIONAL ACTION

### Intergovernmental cooperation

Considerable scope exists for intergovernmental cooperation in the formulation of joint promotion schemes for commodities. Often, developing countries producing commodities cannot match the research, development, marketing and promotional efforts of large-scale enterprises in industrialized countries offering competing products. There are several examples of commodity exports from developing countries, which are lagging behind, resulting in lost markets and to recapture a lost market for basically an unchanged product or commodity requires excessive marketing and promotional efforts and price cuts. The scenario for commodity markets is in the majority of cases not bright, with very depressed price levels and more than ever this situation calls for remedial action to stimulate demand.

**The catalytic role of the ICBs**

Basically, it would be beyond the scope of this paper to discuss the intricacies of developing a marketing and promotional plan. This is to be left to specialists, but it is felt that the task of the ICBs and the industry which is behind the ICBs is to identify areas where common market communication action could be envisaged, and to act as a catalyst in developing viable generic promotion activities. The communication specialists must be fully involved in all facets of a project and they must be given an extremely good briefing on the advantages of the commodity or product which is to be promoted compared to competing products. Such a briefing must be based on sound economic analysis, technical and/or medical facts or research; in other words, the base data gathering has to form part of preparatory activities, or the project itself. On the basis of this set of facts on technoeconomic, health or environmental advantages, the basic messages are developed to influence the decision makers undertaking the purchasing. The target audience for the promotion has of course to be well identified and its behaviour well analyzed through market research or reporting on the market situation by the local trade and industry. The market communication tools, including the appropriate media have to be identified. Again, it is the quality of the briefing given by industry to the market communication agency which is of critical importance. In fact, in most cases, despite considerable preparatory work, the communication agency is likely to require additional information and undertake special investigations about the marketing and promotion techniques utilized for the specific product, marketing channels, consumer attitudes, the decision-making process for purchasing and the profile of the users and buyers.

**Reaching agreement on multinational action**

Another problem in getting a multinational generic promotion project off the ground is to achieve agreement between all parties concerned, both at government and private industry level. Diverse interests are certain to exist, for example the selection of target markets, development of a promotional message or use of media. To achieve an agreement to a generic promotion project, it is important that no specific producer/exporter or country reaps specific benefits out of a campaign but that it influences demand for the promoted commodity in general, and this is the main reason for calling it 'generic promotion'. A campaign fully financed by international funds has of course a better chance of taking off than a campaign where all or a substantial part of the resources come from trade and industry who have to be convinced that by investing in a generic promotion campaign, benefits will be better than if the individual companies were running their own show.

However, a closer analysis of promotion options often points at generic promotion as a highly cost-effective way of stimulating demand for products deriving from basic commodities. For example, it is difficult to imagine that the multinational generic promotion work carried out by the International Wool Secretariat could have been substituted by national and brand promotion. Another example is the low budget PR-campaign carried out by the American Spice Trade Association to promote the consumption of spices in the USA. In the case of spices, the investment in generic promotion represents only a fraction of the media impact. These generic promotion programmes have very efficiently supported the private industry in their efforts to increase demand.

## 4 ISSUES IN PROMOTING CAMPAIGNS

### Investing in generic promotion

It should be noted that the governments and industries in developing countries have very limited options for directly influencing the market situation for the commodities they export. In fact, participation in multinational generic promotion campaigns for specific commodities often represents one of the very few options and, if properly designed and implemented, investing in such campaigns can be very beneficial to the exporting countries.

In most cases, the promotion budget is limited and, in the case of multinational generic promotion action, it is normally very limited, and it is a rather delicate decision to take, when the questions arise, on the use of the funds. What should be the target market or geographical limitation of the promotion campaign? How much can be used for preparatory research and planning of the promotion budget? What should be the complexity of the message and the use of the communication media available, and can be used or obtained at low cost per contact?

Often, considerable financial and human resources are deployed in the preparation of promotional plans. However, if the budgets and the resources required for carrying out the plans are way beyond the capacity of the international community to foot the bill, in the end one could be left with paper and plans but very little action. In any case, it seems to be better to develop plans and projects that have a chance of attracting the necessary resources than something grandiose which does not have a certain security for follow-up in terms of the implementation of market promotion actions.

**The message**

Previously, we have talked about the message. In the great majority of cases, commodities from developing countries have the advantage of being natural products. Thus, environmental and/or health properties can in many cases be attributed to these commodities and at the present time when environment and health are serious preoccupations of individuals and governments, it seems clear that if it is possible and technically or medically justified to base a substantial part of a promotional campaign on such messages, this might be a highly cost effective way of promoting the demand for a commodity. In fact, ITC has developed a certain number of generic promotion projects for commodities and in most cases the natural products and environmental advantages of certain natural fibres such as jute, coir, sisal and silk, which are all competing with synthetic substitutes, have been the key messages in the promotion campaigns. In the case of tropical beverages, such as tea and cocoa, the health aspects are the basic elements of the promotion projects.

**Global versus 'niche' marketing**

What is the most efficient way of informing a target audience about the environmental or health aspects of a commodity? Our experience clearly shows that the global approach where a standard generic promotion plan for all geographical regions is used, this approach can only be considered if the industry is prepared to massively back up on such actions on a global basis. But even in the case of a market niche approach, a certain amount of common features and promotional material developed for the campaign can be adapted to the individual markets. In some cases, particularly when commodities are used in industrial processes, the appropriate media often covers the industry and trade globally or regionally, but reaching the final consumer requires the use of national media.

## Ecology as a key message

Articles, advertorials and promotional material, handouts, posters, etc. have been prepared which have a clear environmental ecological message in the promotion campaigns for natural fibres carried out by ITC. Catchwords (expressions) such as 'natural', 'biodegradable', 'Not harmful to nature', 'No toxic fumes', etc. are essential messages and bring forward the users' environmental concerns for present and future generations. As an example of an article in the field of environmentally friendly products from developing countries, the advertorial entitled 'Sisal wins environmental battle over synthetic twine' is annexed. This article sets out the environmental advantages throughout the entire life cycle of sisal harvest twine compared to the life cycle of synthetic substitutes which definitely falls out to the advantage of sisal twine. Jute geotextiles are promoted with one main message as far as ecology is concerned, namely biodegradability. But of course all other technical advantages have to be promoted as well. The promotional brochure for jute geotextiles is another example.

## The health message

The U.K. Tea Council, in collaboration with the USA tea industry, FAO and ITC, is currently in the process of developing a generic promotion project to promote the health aspects of black tea. The project is divided into two main components: the health research phase and the generic promotion phase. There are believed to be many positive health aspects which can be attributed to the consumption of tea. The medical justification has to be properly established through research. Examples of the areas of research are anticancer, prevention of cardio-vascular diseases, dental caries and gum diseases, etc. As and when the health properties are scientifically proven, this will be incorporated in the promotion campaign messages in the selected pilot target markets.

## Free media space

Obtaining free space in media such as trade magazines, radio or TV through well-prepared Public Relations (PR) activities is possible particularly when the message can be interrelated with subjects of common interest and concern to everybody such as environment, food, fashion, etc. The PR material must be well prepared with some interesting and preferably amusing stories and disseminated to selected target groups of journalists, and followed up by personal contacts. A good example of a highly efficient public relations programme is the American Spice Trade Association's promotion activities for spices in the USA. A detailed description of this programme is contained in the annex.

However, media are in the majority of cases expecting money for their services, so what was originally designed as an article or a TV documentary which was to go into the media without major costs, could end up as an advertorial. Another consideration concerning 'free' advertising space is that you have very little control over the timing or the final content of the message. The journalist's personal views are sometimes added and in the worst of cases, the promotional message could be distorted in a negative direction. In the case of PR activities carried out for technical products, we have experienced that the trade press has been almost impossible to attract to utilize the PR material prepared and if it was included this was only a mention of the promotion activity without going into the argumentation. The space given was also insignificant. Sometimes, as a gesture, a magazine would include some PR articles if, at the same time, advertisements were placed. On the other hand, the use of radio interviews has given very good response. The number of radio stations that have included the interviews in their broadcasting programmes have in some cases been quite impressive. The mailing of information brochures is also possible if you can identify a partner willing to undertake the distribution free of charge. Video used for information or educational purposes is another area to be considered but again the cost of producing a good video film is quite high and there is no security that such a film would be taken up in a TV programme.

The conclusion is that any promotional programme for commodities, particularly if there are significant health, environmental messages or other subjects of common interest such as good food or fashion, could effectively be promoted through a properly staged public relations programme. However, even the initial preparation of the public relations materials such as a press kit can become quite costly as well as the dissemination of the material, for which separate financing has to be found.

## Financing of multinational promotion actions

Another critical area of multinational promotion of demand for a commodity is the financing aspect. To utilize one per cent of sales is often suggested as a modest but reasonable level for such promotional actions by market communication agencies. Depending on the commodity and the country, the amounts can become considerable and tangible results through multinational generic promotion actions could be achieved. Financing through a minor export levy tends to be the standard proposal suggested by consultants or companies preparing promotional surveys and strategy plans. However, such a solution is easier said than done since this will necessitate the agreements of governments. Such actions are time-consuming and in most of the cases the patient has died before the agreement has been reached. It should be noted that the timing of promotion campaigns is very important and financing and implementation of a project should take place as soon as possible after project preparation.

For developing countries trying to find ways of stimulating demand for basic commodities, an alternative is to try to obtain trust fund financing. In most cases the main source of funding, be it a government or an organization, would demand substantial co-financing. The level of requested co-financing can be from 25 to 50% of the total cost of the proposed promotion programme. Again, experience shows that cash contributions from the beneficiaries are very difficult to obtain and in most cases tend to be small or token contributions. However, the trade and industry in the consuming countries are often prepared to contribute in kind. The form of such contributions is to provide market information and the logistic support to the promotion campaign. In some cases, we have seen that the local industry, trade and the cooperative organizations, provide free samples, free space at trade fairs, free space in their membership magazines, free mailing of brochures, providing free staff for demonstrations or lecturers at promotion events, etc. It is possible to evaluate the cost of such support and it can therefore be considered as an important co-financing element of a promotion campaign. If therefore, it is expressed by the main financing body that substantial co-financing should be provided, the formula of incorporating the support in kind that the trade and industry in the importing country can give to the activity as a co-financing element, should be considered.

## 5  CASE STUDIES

In the annexes to this paper, there are a few case studies on generic promotion for commodities

- two with a strong message on environment protection: (1) Promotion of jute geotextiles and (2) Promotion of sisal harvest twine;
- and another on health and food: Promotion of the health aspects of tea.

## 6  CONCLUSIONS

Some important observations can be made in connection with multinational generic promotion of commodities. These are:

1. for most of the commodities, there is a definite need for undertaking actions to stimulate demand;
2. multinational generic promotion of a commodity to support brand, national or other promotional activities is in many cases a low cost and effective way of stimulating demand for a commodity. There are many examples to support these statements, some of them set out in the annexes;
3. the planning and implementation of generic promotion must be done in close collaboration with the trade and industry in the target markets;
4. there is no standard format for promoting the demand for a commodity. The promotion programme has to be designed specifically for the commodity and, in most cases, for the specific target market, although many elements of a generic promotion campaign can be common in different target markets;
5. ICBs can play an important role in drawing the attention of their members to the options existing for generic promotion of their particular commodity and in the preparation of project proposals;
6. the ICBs also have an important role to play in identifying potential financing sources and in negotiating agreements on generic promotion actions with the trade and industry in exporting and consuming countries;
7. funds for generic promotion tend to be very limited. It is therefore of the utmost importance to identify low cost activities which give high returns. Public relations activities and the preparation of press kits and other PR material, passing the message to the consumers on

health, environment and other aspects of common interest and concern to consumers could be one option for undertaking generic promotion;

8. to the extent resources are available, ITC is prepared to assist ICBs in their efforts to identify generic promotion options, for example by carrying out market research and also to prepare project proposals and to identify potential partners for the promotion activities.

# ANNEX I

## Generic promotion of jute geotextiles
### (brief description)

As part of the generic promotion campaign for jute products, ITC has undertaken over the last six years a series of activities to promote jute geotextiles which are now being increasingly used to control soil erosion. The activities included scientific tests whereby the performance of jute geotextiles was compared to those of other natural as well as synthetic geotextiles. The main advantage with jute is that as a natural biodegradable fibre it is ecologically harmonious and decomposes once the protective vegetation has become established. Unlike other traditional jute products which are generally promoted as a commodity, the promotion of jute geotextiles, being an engineering product, special attention was given in focusing the campaign on civil engineers, architects, public works authorities, etc. In addition to the placement of advertisements in specialized technical reviews ITC organized presentation of technical papers in symposiums on geotextiles and organized jute geotextiles promotion stands in technical trade fairs where the promotional theme was to present jute geotextiles as a natural and environmental friendly product. The annual budgets for these activities have been about US$ 60,000 for a three-year period covering selected European markets.

## ANNEX IIa

*Pilot promotion project for sisal
agricultural twine in selected european
countries (summary description)*

The three-year pilot promotion campaign was financed by the Government of Sweden and ABEMS - Brazil (with about US$ 150,000 annually), and supported by the London Sisal Association, the trade and industry and the cooperative movement in the countries where the campaign was implemented.

The main objective was to increase the awareness of farmers in selected European countries of the technical and environmental advantages of using sisal harvest twine in lieu of polypropylene. The main environmental messages were:

- sisal is a natural product;
- sisal is digestible and is not harmful to cattle;
- sisal is produced from renewable resources;
- sisal prevents soil erosion;
- consumption of energy for production is negligible;
- negligible polluting waste.

The main components of the campaign were:

1. preparation of an overall strategy for the implementation of the campaign in collaboration with the trade and industry and advertising agencies in the target markets;
2. the creation of a logo;
3. preparation of information packs to inform the trade and industry world-wide about the campaign, the use of the logo as well as the promotional messages to be used in the campaign;
4. a consultant visited harvest twine machine manufacturers to influence them to adapt the machines to the use of sisal twine;
5. environmental benefits were highlighted through a technical article setting out the environmental benefits. This article appeared in Scandinavian and German farm media as an advertorial.

The campaign was carried out in France, Germany, the United Kingdom, Finland, Sweden and Denmark. The first year's activity in *France* consisted mainly of the placement of advertisements and advertorials introducing the logo and some of the main messages to the farmers. The second and third years were implemented in close collaboration with the French Farmers Cooperative Movement and the trade and industry, the thrust of the campaign being on environmental issues. During both years, folders informing the farmers of sisal's advantages were distributed through the cooperative systems, posters were displayed and articles inserted in the cooperative press. As is common in France, this campaign was based on a lottery formula and the distribution of pins displaying the sisal logo. The number of participants in the lottery is a clear indication that the farming community by and large has received the message of the campaign. Furthermore, the cooperative movement has informed us that the sales of the sisal harvest twine during the last two years, 1991-1992, have stabilized. The promotional activities in the *United Kingdom, Germany* and *Scandinavian* countries consisted of the insertion of advertisements in farm magazines, P.R. activities, posters and pamphlets, and communicating through radio the advantages of using sisal as agricultural harvest twine.

In the light of the rather positive results of the campaign, which was implemented with very limited resources, it is felt that generic promotion of sisal harvest twine is a worthwhile activity in traditional markets, particularly for traditional baling. The technological changes are certainly seriously affecting the overall consumption of sisal twine, but it should be possible to maintain the traditional baling segment of the market for sisal twine, with effective promotional actions.

*Sisal wins environmental battle*
*over synthetic twine*

A silent struggle is under way. In one corner of the ring, the poor farmers of the Third World; in the other, the wealthy petroleum industry. Until now, the petroleum industry, which has captured half the market, has seemed to be the success story, but now the Third World is striking back. Their major weapon is concern for the environment. The struggle focuses on the market for twine.

Concern about the environment is ever-increasing. Besides such threats as acidification, the greenhouse effect and mountains of non-biodegradable waste, the depletion of the ozone layer has become one of the biggest threats to life on earth. It is easy to feel vulnerable. However, our days are not numbered. There is till time to act, and much to do. For example, all those 'ozone friendly' products on the market have already changed our day-to-day shopping habits.

In the past, our efforts to improve the environment were rather more basic - for example, placing filters on chimneys and purifying sewage. The 1980's saw more and more industrialists concentrating on cleaner manufacturing processes. Although there is still much to be done within the industries and utilities, the 1990's have seen a much greater interest in products which affect the environment. Today, environmental factors largely consist of studying the life cycle of products from raw material to waste. Effectively, this means that consumers have been given more power. Today, an increasing amount of people are choosing more environmentally friendly products among, for example, detergents, batteries and fuels. With regard to business, safe-guarding the environment has become a strong factor in competing for customers, and companies with a good environmental image tend to be those that will be most successful.

This has not been the case totally with sisal twine. Despite it being a very natural product for hay and straw bailing, sisal twine has a big competitor in the market: synthetic twine. Despite a drop in demand, sisal is still a very important product. The world's farmers use 200,000 tons every year. If all of this twine was joined together end to end and laid on the ground, it would go around the world 1,000 times. In Brazil, the world's largest producer of sisal, one million people are dependent on sisal cultivation for their livelihood.

In developing countries, subsistence farmers and growers are competing with the wealthy petrochemical industry, whose products are called polypropylene and polyethylene. Until recently, it has been an unequal struggle, if only in view of the resources available for marketing products. Now the United Nations, through its International Trade Centre (ITC), has entered the scene, and with the financial backing of the Swedish Government, is supporting sisal producers. The main arguments used to convince farmers to choose sisal are: sisal is less harmful to the environment than polypropylene; technically it is very sound; it is cost-effective considering its environmental-awareness and finally, it is protecting hundreds of thousands of jobs of poor farmers.

Sisal is extracted from the leaf of a cactus in the Agave family. It grows in desert-like areas where no other form of agriculture is possible. The plant is thought to prevent erosion and desertification and the largest producing countries are Brazil, Mexico, Kenya and Tanzania. For decades sisal twine existed alone, but in the late 1960's, synthetic substitutes were developed which have taken over half of the market. Another opposing silage method has been the introduction of plastic sheeting in the field as well as the machines that prepare giant high density bales that are dependent on the elasticity of synthetic twine. Both sorts of twine, however, can be used in the small and medium-sized harvesting machines. Thus, the battle continues .......

The German environmental institute Environmental Protection Encouragement Agency (EPEA), favours sisal on the basis that it is a natural biodegradable product. The bottom line is that sisal twine only requires land and human effort whereas synthetic twine requires money and petroleum, both as a raw material and a source of energy. In effect, this means that about ten times as much energy is needed to produce one ton of polypropylene as one ton of sisal. Petroleum as a raw material gives off sulphur dioxide and nitric oxides during the manufacturing process, in turn contributing to the acidification of the soil and producing health hazards such as the emission of carcinogens. Problems do not end with the production phase. As synthetic twine does not decompose, there is a huge amount of waste which poses considerable problems of collection, disposal and/or recycling. One particularly nasty aspect of synthetic twine is that the residue can end up in the stomach of cows. Sisal twine residue can be excreted naturally but synthetic twine may remain in the cow until it is slaughtered. Up to 14 kg have been found.

This life cycle illustrates that sisal twine is much healthier for the environment, the only minor problem compared to those of synthetics being that the production requires large amounts of water which becomes polluted under current methods, thus producing organic waste. There are two ways of getting round this problem. One is to purify the water biologically and the other is to use the waste as fertilizer which some manufacturers are already doing.

Economically, sisal twine is now also more cost-effective than its major competitor. Increasingly strict laws regarding waste disposal and environmental taxes, based on the principle that 'the polluter should pay', will favour sisal twine. Polypropylene twine and plastic sheeting for ensilage in the field will become considerably more expensive. This suggests that if developments continue to favour sisal twine, production methods must be modernized. This obviously requires money and the investments in such fields are much valued. Work methods need to be modernized but according to Stephen Klasson, a Swedish development worker, 'There is no alternative to sisal in these dry warm conditions. Therefore, we need more resources to develop our production'.

Ultimately, it will be the consumers, the world's farmers, who will determine whether the future of twine will be polypropylene or sisal. In a world becoming more and more environmentally aware, it is likely that sisal twine will, in general, prove more advantageous than its synthetic counterpart.

## Comparison of properties of agricultural twine

| Properties and other considerations | Sisal | Synthetics |
|---|---|---|
| Natural | Yes | No |
| Biodegradable | Yes | No |
| Harmful to cattle | No | Yes |
| Produced from renewable resources | Yes | No |
| Prevents erosion | Yes | No |
| Farmers economically dependent on production | Yes | No |
| Consumption of energy for production | Negligible | Very high |
| Polluting waste | Negligible | Very high |

*A programme to create an increased demand for tea through a
generic promotion campaign based on the human health
benefits of black tea consumption*

The campaign has two main immediate objectives

- To provide solid and substantiated information on the health effects of black tea consumption;
- To demonstrate the cost effectiveness of a health-based promotion campaign in selected test markets.

The project is designed to run over a four-year period at a total cost of US$ 5.2 million, of which the promotion campaign US$ 2.5 million.

The main components and time frame for the project are set out below.

## Research Activities

- Polyphenolics extracted and ready for use in absorption & metabolism studies
- Early results on colon cancer (i.e. changes in colonic crypts)
- Completion of animal studies on cardiovascular disease
- Completion of studies on tea and oral health
- Completion of studies on absorption & tissue distribution of tea polyphenols
- Completion of human clinical trial on cardiovascular disease
- Completion of activity 1 components of cancer studies in animals
- Completion of human clinical trial on antioxidant capabilities
- Completion of activity 2 components of cancer studies in animals

```
Y E A R 1
Y E A R 2
Y E A R 3
Y E A R 4
```

## Promotional Campaign

- Design of logo and statement
- Testing of logo and statement completed
- Trademark registered internationally
- Printing of operating manuals
- Completion of databases in test countries
- Co-opted trade people to launch logo
- Logo Launched to trade PR organisations
- Active promotion of logo and its message to general public
- Report of impact of campaign on volume of tea sales

# THE CHALLENGE OF MARKETING COMMODITIES FROM DEVELOPING COUNTRIES

JANET FAROOQ AND LAMON RUTTEN[1]

## 1  INTRODUCTION

This paper focuses on the problems arising in the marketing of commodities related to marketing structures, the mechanisms used and the associated government policies. It does not deal with problems of quality control, research and development for new or improved products nor with the ways of selling such new or improved products as these aspects are being covered in other presentations. It is written with the intention of identifying activities that need to be reinforced or initiated in order to assist commodity traders in developing countries who are in a weak bargaining position.

## 2  PRODUCTION AND MARKETING SYSTEMS

It seems rather obvious that marketing problems have a direct relationship with the structure of production. Three basic models of commodity production can be identified: large-scale production; small-scale, but organized production (such as cooperatives); and small-scale, fragmented production. Large-scale production units such as copper or iron ore mines or rubber plantations are in a position to have their own sophisticated marketing department, with well-trained staff and direct access to world-

---

[1] Respectively Chief and Economic Affairs Officer of the Diversification, Processing, Marketing and Distribution Section, Commodities Division, UNCTAD. The views expressed in this paper are those of the authors and do not necessarily reflect the views of the United Nations Secretariat. The designations employed and the presentation of the material do not imply the expression of any opinion whatsoever on the part of the United Nations Secretariat concerning the legal status of any country, territory, city of area, or of its authorities, or concerning the delimitation of its frontiers or boundaries.

wide information and communications networks. With their large-scale production, they can afford to pay for this. They are able to send their staff to overseas training (large oil producers have even set up their own training institute in London) or to visit clients, recruit foreign consultants, undertake market studies, and invest in the penetration of new markets. In many cases, they also have their own agents overseas.[2] Large producers are also able to influence government policies in such a way that they facilitate their activities. For example, infrastructure, such as port, road or railroad facilities, is often specifically constructed to support these producers, and paid and/or maintained out of the government budget.[3] Also, these companies can obtain exemptions from certain regulations, such as allowing them to retain a part of their foreign currency earnings. Government agricultural marketing and pricing policy is often more favourable for large-scale plantations than for smallholders[4]. Large companies are in this privileged situation irrespective of whether they are partly or wholly owned by a TNC or have long-term supply contracts with buyers.

The second way in which production can be organized is through cooperatives or producer associations which group together several small or medium-sized producers for the purpose of providing some common services. One of these services is usually in the marketing area and can range from informal arrangements to coordinate shipments to obtain more favourable transport rates or improve export logistics[5] to having a common marketing service which acts as an agent for the group. There are many examples of this latter case ranging from small cooperatives or producer associations who sell to traders, to large ones who export

---

[2] The large oil producing companies of Mexico, Saudi Arabia and Nigeria and the main Zambian, Peruvian and Chilean copper mining companies all have offices in London; in the case of flowers, some of the largest Colombian producers own import agencies in the USA and have agents in Europe.

[3] This is the case for many mining companies throughout the world and for quite a number of large-scale timber companies.

[4] For instance this was until recently the case of Malawi where tobacco plantations sold directly to foreign buyers, through auctions, while smallholders were forced to sell at a low price to the government marketing board.

[5] For instance, Kenyan horticultural exporters work together to allocate air cargo space.

themselves and in some cases have agents abroad.[6] They can also employ an exclusive agent for their exports[7] and are often sufficiently large and well-known to have access to the services of brokerage houses for hedging or securitization of deals.

The success of cooperatives or producer associations varies considerably and depends on their size, financial situation and marketing experience. Some small cooperatives are well-established and have managed to open direct marketing links with developed country counterparts, in particular alternative trade organisations; some of the larger cooperatives and producer associations are major players on the markets for their commodities.[8] While quite a few cooperatives and producers associations have their own information services, overseas representatives, training programmes, etc., and so are able to function effectively in world markets, many others suffer from a lack of working capital and access to credit, and therefore have severe problems in competing with agents from foreign trade houses who are able to offer prompt payment or even pre-harvest credits.[9] Nevertheless, these types of cooperative arrangements represent a promising way of dealing firstly with the problem of lack of bargaining power for individual producers and secondly, with the problem that the lone small producer or export agent is not considered by most buyers as a reliable counterpart in trade.

---

[6] The first case can be illustrated by Ugandan coffee co-operatives, which, once exports were liberalized in 1990, set up a joint marketing office to organize tenders for foreign buyers. The latter is the case, for instance, in Cameroon, where a co-operative union undertakes CIF arabica exports; in Colombia, where half of the country's coffee is exported by an association of coffee exporters which also undertakes promotion campaigns; or for the South African Sugar Association, which has an office in London.

[7] For example, all Australian sugar was for many years exported by an independent private company, CSR Ltd.

[8] For example in the case of sugar, co-operative groups from Australia, Brazil, Colombia, EEC, Guatemala, India, South Africa and Thailand are among the main sugar exporters; in the case of bananas, Colombian producer co-operatives own importing subsidiaries in the USA and Europe.

[9] In Cameroon, for instance, arabica coffee export co-operatives are well-established and organized, but robusta coffee co-operatives are relatively new, undercapitalized and have little experience in marketing (until 1991, robusta exports were a government monopoly); consequently, they have problems to compete with private buyers.

The third scenario is, clearly, a multitude of small-scale producers (farmers, loggers, fishermen or miners) who usually sell their output to middlemen and are not directly involved in either domestic or foreign markets. These are the groups who often do not have access to market information on an ongoing and up-to-date basis, to credit lines for sales or to other marketing services. Middlemen usually control access to these trade-facilitating factors, and small-scale producers, therefore, often lose out in terms of the part of the final returns for their product that they receive. It was partly to protect the interests of small-scale producers that marketing boards and similar centralized marketing schemes were introduced, be it for cocoa or coffee in Africa, wheat in Canada and Australia, or gold in Latin America. The marketing board was to be an honest middleman, giving a just return to the producer and providing marketing services in a cost-efficient manner. Moreover, because of their size, they would be able to set up offices in the main markets.[10] Serious problems have arisen over how marketing boards set prices for the producers - at what levels are prices set and for what purposes, how frequently are they changed, and when the board accumulates funds, how are these used? But this should not take attention away from the often equally serious set of problems which arise when marketing boards are eliminated - has there been a negative influence on the producers' willingness to continue producing high-quality products, who takes on the collection and sales of commodities and what is the credibility, in domestic and international markets, of these new market players? To quote the industry point of view:

*"The threat that the old-fashioned cocoa boards and their equivalents could disappear, or lose their regulatory powers, is worrying some international buyers. The concern is not only that quality standards may suffer, but that private firms cannot be trusted to meet distant delivery dates. For some chocolate manufacturers a state-run marketing agency still inspires more confidence than a private enterprise."*[11]

---

[10] For example several large cocoa and sugar marketing boards have offices in London, many of the francophone African countries have offices of their cotton marketing board in Paris, and the commodity marketing organisations of China, as well as of the former Soviet Union, are represented in all major markets.

[11] *World Commodity Report*, 15/8/91.

As already evident from the discussion above, these production scenarios lead to at least four marketing scenarios which have different implications for producer price formation. These marketing scenarios are direct sales by producers (plantations, mines or cooperatives) to buyers abroad, purchases from producers by agents of local and foreign firms, centralized market places such as auctions, electronic tender systems or forward markets, and government purchases, through a marketing board or purchasing agency, with or without monopoly power.

When direct sales are made from producers to buyers abroad,[12] prices are in most cases determined through direct negotiations. The bargaining strength and market sophistication of the parties involved is of major importance, especially in the case where a viable 'world market price' is not known.[13] In several markets (such as those for iron ore, phosphates, rubber and tin) price transparency is impaired as deals are usually bilateral and secret.

For a number of commodities such as cocoa, coffee and rubber, a large part of production is bought by agents of foreign companies based in the producing country. Price implications are often negative for the producers who have little bargaining strength because they are rarely informed about market conditions. Moreover, in this marketing situation, producers are directly exposed to world market price volatility.

Both direct sales abroad and sales by producers to agents of foreign companies have, for some commodities, two significant disadvantages. Firstly, when production is scattered, there are high 'discovery' costs for buyers, and high transport costs; and secondly, prices are not transparent, making price negotiations difficult. Centralized market places[14] over-

---

[12] This type of sales prevails in the markets for many metals such as copper, iron ore and tin, for phosphates, for timber, and for a few of agricultural products such as bananas. For most commodities there are, to some extent, direct deliveries from large producers to buyers abroad. For example, in Trinidad and Tobago, small cocoa producers sell to a marketing board while large farmers export directly to merchants and chocolate manufacturers in Europe.

[13] For some commodities a world reference price is widely accepted, such as the LME price for copper, and pricing in most direct deals is related to this reference.

[14] Auctions have existed for quite some time now for tea in most producing countries and for coffee in Kenya; electronic tender systems are being used for cotton (used in the USA and in Tanzania) and organized forward markets for cocoa (Brazil and Indonesia), tin (Malaysia) and cereals & metals (China).

come some of these disadvantages by allowing a central buying point for foreign companies, thus introducing a stronger competition between buyers, while at the same time increasing domestic price transparency. Moreover, such a centralized market place also allows easier access to market information.[15] The producers' bargaining power towards buyers for the international market is thus enhanced. However, centralized markets only function properly when there are sufficient buyers and there is no collusion between them.[16]

Governments can act as a marketing agent on grounds of efficiency (including the perceived necessity to control foreign currency flows, and the fact that a central exporting agency can negotiate better prices, long-term marketing arrangements and exports to non- traditional markets).[17] This type of government marketing board has been set up in a number of sugar exporting countries, for example, Fiji and Mauritius, and also are responsible for coffee and tea trade from India and Sri Lanka with Russia. Four fifths of world raw sugar exports (including from Australia and South Africa) are organized through one export monopoly (government companies in some cases and private companies owned by individual sugar producers/cooperatives in others. This arrangement is widely supported by sugar growers and sugar traders alike because of the large practical advantages it offers.

Another reason for governments to monopolize or control export trade is that control over marketing allows them to directly determine the prices that producers receive. They can, in theory, decide to cushion world market price volatility by taxing producers in times of high prices, and subsidizing them in terms of low prices; the prices paid should then reflect price trends rather than actual prices. In practice, however, political factors have generally played a major role in setting price, with

---

[15] For example since the introduction of organized forward exchanges for metals in China, metal producers, traders and consumers active on the exchanges also have direct, on-line access to the world market prices as formed on the London Metal Exchange.

[16] Tea auctions have for years been criticized because of the power of a few large buyers operating in all of them simultaneously.

[17] Marketing boards are also better able to coordinate export policies among countries. For example, the copra marketing boards of the Solomon Islands, Vanuatu and Papua New Guinea maintain contact throughout the year and try to establish some consensus in their negotiating positions before individual negotiations start. This has often worked quite well.

producer prices being in most cases too low (to generate profits or income for the government or to guarantee a low-price supply to the local consuming or processing sectors) and in some cases too high (to keep producers' political support). If the rationale of government intervention was to protect producers against price volatility, then the methods chosen were often quite costly and usually not very efficient. Government control over the marketing of export crops, or, for that matter, mineral commodities (gold and gemstones are typical examples in this latter category) has often been abused to skim profits from the producing sector. However, even if this practice is disavowed the question remains whether small producers themselves should be left to carry all the risks of price volatility. It should be noted that producers always have to bear quantity and quality volatility; to expose them also to world market price volatility seems socially unjust, and, in fact, is counterproductive in economic terms. As small producers are usually not in a position to cover their own price risks or absorb temporary price setbacks, they have to continuously adapt to changing prices, which can result in large welfare losses for the national economy.[18] There is obviously a marketing dilemma facing countries where small producers are the main providers of commodities: how is marketing best organized so as to protect producers from short-term price volatility, while at the same time keeping prices in line with market trends, avoiding either price levels that are unpractically high (that is, so high that the government cannot afford to maintain them), or price levels that are so low that they do not provide incentives (and means) to producers to continue or to improve their operations.

## 3 RECENT DEVELOPMENTS

This dilemma has been made all the more difficult by some recent developments which risk to reduce even further the bargaining position of commodity suppliers: the liberalization of marketing systems in developing countries, the growing complexity of international commodity trade and the increasing concentration among commodity trade houses.

---

[18] For example, in 1992 most coffee farmers in Laos (where prices directly reflect world market price fluctuations) decided to uproot their coffee trees, in reaction to the low prices offered. While coffee prices recovered since, it will take years to replace these coffee trees.

The first major development is the liberalization of internal and export marketing for commodities in line with the trend of relying on market forces. Much of this liberalization in developing countries has taken place within the framework of IMF/World Bank structural adjustment programmes with the valid intention of making prices and supply more sensitive to world market conditions. Most actions have involved abolishing a government marketing board and fragmenting the system to several, sometimes numerous, internal marketing agents, with no or scanty provision made for the taking over of the functions of the board as a provider of producer and marketing services. In recent years countries in which marketing boards have been abolished or the government lost its trade monopoly include Burundi (a coffee board); Cameroon (boards for cocoa, coffee, cotton groundnuts and palm kernels); Central African Republic (a coffee board); Colombia (a government gold export monopoly); El Salvador (a coffee board); Ghana (a monopoly on coffee exports; for cocoa, there is pressure from the World Bank to liberalize internal marketing, but no changes have been implemented to date); Guinea-Bissau (a board for exports of palm kernels and non-traditional products); Laos (a government monopoly on rice exports); Madagascar (a board for all export crops); Myanmar (a government monopoly on rice exports); Nigeria (five marketing boards, for rubber, groundnuts, cotton, cocoa and palm produce); Pakistan (government monopolies on exports of raw cotton and rice); Uganda (four boards for cotton, tobacco, tea and coffee, and a government monopoly on exports of hides and skins); and Zambia (a gemstone export monopoly).

When these boards had fulfilled price stabilizing functions, one consequence of their abolition is that producers face more unstable prices. Moreover, producers face a higher degree of marketing insecurity as private buyers may not provide the same dense purchasing network as did the government. Market security allows farmers to invest in their production, producing more and selling better quality products. This, in turn, improves the prices that they receive.[19]

---

[19] An interesting example is that of Ghanaian cocoa, which receives a price premium over most other origins because of its systematically high quality. This high quality has been maintained because of dependable purchasing activities (the marketing board organizes weekly purchases at many purchasing points, close to farmers). These activities provide the precondition for quality control by farmers, the first step for systematic quality control throughout the whole production and marketing chain from farmer to quay. In comparison, in Côte

Although quality control mechanisms are not a subject for this paper, it should be stressed that the importance of quality products in international trade is growing. For many agricultural products such as coffee as well as non-traditional ones such as fruits and vegetables, only the market for first quality products is still expanding; the market for products of second quality is declining even in absolute terms. In recognition of this, governments in several countries where marketing boards have been abolished are returning at the quality control level (but not without having lost valuable expertise).[20]

With the abolition of an export monopoly, the private traders who have taken over export marketing are often inexperienced, small-scale private agents who have no commercial standing with buyers, are often restricted in their access to credit, and are novices in their trade dealings. Their small size puts them at a disadvantage in negotiating deals and in using certain marketing techniques. Some marketing techniques such as counter-trade-type transactions are simply too large and complicated for them. For others such as forward and long-term contracts, they are not trusted as counterparts. For a country's economy, long-term, fixed price contracts are often very important.[21] Also small traders often do not have the means to use more complicated pricing mechanisms such as executable orders. In their inland procurement activities, they easily lose out to agents representing large buyers or trade houses who come in better equipped, offering better terms (especially in terms of finance) and have a secure market outlet.[22]

---

d'Ivoire, the quality of cocoa beans is lower because private traders are active more haphazardly, and farmers sell whenever there is a trader near, not waiting for the moment that their beans reach their optimum quality.

[20] For example, in Nigeria, where marketing boards were abolished in 1987 (with disastrous effects on some of the commodity exports), in January 1990, the government stated that it would set up a non-oil export supervision scheme to enforce quality control by issuing quality standard certificates.

[21] In Uganda, the marketing board's long-term contracts for coffee sales have been described as 'Uganda's coffee lifeline.' With them, Uganda has relatively few, very large guaranteed sales, easy to manage, with the possibility to plan ahead.

[22] This is the case, for instance, in Guinea, where local exporters are not able to compete with agents of foreign traders who installed themselves in the country after coffee exports were liberalized in the mid-1980s. In Papua New Guinea, all cocoa exporters are either owned or managed by foreign companies which, according to the Cocoa Marketing Board, have at their disposal highly

This fragmentation of marketing activities in developing countries has taken place at the same time as there has been a growing complexity of international commodity trade: competitiveness has increased, better services are required from exporters (for instance, exporters improve their competitive power if they are able to sell in the currency of their client), and exporters need to follow market developments very closely in order not to sign poor deals.

One factor in this is that the role of futures prices as reference prices for physical trade deals has increased. For most of the important metals, commodity-exchange prices have replaced producer prices as reference prices for international trade.[23] For soft commodities, most of the larger producers and exporters now have direct access to commodity exchange prices, and it has become much more difficult for traders to buy from them for prices which differ in a major way from these 'world market prices'. While the formation of prices on this type of highly visible, transparent market provides additional price information to developing country exporters, it also adds a layer of complexity. Price behaviour on commodity exchanges is quite frequently 'illogical' due to short-term influences of speculative investment fund and trade house activity. This implies that inexperienced exporters from developing countries risk to fix prices at inappropriate moments.

Good knowledge of marketing practices has become imperative, and only those with the possibilities to invest in manpower and in information systems are likely to be able to build up such knowledge. In this situation smaller companies have problems. The fact that they are not easily able to 'buy' protection against price fluctuations through use of futures and options markets (because they do not have the means to deposit the financial guarantees which are required for such use) is only a part of this. Their major problem is that they have no or limited understanding of or access to a sophisticated array of marketing instruments to which their competitors do have access. They regularly have a difficult time evaluating what they are being offered. For example, in many cases option clauses form an implicit, often well-hidden part of physical deals. Several

---

skilled people, good contacts with overseas buyers and good market intelligence on what is happening on terminal markets in various time zones. Domestic traders with these three elements are scarce in PNG.

[23] This happened, for example, in the mid-1960s for copper, the early 1980s for crude oil, and as recent as 1984 for aluminium.

trade houses offer floor prices and shared participation in price increases in their contracts, but this does not comes for free. How can one evaluate the implicit payment involved ? On the other hand, several exporters 'give away' options clauses for free because they do not understand their value; for example, in shipping flexibility. Also, many of the option clauses use futures contract prices as reference prices and there is a need to follow and understand futures markets, even if one is not using them directly for hedging. As a result, less sophisticated exporters frequently lose out in marketing deals, for instance by accepting unfavourable contract clauses, or failing to use opportunities to increase their benefits or reduce their risks.

With more complicated markets, there is a growing importance of knowing how to obtain and use information, especially as practically all commodity markets are segmented in various ways. Questions arise as to which information is needed, how and from whom can it be obtained, who in a country should receive it and what is the best way of evaluating it. The role of information, its collection, processing and dissemination is crucial, and those without the means to handle information flows quickly and efficiently are at a severe disadvantage. Developing country traders have to try to be competitive in an international trading environment where their competitors use the latest technologies available and have the manpower to utilize information to the fullest.

Concomitant with the above developments, there have been some important changes in the world trading structures. The concentration among trade houses traditionally important as intermediaries in the trade of many commodities such as coffee, cocoa and sugar has significantly increased. Several major houses such as Woodhouse, Drake & Carey (soft commodities) and Phibro (soft commodities and metals) have gone out of business, others such as Sucden have given up certain products. Yet others have been taken over by banks (J. Aron by Goldman Sachs, Rouse by Credit Lyonnais). No new large trade houses have emerged, though there are some new traders specializing in niche markets, such as for high quality coffees or specialty sugars. This has given the remaining houses considerable market power and increased knowledge about market plans of major suppliers. One of the primary reasons for this situation was the shaky financial position of several trade houses. Their profit margins declined in absolute terms because commodity prices were low and they were over-exposed to some ill-considered large deals. Banks reacted by tightening the credit lines they give to trade houses, evaluating proposed deals on a case-by-case basis, and insisting on a larger use of risk management instruments. One consequence of this is that entry to the international trade house system has become more difficult; in order to find clients, new entrants either have to accept unfavourable conditions or come up with financial guarantees.

The role of brokerage houses such as Merrill Lynch and Refco and of banks such as Goldman Sachs, Credit Lyonnais, Barclays, or JP Morgan in price formation and physical trading of commodities is also growing quite rapidly. Both groups were not historically involved in commodity trade as such. Brokerage houses have become active partly as a way of diversifying their activities and partly as a result of increasing interest in swaps.[24] A further reason lies in the growing sophistication of many exporters. There seems to be a tendency among exporters, for example in Latin America, to leave the physical side of commodity deals with traders, but to manage price risks independently through brokerage houses. This effectively separates the trading of the physical commodity from its pricing mechanism and so enhances the bargaining power of exporters with traders as compared to their traditional pricing system of executable orders. Banks, through their involvement as intermediaries in the growing longer-term swaps market, see the need to lay off their price risks. This can be done on futures markets, in the over-the-counter market by arranging, when possible, back-to-back deals, but also by getting involved in physical trade. The latter possibility has been found to add considerable extra flexibility and in the early 1990's several moved into base metal physical trading.

## 4  POLICY APPROACHES

Approaches by developing country governments to handling the policy aspects of this new marketing situation have taken three forms. Firstly, the liberalized internal market in a country can be left to sort itself out with only the more viable and experienced traders surviving - this approach was 'chosen', by default, in most African countries. Even with provision of training in modern marketing practices (which in practice has been absent), this is a high cost solution with export earnings for the

---

[24] For example, Merrill Lynch now does a lot of coffee swaps business, with most of the swaps being short term in nature.

country taking a beating for some years.[25] Another disadvantage is that local traders, who have to cope with a generally poor domestic economic environment, have to compete on an uneven footing with representatives of foreign trade houses who have access to all the resources of their parent company. A second approach is to encourage domestic traders to work together through an association of exporters.[26] Even in some of the more advanced developing countries, exporters have often found it essential to cooperate.[27] Associations of exporters in some countries have benefitted directly from government support, both financial and providing access to trade promotion activities abroad.[28]

The third approach, which is complementary to the other two, is to develop an internal market place such as an auction, electronic tender system or a forward market. Several developing countries are following this route to coping with the new internal free market, and are also looking at the possibilities of futures markets. In some cases, the international agency leading the restructuring of a country's export sector has recognized the importance of such a mechanism. For example, in Burundi

---

[25] Nigerian cocoa, for instance, continued to be sold at a high discount long after the initial anarchy which resulted from the dissolution of the Cocoa Marketing Board had been sorted out.

[26] Exporters do not necessarily have themselves to take the initiative in this respect. For instance, in Bolivia, Chile and Colombia, the government took the initiative to set up private entities which provide support to agricultural exports. In South-East Asia, the UN regional economic commission, ESCAP, supports the collaboration between Malaysian and Indonesian palm oil producers with the objective of enhancing the share of palm oil in the world vegetable oil market.

[27] In Colombia, most sugar exporters have joined a sugar export company; palm oil producers have set up their own export marketing company; and many of the smaller emerald exporters have joined in a federation of emerald producers and exporters.

[28] For example, for palm oil, the government of Malaysia and the private sector have worked closely together to promote exports. They undertake activities such as giving large export finance support, including to Russia, for periods up to 2 years, investing in palm oil processing facilities in countries such as Brazil, China and Egypt, and undertaking promotional campaigns in their export markets. In the case of African groundnut and other vegetable oil exports, exports are mainly in the hands of large western transnationals who also trade in other vegetable oils. They have no specific interest in boosting African products. So how can African producers compete? Another example is that of Australian fruit and vegetable exports. The government provides matching funds to those collected by the private cooperative responsible for these exports. Uses of these funds include export promotion.

the World Bank promoted the creation of a coffee auction parallel to the abolition of the marketing board's monopoly power and in Egypt it is considering an electronic tender system to replace the government monopoly for cotton sales.[29] In other cases, actions have resulted from the conscious efforts of certain organizations to overcome marketing problems. Such is the case in Central America, where the Inter-American Institute for Cooperation on Agriculture (IICA), an inter-governmental organization, is promoting the creation of agricultural commodity exchanges. The first ones have already been established, and it expected that they will remedy a situation in which 'a few transnational firms take advantage of the situation to set the conditions for international trade',[30] and ultimately, enhance the competitivity of regional farmers. In the CIS, auctions and forward markets developed more or less spontaneously (as had forward and futures markets in the USA in the 19th century), as a reaction to poor distribution systems.

Under any of these approaches, producers and exporters are more visibly exposed to price risks. Many have expressed interest in learning to cope with these risks by becoming actively involved in using commodity price risk instruments. They are often stymied in doing so not only because of lack of technical knowledge or lack of understanding of which instrument would best respond to their risks, but also because their access to risk markets is hindered by government (and company) regulations and by a lack of understanding on the part of the government of what the private sector wishes to do. Traders in developing countries need assistance in learning how to assess their price risks, and how to institute company policies so as to have a closely monitored hedging strategy and the internal control structure to handle it. They also need to have a good understanding of the range and possible uses of available instruments. Without these tools, there is a large risk that they will end up using risk management instruments as gambling instruments, a means of making money, rather than as insurance. Simultaneously, governments have not adapted to changing market conditions and often do not allow or facilitate the use of modern marketing instruments. They have problems deciding on how best to formulate their policies in the areas of support services

---

[29] P. Varangis, E. Thigpen and T. Akiyama, 'Risk management prospects for Egyptian cotton', *World Bank Policy Research Working Paper*, January 1993.

[30] 'Regional agricultural commodity exchanges promoted', *IICA News*, September-December 1992.

and regulatory policies. These support services involve not only who is entitled to export commodities (public, private firms) but also the conditions they face in terms of access to foreign exchange, laws on use of futures, options, countertrade, tenders etc., and regulations on timing, quality, supply to local market, export taxes and so on. It is clear that it is difficult for governments to develop a policy framework for the use of new marketing mechanisms without sufficient knowledge on the functioning of such markets. Existing assistance and published material does not seem to be adequate for meeting the needs of governments in this area.

## 5  ASSISTANCE REQUIRED

The last issue is, then, to assess what assistance is available to developing countries: its contents and coverage, gaps and ways to fill these gaps. There exists a great variety of bilateral and private sources of assistance of considerable importance. Most developed countries have centres for the promotion of imports from developing countries. There are many private newsletters including from trade houses specializing on specific commodities, and there is a wide array of information vendors such as Reuters who distribute the prices formed on commodity exchanges. Also some commodity exchanges, brokerage and trade houses as well as banks provide training and consultancy services on request. However, the following discussion concentrates on the three main categories of international assistance being given: information dissemination; training; and the organization of market places.

Much attention has been given by the international community to the topic of market transparency. This has been supported through market reviews and statistical work of study groups and international commodity organizations, many of whom are ICB's for the Common Fund. These are basically historical exercises useful for investment planning and considering the supply/demand balance. Market information, particularly on prices, is provided through services such as INFOFISH (FAO) and the Market News Service of ITC which covers tropical timber, spices, rice, hides and skins, fruits and vegetables, flowers and green plants, and fruit juices. It appears normal that those assembling such market information, be it in the UN system or not, charge a reasonable fee for the service, especially when it is provided frequently and rapidly. However this raises problem of costs involved in obtaining information - how are these to be met in a country and who should pay. Some possible solutions have been tried. One option is for the government to bear the costs of buying the information that its producers think should be publicly available. It can then disseminate it through various means such as putting price information on the radio in local languages (this has been done for fish). This option helps the small producer to bargain better with the intermediaries. A second is for a organization such as a government department, a large commercial firm or a cooperative to buy the information and to sell it on to others. However, start-up costs for service remain a problem and in this respect, for products where up-to-date market information is scattered or scarce, the Common Fund could, through an ICB-sponsored project, help a new service get established with the intention that it become self-financing within a couple of years. Such projects seem good candidates for loans rather than grants.

A second area of assistance which has expanded tremendously over the last few years is training for traders, covering a variety of important topics. The ITC has been particularly active in this field with its series of traders manuals and associated dissemination seminars. The commodities they have covered include cocoa, coffee, cotton, flowers, fruit juices, and vegetable oils. These manuals which cover topics such as importing channels in main markets, product promotion, ways of adding value, contract specifications and shipping, payment and insurance terms, have been highly appreciated. One problem with this approach is the cost of keeping the manuals up to date, given the rapid changes in international marketing. Up until now the manuals have been provided free of charge to developing countries in line with UN regulations. The ITC has helped several ICB's develop proposals for new or revised manuals for Second Account funding which have run into approval problems. It seems that another approach needs to be taken, perhaps following the example of GEPLACEA some years ago when it developed, with funds from its members and sponsoring from private trade companies, a Handbook on International Sugar Marketing. It still sells this handbook for about US$85. Could not an ICB consider providing funds to finance the development or revision of a Traders Manual for its commodity with the Common Fund supporting 2 or 3 dissemination seminars, particularly for LDC's exporting that commodity? One could, in this way, draw on the trade expertise of the ICB members (both exporters and importers) through contributions in kind (making available experienced traders either to work on the manual or to animate the seminars). Since having more aware traders on both sides of a market will help the market function better, it would seem that both producers and consumers represented in an ICB should be willing to support such an endeavour.

UNCTAD has taken a slightly different, though complementary approach, in developing its commodity trading packages. The focus has been on computer based training for using risk management instruments (futures and options) for traders in relation to their specific commodity in order for them to be able to execute trade deals efficiently and to provide advice to their companies on marketing opportunities. To date courses have been developed for cocoa, coffee, cotton, sugar and palm oil in the framework of the TRAINFORTRADE programme which is designed to provide for dissemination through regional training centres.[31] The intention is to make the training as self-financing as possible through training local trainers and through charging fees for participation in training sessions. The existing courses are being integrated with computer-based modules on physical trade mechanisms so that the interlinks are clear and the use of futures and options is related to actual trading situations of participants. At the moment there is a need to further improve the courses developed as well as expand coverage to other commodities. Both initiatives could be envisaged as projects for the Second Account as they are time-bound in nature and of interest to many commodity traders in a range of countries including LDC's.

Through undertaking this work, UNCTAD has become very conscious of two other gaps in existing assistance in the area of training, which it is making a very modest start to fill. The first concerns an urgent need to develop a course for executives of companies engaged in commodity trading on how to draw up a trade strategy with proper control structures to limit financial risks, including those associated with the use of risk management instruments. One major problem in firms in both the North and the South is that senior management in many cases does not understand the marketing instruments being used and does not have a formalized strategy. This can result in abuse by trading staff and large speculative losses.[32] Hedging strategies in particular need to be thought through

---

[31] This programme has benefited from finance provided by the EEC and the governments of France, Switzerland and Luxembourg in particular for course development, establishment of regional centres and scholarships for African traders.

[32] To give a few examples: in 1988, it was discovered that German trade company Klockner had accumulated 600-700 million DM of 'paper' losses on the Brent oil forward market and on the crude oil futures markets; these losses had

and internal controls developed, with limits put on trading positions of any individual and checks and balances instituted on decisions taken. A course in this area needs finance to be developed and then its delivery could be more or less self-financing through fees charged for participation.

The second area concerns a course for policy makers in governments, including Central Banks and Ministries of Finance, Trade and Development Planning, who need to understand the uses that can be made of various instruments in the area of international trade, including risk management instruments, and, in this connection, ensure the necessary conditions for appropriate use of these instruments. UNCTAD has started developing one course in this area for countries in Africa with large coffee exports. Using the exchange of experience with countries where governments have recently gone through a reformulation of their export marketing and risk management policy framework, it is hoped that this course will help African governments improve their policy framework, thus enhancing the competitiveness of their exporters.

A proper and judicious use of modern marketing and risk management instruments seems to be in the interest of all trade partners as it leads to a better functioning of markets. For traders and consumers, it facilitates and securitizes deals; in the case of commodity exchanges it improves their operation, giving additional returns to many of the intermediaries and resulting in better price formation; and for exporters, it improves their access to export credit, puts their relationships with trade partners on a surer footing, and enhances their bargaining position. Therefore, the development of these three types of courses for a commodity could be an ideal project format for the Second Account. A further consideration is that limited finance is needed for the development of each course (about $100,000 per commodity to develop a standard course and organize a first validation of it).

---

previously gone unnoticed because the 'rolling over' of positions allowed keeping such unrealized losses out of the account books. Similarly, Showa Shell, Shell's Japanese oil import subsidiary, accumulated over a period of four years losses on unauthorized foreign currency transactions amounting to over $US 1 billion, without the knowledge of anyone outside the small group of staff involved in the company's foreign currency dealings. British food company Allied Lyons lost $US 268 million on foreign currency dealings, which was discovered accidentally when the company's main trader was home ill and one of his colleagues had to know which contracts the company had outstanding.

It should be pointed out in this regard that the World Bank has started a country level programme in a few commodity-exporting developing countries (Colombia, Costa Rica and Papua New Guinea) which involves the identification of risk distribution in national economy, the identification of laws and regulations, an assessment of benefits and costs of hedging, an identification of necessary changes in the legal and institutional frameworks and training, and a pilot programme including the introduction of new accountancy and company control systems. This is done under the World Bank's country programme, covering commodities of importance to the country. Every country intervention has a duration of at least 2 years. This intensive approach is useful in that it integrates consideration of country debt and budget management, but it does not lend itself easily to commodity-focused assistance through ICB's.

The last area which needs attention, much more than it is receiving now, is the organization and operation of internal or regional market places. This includes support for exporter associations and support for auctions, forward markets, etc. for organizing internal marketing. The establishment and operation of exporter associations is clearly a country-level activity, but it could be positively encouraged through exchange of experience among traders from several countries exporting the same commodity. This exchange could focus on modalities, financing mechanisms, services provided and experiences in export markets, and this could be arranged under the auspices of an ICB. Similarly, the setting-up of national or regional centralized marketing places would benefit inter-country discussions on advantages, problems, feasibilities etc. This is already happening in Central America (see above) and South-East Asia where countries are involved in ongoing discussions about ways of cooperating in the creation of regional commodity contracts and exchanges. Also, such market places would benefit from being electronically interlinked, providing direct price information to different countries, allowing a larger and not locally restricted use of the market, and making it possible to be connected to major futures contracts traded elsewhere. Again, this area could form the basis for ICB sponsored projects.

It is our distinct impression that the challenge of marketing commodities from developing countries in an increasingly competitive and complicated setting is an area where more attention needs to be focused. However, most of the activities we see as required do not involve large sums of money, nor a long time frame. They would be of concrete value to a large number of producers and traders from many commodity supplying countries, who should bear some of the costs, and, in our experience, are willing to do so. They would have, as far as we can tell from contacts with the trading community in the North (trade houses, brokers and banks) much support from this group as better functioning market and traders are also crucial to their survival. Thus this area appears to hold promise for ICB/Common Fund support.

# ECONOMICS, POLITICS AND ETHICS OF PRIMARY COMMODITY DEVELOPMENT: HOW CAN POOR COUNTRIES AND PEOPLES IN NEED BENEFIT MOST?

UMA LELE[1], JAMES GOCKOWSKI[2] AND KOFI ADU-NYAKO[3]

## 1 INTRODUCTION

The poorest countries depend preponderantly on a limited number of agricultural commodities for exports, employment, income, government revenues, savings, and investment (Table 1). In these economies a small percentage change in the output or prices of these major commodities has a large macroeconomic effect, in contrast to nontraditional commodities or services which typically play a small role in the economy. This means that commodities most important in production and exports must receive high priority in improving production or exports if economic transformation is to be achieved. This is a rather obvious fact, but one which is often overlooked in the consideration of economic diversification strategies of poor countries.

[1] Director of International Studies and Programs and Graduate Research Professor, Department of Food and Resource Economics, University of Florida, Gainesville, Florida 32611, and Visiting Research Scholar at the International Monetary Fund when this paper was prepared.

[2] Graduate Student, University of Florida

[3] Research Associate, University of Florida.

The authors are grateful to Peter Wickham, Chief of the Commodities Division at the International Monetary Fund, for his comments on the earlier draft of this paper. Views expressed in this paper are those of the authors and do not necessarily represent the views of the International Monetary Fund.

*Table 1:* Percentage of Export Earnings from Major Agricultural Export
Commodity among Least Developed Countries.

| Country | Major Agricultural Export | Per cent of Total Export Earnings | |
|---|---|---|---|
| | | 1984-85 | 1985-86 |
| Benin | cotton | 31.5 | 26.3 |
| Burkina Faso | cotton | 46.7 | 37.2 |
| Burundi | coffee | 84.0 | 86.7 |
| Cen. African R. | coffee | 35.4 | 30.1 |
| Ethiopia | coffee | 62.7 | 69.8 |
| Gambia | oil seeds | 24.8 | 21.6 |
| Ghana | cocoa | 66.1 | 60.7 |
| Guinea-Bissau | oil seeds | 64.3 | 54.4 |
| Haiti | coffee | 26.7 | 29.3 |
| Kenya | coffee | 27.3 | 34.5 |
| Liberia | rubber | 19.0 | 18.7 |
| Madagascar | coffee | 39.0 | 40.5 |
| Malawi | tobacco | 48.0 | 49.8 |
| Mali | cotton | 56.0 | 37.0 |
| Niger | cattle | 14.2 | 18.9 |
| Pakistan | cotton | 10.6 | 15.1 |
| Rwanda | coffee | 43.0 | 64.0 |
| Somalia | cattle | 79.4 | 79.3 |
| Sierra Leone | coffee | 12.7 | 18.9 |
| Sri Lanka | tea | 39.2 | 31.4 |
| Sudan | cotton | 47.7 | 44.3 |
| Tanzania | coffee | 39.1 | 50.2 |
| Togo | cotton | 11.3 | 15.5 |
| Zaire | coffee | 19.0 | 24.4 |

*Source:*    UNCTAD, *Handbook of International Trade and Development Statistics*, 1988 and 1989.

Many of these primary commodity nations are in Africa. Their immense diversity in terms of soils, climate, institutions, political regimes, and international marketing systems inherited from the colonial era mean that the set of development approaches and the subset of commodity strategies will also be heterogeneous and large. Notwithstanding their differences, agricultural commodity dependent countries share several common features. They have extremely limited human and institutional capital. They have become marginalized in the share in world exports, with a few notable exceptions, yet have increased their dependence on food imports. As a group, terms of trade changes have affected them more adversely than their higher income Asian or Latin American counterparts. They are highly dependent on a fragmented donor community for concessional assistance, at levels which were already high by the end of the 1970s (up to 10 to 15% of GNP) (Lele, 1992.), but which have now reached over 50% of GNP in some countries (*e.g.*, Mozambique). These increases have been in response to a higher demand for rehabilitation of infrastructure following wars and political disruptions, balance of payments difficulties, and frequent external shocks such as the recent decline in terms of trade, international interest rate fluctuations and droughts. Indebtedness has doubled as a share of exports for many countries in this group in a short period since the mid 1980s in spite of a combination of debt forgiveness, reschedulings and increased concessionality of the more recent economic assistance. In combination with political chaos these factors have generated donor fatigue, and have resulted in reduced political support for reforms at home.

While increased aid flows have been necessary, they have also brought a broad range of donor conditionalities and other costs. External resources provided by the donor community demand a huge amount of the limited capacity of governments that should ideally be allocated to the macroeconomic management and long term development of their economies. Apart from the administrative demands, advice and assistance is often inconsistent and conflicting both among donors and even by the same donor over time although much progress has been made in recent years in coordinating and implementing donor advice with respect to the specifics of macroeconomic reforms. However, absence of institutional memory is a pervasive problem in donor agencies, as shown in this paper. Long term consistent strategies are important for achieving broadbased sustained growth in the production of commodities.

Reaching previous peaks in agricultural exports is relatively easy by implementation of macroeconomic reform programs via the depreciation

of the exchange rate and reduction in budget deficits, as the experience of
the last decade has shown. When significant policy distortions existed
prior to reforms as in the case of Ghana or Tanzania, large shifts in
output from parallel markets to the official economy, the planting of new
trees, and greater application of variable inputs by farmers have produced
a significant export supply response. Maintaining these rates of agricultural production and exports however often requires the removal of
structural constraints once initial reforms have been implemented. In
Kenya and Malawi, macroeconomic policies were not highly distortionary
when external shocks began to affect them in the late 1970s, and their
agricultural export performance has been respectable by general standards
of developing countries (Lele and Meyer, 1989). However, their over-
whelming problems have been of an institutional nature, *e.g.*, discriminatory policies towards small farmers leading to unequal distribution of
benefits, inefficient public enterprises, weak ministries of agriculture and
the non-viability of financial institutions serving the agricultural sector
(Lele and Nabi, 1991). Their reforms raise complex issues which have
not yet been fully explored by donors from a long-term growth perspective. Sustained and broadbased agricultural growth in food and export
crop production for these low income countries will depend on the extent
to which governments of both industrial and African countries undertake
reforms, both of a price and nonprice nature, and most importantly, the
extent to which they rely on the historical experience of agricultural
development in Africa and throughout the developed and developing
world to learn and implement relevant policy lessons.

A comprehensive treatment of the issues affecting commodities is
overdue. In the past, approaches to the issues have been piecemeal and
subject to change. In the 1950s and 1960s questions were often raised
concerning limited international market prospects. In the 1970s, integrated
rural development projects aimed investments at achieving the goal of
domestic food self-sufficiency among the poorest households in resource
poor regions in Africa. That strategy when it ignored the importance of
export agriculture or macroeconomic policies produced disastrous results.
Macropolicy reforms geared to export incentives became the motto in the
1980s, with a winding down of agricultural investment portfolios by
donors in Africa. Introduction of safety nets particularly to protect the
urban poor came in vogue in the latter half of the 1980s, after criticism of
donors mounted that their export-oriented adjustment programs lacked a
human face. Concern for the environment has become the preoccupation
in the 1990s. These piecemeal approaches and changing fashions have

lacked an appreciation of the essential balance and complementarity between (a) price and non-price factors, including particularly the roles of human capital, development of the factor and product markets, public enterprises, infrastructure, technologies; and most importantly (b) the fundamental role of government *vis á vis* the private sector in the development of smallholder agriculture.

Governments are viewed as inefficient rent-seeking bureaucracies and in some cases with justification. But this view poses a fundamental dilemma. Without acknowledgement of the legitimate strategic role of governments *inter alia* in the development of markets, there is little hope of agricultural development in Africa. Yet without sharply increased investment in the training of nationals, retention of the qualified personnel in the public sector and accountability of governments, they cannot play the essential active facilitative role.

## 2 THE INHOSPITABLE INTERNATIONAL MARKET ENVIRONMENT

Poor countries depending on agricultural commodities face a host of constraints in the international market place including:

- inelastic world demand for their products *e.g.*, tea, coffee and cocoa;
- rapid technological change in competing countries;
- tariffs on processed agricultural commodities in OECD countries;
- growth of substitute products in importing countries *e.g.*, sweeteners and beet sugar;
- growing environmental concerns associated with their production;
- health concerns associated with their consumption *e.g.* tobacco, palm oil and sugar;
- increasingly oligopolistic market structures in OECD countries;
- restrictions placed upon their production by aid-giving countries to appease their own internal environmental lobbies while subsidized production of the same products continues at home *e.g.*, the U.S. stance towards the support of tobacco production in Africa;
- reduced import demand by Eastern European and Russian consumers due to severe income compression;
- and not the least important, the protectionist policies of OECD countries towards the production of all major and minor cereals, livestock and dairy products, sugar, edible oils, etc.

As a result of these conditions, growth in the demand for the raw and processed commodities of the poorest countries has been constrained and has greatly reduced production incentives for rural households. Witness for example the adverse effects of the exports of frozen meat carcasses by the EC and the dumping of surplus cotton by the U.S. and China over the last several years on African production and the financial health of its commodity-based institutions (Delgado, 1993; Lele, *et al.*, 1989a).

Agricultural policies of industrial countries are intended to protect the traditional small family farm 'way of life' at home. Yet in reality a large share of the benefits of support prices, government payments and export subsidies accrue to a handful of politically well organized large producers, processors and exporters. Various estimates of the likely increase in international prices from liberalization of OECD food policies exceed well over 25%, depending on the different assumptions of the models (Anderson and Tyler, 1990). Recent studies also show the high cost of budget deficits in OECD countries on the demand for primary commodities via the effect on the levels of real interest rates (Duncan, 1993). According to these studies an increase in the fiscal deficits of G-5 countries by 1% of their GDP causes a reduction of 2% in the relative prices of commodities. Changes in OECD fiscal deficits explained 40 to 50% of the changes in the real commodity prices over the sample period. Monetary expansion has the opposite effect.

In many commodity markets, the consumer benefits from recent price declines in raw commodity markets have been minimal in comparison to those of marketing agents (multinationals and trading houses), perhaps due to the high degree of concentration. For example, over 70% of the world instant coffee market is controlled by 4 multinational corporations. The World Bank's latest commodity report observes that between 1988 and 1991 retail prices of coffee to consumers declined by only 5 to 7% in the U.S., France and Germany, although international arabica coffee prices declined by 40% in the same period (World Bank 1992). An important consequence of the price declines has been the large growth in coffee stocks in importing countries. Whereas the price elasticities of demand for consumption range from only 0.1 to 0.3, for stocks they range from 0.4 to 1.0 (World Bank, 1992). A consequence of oligopolistic marketing sectors and unnecessarily high margins is the substitution away from primary commodity consumption by consumers in developed countries.

One of the rationales for international commodity agreements is to countervail against the market power exerted by the industrial nations and their marketing sectors. However given the inherent instability of cartel schemes, they have usually failed to be effective and when they have been enforced have had the same deleterious effects on consumption demand as oligopolistic marketing sectors. One solution to this difficult dilemma is for primary commodity producing countries to attempt to integrate upstream into the marketing sector of industrial countries as for instance Brazil has managed in the coffee sector. However, because of the small size of many commodity producing countries, their ability to achieve the economies of scale necessary to compete in the food processing industry is limited. In these cases regional economic cooperation and the development of infrastructure such as roads and other communication processes linking these small economies becomes fundamental. But these are by no means easily implementable solutions. Regional economic cooperation has not worked in Africa before, even among a few countries (*e.g.*, the breakdown of the East African Community), and although major new efforts are underway (*e.g.*, SADCC), the country groupings are often too large to achieve the necessary political consensus.

The indirect dynamic effects of these international distortions on poor low income countries can be as significant as the direct and indirect taxation in developing countries whose removal has correctly been a cornerstone of adjustment programs. It is necessary, therefore, that the Bretton Woods institutions promote free trade and competitive markets not only in the distorted economies of developing countries, but in the distorted markets of OECD countries as well by: supporting GATT; opening the European Common Market to developing and former Eastern Block countries; encouraging more stable monetary and fiscal policies in the OECD countries; reforming OECD farm programs; and by assisting poor developing countries in increasing value added. The potential global welfare gains from reform of policies of industrial countries, namely from a combination of liberalization in trade regimes, more stable monetary and fiscal policies and shift to direct income transfers to the needy small family farms are large. Such reforms will lower input use, budget outlays, and improve environmental quality in industrial countries. They will also mean higher and more stable prices to the low income producers in developing countries, an increase in global allocative efficiency, reductions in fiscal deficits and reduced aid dependence. These gains are larger than the roughly fifty billion dollars of concessional aid industrial countries provide to developing countries annually, much of which now goes to low income countries in Africa.

**Balance of payments performance**

The impact of the growing food demand of low income countries on the microeconomic dynamics of the farm household and the balance of payments are important in the discussion of commodities, which tends narrowly to be focused on the problems of export commodities. Stagnant growth in productivity of African agriculture coupled with rapid population growth, high rates of urbanization and the different preferences of urban consumers have lead to increased levels of cereal and livestock imports. For the first time developing country food imports exceeded developed country imports in 1990. The share of Asia in world cereal imports increased from 37% to 60% in 1992, and that of Africa doubled from 6% to 12%. Even with the doubling of food imports Africa's food aid requirements - estimated to be 6 million tons in 1991-92 simply to maintain per capita consumption and 11.4 million tons to meet UN calorie requirements - could not be delivered due to extremely inadequate port capacity and related distribution infrastructure. It has been estimated that if current population growth and export earning rates continue, African food imports could rise from their current 5% of export earnings to 20% by the year 2000 - a level never before approached (Delgado and Pinstrup-Anderson, 1993). Unless efforts are made to increase food crop productivity, with the rapid increase in population and the consequent increased pressure on the land it is likely that there will be more pressure on Africa's export sector.

Under a similar set of conditions Asian countries were able to finance rapidly rising food imports because of their spectacular success in *both* food and export agriculture and the rapid overall economic growth associated with that impressive and broadbased growth of the agricultural sector. From 1965 to 1990 the world export volumes of agricultural commodities grew at an annual rate of 2.6%. During this period, Asia increased its volumes at an average growth rate of 3.9%, (Figure 1) and gained market shares dramatically in oil palm products, robusta coffee and cocoa, all traditional African exports. Asian shares of non-traditional agricultural and manufacturing sectors also increased. Per capita food production also accelerated in Asia following the widespread introduction of high yielding varieties in the mid 1970s. The food and export crop growth in Asia was accompanied by rapid and broadbased growth of income and employment in the rural sector and provided a stimulus to the growth of the nonagricultural sector through an elastic supply of labour, food and rural savings (Figure 2). This in turn has led to reductions in the numbers and proportions of people living in poverty. In contrast, Africa experienced an annual decline in export volumes of 1.3% and nominal agricultural export earnings showed practically no growth during the 1980s, as compared to nearly 4.6% average annual growth in Asia. Individual countries in Africa *viz.* Kenya, Côte d'Ivoire, Cameroon, and Mauritius experienced growth throughout this period. Others such as Ghana, Sudan and Zambia have showed growth in exports since the adjustment process began (Lele and Adu-Nyako, forthcoming).

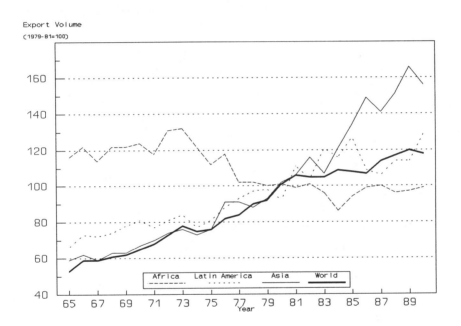

*Source:* FAO, *Yearbook of Agricultural Trade*, 1991

*Figure 1:* Agricultural Export Volumes, 1979-90

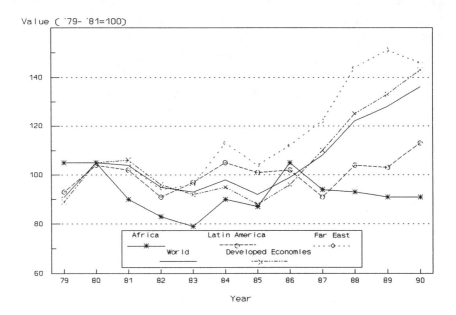

*Source:* FAO, *Yearbook of Agricultural Trade,* 1991

*Figure 2:* Agricultural Export Values, 1979-90

3  SUPPLY RESPONSE: ROLES OF PRICE AND NONPRICE FACTORS AND THE
RECORD OF MACROECONOMIC AND SECTORAL ADJUSTMENTS DURING
THE PERIOD OF ADJUSTMENT

It is clear that to compete in an inhospitable global market, Africa urgently needs to augment factor productivity which lagged behind that of Asia and Latin America in the 1970s and 1980s and was a significant factor in explaining its declining market shares and loss of competitiveness in primary commodity production. As seen in Figure 3, African labour productivity measured as wheat equivalent units per agricultural worker declined slightly from 1976 to 1989, meanwhile labour productivity in Asia and Latin American registered significant increases. This was especially the case in Latin America, the only region where the land-labour ratio (A/L) has been increasing. The most striking observation drawn from Figure 3 is the large jump in land productivity in Asia between 1980 and 1985. This gain may be explained by several factors. One important occurrence over this period was the significant increase in productivity of Chinese agriculture as the result of gradual reforms begun in the late 1970s in the output and input markets. Secondly, there has been the diffusion and adoption of a second generation of high yielding varieties including hybrid varieties of rice developed by the national agricultural research and extension services which are more site specific, higher yielding and more pest resistant than the original Green Revolution varieties (Byerlee, 1993). Certainly another factor has been the decreasing land labour ratio in Asia. The fact that this ratio continues to decline indicates that Asia especially South Asia still has a lot of labour in agriculture waiting to be drawn into the industrial sector. A major impact of increased agricultural productivity in smallholder agriculture is to increase food security at the household level and free rural labour for production in the export crop sub-sector.

Most evidence on supply response of agriculture to price indicates that aggregate supply elasticities tend to be rather small, almost close to zero (Binswanger, 1989; Faini, 1992). Supply response is higher in the long run than in the short run. Moreover, particularly in the long run, supply is more responsive to nonprice than price factors, and this is more true in Africa than Asia. Asia is better endowed with infrastructure, institutions and investment in technology, (see below for more details) and factor and product markets are more competitive there with greater scope for price responsiveness. This means that investments in productivity-enhancing agricultural research, extension, input supply, feeder roads, institutions

and human capital in Africa will have a greater impact than price adjustments, although the latter are by no means unimportant given the importance of profit incentives in technology adoption, and the fact that price
distortions have been more acute in Africa than Asia.

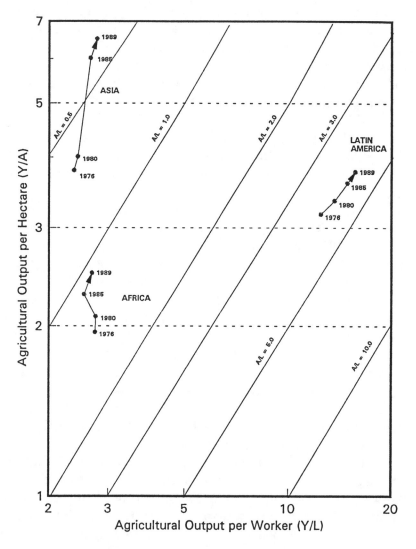

*Notes:*   Output measured in wheat equivalent units.
           *A/L* = hectares of arable land per worker.

*Figure 3:* Changing Productivities and Land-Labour Ratios in Asia, Africa
            and Latin America

## The extent of price distortions

In a cross-country study on the level of government intervention in agriculture, Krueger *et al.* (1991) found the level of producer taxation in the three sub-Saharan countries to be double the levels of the Asian and Latin American countries included in the study at 51.6% of border prices at the official exchange rate.[4] Differences in the levels of indirect intervention mainly from overvalued real exchange rates and industrial protection were roughly equivalent among regions - averages ranging from 21.3% among the Latin American countries to 28.6% within African countries. The main difference between regions was in the level of direct taxation, which was roughly eight and three times higher in the African countries as compared to Asian and Latin American countries. This difference explains why both sectoral and macroeconomic policy reforms were needed in Africa leading to the adoption of structural adjustment programs. Krueger's, *et al.* findings have been corroborated by the MADIA studies[5] of six African countries, as well as by others (Lele, 1989; Lele, 1992; Langham and Kamajou, 1992). To date the debate has focused on the removal of price distortions more than on the quality and quantity of public expenditures. Before proceeding to those important issues, we explore the recent record of African countries in the reform of prices since the adjustment process began.

## Record of price adjustments

In a study of 24 adjusting and nonadjusting countries, Lele and Adu-Nyako show that real exchange rates have depreciated in most countries except those with the CFA currency which has experienced a strong appreciation since 1985-86 with substantial cost to external competitiveness. But when price adjustments are reviewed more closely, progress on reforms is more disappointing. Nearly half the 20 adjusting countries undertaking exchange rate adjustments have not passed on the increased prices to producers. Gains appear to have either been absorbed

---

[4] Countries included in this study were: Côte d'Ivoire, Ghana, Zambia, South Korea, Malaysia, Pakistan, Philippines, Sri Lanka, Thailand, Argentina, Brazil, Chile, Colombia, and the Dominican Republic.

[5] See Uma Lele, ed., 'Managing Agricultural Development in Africa,' Discussion Papers 1 through 12, The World Bank, Washington, D.C.; see also *Aid to African Agriculture: Lessons from Two Decades of Donors' Experience*, 1992, The World Bank, Washington, D.C.

by marketing boards, or to have resulted in higher costs of marketings associated with devaluations and the high import content of transport. Nominal producer prices deflated by CPI indices decreased in 10 out of 18 countries for which data are available (*e.g.*, Cameroon, Côte d'Ivoire and Senegal), although often the share of producer price to border price increased due to a combination of worsening international terms of trade and appreciation (or inadequate depreciation) in the exchange rates. Real producer prices in Ghana and Madagascar improved despite a decline in producer to border price ratios, due in part to large devaluations.

**Movements of input prices**

The effects of declining real producer prices were aggravated in several countries by increases in the real prices of fertilizers and pesticides due to a combination of devaluations and removal of subsidies. Notwithstanding the decline in the world market prices of fertilizers, prices often doubled. An important development in virtually every country has been the widening role of the private traders in the sale of improved seeds, pesticides and fertilizers. However, the high cost of internal transportation, the inadequate access of traders and producers to credit, and lack of lucrative opportunities in input trading vis a vis other alternatives means that private trade will not by itself be able to meet the large input needs of a modernizing agriculture. Later in the discussion of microeconomic issues we stress the risk aversion of small farmers in remote areas with few savings or access to credit and the fundamental importance of increased fertilizer use as a means of increasing land and labour productivities, and particularly women's labour productivity.

**Availability of credit**

Low profitability in agriculture implies low rural savings rates and liquidity constraints for expenditures on agriculture. Limited credit availability to rural households has remained a common feature with only a mixed record of implementation of financial reforms. In 1989, the ratio of the value of agricultural production to domestic credit supplied was only 0.17 in Senegal, but as high as 1.48 in Ghana. However in these countries, the share of credit reported to have been allocated directly to the institutions handling needs of the agricultural sector did not exceed 12% of the total credit created on average (Lele and Adu-Nyako).

A strong positive development has been the increased access of private traders to credit, whereas the public sector dominated before. The increasing importance of commerce is beneficial to agriculture particularly as privatization of trade shifts handling of the marketed surplus from the public to the private sector. Yet the declining share of agricultural credit in total domestic credit is worrisome. The financial sector tends to prefer the urban and industrial trading sector characterized by less risk and higher returns as opposed to the agricultural production and trading sector influenced as it is by the vagaries of weather, poor transportation and inadequate market information.

While there has been widespread questioning of directed provision of credit through specialized credit agencies in the drive to liberalize financial markets, in reality the past problems of nonrepayment of credit of these specialized agencies have often resulted from credit given to large and politically more influential producers. For instance, despite four IDA credits to Kenya's Agricultural Finance Corporation (AFC) amounting to well over $65 million in a decade between 1975 and 1985, the World Bank was unable to persuade the government of Kenya to make credit available to small farmers with less than five acres of cultivable land even though they constitute nearly 90% of farms
in Kenya (Lele and Meyers, 1989). The bulk of overdues of AFC were associated with large commercial and politically powerful farmers.

Liquidity constraints are of course the greatest at the lower socioeconomic levels. Development strategies targeting the very poor must address this fundamental characteristic if they are to participate in the development process. A commodity-based development strategy can directly and indirectly improve the incomes of these households even though they are typically not commodity producers. Directly real wages of labourers in the commodity sector increase as the demand for their labour increases. Indirectly, incomes of the landless rural class can increase through growth effects on the demand for rural goods and services - provided they are not denied access to entrepreneurship by financial, human capital or other constraints.[6] In most developing countries the financial needs of this group are not met by the formal financial sector because of the high costs of administering credit in a Western-style to numerous low asset borrowers in an environment of poor infrastructure, information etc. A chief obstacle for many poor households in

---

[6] For discussion of the these dynamic relationships see Mellor and Lele's article "Growth Linkages of the New Food Production Technologies." *Indian Journal of Agricultural Economics* 28 (January-March 1973): 33-55.

accessing formal financial markets is the requirement of collateral. Its absence is the result of the past inability of households to accumulate assets, in turn a result of past liquidity constraints and the high costs of borrowing in informal markets. Credit schemes targeted to low income households can lead to broad participation of the rural population in a primary commodity development strategy.

Such liquidity constraints of the poorest rural households have been ameliorated in Bangladesh by the provision of collateral-free loans from the Grameen Bank enabling marginalized members of the Bangladesh society to benefit from the growth in the agricultural sector generated by high yielding grain varieties (Hossain, 1988). Small Bank-financed investments, especially by women, in various commercial and cottage enterprises in the rural nonagricultural sector have led to significant increase in incomes, capital accumulation, and employment among households receiving loans. The average amount of working capital increased nearly 4 times per borrower household after a period of two years with the Bank and total capital accumulation among borrowers increased at an average rate of 52% over the first three years of membership in the Bank. This highlights the collateral dilemma facing the poor in obtaining formal sector loans. The Bank's excellent loan repayment performance[7] has been attributed to : (a) the small size of weekly repayments; (b) confining loans to the extremely needy[8]; (c) provision only for activities that generate a regular income; (d) the use of peer group liability (as a substitute for collateral); (e) the small size of the initial loans with subsequently larger loans available contingent on past loan repayment performance; and importantly (f) a highly trained and dedicated staff. In Madagascar and Malawi, similarly high loan repayment rates based on peer monitoring have been documented (von Braun, *et al.*, 1993; Lele, 1989b). On a percentage basis, the costs associated with targeted credit to the poor are necessarily higher than for credit administered to large borrowers, mainly because of the increased managerial demands of numerous small transactions. In Bangladesh borrowers pay interest rates equivalent to the commercial rate of 16% which only covered 49% of the total costs of the credit program in 1986. Thus the implicit subsidy rate is approximately

---

[7] Hossain (1988) found that only 0.5 percent of the loans to 975 surveyed borrowers were overdue.

[8] Those families with less than 0.5 hectares of land (comprising 46% of all rural households). Hossain, p. 15, 1988.

51% at the opportunity cost of funds (Hossain, 1988). By recognizing and removing supply constraints inhibiting the linkage between commodity-led growth and increased demand for rural goods and services, carefully targeted subsidized credit can enable resource-poor rural inhabitants to participate in the development process.

As the recent insolvency of private OECD financial institutions illustrates, weak and insolvent private banks seem no less susceptible to bad loans and undue influence of the politically powerful elite than government institutions. Stiglitz (IMF, 1993) and others (Floro and Yotopoulous, 1991) have begun to question the wisdom of rapid financial liberalization, making a strong case for an active role for governments in creating financial institutions in developing countries that can supply funds for long-term investments, and provide a strong regulatory presence to prevent the disruptive macroeconomic consequences of financial market failure. Stiglitz also questions the response of savings to high interest rates while stressing the adverse effects of high costs of loanable funds on investments.

A combination of volatile and declining international prices, inadequate and haphazard implementation of price and exchange rate reforms, growth and equity considerations and institutional uncertainty calls for development of specialized credit agencies in Africa which would make credit directly available to small farmers. Given the weak private sector and the large financial requirement of agriculture they will have to be government institutions.

**Public expenditures and investment**

The checkered record of adjustment is also evident from the performance of these countries with regard to balance of payments and fiscal deficits. While Ghana and Tanzania were able to reduce fiscal deficits which exceeded 6% of GDP, at the same time their current account balances deteriorated. In contrast the situation was reversed in Kenya and Zimbabwe. This is in part because terms of trade changes affected each of the countries differently depending on their export portfolio. For instance Ghana with a high agricultural export concentration in cocoa was more affected by the price decline than others. Aid inflows were large and increased during the period to compensate for the loss in international terms of trade. For a group of 24 sub-Saharan countries, net overseas development assistance (ODA) adjusted for terms of trade effect increased from an annual average of $5.9 billion (in constant 1987 prices) in 1981-

86 to \$8.5 billion in the 1987-91 period. Net transfers in real terms also increased on average by 42% annually over the same period.

Reductions in the fiscal deficits among countries undertaking reforms were mainly the result of decreased public investments and expenditures. Governments in Africa have tended to freeze the wage portion of the recurrent budget, thus reducing real wages of government employees while cutting support for maintenance and operations. As consequence of the declining real wage in government many qualified professionals have fled from public service further reducing the effectiveness of the public sector, when indeed agriculture requires a strong, effective albeit small public sector, as the record of every country successful in agricultural development testifies time and again.

As the result of reductions in public investment spending on infrastructure and other public goods by government, restrictive credit policies and declining export earnings, gross domestic investment as a ratio of GDP declined in 11 of 12 countries classified as early intensive adjustors over the 1983 to 1990 period (Lele and Adu-Nyako, forthcoming). Faini (1992) also presents evidence that the level of investment in SSA has declined with the adoption of adjustment programs and restrictive credit programs. Empirical evidence of the relationship between net domestic investment (*NDI*) and export earnings (*EE*) was obtained using World Bank statistics by regressing the level of *NDI* for 25 African countries from 1980 to 1987 on *EE* and a constant term. The results (*t*-ratio in parentheses):

$$NDI = 1.58 \cdot 10^8 + \underset{(24.3)}{0.521}\, EE \qquad \text{Adjusted } R^2 = 0.77$$

indicate a significantly positive relationship between the two variables for the group of African countries. The negative effects of structural adjustment and declining rates of export earnings on rates of investment in African countries is of great concern to the future growth prospects of these economies.

We now move on, first to discuss the issues of economic diversification at macroeconomic and microeconomic levels, before ending the paper with an exploration of their implications for future price and nonprice policies for vigorous and sustained growth of smallholder agricultural productivity.

## 4  THE FALLACY OF COMPOSITION AND ECONOMIC DIVERSIFICATION

We have seen above that lower levels taxation of agriculture can result in significantly higher rates of exports. Nevertheless when devaluations and reductions in taxes are carried out simultaneously by a large number of 'small' developing countries as has been the case in the decade of adjustment, the price effect of supply shifts given inelastic income and price elasticity of demand and oligopolistic import markets on the international terms of trade must inevitably be significant. This old notion of fallacy of composition, first articulated by Singer (1950) and Prebisch (1950), has recently been supported by policy simulation models of the removal of export quotas and taxes for tree crops (tea, cocoa and coffee) in Africa (Panagariya and Schiff, 1992; Evans, *et al.*, 1992). They show declines in the combined income of producers as a result of removal of taxes and quotas. As ameliorating strategies the authors suggest export diversification and supply control through a cartel taxation scheme. Duncan (1993) and others argue and we concur that such schemes have tended not to benefit small producing countries, which often lose market shares as the breakdown of the coffee agreement shows. Increasing efficiency is the more effective way of maintaining competitiveness in periods of declining commodity prices, a strategy effectively pursued by the leaders in commodity exports in Asia (Malaysia and Indonesia) and Latin America (Brazil and Colombia).

In another study when the effect of a 5% increase in the supply schedules of African countries for the 6 most important African commodities was simulated, only cocoa export revenues declined in the short-term (Koester, *et al.*, 1988). In the long-run after other producing countries had adjusted to the new world prices by decreasing their production, the effect on export earnings was positive in all cases. This in turn leads one to explore which exporting countries are likely to reduce their production for the inadvertent benefit of African countries. Brazil, Colombia, Costa Rica and Malaysia are seen to be likely candidates for production cutbacks, due to higher returns in alternative activities and rising domestic wage costs (World Bank, 1992). Export diversification and trade expansion in these countries has been stimulated by increasing international capital flows following trade liberalization. The positive effects of a GATT-style trade liberalization via increased real wages in middle income countries and their resultant shifts out of traditional exports could be large for poor countries. But several of these countries have chosen to remain as major producers by increasing efficiency through a strong emphasis on improvement of technology in production, harvesting and processing. They have also continually shown a willingness to adjust their macroeconomic parameters and promise to be tough competitors for low income Africa especially countries with the fixed CFA currency. Nor are Viet Nam, Indonesia, India, Sri Lanka or China - major primary commodity producers with large pools of underemployed labour in agriculture - likely to shift out of primary commodities in the next decade or more.

**Diversification within and outside agriculture: lessons of recent history**

Over the past two decades donors have gone through several short cycles in advising poor countries on diversification strategies, without a long term view of the role of primary commodities in the overall economic transformation. The Singer/Prebisch export pessimistic consensus of the 1960s led the World Bank and the IMF to sound a cautionary note on primary export crop promotion and to promote export diversification.[9] On the advice of the FAO, in 1973 the World Bank adopted a policy to restrict investment lending in support of the expansion of coffee, tea and cocoa except in cases when countries lacked any alternatives in production (Lele, 1992). However World Bank assistance in the establishment of tea processing capacity in Kenya had the inadvertent beneficial effect of stimulating domestic production. Kenya ignoring the conventional wisdom consistently encouraged smallholder production and productivity growth of export crops and increased world market shares in tea and coffee. This export drive was mainly the result of internal political pressure which opened the access of small African farmers to the production of the crops, the rights to which had been denied to them in the colonial period, and provided the same international price at auctions as in the estate sector. In contrast the taxation of smallholder tobacco in Malawi was much greater than the estate tobacco sector and farmers' rights to grow some export crops were restricted (Lele and Meyers, 1989).

Three types of diversification strategies are pertinent:

---

[9] In a special report to the IMF executive directors in 1969 staff expressed support for "reducing those commodities which were in serious oversupply by domestic taxation" (e.g. coffee). The report went on to observe, "However, there have been several countries in which is has not been feasible to use the tax system directly and where the Fund has approved exchange measures involving the imposition of substantial taxes through the exchange system." (IMF, 1969).

(a) diversification within the rural economy of activities already undertaken by farmers, *e.g.*, food crops to meet growing local demand. In
Africa given growing food imports such diversification can be of
major significance in improving balance of payment problems;
(b) diversification within agriculture to new higher value activities for
either domestic largely urban consumption *e.g.*, dairy, and poultry or
for export, *e.g.* horticulture, nuts, fruits, and livestock; Diversification prompted by a strong demand pull as a result of a growing
population pressure and urbanization is evident in much of Africa and
could be boosted further by more reliable functioning of markets,
*e.g.*, by stabilizing the supply of feedstock for poultry which tends to
be a serious constraint to its growth; and
(c) diversification outside agriculture through import substituting industrialization, acute forms of which have been pursued by African
countries with disastrous consequences for agriculture although in
China development of rural enterprises has proven successful.

Past diversification attempts have been of all three kinds. Numerous small
successes can be cited in diversification to non-traditional activities, such
as the shift out of sorghum and millet to hybrid and improved open
pollinated varieties of maize throughout Africa, or the growth of poultry
and small scale irrigated rice in Nigeria to meet the growing urban
demand, or of horticultural crops for exports as in Kenya. However, the
macroeconomic effects of these efforts on the balance of payments,
employment, income, and government revenues initially tend to be small
and take a long time to achieve significant results. With a longer time
horizon, colonialists exhibited more patient in this regard than donors in
the development of African agriculture (see Lele and Meyers, 1989).

The major purpose of export diversification within agriculture is to
achieve a cushioning effect on trade balance fluctuations through a
diversified portfolio. However, this result is contingent on negative
correlation of the net returns in the export portfolio. Temporal prices of
agricultural commodities tend be positively correlated, while within
national borders yields are spatially and temporally positively correlated,
thus reducing the scope for revenue cushioning within the agricultural
sector.[10] Within a particular commodity sub-sector, diversification of

---

[10] In an examination of 26 agricultural commodity prices from 1958-1990
commonly produced in Africa, the typical commodity was negatively correlated
at the 10 percent significance level with fewer than 4 of the 26 commodities.

marketing strategies through increased use of futures markets, forward contracts and commodity options can have some of the desired risk reducing effects probably at a much lower cost than production diversification. The opportunity costs of production diversification can be very high especially when national research capability is a constraint. These costs are mainly from a reduction in specialization, lower research expenditures on a per crop basis, and the resulting decrease in productivity growth.[11] An acute concern in developing countries is that it is easier to improve productivity of crops already in place than that of new crops where expertise is limited.

Kenya which pursued its comparative advantage in traditional export crops diversified its agriculture and economy more rapidly than Tanzania, which overlooked its comparative advantage, neglected smallholder agriculture and embarked on an active program of acute import substitution. Tanzania placed emphasis on the development of food production in marginal areas with few obvious technological possibilities, and embarked on regional diversification in the Southern Highlands remote from the major centres of consumption. Quite paradoxically, the neglect of Tanzania's traditional export sector and of food production in the established high potential areas increased the share of agriculture in a declining GNP and exports by the end of the 1970s. Emphasizing productivity gains among food and export crops with a demonstrated comparative advantage while carefully identifying the location-specific costs and benefits of alternative strategies is the most effective means of diversifying into new crops, undeveloped regions and industry. Efforts to increase productivity of traditional food crops *i.e.*, sorghum, millets and cassava and diversification out of agriculture through industrialization have had very limited success. Despite low international prices traditional export crops will have to be the important means of Africa's economic growth.

---

Specifically, arabica coffee, robusta coffee, cotton, cocoa, tea, and palm oil were negatively correlated with 0, 8, 0, 4, 5, and 8 commodities, respectively (Langham, 1992).

[11] The effect of diversification on total factor productivity growth in U.S. agriculture was negative and quantitatively large in a panel data study of the 50 states (Habasch, 1989).

## 5 LESSONS OF SUCCESSFUL AGRICULTURAL DEVELOPMENT EXPERIENCE AT THE MICRO LEVEL

### Food insecurity and the labour constraint

Increasing factor productivity of both traditional food and export agriculture are essential and complementary rather than dichotomous goals. Agriculture of early developing countries is characterized by a large number of geographically dispersed households with low factor productivity and incomes in which food security considerations dominate production decisions. These households face risky production conditions, and poorly developed or nonexistent markets for commodities and factors of production. Labour constitutes up to 80% of value added in low-income African agriculture, compared to 50% or less in low-income Asia. A combination of lower rural population densities and higher labour intensity means considerable shortages of labour at peak periods of land preparation, planting, weeding, and harvesting although densely populated rural areas in Africa are increasing *e.g.*, the Machakos district in Kenya, the Southern Region of Malawi, the Western Highlands of Cameroon and most of Rwanda and Burundi. Labour is a major bottleneck for the development of export agriculture by small farmers, which can be relieved by labour saving innovations in food crop technologies and other household activities such as food processing, fuel and firewood collection and water supply thereby releasing labour for export crop production. For example, small farmers in the Mwanza region of Tanzania increased cotton production in the 1960s because introduction of hybrid maize released labour from the previously arduous dependence on sorghum (Lele, 1975).

Ensuring the reliable supply of purchased foods at reasonable prices throughout the year is also essential for small farm households which often spend up to 50% of their income spent on food. The income and nutritional effect of high food prices and food shortages can seriously affect the allocation of productive resources to cash crop production by rural households.

### The role of infrastructure in market integration

Improvement of fragmented food markets is clearly one way to improve food security. Priority to the development of rural feeder roads is essential to the development of competitive food markets and the stimulation of production. Gaviria, *et al.*, (1989) documented that the density of rural roads in the latter half of the 1980s in Nigeria with a population density similar to India's in the 1950s was substantially lower than India's in the 1950s. Ahmed and Donovan (1992) make the same point more generally in Africa *vis á vis* Asia. For example, paved roads and rails per 1000 hectare of cultivable land averages 1.1 kilometre in Africa and 5.3 kilometre in Asia. Elasticity estimates of the impact of rural roads on aggregate agricultural output and fertilizer use were as high as 0.37 in the case of output and 0.44 for fertilizer (Antle, 1983; Binswanger, *et al.*, 1987; Binswanger, *et al.*, 1989). Inadequacy of rural infrastructure results in higher cost of services including transportation and marketing and retards adoption of new technologies and inputs.

A recent study of countries in the CFA currency zone found that the cost of transportation from farm to local markets was five times the cost from one regional capital to another (Bonnafous, 1993). Yet development of trunk routes has received more attention by governments and donors. Planning and implementation of rural feeder roads is a function most effectively conducted by local government even though private sector contractors, where they exist, may be employed to carry out the actual work. Kenya and Malawi have shown an effective capacity to develop and maintain rural feeder roads, in Kenya's case thanks to the superb work of the International Labour Organization in developing local planning and implementing capacity over more than a decade. Nigeria and Tanzania have had less success in part due to the erosion of their local government institutions (Gaviria, *et al.*, 1989). In Tanzania the decline of local institutions occurred even though the government's vastly more effective rhetoric of local participation attracted nearly twice the level of per capita foreign aid as in Kenya. The actual record on the functioning of the participatory institutions in Kenya such as the Harambee schools and health clinics and the farmer-based cooperative credit/marketing organizations has been consistently stronger than in Tanzania. Donors need to evaluate their expectations of democratic governments not simply in terms of the presence or the absence of a free press or a multiparty system, but the extent to which local rural institutions operate effectively. Kenya receives far higher marks on this score than recent reports in the Western press would lead one to believe.

### The role of stable and unstable prices

When is there a role for governments to intervene in markets? Tree crops are characterized by higher unit value even at the current depressed international prices when exchange rates are close to market rates and producers receive a high share of the price relative to food crops. Tree crops entail long term investment in a stock of capital. Price variability results in a strong supply response in the upswing and decreased levels of variable inputs into production on the downswing. For example, during the coffee boom in 1977, when coffee plantings increased, the relative coffee price/maize price ratios in Kenya, which has had a history of low taxation, appropriate exchange rate adjustments and low internal food prices, were 45 to 1 compared to only 7 to 1 in Cameroon with an overvalued CFA, higher direct tax on coffee, and higher internal food prices (Lele 1992). As a result Kenyan yields of smallholder coffee farms are three times those in Cameroon and the per hectare or per labour day returns to coffee have been much higher (Lele 1989). Tree crop production does not therefore require price stabilization as a way of providing an incentive to producers. It is only when prices remain depressed over a long period and monopolies tax export agriculture particularly *vis á vis* other alternatives that farmers switch to other crops, as is the case with coffee in Tanzania in 1993.

This principle, however, does not apply to annual crops. Even when competitive markets exist, privatization of marketing still does not solve the problem of intertemporal price instability common to agricultural production especially in low rainfall areas. In the case of coarse grain staples in East and Southern Africa and the Sahel, production is highly variable. In Southern Africa surplus production prompted by favourable weather or high prices results in low maize prices causing farmers to switch out of maize after ensuring domestic food needs; the subsequent rise in market prices that results generates a cyclical 'cobweb' pattern of price and supply variation. Such price and supply variability is, however, not dampened by private trading stocks across years in developing countries due to the high opportunity cost of capital. Major benefits of year-to-year price and supply stability include the inducement to producers to adopt uncertain technologies and macroeconomic stabilization from reduced variations in the balance of payments accounts from fluctuating food import bills. Stable prices and supply are also beneficial to annual cash crop sectors such as cotton, jute and sisal that require further processing and call for a stable supply of throughput to the processing units in order to achieve full capacity utilization and economies of scale.

Food security stocks and stable prices are also needed to ensure the level of consumption of the rural poor as already noted above. When food security is guaranteed by stable rural markets, producers are more willing to devote resources to cash crop production, as is witnessed in the Central

Province of Kenya where coffee farmers' food needs are ensured by the government's maize stabilization program. Crisis distribution systems and food safety nets are as essential in low rainfall areas of rural Africa as in urban areas which have been the focus of donors and governments. This is perhaps because opposition to reforms tends to originate in urban concentrations, and interaction in food and export crop production at the farm level through the nexus of food insecurity and labour constraints is not widely understood.

Although Timmer (1988 and 1993) argues that much of the success of Asian countries in agriculture is attributable to the existence of a stable food price environment, others have argued on theoretical grounds against domestic price stabilization through the holding of food stocks by government (Newberry and Stiglitz, 1981). Providing a stable price environment requires an integrated and comprehensive approach with important roles for both the private and public sector. For countries with unsustainable costly parastatal marketing systems the example of China highlights the benefits of a gradual transition towards privatization rather than a 'big bang' approach in maintaining food security while new marketing institutions develop. In contrast, liberalization of Malawi's grain marketing in a market environment characterized by liquidity constraints, poor market information and high transport costs, coupled with an influx of 700,000 Mozambique refuges resulted in maize shortages and prices 3 to 4 times the previous official price (Lele, 1989b).

Spatial stability of prices and market supply are highly correlated with the level of infrastructure. When adequate feeder roads exist, credit markets function, and market information flows adequately price variability between regions will be substantially reduced as food flows respond to price signals. The role of government in the distribution system in such a situation is considerably reduced, but is of course crucial in ensuring the required infrastructure and information flows. The government must also ensure that collusive behaviour by traders does not interfere with the flow of food. Intertemporal price variability may still threaten food security even in countries with high infrastructural development. Here again, speculative and collusive behaviour by private traders can be highly destabilizing and add to climatic-induced variations compounding the risk of famine. To provide stable prices both spatially and intertemporally, Dréze and Sen (p. 95, 1989) argue for active government participation in food trade and storage, noting that... 'The existence of public stocks can go a long way towards reducing fears of future scarcity and defeating the manipulative practices of private traders.' The issue of food security and the relative role of government and the private sector must be addressed on a country-by-country basis. Donor agencies often have not distinguished between the differential causes of marketing parastatal losses which can range from external shocks, inappropriate government policies, transportation and other infrastructural bottlenecks, provision of non-commercial services such as the maintenance of rural feeder roads, incompetence, or corruption - each of which requires a different intervention.

While serving many beneficial roles, price stabilization policies have fallen out of favour because of the high fiscal costs incurred by marketing parastatals.[12] Implementation of a stable price environment while likely requiring some degree of government subsidization has proven to be more costly than is necessary for several reasons. In Kenya the deficits of the National Cereals and Produce Board have been attributed to: (a) poor management; (b) a stringent economic environment; (c) a lack of equity capital leading to excessively high financing costs of operation; and (d) restrictions on inter-district movements of grains and monopsony control of purchasing (Lele and Christiansen, 1989). Many African governments have attempted to maintain a single official price through costly buffer stocks rather than encouraging private trade through infrastructural development and allowing prices to move freely while acting as a buyer and seller of last resort to maintain a relatively wide price stabilization band. The costs of maintaining buffer stocks can be reduced by substituting financial stocks and trade for physical stocks especially as import displacement times are reduced by the crucial development of public infrastructure. Use of forward markets can prevent costs due to short-term market fluctuations (including exchange rate variations). Further savings can be generated by the interest earned on financial stocks invested in international credit markets until they are needed. Public investments in irrigated agriculture reduce the variability in food stocks and increases greatly the level of food security. It is also important to note that the costs of administering an effective price stabilization program increase in some proportion to the divergence between the internal and world price. Thus

---

[12] In Tanzania economic losses of the National Marketing Corporation in 1983 were around $250 million; while total central government expenditures on agriculture were around $49 million. In Kenya the accumulated losses of the National Cereals and Produce Board were about $300 million in 1986 while government agricultural expenditures were only $8 million (Lele, 1989).

stabilization around long-term world prices will be lower in administrative costs than when there is a significant divergence.

The adjustment costs of privatizing parastatal marketing systems can be high especially when the change is sudden and entrepreneurial capacity is low. As primary commodity producers privatize, training their new traders in the use of increasingly sophisticated trade instruments and contracts will alleviate some of these adjustment costs. In certain cases privatization has resulted in a lowering of quality standards as in the case of Nigerian cocoa, where the government has had to again assume the role of regulating quality. In contrast to direct government quality regulation, in Kenya small-farm tea auctions assure this role by paying quality premia to smallholders often 15% above the price received by large estates.

To rely in a purist fashion on either the state or the market mechanism will not ensure food security. The challenge of establishing a stable least-cost price environment based on a combination of the public and private sector and the effects of such an environment on productivity growth should be one of the most interesting issues for professional economists.

**Research and extension**

Much of the evidence for sources of total factor productivity (TFP) growth comes from Asia (Azam, Bloom and Evenson, 1991; Rosegrant and Evenson, 1992; Evenson and Rosegrant, 1993). These studies show that the main sources of growth in TFP are research and extension expenditures and imports of foreign innovations (measured as patented inventions of agricultural implements). These three factors alone accounted for 87% of the growth in TFP in India which averaged 1% annually from 1956 to 1985 (Rosegrant and Evenson, 1992). In Africa preliminary estimates of TFP growth show stagnant rates from the early 1970s to the early 1980s with positive rates in more recent times of approximately 1.6% (Delgado and Pinstrup-Anderson, 1993). The factors explaining the slow growth in TFP in Africa have not been analyzed statistically but certainly the ineffectiveness of research and extension systems would head a list of possible factors.

While donors and African governments have devoted substantial resources to agricultural research in Africa, many of these investments have suffered from excessive use of short term consultants, over-emphasis on construction of buildings, lack of a long-term commitment and especially the lack of effective incentive structures for national research scientists (Lele and Goldsmith, 1989) The building of effective sustainable research institutions requires a cadre of indigenous researchers working collaboratively with experienced and qualified international scientists with a long term outlook towards solving technological constraints. In addition it requires a sustaining environment where farmers are commercially oriented and willing to adopt and indeed demanding of innovations. A research policy drawn up by qualified, well trained and experienced nationals cognizant of farmers' needs and demands is required to address these complex problems of agriculture and rural development. Close collaboration with extension systems can increase the effectiveness of research. The recent experiences of the World Bank's Training and Visit Extension program and the Global 2000 program in Africa indicate the positive results that can be achieved. Experience suggests the need for a unified and politically supported strategy of research and extension which draws on the best of various systems rather than a rigid adherence to a single approach.

### Input intensification and environmental concerns

In most areas of the developing world, environmental degradation can be linked to the inability of agriculture to provide the surplus necessary for the structural transformation. In the face of slow productivity growth and rapid population growth the extensive agricultural margin is expanded into environmentally fragile lands. The best strategies to preventing the mining of marginal agricultural lands are: (a) to attempt to increase the productivity of existing lands; and (b) attempts to slow population pressures. African governments must insist on - and donors must support their need for - increased access to chemical fertilizers and pesticides. Africa's per hectare fertilizer consumption is the lowest in the world (Lele. *et al.*, 1989b). While there are major country differences, the sharp rise in internal fertilizer prices together with haphazard adjustment of producer prices and the uncertainty in input and output markets have increased the risks in fertilizer application (Lele, *et al.* 1989). Often a decline in the consumption of fertilizer means increased substitution of (largely female) labour into production and the expansion of the agricultural frontier. To prevent this expansion and the resultant degradation will require attention to expanding productivity growth through investments in research, extension and rural infrastructure while concurrently improving input delivery systems and the access of farmers to these inputs.

6  SUMMARY AND CONCLUSIONS

In conclusion it is clear that agricultural development through the commodity sector requires very careful consideration of a highly diverse set of issues including *inter alia* technology, institution building, management, human capital development, resource allocation systems (pricing/marketing systems for allocations of private goods *vs.* nonmarket allocation systems for public goods), financial systems, household constraints, natural resource management, and not the least important the location-specific determination of the sets of public and private goods. We have examined a broad range of policies addressing the role of commodities in agricultural development strategies that provide numerous important lessons. The successful smallholder commodity development in Africa to the extent that it has occurred stresses the importance of high quality location-specific research and extension, rural infrastructure, producer and processor access to finance, processing and marketing arrangements that take into account scale economies in processing, and appropriate price incentives. Most importantly, developing countries require competitive global markets which would allow the full expression of consumer demand and the possibility of vertically integrating commodity processing enterprises into these markets to the benefit of the citizens of developing countries as well as consumers in the industrial economies.

Information is critical for developing a thriving export sector. This calls for a pragmatic partnership of public and private institutions, rather than ideologically based preferences for the private or the public sector. It also requires a zealous commitment to the collection and dissemination of relevant information to all concerned actors. International flows of the necessary technical, organizational, financial, managerial, environmental and international market knowledge must be encouraged. And that knowledge used: (a) to develop and provide access to technology and (b) in the training of new forms of management, information systems and export strategies within the commodity sector. Governments need to be skilled at borrowing knowledge, in employing experienced international personnel and distinguishing from the ill-equipped, inexperienced technical assistance with little institutional memory that has often accompanied foreign aid programs.

Developed country governments need to undertake a fundamental assessment of: (1) the effects of trade policies on their own consumers and the developing countries, and (2) their foreign aid policies; in order to determine what might place low income countries on a sustained growth path, while remaining politically feasible at home. Most importantly, the governments of the least developed African countries need to review the experience of other developed and developing countries and to change the fundamental way in which agriculture now operates.

**Bibliography**

Ahmed, R. and C. Donovan (1992). 'Issues of Infrastructural Development', Washington D.C.: International Food Policy Research Institute.

Anderson, K and R. Tyers (1990). 'How Developing Countries Could Gain from Trade Liberalization in the Uruguay Round.' In *Agricultural Liberalization: Implications for Developing Countries*. ed. Ian Goldin and Odin Knudsen, Paris, OECD.

Antle, J. (1983). 'Infrastructure and Aggregate Agricultural Productivity: International Evidence.', *Economic Development and Cultural Change*, 31(April): 609-19.19.

Azam, Q.T., E.A. Bloom and R. Evenson (1991). 'Agricultural Research Productivity in Pakistan', Economic Growth Discussion Paper No. 644, Yale University.

Binswanger, H. (1989). 'The Policy Response of Agriculture' in Proceedings of the World Bank Annual Conference on Development Economics, supplement to the *World Bank Economic Review and the World Bank Research Observer*: 231-58.

Binswanger, H., M.C. Yang, A. Bowers, and Y. Mundlak (1987). 'On the Determinants of Cross Country Aggregate Agricultural Supply', *Journal of Econometrics*, 36(1): 111-31.

Binswanger, H., S. Khandker, M. Rosenzweig (1989). 'How Infrastructure and Financial Institutions Affect Agricultural Output and Investment in India', World Bank Working Paper Series No. 163. Washington, D.C.: World Bank.

Bonnafous, A. (1983). 'Trucking in Sub-Saharan Africa: What Deregulation?', in *Regulatory Reform in Transport: Some Recent Experiences* ed. Jose Carbajo, World Bank Symposium.

Byerlee, D. (1993). 'Modern Varieties, Productivity and Sustainability: Recent Experiences and Emerging Challenges', Presented at AAEA/IPFRI Workshop (Post-Green Revolution Agricultural Development Strategies in the Third World), Orlando, Florida, July 30-31.

Delgado, C. (1993). 'Coastal Demand Constraints for Sahelian Livestock Products', In Delgado, C. and O. Badiane, eds. *Regional Integration of Agricultural Markets in West Africa*, (Book manuscript in preparation).

Delgado, C. and P. Pinstrup-Anderson (1993). 'Agricultural Productivity in the Third World: Patterns and Strategic Issues', Presented at AAEA/IPFRI Workshop (Post-Green Revolution Agricultural Development Strategies in the Third World), Orlando, Florida, July 30-31.

Dréze, J. and A. Sen (1989). *Hunger and Public Action.* Clarendon Press, Oxford.

Duncan, R.C. (1993). 'Market Diversification and Agricultural Export Prospects in Sub-Saharan Africa', in Nathan C. Russell and Christopher R. Dowswell ed. *Policy Option for Agricultural Development in Sub-Saharan Africa.* CASIN/SAA/Global 2000.

Evans, David, Ian Goldin and Dominique van der Mensbrugghe (1992). 'Trade Reform and the Small Country Assumption', in Ian Goldin and L. Alan Winters (eds.) *Open Economies: Structural Adjustment and Agriculture.* Cambridge: Cambridge University Press.

Evenson, R.E. and M. W. Rosegrant (1993). 'Determinants of Productivity Growth in Asian Agriculture Past and Future', Presented at AAEA/IPFRI Workshop (Post-Green Revolution Agricultural Development Strategies in the Third World), Orlando, Florida, July 30-31.

Faini, R. (1992). 'Infrastructure Relative Prices and Agricultural Adjustment', in Ian Goldin and L. Alan Winters (eds.) *Open Economies: Structural Adjustment and Agriculture.* Cambridge: Cambridge University Press.

Floro, S. L. and P. Yotopoulos (1991). *Informal Credit Markets and the New Institutional Economics: The Case of Philippine Agriculture.* Boulder, Colorado: West View Press.

Habasch, Mona (1989). 'The Impact of Diversification on Productivity in U.S. Agriculture', unpublished M.S. thesis, Gainesville: University of Florida.

Hayami, Y. and V. Ruttan (1985). *Agricultural Development An International Perspective,* Baltimore: John Hopkins University Press.

Hossain, M. (1988) 'Credit for Alleviation of Rural Poverty: The Grameen Bank in Bangladesh', Research Report No. 65, International Food Policy Research Institute in collaboration with the Bangladesh Institute of Development Studies.

IMF (1993). *IMF Survey,* May 31.

Koester, Ulrich, Hartwig Schafer and Alberto Valdez (1989). 'External Demand Constraints for Agricultural Exports: An Impediment to Structural Adjustment Policies in Sub-Saharan African Countries?', *Food Policy* 14(3).

Krueger, Anne, Maurice Schiff and Alberto Valdés (1991). *The Political Economy of Agricultural Pricing Policy*, Baltimore: The John Hopkins Press for the World Bank.

Langham, Max (1992). 'Determinants of Productivity in the Agricultural Sector with Implications for Research Policy and Analysis', in Langham, Max and François Kamajou (eds.) *Agricultural Policy Analysis in Sub-Saharan Africa*, Gainesville: Office of International Programs, University of Florida.

Langham, Max and François Kamajou (1992). 'Price Policy in the Cameroonian Coffee Sub-sector with Emphasis on Arabica: Producers' Returns Versus Government Revenues', in Langham, Max and François Kamajou (eds.) *Agricultural Policy Analysis in Sub-Saharan Africa*, Gainesville: Office of International Programs, University of Florida.

Lele, Uma (1975). *The Design of Rural Development*, Baltimore: John Hopkins University Press.

Lele, Uma (1989a). 'Agricultural Growth, Domestic Policies, the External Environment, and Assistance to Africa: Lessons of a Quarter Century', MADIA Discussion Paper No. 1, Washington, D.C.: World Bank.

Lele, Uma (1989b). 'Structural Adjustment, Agricultural Development , and the Poor: Some Lessons from the Malawian Experience',, MADIA Discussion Paper Washington, D.C.: World Bank.

Lele, Uma (1992). 'Structural Adjustment and Agriculture: A Comparative Perspective on Response in Africa, Asia, and Latin America' International Working Paper Series, Gainesville: Food and Resource Economics Department, University of Florida.

Lele, Uma, ed. (1992). *Aid to African Agriculture: Lessons from Two Decades of Donors' Experience*, Baltimore: John Hopkins University Press for World Bank.

Lele, Uma and Kofi Adu-Nyako (1992). 'Approaches to Poverty in Africa', *Food Policy*, Volume 17, Number 2.

Lele, Uma and Kofi Adu-Nyako (forthcoming), 'Adjustment and Agriculture in Africa'.

Lele, U. and M. Agarwal (1989). 'Smallholder and Large-Scale Agriculture: Are There Tradeoffs in Growth and Equity?', MADIA Discussion Paper No. 6, Washington, D.C.: World Bank.

Lele, U. and R. Christiansen, (1989). 'Markets, Marketing Boards and Cooperatives in Africa: Issues in Adjustment Policies', MADIA Discussion Paper No. 11, Washington, D.C.: World Bank.

Lele, U., N. van de Walle, and M. Gbetibouo (1989b). 'Cotton in Africa: An Analysis of Differences in Performance', MADIA Discussion Paper No. 7, Washington, D.C.: World Bank.

Lele, U. and R. Christiansen, and K. Kadiresan (1989b). 'Fertilizer Policy in Africa: Lessons for Development Programs and Adjustment', MADIA Discussion Paper No. 5, Washington, D.C.: World Bank.

Lele. U. and A. Goldsmith (1989). 'The Development of National Agricultural Research Capacity: India's Experience with the Rockefeller Foundation and its Significance for Africa', *Economic Development and Cultural Change*, Volume 37, Number 2 (January): 305-343.

Lele, Uma and I. Nabi eds. (1991). *Transitions in Development: Role of Aid and Capital Flows*. San Francisco: Institute of Contemporary Studies.

Lele, U. and L.R. Meyers (1989). 'Growth and Structural Change in East Africa: Domestic Policies, Agricultural Performance, and World Bank Assistance, 1963-86', MADIA Discussion Paper No. 3, Washington, D.C.: World Bank.

Mellor, J. and U. Lele (1973). 'Growth Linkages of the New Food Production Technologies', *Indian Journal of Agricultural Economics*, 28 (January-March):33-55.

Newberry, D. and J.E. Stiglitz (1981). *The Theory of Commodity Price Stabilization: A Study in the Economics of Risk*. Oxford: Clarendon Press.

Panagariya, Arvind and Maurice Schiff (1992). 'Taxes versus Quotas: The Case of Cocoa Exports', in Ian Goldin and L. Alan Winters (Eds.) *Open Economies: Structural Adjustment and Agriculture*. Cambridge: Cambridge University Press.

Prebisch, Raoul (1950). *The Economic Development of Latin America and Its Principal Problems*. New York: United Nations.

Rosegrant, M. and R. Evenson (1992). 'Agricultural Productivity and Sources of Growth in South Asia', *American Journal of Agricultural Economics*, 74(3): 257-61.

Singer, Hans W. (1950). 'The Distribution of Gains Between Investing and Borrowing Countries', *American Economic Review*, 40 (2): 473-85.

Timmer, P. (1988). 'The Agricultural Transformation', in ed. H. Chenery and T.N. Srinivasan, *Handbook of Economics*, Volume 1. Amsterdam: North-Holland.

Timmer, P. (1993). 'Food Price Stabilization: The Relevance of the Asian Experience to Africa', in Nathan C. Russell and Christopher R. Dowswell eds. *Policy Option for Agricultural Development in Sub-Saharan Africa*. CASIN/SAA/Global 2000.

von Braun, J., S. Malik, and M. Zeller (1993). 'Credit Markets, Input Support Policies, and the Poor: Insights from Africa and Asia', Presented at AAEA/IPFRI Workshop (Post-Green Revolution Agricultural Development Strategies in the Third World), Orlando, Florida, July 30-31.

World Bank (1992). *Market Outlook for Major Primary Commodities Vol. II: Agricultural Products, Fertilizers, and Tropical Timber*. International Trade Division, International Economics Department.

# PART V

---

# SUMMARY AND CONCLUSIONS,

# PARTICIPANTS

# SUMMARY AND CONCLUSIONS
## BY THE MODERATOR

## 1 THE GLOBAL COMMODITY SITUATION

The decline in rates of economic growth, especially in the developed countries, along with the dislocation of production in Eastern Europe and the former USSR have depressed demand for commodities, and have increased supply availabilities in certain cases. Some commodities were particularly affected, such as natural rubber and other agricultural raw materials as well as animal feeds, and several non-ferrous metals, such as lead, zinc and tungsten. For some agricultural commodities such as jute and hard fibres competition from synthetics was very manifest. Further, there was a negative impact on demand for some commodities stemming from changes in manufacturing technology.

The level of real export prices of agricultural, fishery and forestry products in 1992 was estimated in the Review of the World Commodity Situation and Outlook by FAO to be 25 per cent below that at the start of the 1980s. Relative to average prices over the years 1979 to 1981, the index of real prices for exports of developing countries was down by 38 per cent and for that for developed countries down by 18 per cent. The decline in real prices reflected several factors. For many commodities a major change was the technologically driven increase in yields. Over the years to 1991 the percentage increase in output per hectare of many of the commodities was over 20 per cent. Further, increases in production exceeded increases in yield for each of the commodities except cotton. Demand, however, grew at a slower rate. The growth in income in the mature markets added little to the level of demand that was near satiety as reflected in low income elasticities of demand. Exacerbating the decline in prices was the characteristic unresponsiveness or inelasticity of consumption to price. Protectionism by a number of industrialized countries also contributed to the weakness of several agricultural commodity prices.

Explanations of the persistence of production in these circumstances included: (i) the durability of productive capacity and thus the slowness of response to declines in the incentives for production; (ii) high capital investment and consequently high fixed costs; (iii) cost reducing changes

on the supply side over and above those stemming from yield increases;
(iv) distortions in the relationship between production incentives at the
farm level, prices quoted on markets of international significance and
those paid by consumers.

## 2  DEVELOPMENTS IN PRODUCER/CONSUMER COOPERATION

There had been a clear weakening of efforts to agree upon and implement
policy actions in the field of commodities in the 1980s and the early
1990s. The international agreements for price stabilization broke down or
appear to face a bleak future.The formulation of a strengthened international commodity policy must take account of the changed circumstances
and identify strategic areas where action can remove the main obstacles to
international cooperation. The revitalization of producer/consumer
cooperation is crucial given the oversupply situation for many commodities. The Cartagena Commitment of UNCTAD VIII and its follow-up
provided both a reaffirmation of the will of the international community
to persevere in the attainment of enhanced cooperation in the area of
commodities and a number of concrete orientations and guidelines to
implement that will.

The more concrete identification of operational areas for pro-
ducer/consumer and producer cooperation include:

- Supply management and rationalization;
- Improvement in market transparency;
- Research and development;
- Promotion of local processing;
- Market promotion;
- Improvement in and rational use of marketing systems and practices;
- Ensuring the sustainability of commodity-based development;
- Environmental aspects.

Producer cooperation should aim at objectives catering for immediate
improvement (such as the elimination of stocks overhanging the market)
and/or for long-term improvement (such as investment and production
policies, marketing strategies and research and development). The most
striking positive development in the 1980s is the growing awareness of
the need to cooperate internationally to improve transparency in commodity markets and industries, and the growing number of concrete efforts in
this direction that are taking place e.g. in various metals and minerals and

in a number of agricultural commodities. Also striking is the movement that has taken place in the field of international cooperation for supply management and rationalization. Although some producing countries have done rather well through productivity growth, there still remains the conviction that, especially in the case of the Least Developed Countries, depressed prices in the long term are not in the interest of producers, and perhaps even of consumers. Accordingly, production policies and supply rationalization deserve support from the international community. Equally promising is the upsurge of interest in cooperation for improvement in, and rational use of, marketing systems and practices. This should include training activities in the marketing areas.

## 3 SPECIFIC MARKET PROBLEMS FACED BY COMMODITIES COVERED BY INDIVIDUAL ICBs

As mentioned above, most agricultural and non-agricultural commodities continued to suffer from declining prices both in nominal and real terms. While there is a need to improve productivity in both the agricultural and processing sectors, and thus add to the value-added accruing to developing countries, supply rationalization may be required to improve or at least maintain returns to producers. This is particularly important in the case of commodities with inelastic demand, or those where production growth might be expected to outstrip the growth of demand. Nevertheless, lower prices resulting from improved productivity might also stimulate demand by processors and producers of semi-manufactured goods. Processing activities within developing countries should be stimulated and processed goods from their countries should be provided better access to markets of developed countries. In general, efforts to improve market transparency should be given continuing priority with a view to assisting a rational and economic utilisation of resources. Development activities need to be considered within the context of promoting sustainable agriculture and extractive sectors.

Apart from these general problems which apply to a range of commodities, specific problems identified by ICBs include: in the case of jute and hard fibres, competition with synthetics and structural decline in demand in traditional end-uses; in the case of tea and cocoa, inelastic demand combined with a decline in the demand from former East European Countries; in the case of bananas, danger of black sigatoka disease; in the case of sugar, cotton and wheat, protectionist policies of OECD countries combined with commodity specific constraints; for timber, environmental concerns; for fishery products, the change in quality control systems in some of the main importing countries; for lead, zinc and rubber, recessionary economic conditions in consuming countries, and in the case of the first two, substantial supplies coming from countries which traditionally were net importers; for minerals and metals, competition from new materials, lack of basic geological information, physical infrastructure and environmental problems.

## 4  GLOBAL COMMODITY STRATEGIES

A global commodity strategy should be viewed as a dynamic instrument, presented as a concise brief statement, of an action programme to channel needed assistance of all types and from all potential sources to a specific commodity. It is not a means to intervene directly in a commodity market, but rather the product of a consensus among those involved with that commodity in terms of its prospects and problems, and the measures needed to realize and address them respectively. It should include a brief assessment of the supply/demand and price situation and prospects, and when appropriate an assessment of the particular situation of individual producing or consuming countries, and should, through its analysis of the following elements, lead to a prioritization of actions required.

Brief comments on some elements of a commodity strategy are presented below. It is recognized that Research and Development and Human Resource Development are significant components of the elements mentioned, while commodity development should take place in a manner compatible with Sustainable Development.

*Productivity Improvements.* Part of the strategy should be an assessment of the prospects for productivity improvements, and the measures needed to achieve these. In rice research, for example, some 25 to 30 per cent increase in (land) productivity can be expected to come from hybrid and new varieties. In that and other cases, further substantial contributions are expected to come from improved farming systems, while new frontier technologies like nitrogen fixation can lead to considerable reduction in fertilizer inputs. Genetic improvements hold promise for further increase in yields. Productivity improvements are advantageous for various reasons. For a number of commodities, they may be necessary to sustain competition with other products such as synthetics. For many if not most commodities, increased productivity and lower unit costs should lead to economy in resources. The concept of productivity should also embrace the development of alternative end-uses, as was demonstrated for sugar. Productivity improvements are also desirable in order to meet increased demand (as mentioned for rice) and, finally, the reduction of inputs without a reduction in production can be beneficial from an environmental point of view. The need for and consequences of productivity improvements will be different for each commodity and would require careful assessment in every case.

*Trade Policies.* The strategy should encompass an approach to making the trade policies of consumers and producers consistent and compatible with the pattern of growth in supply and demand foreseen in the commodity. This implies that trade barriers at various stages of processing of consuming countries as well as production incentives, subsidies and taxes imposed by producing countries should be reviewed with a view to identifying problems and constraints and possible actions to address these.

*Marketing Systems.* The structure of the marketing systems and price formation mechanisms in use for a commodity should be considered in the light of criteria for efficiency and transparency. This may lead to proposals for building up or reforming marketing systems such as auctions, terminal, forward or futures markets or for the organization of exports from producing countries through cooperatives or trading firms. Needs for training, advice and exchange of experience in these areas can be addressed at the level of operators (traders) in terms of techniques, management of exporting firms in terms of options available, strategies and internal control mechanisms, and government officials in terms of policy and regulation implications.

*Product and Market Development and Promotion.* Maintenance and/or improvement of product quality, development of new end- uses, finding new markets and promoting the consumption of commodities, their by-products and derivatives, should form an integral part of the development strategies for commodities. Of special concern are: quality enhancement; improvement of processing methods; development of new end-uses for commodities and their by-products; identification and the development of new markets to enhance competitiveness. Market information projects are well suited to develop these areas. Governments, ICBs and the industry behind the ICBs should consider demand stimulation through multinational generic promotion as an important option to support brand and national promotion activities for commodities in order to improve the competitiveness of natural products vis-à-vis synthetics and substitutes; to take advantage of any improvement of access to export markets; and to develop exports of products resulting from diversification programmes. These generic promotion programmes should be based on an in-depth assessment of the market potential and utilize modern market communication tools and techniques to stimulate demand. In particular, public relations activities passing the message to consumers on health, environmental and other aspects of common interest and concern have been identified as effective and low cost options for multi-national action.

*The Regional Dimension of Global Strategies.* While developing international strategies for specific commodities, it is important to take into account the possibilities or existence of regional strategies and integrating them into the global strategy. Just as each commodity would require a separate strategy in view of its peculiar dynamics and problems, the diversity among regions should be reflected in global strategies. In order to achieve a coordinated approach at various levels, it is important to involve regional organisations such as ESCAP, ECA and ECLAC. Some of the regional commissions have been addressing commodity issues effectively at the regional level, and are involved in developing strategies for expanding intra-regional trade in specific commodities which are of significant socio-economic interest to the developing countries in their regions.

*The Links between Commodity Development and Economic Development.* Commodity Development strategies should take explicit account of the vital role of the commodity sector for overall economic development, especially in least developed and low income countries. In many of these countries, a limited number of primary commodities make a large contribution to employment, income, exports, government revenues, and raw materials for the industry. The poorest countries depend on agricultural (food and export) commodities for their employment, revenues, exports and imports. Therefore, macro-economic policies (i.e. exchange rate and trade regimes, patterns of public expenditures, etc.) influence the performance of major commodities. Furthermore, since many agricultural commodities are grown by a large number of small producers, improvements in the employment and income which they generate, are critically dependent on the policies towards the development of commodities. Furthermore, with rapid population growth, failure to increase productivity of commodities tends to result in bringing marginal areas unsuitable for cropping under cultivation, damaging natural resources. Thus, on grounds of overall economic growth, equity as well as environmental sustainability, commodity development must be viewed as an integral part of macroeconomic management as well as an overall long term economic development strategy. By pursuing macroeconomic policies adverse to the development of commodities, some developing countries have experienced slow economic growth and stagnant exports. By the same token, countries successful in overall economic development have pursued policies strongly conducive to a broad-based development of commodities, in particular and the agricultural sector in general.

## 5 ROLE AND OPERATION OF THE COMMON FUND

The general utility of the Common Fund as a focus for action in the commodities field was acknowledged.

*Second Account.* It was noted that the start-up phase in the commencement of the operations of the Second Account had been completed with the adoption of the Rules and Regulations as well as Guidelines and Criteria for the Determination of Priorities. A Manual for the Preparation and Management of Projects had also been recently prepared, which would provide much needed guidance to the ICBs.

With the adoption of these basic instruments, the Second Account has now become fully operational. After a somewhat slow start, project approvals and financing are picking up speed. The approved projects, with a total value of about USD 8,500,000, are located in more than twenty countries in Africa, Asia (including the CIS), Europe and Latin America. They concern vital commodities of interest to developing countries including cocoa, coir, cotton, jute, olive, rubber and zinc. The quality and relevance of project proposals received by the Fund has also improved. Last year, five projects were approved for financing in contrast to one the previous year. It is hoped that in 1993, more than ten projects will be approved. Out of the twenty-one ICBs designated by the Fund, nineteen have sponsored project proposals to the Fund. These ICBs had sponsored more than one hundred (100) project proposals and profiles.

Forty (40) project proposals with a total value of USD 100,000,000 are known to be currently in the pipeline for consideration for financing. Out of these projects, several will qualify for financing in the immediate future and/or sometime in 1994. They aim at improving productivity, quality, expand local processing, diversification of commodity production and exports, market promotion, research and development into new end-uses as well as controlling disease.

It was felt that there was need to speed up the project pipeline for approval by the Executive Board; towards this end a number of useful recommendations were made at the Seminar.

It was stressed that the Common Fund could play a useful role in providing a forum for inter-ICB dialogue on the implications for development of the world commodity situation and prospects. By this means, it can bring to the systematic attention of ICBs the analytical work being done by a number of international organizations. The dialogue could also assist with identifying the steps needed to ensure the most effective utilization of the resources of the Common Fund in fulfilment of its objectives. It was felt that both the first Seminar organized in Amsterdam as well as the present Seminar had contributed to a better understanding of the respective roles which the Common Fund and the ICBs could play in the area of commodity development. It was hoped that such seminars would become a regular feature in the future. A suggestion was made that the annual seminar could be combined with a one-day meeting of executive heads of ICBs and the Fund.

The need for closer interaction between the Common Fund and the ICBs on a continuing basis was emphasised. It was felt that such interaction, particularly in the early stages of project identification can greatly facilitate the task of the ICBs in coming forward with projects which the Common Fund can finance. It was noted that the ICBs are currently invited to the meetings of the Consultative Committee whenever projects submitted by them come up for consideration. The Management was urged to consider ways to further intensify the dialogue with the ICBs.

It was noted that one of the constraints which had been encountered in the past in the formulation of projects which fully meet the criteria of the Common Fund, had been the inability of the ICBs to commit the requisite resources for the purpose. In this context, the need for providing technical assistance to the ICBs for project preparation was stressed. Such assistance is provided in some form or another by other international financial institutions. It was noted that the Common Fund Secretariat had submitted to the Executive Board a paper setting out a number of options for providing the necessary resources. It is imperative that an early decision be taken in this regard.

The need for close collaboration between the Common Fund and other international and regional organizations active in the field of commodities was stressed. The latter could, for example, co-sponsor workshops and training sessions with the Common Fund. They could also provide valuable assistance in the preparation of projects to be financed by the Common Fund.

*First Account.* In view of the interest in supply/production management now being shown by producers and consumers of some commodities, as well as the momentum which is likely to build up for using the resources of the Second Account for financing development measures, member states of the Fund should be encouraged to turn their attention to the use which may be made of the resources in the First Account. Among some of the ideas mentioned in that regard are the following, although some of them may require amendments to the Agreement:

- financing security stocks, which to the extent that they improve reliability of supply, can work in the interests of both consumers and producers;
- financing internationally coordinated production management measures capable of utilizing short term revolving finance;
- using the income derived from investing First Account subscriptions to finance Second Account projects;
- freezing the uncalled portion of the paid-up capital of the First Account, replacing it by an equivalent amount of voluntary contributions to the Second Account.

# LIST OF SEMINAR PARTICIPANTS

Honorary Chairman - Mr. Erik Derycke
Secretary of State for
Development Cooperation

Chairman - Mr. Budi Hartantyo
Managing Director, Common
Fund for Commodities

Moderator of the Seminar - Sir Alister McIntyre
Vice Chancellor, The University
of the West Indies

## 1 INTERNATIONAL COMMODITY BODIES

International Cocoa Organization - Mr. P.O. Ononye
Head of Economics and Controls
Division

International Cotton Advisory - Dr. Lawrence H. Shaw
Committee Executive Director

Intergovernmental Sub-Committee - Ms. Helga Josupeit
on Fish Trade (FAO) Fishery Industry Officer, Fish
Utilization and Marketing Service

International Jute Organisation - Mr. Md. Shamsul Haque Chishty
Executive Director
- Mr. A.J. Brown
Director
- Mr. Khaled Rab
Chairman of the COP

International Lead & Zinc - Dr. Rolf W. Boehnke
Study Group Secretary-General

International Natural Rubber - Mr. C.C. Goldthorpe
Organization Senior Rubber Industry
Development Officer

- Dr. P.W. Allen
  Secretary, International Rubber
  Research and Development Board

International Olive Oil Council          - Mr. Fausto Luchetti
                                           Executive Director

International Rubber Study Group         - Tan Sri Dr. B.C. Sekhar
                                           Secretary-General

International Sugar Organization         - Mr. A.C. Hannah
                                           Head, Economics and Statistics
                                           Department
                                         - Mr. Pedro Pablo San Jorge
                                           (MINCEX)
                                         - Ms. Dora Papini
                                           (GEPLACEA)

International Tropical Timber            - Mr. Lachlan A.J. Hunter
Organization                               Assistant Director for
                                           Management Services

Intergovernmental Group of Experts -    Mr. Fat-Chun Leung Ki
on Tungsten (UNCTAD)                       Economic Affairs Officer


## 2  INTERNATIONAL ORGANIZATIONS

African, Caribbean and                   - Dr. Ghebray-Berhane
  Pacific Group of States                  Secretary-General
                                         - Mr. Ilyas K. Besisira
                                           Expert in Charge of Development
                                           of Trade and Services
                                         - Mr. Alhaj Alhousseini
                                           Expert in Charge of Commodities

African Development Bank                 - Mr. S. Owusu
                                           Division Chief in the Development
                                           Research and Policy Department

Economic Commission for Africa           - Mr. Janvier D. Nkurunziza
                                           Economic Affairs Officer in the
                                           Trade and Development Finance
                                           Division

| | |
|---|---|
| Economic and Social Commission for Asia and the Pacific | - Mr. Ravi Sawhney<br>Chief in International Trade and Tourism Division |
| European Economic Community | - Mr. Hans Smida<br>Director<br>- Ms. Myfanwy van de Velde<br>Principal Administrator<br>- Mr. Richard Wyatt<br>Principal Administrator<br>- Mr. Derek Taylor<br>Principal Administrator<br>- Mr. Heinz Helmert<br>Principal Administrator<br>- Mr. Winfried Deutzmann<br>- Mr. Roger Booth<br>Head of Unit |
| Food and Agriculture Organization of the United Nations | - Ms. Paula Fortucci-Marongiu<br>Chief, Raw Materials, Tropical and Horticultural Products Service, Commodities and Trade Division<br>- Mr. W. A. Lamadé<br>Chief, Basic Foodstuffs Service Commodities and Trade Division |
| General Agreement on Tariffs and Trade | - Ms. Christine Schröder<br>Counsellor, Agriculture and Commodities Division |
| International Nickel Study Group | - Mr. Glen E. Wittur<br>Secretary-General |
| International Trade Centre UNCTAD/GATT | - Mr. Björn Olsen<br>Chief - Market Development Section (Commodities and Agrobased Products)<br>Division of Product and Market Development<br>- Mr. Bertil Byskov<br>Senior Market Development Officer |

The OPEC Fund for International          - Mr. Mu'azu Abdul-Malik
                                           Development Legal Counsel

United Nations Conference on             - Mr. Carlos Fortin
                                           Trade and Development Deputy to
                                           the Secretary General of
                                           UNCTAD
                                           Director, Commodities Division

The World Bank                           - Mr. Etienne Linard
                                           Business Affairs Adviser
                                           (European Office)


3  OBSERVERS

Embassy of Cuba                          - Mr. Alvarez Portela
                                           Counsellor

Ministry of Economics, Germany           - Dr. Karlheinz Rieck

Representative of LDC Group              - Mr. Syed Jamaluddin
     of countries                          Economic Affairs Minister
                                           Permanent Mission of Bangladesh
                                           at Geneva


4  HOST COUNTRY

Cabinet of the Secretary of State        - Ms. S. Gerlo
     for Development Cooperation            Chief of Staff
                                         - Mr. T. Vanelslande
                                           Attaché

ABOS - AGCD                              - Mr. Roger Lenaerts
     (Aid and Development                  Administrator-General of
     Cooperation Administration)           A.G.C.D.
                                         - Mr. H. Santkin
                                           Director-General
                                           General Directorate of Direct
                                           Bilateral Assistance

- Mr. P. Lelièvre-Damit
  Director-General
  General Directorate of Direct
  Bilateral Assistance
- Ms. M.-L. Van Den Bergh
  Acting Director-General
  General Directorate of Indirect
  Assistance
- Ms. A. Ribeiro-Vanderauwera
  Acting Director of Administration
  Directorate of Relations with
  International Organizations
- Mr. R. Van Landuyt
  Adviser United Nations and
  Specialized Agencies
- Ms. R. Schoofs
  Bureau, Specialized Agencies
- Mr. Dany Ghekiere
  Adviser

Ministry of Foreign Affairs

- Mr. H. van Houtte
  Administrator-Director-General
  General Directorate for Foreign
  Economic Affairs
- Mr. L. Jansen
  Director of Services
  Service Directorate of Multilateral
  Economic Affairs
- Mr. J. L. Tordeur
  Deputy Adviser
  Commodities & Agricultural
  Products
- Mr. Eugene Schoffers
  Administration Secretary-
  Economist for Basis Products
- Mr. Koen Adam

Others

- Prof. L. Berlage
  K.U.L. - Centre of Economic
  Studies
- Prof. P.K.M. Tharakan
  UFSIA
  Department of Third World
  Affairs
- Mr. X. De Clercq
  Representative of Belgian NGOs,
  Oxfam, Belgium

## 5  GUEST SPEAKERS

- Mr. José A. Cerro
  Executive Secretary,
  Group of Latin-American and
  Caribbean Sugar Exporting
  Countries
- Ms. Janet Farooq
  Chief - Diversification,
  Processing, Marketing and
  Distribution Section, UNCTAD
- Mr. Gabriel D. Kouthon
  Senior Officer,
  Food and Agriculture Industries
  Service
  Food and Agriculture Organization
  of the United Nations
- Prof. Uma Lele
  Director of International Studies
  and Programs and Graduate
  Research Professor,  University of
  Florida

## 6  MEMBERS OF CONSULTATIVE COMMITTEE

- Mr. Werner Gocht
  (Vice-Chairman)
- Mr. Dale Andrew
- Mr. Fernando A. Bernardo
- Mr. Indrajit Singh Chadha
- Mr. Ibrahim Gusau Garba
- Mr. Edmond de Langhe
- Mr. Takahiko Haseyama
- Mr. Mikhail S. Pankine
- Mr. Demeke Zewolde

## 7  SECRETARIAT OF THE COMMOND FUND FOR COMMODITIES

- Mr. Henrik Skouenborg
  Chief Operations Officer
- Mr. My Huynh-Cong
  Chief Finance Officer
- Mr. Getachew Gebre-Medhin
  Senior Project Officer
- Mr. Reuben Navarro
  Senior Economist
- Mr. Tailai Lu
  Assistant Project Officer
- Mr. Hans Nusselder
  Project Assistant
- Ms. Michèle Schwarz
  Accounting Assistant
- Ms. Olga Da Costa
  Conference Assistant
- Ms. Sylvia Lagerquist
  Secretary, Operations Unit
- Dr. Hidde P. Smit
  Vrije Universiteit, Consultant
- Mr. Kees Burger
  Vrije Universiteit, Consultant